THE
COMPLETE BOOK OF
HOUSEPLANTS
& INDOOR
GARDENING

THE
COMPLETE BOOK OF
HOUSEPLANTS
& INDOOR
GARDENING

Consultant Editor Edwin M. Steffek
Former Editor of 'Horticulture' magazine

CROWN PUBLISHERS, INC.
New York

CONTENTS

First published in the United States of America by
Crown Publishers, Inc., one Park Avenue,
New York, N.Y. 10016
© Octopus Books Ltd.
ISBN 0517-52614 X
Library of Congress Catalog Card
Number 76-7415
Produced by Mandarin Publishers Limited
22A Westlands Road,
Quarry Bay, Hong Kong
Printed in Hong Kong

CHAPTER 2:
BEAUTIFUL PLANTS FOR AN EFFECT
William Davidson

CHAPTER 3:
INDOOR PLANT GARDENS
Frances Perry

CHAPTER 4:
CONTAINER GARDENING OUTDOORS

CHAPTER 5:
CONSERVATORIES AND GREENHOUSES
Roy Hay & John Negus

INTRODUCTION

Houseplants are a fascinating subject,
and the popularity of indoor gardening books
grows because people want to learn
more about choosing, caring for and using
plants in their home.

I have seen and read many books on
indoor gardening, and this one brings together
all the possibilities that can be undertaken
in this rewarding pastime. Well-known
authors have been asked to write on
the subjects in which they are experts. The
whole field is, therefore, covered in
detail in this one volume with the accuracy
one would expect from such writers.

Many of those questions we ask ourselves
are answered, and, as a book of
reference, *The Complete Book of Houseplants
and Indoor Gardening* should be in the
possession of all those who have an interest in
the culture of indoor plants.

I recommend this exciting book to all
plant lovers.

Thomas Rochford

CHAPTER 1
CHOOSING PLANTS FOR THE HOME

It is possible to imagine that since time
immemorial there have been
potted plants growing in some house
somewhere – *Cycas revoluta*, the
oldest plant in the world, for example,
could not have gone through its
earlier years without some ancient or
other putting it in a container of some
kind to improve the appearance
of the homestead. But it is only in
the last quarter of a century
that houseplants have really come into
their own to form an essential part
of the living requirements of
the many people who positively
enjoy having them around.

Flowering houseplants

Quality plants are always the first to sell in the florist's shop, and quality plants will always give the best results, so do not necessarily think that you are getting the best of bargains when you acquire the cheapest of plants. And, if you are a beginner with plants, then it is wise to make your initial experiments with the easier subjects, and to leave the more difficult until a reasonable amount of knowledge concerning the needs of indoor plants has been accumulated. In the pages of this book there are hundreds of plants described, with much emphasis on whether they are easy or difficult to manage, so there is no need to go to the flower shop feeling ignorant about what should be chosen for the initial steps in this fascinating hobby.

A requirement that is as important as the plant selection is the environment in which the plant will be expected to live. And, quite frankly, if your living room is dingy, dark and airless then it could well be a complete waste of time for you to contemplate the prospect of growing any sort of living plant. Only the very toughest of plants, such as the cast iron plant, *Aspidistra elatior*, will survive for any length of time in very poor light. Ideally, rooms should be light and airy so that a buoyant, rather than stuffy atmosphere prevails.

Given reasonably good light and adequate ventilation on warmer days the next most important need that the householder can have some measure of control over is the temperature at which the room is maintained. And maintained is an important word in this instance, as it is not only important that plants should enjoy adequate temperature, it is also essential that it is maintained constantly during the day. Temperatures that go up and down like a yo-yo can only be harmful in the end. It will lead to much greater success if a temperature range of 15-20°C/60-68°F can be maintained rather than having rooms baking hot in the evening and as cold as the grave at other times of the day.

Few plants thrive in very high temperature, as the atmosphere dries out more and more as the warmth of the room gets higher and higher, and in very dry conditions there is a tendency for plants to become dehydrated. There is also much more risk of them being attacked by pests such as red spider mite which relish very dry surroundings. Also in relation to heating, it is wise to keep more delicate plants well away from radiators, and particularly important that plants should not be placed immediately above heating appliances in the stream of ascending hot air.

Water, water everywhere and not a drop to drink – in the case of most houseplants there is far too much water and far too much to drink. So when dealing with plants great care must be exercised in ensuring that they have sufficient water for their needs, but are not permanently waterlogged. It is not easy to give precise directions concerning the needs of plants that are so varied in themselves in their requirements. But, unless instructions are given to the contrary, then it is best to water plants and to allow them to dry out a little before watering again. Treated in this way roots will remain much more active and the plants generally will be very much crisper in their appearance than if watered in small amounts at irregular intervals.

Good drainage is an essential need whether you are planting corn in a ploughed field or potting an African violet in a pot. It is not only important that plants should be properly watered, it is equally important that the water when poured into the container should drain sharply through the soil. If water remains on the surface of the soil for any length of time it will be wise to remove the plant from its pot to see if there is anything impeding the drainage – it could, for example, be a worm cast blocking the holes in the bottom of the pot. Tepid water is preferred to cold, and rainwater should be used wherever possible because it is purer.

Feeding is also important and if done properly there should not be so much need for potting plants on into larger pots. Young and established plants should be fed with a balanced fertilizer used as directed when plants are in active growth, usually during the spring and summer. Plants in larger pots of 25cm/10in size and upwards can be maintained for many years in perfect condition simply by feeding them regularly. Some of the smaller plants, however, may have to be potted into slightly larger containers almost as soon as they are purchased – chlorophytum, *Begonia rex* and many of the flowering plants like cinerarias which come in particularly small pots are good examples.

Whatever the time of year or whatever the plant it is important that the existing pot should be well filled with roots before any potting on operation is considered. And, when potting on, the new container must not be too much larger than the one the plant is being transferred from. If the new pot is made of clay then a few pieces of broken flower pot will have to be placed in the bottom of the pot to aid drainage

Below: An azalea laden with pink blooms

before introducing any soil; plastic pots have sufficient holes in the base to offset the need for 'crocks'. When potting, a properly prepared and sterilized mixture must be used, and for houseplants that are expected to remain in the same pot for some time a soil mix with a reasonable amount of loam in its preparation is beneficial. Most plants will get along very well on a mix of two parts loam-based mixture and one part peat–soil from the garden is very seldom suitable.

Most plants indoors will benefit if they can be grouped together rather than dotted about the room. One method of grouping is to place them on a bed of moist gravel in a waterproof tray. A second method, providing humidity, is to plunge the pots to their rims in a bed of moist peat or moss.

The familiar name, where applicable, minimum winter night temperatures, place of origin, are given for each plant described.

Winter flowering plants

Ardisia crispa

[7°C/45°F; East Indies] Compact evergreen shrub that may in time attain a height of some 1.2m/4ft, but this would take several years as the ardisia (also known as *A. crenula*) is a slow growing plant. Leaves are leathery, glossy green and slightly waved at their margins. Fragrant white flowers in summer are insignificant, and the principal attraction is the clusters of scarlet berries that appear in autumn and will remain on the plant for many months. New plants can be raised from seed, but plants raised from cuttings are easier and quicker. Require cool, light conditions, a gritty, loam-based mixture and moderate watering. Feed with liquid manure every two or three weeks during the growing season.

Azalea indicum

[10-15°C/50-60°F; China] These tender azaleas, correctly known as *Rhododendron simsii* (Indian azaleas), are grown out of doors during the summer months and under glass from autumn until flowering in December. They are the aristocrats of the winter-flowering range of pot plants, laden with red, pink or white blooms. When purchasing it is important to look for plants with an abundance of buds as plants that are too backward may not flower satisfactorily indoors, while those that are too advanced in flower will give pleasure for a shorter length of time.

The most important requirement in order to succeed with azaleas indoors is to ensure that the mixture is kept permanently moist as any drying out will result in foliage shrivelling and flowers wilting. The best way of watering is to plunge the plant pot in a bucket of rainwater – treatment that larger plants may require two or three times each week. Indoors, good light and cool growing conditions are also essential, as plants seldom do well in very hot, airless situations. After flowering, plants may be put out in the garden for the summer months where they should be kept moist and sprayed over periodically. When potting on use a mixture composed almost entirely of leafmould and peat or a proprietary lime-free peat mix. Propagate from cuttings taken with a piece of old wood (a heel) and about 8cm/3in in length during the summer. Insert cuttings in equal parts sharp sand and peat and maintain a temperature in the region of 15°C/60°F until the new plants are established.

Begonia glaucophylla

[13°C/55°F; Brazil] One of the many fibrous-rooted begonias that are excellent value both in respect of attractive foliage and colourful flowers. These are particularly suitable for hanging pots and baskets as the thin long stems droop naturally. Leaves are pale green and glossy with waved margins and darken as they mature, and clustered brick-red flowers are a welcome sight during the month of February. Being a natural trailing plant it is seen at its best when several plants are put in a hanging basket during the summer to flower the following year. Use a peaty mixture when planting, set in good light and keep evenly moist, especially while flowering. Increase plants by inserting pieces of stem with one or two leaves attached in a peat and sand mixture – a heated propagator will speed the rooting time.

Left: This group of cyclamens shows the variety of leaf markings and flower shades.
Above: *Primula malacoides*

Camellia japonica

[Hardy; China/Japan] Cool, dark green, glossy leaves and exquisite single and double wax-textured flowers that often seem too perfect for words. There are many fine hybrids in shades of pink, red and white to brighten your home during the more dismal months of the year – by careful selection you could obtain a collection of plants that would provide flowers from October through until the spring. However, to grow them well it is essential to have a balcony or terrace out of doors where plants could spend most of their time, bringing them indoors while they are in flower or to protect them from the more severe weather conditions. Indoors during the winter months they should enjoy the lightest possible location in a room that is cool and airy. In rooms offering excessive temperature and poor light, loss of leaves and flower buds is inevitable. Surprisingly, as one is forever being warned about the dangers of potting plants into containers that are too large, camellias in pots seem to do better when in large pots that would seem out of proportion to their size.

A lime-free mixture is essential, and one containing a high proportion of well-rotted leafmould would be ideal. Water to keep the soil moist at all times, preferably with rainwater, and during the summer months top the soil with moist peat to keep the roots cool.

Propagate from cuttings with three or four leaves attached, insert in small pots filled with peat and sand mixture and keep in a closed glass frame out of doors in a shaded part of the garden. Plants that do not seem to be taking too kindly to being planted in pots can be put out in the garden against a north-facing wall in lime-free soil.

Cyclamen persicum

[10-15°C/50-60°F; Syria] When purchasing cyclamen it is important to select those that are of full appearance and to avoid those that have a soft look about them. In particular it is wise to remove plants from protective paper sleeves before purchasing. The latter exercise will allow you to inspect the plant from underneath and to see that there are plenty of flower buds in evidence which will provide the flowers of the future.

Cyclamens are among the most popular, albeit difficult plants for winter flowering. They have attractive dark green rounded leaves, marbled with white or silver, and the pink, mauve, crimson or white flowers are carried high above the foliage.

They are very much better in a room or entrance hall where the conditions are light, airy and, above all, not excessively hot. Much is said, and often rightly so, about the danger of placing plants in positions where they are likely to be in a cold draught, but it is seldom that a cyclamen objects to windows being opened when weather conditions permit. In moderately cool rooms plants will remain in flower for very much longer and will have a generally more healthy look about them than they do when exposed to hot, airless conditions.

Cyclamen can be watered safely either from above or by standing the pot in water. Make sure that the roots of the plant are thoroughly wetted each time, but do not overwater as water left on the surface may cause rotting of the corm with subsequent rapid death. Care should be taken to ensure that the potting mixture does not 'dry out completely.

When flowers are over and foliage turns yellow, cyclamen can be put out of doors and pots placed on their sides so that the mixture remains dry. When new growth is noticed in the centre of the corm the old mixture should be completely removed and the plant potted up freshly, and watering and feeding restarted. Cyclamens are difficult to keep growing from year to year but it is worth trying.

Propagation is by seed, which germinates quite readily in a little heat and humidity.

Euphorbia pulcherrima (Poinsettia)

[Christmas Flower; 15°C/60°F; Mexico] Whereas most of the winter-flowering plants require cool and airy conditions indoors to maintain them in good condition, the poinsettia is the exception to the rule and must have reasonable warmth if it is to prosper. Although excessive temperatures are not required, it is important that the minimum should not fall much below that recommended above for any length of time. The growing position must be the lightest possible, and full winter sun will not present any problems, although if the plant is kept after flowering it should be shaded from strong sunlight in summer.

The bright green leaves are surmounted by large brightly coloured flower bracts. Bright red or scarlet is the usual colour, but pink and white forms are also available.

However, in spite of its need for more preferential treatment, the modern poinsettia is a very much more durable plant than its predecessors of two decades ago. In those days the varieties that were grown needed constant

Below: *Solanum capsicastrum,* a cheerful and welcome gift plant at Christmas.
Above right: *Euphorbia pulcherrima*

attention and constant temperature if their leaves were not to shower off. The modern plants are not only very much more attractive as pot plants, they are also very much easier to care for both in the home and in the greenhouse. Need for careful watering is reasonably critical, and one must practise a programme that permits the mixture to dry out between each watering, so that the soil is kept just moist; over-watering and badly drained soil will cause the leaves to lose their colour and eventually fall off. How to get plants to flower again for a second time has become an almost standard question when poinsettias are under discussion – many indoor plant growers can get them to grow perfectly well for a second and third year in their homes, but no flowers will appear.

To encourage flowering the simple answer is that the plant from mid-September onwards should not be exposed to artificial light in the evening, as additional lighting simply results in the plant producing more and more leaves at the expense of flowers, or bracts. Even a street light outside the window of the room in which the plant is growing will prevent it from flowering. A weekly dilute feed during the summer months should also encourage new flower production.

Poinsettias are propagated from tip cuttings, that is to say the top section of a growing shoot is removed with three or four leaves attached, and the lower leaf is removed before inserting the cutting in a small pot filled with equal parts peat and sand. Cuttings do better if they are in a mist propagating unit so that the leaves are continually moistened with a fine spray of water. Even in these conditions cuttings will often go limp and seem quite dead only to rally in a few days and begin to root in about a fortnight. Once rooted they should be potted into gradually larger containers using a loam-based mixture – addition of a little extra peat will do no harm.

Primula

[10-13°C/50-55°F; China] With the winter-flowering primulas the principal requirement for success is cool and airy conditions, and they will do better for being in good light. Moist conditions at their roots and a moist atmosphere surrounding plants will also be beneficial, as will a soil mix with a reasonably high proportion of peat–most kinds will do well in an equal mixture of loam-based mixture and peat. Often you will find that very large plants are being sold in relatively small pots with not enough soil to keep the plants healthy. Such large plants are best potted on into larger containers as soon as they are acquired–you may then witness an improvement. The principal species are *P. malacoides*

and *P. obconica,* both with light green hairy leaves in a rosette shape. The flowers, on tall stems above the leaves, are in large clusters and come in a wide range of colours; many are highly fragrant. The plants are treated as annuals and usually discarded after flowering.

People with sensitive skin would be well advised not to purchase or handle *P. obconica,* as there is every chance that quite severe skin irritation will be the result.

New plants are propagated from small seeds, but it is often better to purchase small plants and to grow them on if only a modest quantity is required.

Solanum capsicastrum

[Winter Cherry; 10°C/50°F; Brazil] With their bright red or orange fruits these are very cheerful subjects at Christmas, but it is important that they should enjoy the maximum amount of light and fresh air if they are to retain the appearance. In poor light, they will shed their berries quickly, so the light and airy windowsill is absolutely essential. Raised from seed these plants should be grown on into small pots of loam-based mix before being transferred to sheltered outdoor conditions for the summer months. Bring them under cover, in the home or a greenhouse, when nights become colder. Keep plants moist at their roots throughout the growing season and spray the foliage over regularly once the flowers appear in summer, in order to improve pollination and help berries to set. Plants can be propagated from cuttings taken from plants kept from the previous year. However, it is usually better to treat them as annuals and dispose of them once their attraction has gone, and to raise new plants from seed annually in spring.

Spring flowering plants

Aeschynanthus (syn. Trichosporum)

[13°C/55°F, South East Asia] A trailing plant that is at its best when several have been planted and allowed to develop in a hanging basket, *A. speciosus* (*T. speciosum*) has untidy growth that may in time extend to some 60cm/2ft long branches. Leaves are pale to dark green in colour (often depending on available light) and lanceolate in shape. Big attraction is the cluster of tubular flowers which have flame-orange and yellow as the principal colours. Keep the peat-based mixture moist and general conditions warm and as humid as possible. New plants are raised from cuttings a few cm in length and inserted in peat in a warm propagator.

There are a few other aeschynanthus that are occasionally available and flower at different times of the year – all require similar conditions in which to grow.

Allamanda neriifolia

[13°C/55°F; Tropical South America] This shrubby species requires a lot of space and much water and fertilizer. The mid-green lance-shaped leaves are set in whorls of three or four. The plants will in time attain a height of some 1.2m/4ft, by which time it will probably be in a container of 25cm/10in in diameter. Consequently, it is not the plant for the room that is limited in size. Small, rich yellow flowers are attractive, but not very spectacular considering the size of plant that is needed to bear them. A location offering light shade is best and a rich loam-based soil. Water freely in spring and summer, but keep on the dry side in winter. Propagate new plants from 8cm/3in long cuttings inserted in peat and sand in a warm propagating case. There is also *A. cathartica* that one may be tempted to purchase, but it really is best suited to the hot greenhouse where the climbing growth can best be accommodated – flowers of this one are large, golden-yellow and most impressive.

Anthurium scherzerianum

[Flamingo Flower; 13°C/55°F, Tropical South America] Although this plant may be had in flower at almost any time of the year, it is at its best during the spring months. In common with all aroids it will do that much better if the general conditions are moist and humid with reasonable warmth. Conditions that are very hot with little moisture are almost as bad as conditions that are cold and unfeeling. The growing medium should contain a high proportion of peat, and the plant pot should be plunged in a larger container that is filled with peat or moss and kept moist. Large lanceolate leaves are dark green in colour and not unattractive, but the principal feature of this plant is the brilliant scarlet flower with curled spadix. Although smaller flowers on short stalks will be adequately supported, if larger flowers need some form of support, a cane that is tied in position just under the flower will be ideal. Older plants may be split up to produce new plants, but as this is not easy to do, raise new plants from seed sown in peat in warm conditions as soon as the seed becomes available. If practical, use rainwater with the chill off when watering, moderately in winter, and freely during the growing season.

Astilbe

[Hardy; Japan] Naturally flowers in the garden much later in the year, but many of these plants, with their handsome plumed flowers, in shades of white and pink, are forced into flower by the nurseryman to be sold at Easter. Their principal need is water – lots and lots of it – as any drying out of the mixture will surely result in the shrivelling of foliage and general deterioration of the plant. If plants are in small-ish pots when purchased it will be wise to transfer them to slightly larger containers using a loam-based mixture. Having finished flowering indoors, it is advisable to find a moist and shaded spot in the garden and to plant them there permanently. New plants are produced by dividing the old clumps and planting them up in smaller sections.

Below: Brilliant scarlet flowers are the principal feature of *Anthurium scherzerianum*.
Above: *Allamanda cathartica* 'Hendersonii'.
Opposite top: *Calendula officinalis* 'Double Golden'.
Opposite bottom: *Aeschynanthus speciosus*

Calendula officinalis

[Pot Marigold; Hardy; Southern Europe] Pot marigolds in their many fine colours are excellent value as potted plants and are comparatively inexpensive to purchase. They require a cool light place indoors, and the soil mix must at all times be kept moist.

Having finished flowering they should be disposed of because they are annuals; however, if it is not too late in the year they can be planted out in the garden after careful dead-heading and may then produce a second show of flowers.

Clarkia

[Hardy; California] Another cheap and very cheerful annual that, if seed is sown in September, will provide attractive pot plants for the spring of the following year. Plants should be grown in cool conditions, transferring them to gradually larger size pots as the need arises due to being pot bound.

There should be good light, as plants that are grown too hot, or in poor light, will become much too long and leggy, so much less attractive as pot plants. There is a wide range of colours available, separate or mixed and borne in dense spikes. Discard after flowering.

Columnea

[13°C/55°F; Tropical South America] As hanging basket and hanging pot plant subjects become more and more popular it surely cannot be long before much more attention is given to these superb natural trailing plants. They are not especially easy to grow, but given that extra bit of care, the rewards can be quite spectacular. Adequate and steady temperature is absolutely essential, as is the need for moist and shaded conditions. Given these, then ensure that plants are potted or planted into an open peaty mixture – working in a little charcoal (to prevent the mixture turning sour) and fresh sphagnum moss. There are a number of sorts that may be obtained, and one of the best is still the old favourite, C. × banksii, which has rich dark green foliage and brilliant orange flowers. There is also C. microphylla which has smaller leaves that are a lighter shade of green and hangs straight down from the container in which it is growing. The latter flowers very freely and is a most impressive plant when properly cared for. To encourage flower production it is advisable to keep the mixture on the dry side for several weeks prior to the plant's natural flowering time. New plants are raised from small cuttings, but preferably not from growth that is bearing flowers.

terrace plants, the hydrangea bought for room decoration may, when finished flowering indoors, be planted out in the garden.

Iberis amara

[Candytuft; Hardy; Western Europe] Cheap and cheerful annual plants with a nice clean appearance are often more worthy of a place on the windowsill indoors than is sometimes imagined, and the pleasantly scented white flowers of the humble candytuft can add that nice touch of difference at very little cost. Sow seed in early spring in cool conditions and pot on as necessary until plants are in 13cm/5in pots – a loam-based mixture with a little extra peat added will be fine for potting at all stages of development. After flowering, plants should be disposed of and a new start made with fresh seed in the next season.

Jasminum mesnyi (syn. primulinum)

[10-13°C/50-55°F; China] In ideal conditions these can become quite rampant climbing plants that will cover the wall of the conservatory or garden room in no time at all, even when their roots are confined to pots, or similar containers. Fortunately, harsh pruning seems to cause very few problems provided it is done after plants have flowered, and only the shoots that have flowered are removed. Some of the prunings can be used for propagation purposes by using pieces a few cm in length and inserting them in a sand and peat mixture. Cuttings can be taken at any time during the spring and summer months.

Cool, light and airy conditions will suit them at all stages of growth, as plants tend to become thin and drawn when grown in high temperature. Delicate primrose-yellow flowers are produced singly among the dark green trifoliate leaves. For best results use a good loam-based soil mix kept moist. When grown in pots it is essential to provide a framework, possibly in the shape of a miniature trellis, which growth can be trained to as it develops. After flowering, plants may be placed in the garden against a sheltered wall until mid-September when nights become colder and then taken indoors to a cool, light room.

Medinilla magnifica

[15°C/60°F; South East Asia] A choice plant that will need ample space in which to grow and better than average conditions in order to survive at all indoors. Thick, almost coarse leathery leaves are supported by strong, woody stems. The enormous flower clusters in late spring are the attraction as they hang from the plant in similar fashion to bunches of grapes on a vine – the large bract is pink in colour and the individual flowers a showy carmine-red. Plants are seen at their best when they have

Hydrangea

[Hardy; China/Japan] When purchasing hydrangea plants for room decoration it is important that pre-wrapped plants are not selected, as many of these are very badly grown in conditions that are much too cold, with the result that they become hard in appearance and lose many of their lower leaves. A seemingly innocent protective paper bag can conceal many ills, so it is wise to insist on seeing the actual plants and not just the few flowers that are showing at the top of the wrapping. With hydrangeas, a good buy is a plant no more than 60cm/2ft tall having stems well furnished with rich green leaves and at least five flower heads, some open with others to follow. It should also be in a pot of not less than 13cm/5in in diameter – there is seldom sufficient goodness in smaller pots to maintain hydrangea plants for any length of time. Colouring of hydrangea flowers is also very variable so one should seek out those with a blue, pink or white colouring that is well defined.

Indoors, the principal requirement of the hydrangea plant is a light and cool position in which to grow and an abundant supply of moisture at its roots while in active growth – during the winter the plant can be allowed to dry out completely. Whether plants are needed for growing or for taking cuttings from in the spring they should be placed out of doors during the winter and will benefit if they can have the protection of a glass frame while outside. In early spring they should be taken indoors again and watering should be started. Once a reasonable amount of growth has developed plants can be potted on into larger containers using a loam-based mixture, lime-free for blue-flowered forms to maintain the colour. New growth will quickly develop, and when it is obvious which of the shoots are going to produce flowers, select those that are blind for taking cuttings from to make new plants for the following year. Cuttings root reasonably easily in a warm propagator in a peat and sand mixture.

Besides being fine room, conservatory and

attained their maximum height of some 1.8m/6ft – huge clusters of pendulous flowering bracts hanging from such plants can be most spectacular. Let it be said, however, that these are plants for those with some knowledge and not the beginner with indoor plants. Consistent warmth, light shade and reasonably high humidity are essential needs, as is the need for potting plants on into larger containers as they fill their existing pots with roots – use a loam-based mixture with a little additional peat. Once plants have been put into containers of about 25cm/10in in diameter they can be maintained by regular feeding with a balanced liquid fertilizer. New plants are raised from cuttings of young growth using two leaves with a piece of stem attached. However, high temperatures and a propagator are needed.

Primula vulgaris

[Hardy; Europe] In most respects this primula (syn. *P. acaulis*) is a trimmed-down version of the garden polyanthus, as it has leaves, flowers and flower colours that are very much the same. The principal difference is in the size, especially in the length of the flower stalk which is very much shorter. The more compact habit makes this plant a very good subject for small plant gardens. Very easy to care for, it requires the almost standard treatment for hardy plants that are also utilized as potted plants, in that cool, light and airy conditions are preferred. The loamy mixture should be

Opposite: Select a hydrangea that is bearing at least five flower heads.
Below: Schizanthus, or Butterfly Flower.
Right: *Medinilla magnifica*

moist all the time and when the plant has outlived its usefulness indoors it can be planted in a moist, shaded part of the garden. New plants are raised from seed and older ones may be split up if only a small number are required.

Schizanthus

[Butterfly Flower; 10°C/50°F; Chile] The dwarf forms of these very floriferous half hardy annuals will provide a wealth of colour in the spring. The larger schizanthus tend to be much too space-demanding for the average size room. Again there will be the need for light and airy conditions if plants are to remain compact and attractive – in hot conditions the plants tend to become much too loose and open, so much less attractive. The colour range of *S. pinnatus* and its named dwarf varieties is almost infinite, and the delicate single 'butterfly' flowers are most effective set off against the fern-like foliage. Grow in a loam-based soil mix and pinch out the tips of young plants to encourage bushy growth. Discard after flowering.

21

Achimenes

[Hot Water Plant; 13°C/55°F; Mexico] Mostly compact little plants that produce an endless succession of tubular or trumpet-shaped flowers in many colourful shades. At their best during the summer months when they should have a light airy window position, moist though not saturated peat-based mixture, and regular feeding. When flowering has finished in September, dry off the tubers and store in a frost-free place until starting new growth. New plants raised in a number of different ways: from seed sown early in the year, from cuttings a few cm in length as they become available, or by splitting up the scaly rhizomes from which growth develops. Immersing plant pot, in which the rhizome is contained, in warm water when starting dormant plant into growth in February will encourage plants to develop new growth more rapidly – hence the common name of Hot Water Plant.

Begonia

[5°C/41°F] Most of the tuberous begonias are of hybrid origin. They can be purchased either as seed or tubers, the latter producing mature plants much more quickly – and, in theory, the more you pay for seed and tubers, the better the resultant plants ought to be! Seed is very fine and requires to be sown in warm, moist conditions, while the tubers are started into growth in shallow boxes filled with peat in February. The pendulous varieties can be started in the same way, and are among the most spectacular plants to have growing in a hanging basket. Reasonably warm conditions are required in the early stages; when

Summer flowering plants

Above: *Capsicum annuum.*
Below: *Tuberous begonia* 'Guardsman'.
Opposite: Achimenes Little Beauty'

growth is well established, pot the tubers up singly in the soil mix and move them into larger pots as necessary. Cool and lightly shaded locations suit them best. Keep moist and well fed while in active growth, and store tubers in dry conditions in winter after they have naturally died down. Potting on must not be neglected, so as soon as plants have filled

their existing pots with roots they should be transferred to slightly larger containers–a suggested mixture is two parts loam-based to one part fresh peat. The large double flowers, resembling a rose and sometimes frilled, range from white through yellow to shades of pink, red and orange. The pendulous varieties are small-flowered but if possible produce these even more abundantly throughout summer.

Campanula isophylla

[Bellflower; 7°C/45°F; Italy] There are two varieties that one may occasionally see offered for sale: *C. isophylla* 'Alba', and *C. isophylla* 'Mayii'. As the name suggests the first mentioned has white flowers and is reasonably easy to care for, while the latter has pale blue flowers and variegated, heart-shaped leaves; it is a trifle more difficult to manage. Both may be increased by means of cuttings inserted in a peat and sand mixture in spring. The white form is a particularly fine plant when employed as part of a mixture in a hanging basket, or as an individual trailing plant in a 13-18cm/5-7in pot. After flowering plants should be cut hard back in the autumn and kept very much on the dry side until the following spring when watering should be gradually restarted to bring plants back to life. Once they have produced a reasonable amount of growth plants should be removed from their pots and the old soil gently teased away before potting in fresh loam-based mixture, using the same container. Once growing away in the fresh medium it will be essential that watering should at no time be neglected. It is also important to clean plants over and remove all dead flowers regularly.

Capsicum

[Peppers; 10-15°C/50-60°F] Raised from seed sown in gentle heat in the spring, the plants are not in themselves attractive and are mainly grown for the different coloured and shaped fruits that they produce. Once seedlings are of reasonable size they should be potted into small pots of loam-based mixture and gradually into larger ones as required. Syringe the leaves daily during the flowering period to assist fruit-setting. Give a dilute liquid feed at ten-day intervals when the fruits first appear and until they show colour. In summer they may be placed out of doors where they can have the protection of a sheltered wall. They are best treated as annuals and should be disposed of when the ripe fruits have been harvested.

Celosia

[Cockscomb; frost-free; South East Asia] There are many varieties of this annual, but the one that is most often seen offered for sale is *C. argentea* Cristata, which has red or yellow cockscomb flowers from July to September. New plants may be grown from seed sown in gentle heat in the spring, but it is usually easier to buy one or two plants in pots if they are wanted for room decoration. It would be wise to pot them on into loam-based mixture as soon as purchased, using a slightly larger pot – this will obviate the need for too frequent feeding. Place in a well-lit position and keep thoroughly moist. After flowering plants should be disposed of.

Citrus mitis

[Calamondin Orange; 15°C/60°F; Philippines] One of the more choice of the potted plants, this ornamental orange has many attractive qualities. Small glossy green leaves are attractive in themselves, and the plant retains a reasonably compact habit if the growing conditions are fairly cool (about 13°C/55°F). White, heavily-scented flowers are mostly produced in the summer, but you may chance to have a crop of flowers at almost any time of the year for no apparent reason. Flowers are normally followed by small green fruits that will in time ripen to become perfect miniature oranges. These are bitter tasting but quite edible. New plants may be raised from seed or from cuttings about 8cm/3in in length – firm young shoots root fairly readily at any time of the year if a heated propagator is available. The best method of cultivation is to pot the plant on almost as soon as it is purchased if it is growing in a relatively small pot, which is usually the case. Two parts of loam-based mixture to one part fresh peat will do them well. To counteract the possibility of plants becom-

ing top-heavy it is advisable to use clay pots. Another important requirement is that plants should be placed out of doors during the summer months, as they will need all the sunshine that is available to keep them in good condition. Watering should not be neglected, but by the same token it must not be overdone, as the Calamondin Orange has a comparatively weak root system that may easily be damaged by overwatering and equally easily by frequent and careless potting. Regular feeding of established plants with weak liquid fertilizer will do no harm. With watering and feeding with liquid fertilizers, it is very important that the water should drain freely through the soil

24

and not lie on the surface—an open soil and provision of adequate drainage in the bottom of the pot will assist in this matter.

Crossandra

[13°C/55°F; India] The variety most often seen is *C. undulifolia* 'MonaWalhed', which is a compact little plant that seldom attains more than 21cm/8in in height, and is well suited to the dish garden or the crowded windowsill where only small plants can be accommodated. Leaves are a dark glossy green in colour and the orange flowers are colourful for a long

ence, but may be sown later to give a succession of flowering plants. A peaty mixture is needed and plants should be potted on into slightly larger pots as required. Good light, but shaded from hot sun, and a moist mixture is important and dead flowers should be regularly removed to prevent them rotting leaves. As plants develop a tuber is formed from which leaves and flowers are produced. Give a weekly feed when buds appear. When flowers and leaves naturally die down in the autumn of the year the mixture should be allowed to dry out, and the tuber, or corm, should be stored

though a few are variegated; the flowers of many of the hibiscus are quite breathtaking, and come in many shades of yellow, red and orange in both single and double forms. In most instances the flowers of these shrubby *Hibiscus* last for up to one week at least, depending on conditions. But the short life of individual flowers should not deter you from acquiring these plants, as there is a continual succession of flowers on healthy, vigorous plants. To keep plants in good order they require lots of water during the spring and summer months, with a little less in winter.

Opposite above: *Hibiscus rosa-sinensis.*
Opposite below: Gloxinia.
Above: *Celosia plumosa.*
Right: *Citrus mitis*

period during the summer months. A peaty mixture is ideal and it must be kept moist during the summer and a little on the dry side in winter. Feed while actively growing and provide a light position that is shaded from the sun. Propagate from cuttings 10cm/4in in length in warm conditions in spring.

Gloxinia

[13-18°C/55-64°F; Brazil] The florist's gloxinia should be more accurately described as *Sinningia speciosa*, but few florists would recognize the plant by the latter name, so gloxinia it is. Very fine seed is thinly sown in warm conditions in the spring of the year for prefer-

in a dry, warm place until the following spring when it can be started into growth by placing in a box or pot filled with moist peat. A temperature of not less than 20°C/70°F should be maintained until growth is established. Green leaves that are large, velvety and very brittle should be handled with the greatest possible care. Many named varieties are available, all with clusters of trumpet-shaped flowers in shades of red, purple, pink and white, single or double and some with frilled edges.

Hibiscus

[Rose Mallow; 7-16°C/45-61°F; South East Asia] Most varieties have green leaves, al-

In winter the mixture may be allowed to dry out so that plants shed their leaves and remain dormant until watering begins in the early spring; at the higher temperature the plants will retain their leaves. A light position and regular feeding are essential needs, and when potting plants on into final containers it is best to use a peat-based mixture. Plants are increased by taking cuttings about 10cm/4in in length and inserting them in a peat and sand mixture in a warm propagator. Plants develop into bushes 1.8m/6ft in height when grown in larger containers, but may be kept in check by regular pruning which is best done in spring as growth restarts.

Hoya

[Wax Flower; 10°C/50°F; Queensland] There are numerous species with both green and variegated leaves, but by far the most popular is *H. carnosa* which makes a fine climbing plant. For this reason, it requires reasonably tall canes or a framework for climbing stems to twist around. A light position is needed and a careful check must be maintained for mealy bug pests which frequently inhabit the areas between the twisting stems and plant support. Leaves are leathery, elliptic and green in colour. The pendent clusters of star-shaped waxy flowers are, however, the main feature, and are so perfect as to seem quite unnatural. Use a peat-based mixture when potting and be sure that the pot has ample drainage. New plants can be raised from cuttings which can be taken at almost any time in summer if a heated propagator is available–cuttings should be made from firmer growth and not from soft stems at the top of the plant. Flower fragrance is an added bonus with this plant. Variegated forms tend to flower less freely, but are valuable on account of their attractive leaf colouring.

Hypocyrta glabra

[Clog Plant; 13°C/55°F; Tropical America] New plants are raised from cuttings inserted in small pots filled with a peat and sand mixture–several cuttings per pot is preferred. Leaves are attractive glossy green, and have a puffed up, almost succulent appearance. Attractive tiny orange-coloured flowers are produced in great numbers over a long period in the axil of the topmost leaves and vaguely resemble clogs, hence the common name. Although reasonable temperature is advised, one should guard against very hot and stuffy conditions, as plants prefer a light and airy location if they are to give good results. Peaty mixture essential when potting, and frequent feeding of established plants with weak liquid fertilizer will be beneficial when plants are in active growth during the summer months.

Passiflora caerulea

[Passion Flower; Hardy; Brazil] Very vigorous plants that will need a framework of some kind for the tendrils to cling to as the plant develops. Foliage of five-lobed dull green leaves is not particularly attractive, but this is more than compensated for by the exotic flowers that were symbolic for Christian missionaries. They saw in the petals the ten apostles of the Crucifixion, in the five anthers the five wounds, in the three stigmas the nails, in the purple rays of the corola the crown of thorns. In the tendrils they saw the cords and whips and the five-lobed leaves resembled the cruel hands of the persecutors. Given a light airy window position, a gritty, loamy soil and reasonable watering and light feeding, these are fairly easy plants to care for. When too large for indoors they may be planted against a sheltered wall in the garden.

Stephanotis

[Madagascar Jasmine; 10-15°C/50-60°F; Madagascar] As climbing plants with exquisitely scented white tubular flowers borne in clusters, *Stephanotis floribunda* stand supreme. Leaves are leathery and glossy green and, being a natural climber, it is important that adequate supports are provided for the twining stems of the plant to twist around. In winter they should have a light position that is not too hot, and the loam-based potting mixture should be kept only just moist. During spring and summer much more water will be needed, but it is important that the mixture should be free draining to avoid root rot that will result in discoloration and eventual loss of leaves. New plants may be raised from cuttings in a warm propagator in a peat and sand mixture, or they may be raised from seed if seed can be obtained. By cross pollination of flowers you may be able to encourage your own plants to produce seed – the seed pod resembles a large oval-shaped green fruit and should be left on the plant until it turns yellow and actually splits open. It is quite an exciting experience to see the silk-like textured seed 'parachutes' slowly expand and eventually emerge from the seed pod.

Thunbergia alata

[Black-eyed Susan; 7°C/45°F; Tropical Africa] Rather thin, spindly plants whose leaves are not particularly attractive, but the brown-centred orange-yellow flowers are produced in abundance throughout the summer. They may be encouraged to trail or climb, and can be planted out of doors against a sheltered wall for the summer months. Raised from seed sown in a warm propagator in the spring, they should be gradually potted on until they are in 15-20cm/6-8in pots of a good loamy soil. Once established in their final pots they will need to be watered and fed regularly to keep the flower production constant. Throw out once all the flowers have faded.

Below: *Thunbergia alata*, or Black-Eyed Susan; Above: *Passiflora caerulea*, the Passion Flower

Half and year round flowering plants

Aphelandra

[10°C/50°F; Tropical South America] Not many of our flowering houseplants have the added advantage of possessing decorative foliage as well, but in the two most popular varieties of aphelandra we have just such plants. Both have green leaves with prominent white stripes; *A. squarrosa* 'Louisae' is free flowering and may attain a height of some 60cm/2ft, while *A. s.* 'Dania' is smaller and more compact

with more silvery foliage, but is less free with the colourful yellow flower spikes that are the crowning feature of these two fine pot plants.

With both plants it is essential that the soil is kept permanently moist and that plants are regularly fed with a balanced liquid fertilizer – the amount recommended by the manufacturer can be slightly increased and no harm will be done. Aphelandra plants make a mass of roots, hence the need for extra feeding – it is also the reason for using a soil that is loam-based when potting plants on into larger containers, annually in spring.

In summer provide some shade from strong sunlight, but keep the plants away from draughts or they will lose their lower leaves. When the plants have finished flowering it is best to remove the dead flowers and to cut the main stem at the top of the plant back to the first pair of sound leaves, from the axils of which new growth will develop. When these new shoots have developed two pairs of leaves they can be removed and put individually in small pots filled with a peat and sand soil mix –in a heated propagating case they will root in some six weeks.

Begonia

[10°C/50°F; C. & S. America] There are a number of begonias that can be relied upon to produce at least a few flowers for much of the year, but the German Rieger strain of begonia is far and away the most important of commercial flowering begonias. And, like it or not, the commercially important ones are those that the average indoor plant grower is most likely to be able to acquire. In different parts of the world the begonias have been given different names, but the most appropriate to my way of thinking is *B.* 'Fireglow', which captures well the rich, almost glowing colouring of the flowers. These are produced in small clusters from the leaf axils over many months given the right conditions. Red is the most popular colour, but there are also a number of shades of salmon and orange.

Plants are normally sold in 13cm/5in pots and are very dependable indoors. They are quite capable of flowering for most of the year if given a cool, lightly shaded location, a moist peat- or loam-based mixture and regular feeding with weak liquid fertilizer. Dry air is a killer of these plants and often causes flower buds to drop off; therefore, provide as much humidity as possible by setting the pots in moist peat or on trays of pebbles and water. Care should be taken to avoid stuffy condi-

Above: Beloperone guttata.
Right: Flowering begonia

tions as mildew on the leaves can be troublesome – this is also a good reason for keeping water off the leaves at all costs. Mildew can be treated with one of the many fungicides that are available, but even if eradicated it leaves the foliage looking much less attractive. New plants are grown from cuttings of non-flowering shoots taken at almost any time of the year – use cuttings about 8cm/3in in length inserted in a mixture of peat and sand in reasonable heat.

Beloperone guttata

[Shrimp Plant; 70°C/45°F; Mexico] A plant that is forever in keen demand. Soft green leaves are produced on stiff, wiry stems that need no support until plants reach a height of some 45cm/18in. The flowering bracts are a rich shade of brown overlapping white tongue-like blooms and resemble shrimps – hence the common name. They appear almost continually throughout the year. Plants can be pruned to shape after flowering in early spring, and throughout the growing season they will require regular feeding. Potting on into a loam-based mixture with a little extra peat should not be neglected if larger plants are required. To produce larger plants it will also help if the bracts on young plants are removed for the first few months; the plant will then put all its energy into producing more lush foliage. Propagate from cuttings inserted in fresh peat in a propagator, and pot into gradually larger pots as plants fill their existing containers with roots.

Calceolaria

[Slipper Flower; 10-15°C/50-60°F; South America] In common with the majority of flowering pot plants, the calceolaria abhors very hot conditions, and much prefers the cool room that is light and well-ventilated. It is important to keep plants moist at all times and to feed them well. Small plants when first purchased will benefit if potted immediately into a loam-based mixture – this will reduce the need for feeding and encourage plants to retain their rich green colouring. Keep a watchful eye for greenfly and treat immediately. Discard plants when they have finished flowering. Most calceolarias are of hybrid origin and have soft, slightly hairy leaves. The pouch-shaped flowers, borne in large clusters on top of the plants, are usually in shades of red, orange or yellow marked with contrasting colours.

Chrysanthemum

[Hardy; China/Japan] An almost foolproof plant indoors provided it is purchased in the right condition – that is with several flowers well open and lots of buds to follow that are showing colour. In winter, if in too backward condition, flowers will frequently fail to form properly before turning black. So buy in good condition to begin with, then keep moist in a cool room that is well-ventilated and as light as possible. After flowering, either plant in the garden or discard.

Left and above: Beautifully coloured chrysanthemums are popular gift plants.
Top: The pouch-shaped calceolaria flowers.
Opposite above: *Cineraria cruenta*.
Opposite below: *Impatiens sultani variegata*

28

that has weak, spindly growth in most instances, and tubular cigar flowers that are scarlet, black and white in colour and appear from April until December. The shape of the flower and the presence of the white lip of the flower give the plant the appearance of a miniature cigar end glowing. Can be propagated from seed or cuttings in the spring and requires cool and reasonably light conditions in the home. Grow mature plants in good loam, moist and fed during the growing season.

Exacum affine

[13-16°C/55-61°F; South East Asia] Compact flowering plant that seldom attains a height of more than 24cm/9in, and has bluish-lilac flowers that are pleasantly fragrant. Small, glossy green leaves are in themselves attractive. Grows best in cool and light conditions, and requires regular watering and feeding. Propagate from seed at gentle heat in spring or summer and pot on into a loam or peat soil. Although they are perennial it is better to raise new plants each year.

Impatiens

[Busy Lizzie; 10-13°C/50-55°F; Tropical Africa] Known to everyone, Busy Lizzies propagate like weeds either in water or more conventionally in pots of potting mixture. Once cuttings have rooted well their tops should be pinched out to provide more bushy plants. Thereafter, pot on as required and keep the peat- or loam-based soil moist at all times. Feed well when plants are in their final pots. Many excellent varieties to choose from, the colour range spanning white, pink, red, deep crimson, orange and purple. They flower almost continually and are all easy to grow in the pleasant warmth of a bright room that is well-ventilated on warmer days.

Lantana

[7°C/45°F, Tropical America] Tall and woody evergreen shrubs with somewhat coarse and unattractive appearance as far as foliage goes, but more appealing once flowers appear. Individual flowers are small and tubular, but form a pleasing globular head and are available in a wide range of colours from white through bright yellow, pink, orange and bright red, over many months. Can be grown out of doors in summer, and need cool and light conditions in the home. Principal drawback is the uncanny numbers of whitefly that the plant is capable of becoming host to—these should be got under control as soon as detected. Propagate from seed sown in spring or from cuttings taken in late summer. Provide a gritty loam-based soil and good light; water freely, but keep just moist in winter and feed every two weeks once the flower buds begin to form.

Cineraria cruenta (Senecio cruentus)

[8°C/46°F; Canary Islands] A superb perennial flowering plant, producing masses of daisy-like flowers in a range of bright colours. It is best treated as an annual and discarded after it has passed its best. Easily raised from seed sown at any time in the spring in cool conditions – April sowings will, if you are fortunate, provide flowering plants for late December. Indoor plants when mature should enjoy lightly shaded and airy conditions, and should be kept just moist and well-fed with a balanced liquid fertilizer.

Cuphea ignea

[Cigar Flower; 7°C/45°F; Mexico] An amusing rather than attractive evergreen plant

Pachystachys lutea

[Lollipop Plant; 15 C/60 F; Tropical South America] This produces curious upright cones of yellow-flowering bracts with protruding white flowers throughout the summer months and likes to be permanently moist and fed regularly. Pot on when well rooted in a loam-based mixture. Cuttings of non-flowering shoots a few cm in length may be taken at any time if a warm propagating case is available. Develops to a shrub of some 1.2m/4ft in height, but can be kept under control by pruning after flowering. A light, warm position is needed indoors with shade from hot sun.

Saintpaulia

[African Violet; 13°C/55°F; Central Africa] The man who first set eyes on some scruffy little violet-like plants in what was Tanganyika could not possibly have realized what a startling discovery he had made. Countless millions are produced by the commercial growers annually, and countless millions more are raised by almost everyone who has a windowsill and an interest in these amazing plants. The numerous varieties come in single- or double-flowered forms, the violet-shaped flowers ranging from white through shades of pink, red, purple and blue. Leaves are almost round in shape, light or dark green according to the variety, and are covered in fine hairs. There are also varieties with leaves that are cristated, waved and what have you, but most are as described.

Leaves that are fresh, of good colour and generally sound will root with little bother in small pots filled with a peat and sand mixture. They can be rooted in water, but the soil mixture method is best. A small, heated propagating case will speed the rooting process, as will treating the ends of the cuttings with rooting powder. When little bunches of leaves have formed at the base of the leaf stalk (don't poke about in the soil, they will come naturally in their own good time!) the plant should have all the mixture gently teased away and the young plantlets can then be gently separated and planted up individually in shallow pans of peat and sand. When of reasonable size, pot them in soilless mixture individually, and keep them in the propagator if possible until they have become established. Treated in this way plants of more attractive appearance will result – it will take longer to get plants of any size but they will show off their flowers very much better.

Saintpaulias are best grown in a peat-based soil; they must have adequate light, and this will mean the light windowsill during the day (but shaded from sun scorch) and going underneath a light of some kind in the evening

during winter. Placing plants on a bed of moist pebbles will help to provide the essential humidity and they should ideally be watered with tepid, rather than cold water. Keep water off leaves and flowers – it is usually best to stand the plant in a saucer of water and allow it to draw up all that is required by capillary action.

Established plants will benefit from feeding with a balanced liquid fertilizer. But if plants produce lots of lush leaves and seem reluctant to flower it may help if the fertilizer normally used is changed to a tomato fertilizer. Use the latter at weak dilution and feed with a weak dose fairly often – every week – rather than give heavy doses occasionally.

Salpiglossis

[10°C/50°F; Chile] These are good examples of half-hardy garden annuals that may be put to excellent use as pot plants. Indoors, they

require cool, light and airy conditions with a watering programme that is never neglected. Salpiglossis, with brightly-coloured flowers, make fine feature plants up to 60cm/2ft high in the entrance hall of the house, if this is properly lit. Seed may be sown at any time between February and September, and if sowing can be staggered over this period then plants may be had in flower from July and through to the following spring. When potting use a loam-based mixture.

Spathiphyllum

[White Sails; 13°C/55°F; Tropical America] These are two that the houseplant grower is likely to come across: S. *wallisii* growing to a maximum height of about 46cm/18in and S. × 'Mauna Loa', a much more majestic plant with flowering stems that may attain a height of 91-122cm/3-4ft in good specimens. Being aroids both require moist conditions at their roots and a humid atmosphere, as well as light shade in preference to strong light. When potting use a peaty mixture and to increase plants the roots should be divided and pieces potted up individually. This can be done at any

time if plants are not in flower. The flowers are white in colour and consist of a waxy upright spathe and give an exotic touch to a plant collection; even after losing their white colour they retain a dull green colour that has a certain amount of appeal with their bright green shiny leaves.

Streptocarpus

[Cape Primrose; 10°C/50°F; South Africa] In recent years there has been a considerable improvement in the range of streptocarpus. A major factor in favour of these pleasing plants is that they flower over a very long period, from late spring to autumn. In spite of the newcomers, the old variety, S. × *hybridus* 'Constant Nymph', is still a firm favourite with its attractive blue flowers that bloom freely from May to October or even later. New plants may either be raised from seed or leaf cuttings. In the home they require good light and reasonably cool conditions in which to grow. Neither watering nor feeding should be excessive. A loam-based mixture with a little additional peat should be used when potting.

Opposite above: *Spathiphyllum* × 'Mauna Loa' may grow to a height of 90-120cm/3-4ft.
Opposite below: *Pachystachys lutea*.
Above: Salpiglossis require cool, light conditions.
Left: Saintpaulias, or African Violets, are sometimes difficult to flower, but a tomato fertilizer will help

Foliage houseplants

Aglaonema

[16°C/61°F; South East Asia] There are a number of aglaonemas to be seen in tropical collections, but not many that are commercial propositions so they are not often offered for sale. All of them require warm, shaded and humid conditions if they are to succeed. The mixture, which should contain a high percentage of peat, must be kept moist at all times, but saturation for long periods should be avoided. Wait four to six months before feeding newly potted plants, and thereafter at three-month intervals. Mealy bug is a troublesome pest that is difficult to eradicate – bugs are found among the closely-grouped leaves, which makes the essential contact with insecticide difficult to achieve. *A. commutatum* 'White Rajah' (*A. pseudobracteatum*) grows 30-60cm/12-24in tall, has spear-shaped leaves variegated with gold and cream and is generally more colourful than most aglaonemas which are mottled shades of green and grey. Curious white or yellow flower spathes appear on mature plants. New plants may be raised either from cuttings or by division of clumps of mature plants. When propagating, warm, moist and shaded conditions are essential. Fresh sphagnum peat will be the best medium to start plants off in.

Araucaria excelsa

[Norfolk Island Pine; 7°C/45°F; Norfolk Island] Typical needle pine leaves are shaded dark and light green and develop on horizontal branches that radiate from the main stem. The spaced tiers of leaves are the principal attraction of this plant which is one of the true aristocrats among the foliage plants that are suited to cooler room conditions. Set in a well-lit airy position, watering freely in spring and summer, less in winter. New plants may be raised from cuttings of stem tips, or from seed – the latter method produces plants with more attractive symmetrical growth. However, seed is very difficult to obtain, so it is often better to seek out young plants that may be grown on. When potting, clay pots will help to balance plants better than plastic ones as plants are inclined to be top heavy. Although plant growth will be slower in loam-based mixture, a better plant will result than if the plant is grown in a peat medium. Clay pots must have a good layer of broken pots placed in the bottom before soil is introduced, as good drainage is most important. (This advice applies in particular to araucarias, but should be standard practice with clay pots, especially when using a loam-based mixture.)

Asparagus

[7°C/45°F; South Africa] *A. medeoloides* (smilax) and *A. plumosus* (asparagus fern) make very effective potted plants, or plants for the wall of the heated conservatory, but are most frequently seen as cut foliage in floral arrangements and other designs created by the florist. One of the most durable of potted ornamental asparagus, and the one most frequently seen, is *A. sprengeri*, which can either be grown as a trailing plant or encouraged to climb a plant frame. Choose a loam-based soil and a well-lit spot, shaded from direct sun. Feed every two weeks and give plenty of water in spring and summer. Keep just moist in winter. New plants may be raised from seed sown in a temperature of around 20°C/70°F in the spring, but it will be much simpler to propagate by division of roots in the spring.

Aspidistra elatior

[Cast Iron Plant; 7°C/45°F; China] The great favourite of the Victorian era, the aspidistra still has much to commend it and is most effective when seen in its traditional setting – that is atop its Victorian plant pedestal and growing in its rather grand and flowery Victorian plant pot. The oblong-lanceolate leaves, up to 50cm/20in long, are green and somewhat coarse in appearance and are produced on short stalks that emerge directly from the soil in which it is growing. There is a rare variegated form. Easy to care for in shaded conditions, but one should avoid getting the loam-based mixture sogging wet, and at no time should the leaves be cleaned with anything other than a sponge moistened in water. Propagate at almost any time by dividing older clumps and potting them in a rich loam-based mixture.

Begonia rex

[15°C/60°F; South East Asia] The king of the begonias is grown entirely for its colourful foliage. Blended into or overlaid on the green wrinkled leaves can be found a kaleidoscope of colours – red, pink, silver, cream, grey, lavender and maroon. Although plants may be encouraged to grow to 60cm/2ft in height and 60cm/2ft in diameter in ideal conditions in the greenhouse, they are usually seen as much smaller plants decorating window ledges and in mixed arrangements with other plants. Mildew on leaves, which appears as white circular spots, is one of the most troublesome problems and is most prevalent in surroundings that are dank and airless. So a buoyant humid atmosphere and reasonably light conditions are needed, but strong sunlight must be avoided. A peaty soil is essential and it should be kept moist, but never soggy wet.

Raise new plants by slitting the veins on the undersides of a mature leaf in places before placing it on a mixture of peat and sand. It may be necessary to peg the leaves down with hairpin-shaped wires, or by placing small pebbles on top of the leaf. Alternatively, the stronger and older leaves may be cut up into 2.5cm/1in-wide squares and simply placed on moist peat and sand. This is a fascinating means of propagation, but it is extremely important that the propagating medium must at no time dry out as the small leaf sections will quickly shrivel up and die. Moistness of a happy medium should be the aim, as leaf sections will also rot readily in very wet conditions. When potting on larger plants a peaty, open soil is essential. It will be found that freshly-bought plants are often in pots that are much too small for them, making it necessary to pot the plants on almost as soon as they are acquired.

Calathea

[13-16°C/55-61°F; Brazil] Exotically-coloured leaves in many shades of green and brown are the order of the day here, and *C. makoyana* (Peacock Plant) with its exquisitely patterned leaves is one of the most striking of foliage plants. It fully justifies its common name of Peacock Plant. The leaves of *C. zebrina* are light and dark green and have a texture that is reminiscent of velvet. *C. insignis* has narrower more densely clustered foliage that is also very impressive. Not plants for the beginner, the suggested minimum temperature must be maintained, and the general conditions surrounding the plants should be moist and shaded; ideally water and spray with rainwater as tap water may leave white marks on the foliage. Propagate by division of the rhizomes in summer, and at all stages of growth a peaty, open soil must be used.

Opposite: The wrinkled green leaves of *Begonia rex* are overlaid with a kaleidoscope of red, pink, silver, cream, grey, lavender and maroon. Above: Everyone's favourite houseplant,

Chlorophytum elatum, and a variegated hedera. Above right: *Aspidistra elatior*, very popular in the Victorian era, is easy to care for in shaded conditions

Ceropegia woodii

[Hearts Entangled; 10°C/50°F; South Africa] The leaves of this plant are a mottled grey-green in colour and heart-shaped with a puffed-up succulent appearance. Flowers in autumn are brown and insignificant. Essentially trailing plants, one of the principal fascinations, as the common name suggests, is the way in which the slender trailing stems and leaves entwine around one another. Easily grown in almost any light position where the trails can hang over the sides of the pot. Plants in pots of comparatively small size will produce yards of growth. Water sparingly in winter. To increase, insert individual leaves with a piece of stem attached in small pots filled with moist peat. Grow on in a rich loam-based soil.

Chlorophytum elatum

[Spider Plant; 7°C/45°F; South Africa] Everyone's favourite, this very graceful green and cream striped grass-like foliage plant, also listed as *C. comosum* or *C. capense*, can be seen on the windowsill of almost all who keep plants indoors. There are several reasons for this and chief among them are the facts that the Spider Plant is extremely easy to grow, and can be propagated by a novice. To grow them successfully they need little more than a light windowsill position, ample watering in spring and summer, and feeding with liquid manure once a week in summer – it is also advisable to pot them on into larger containers annually in March or April using a loam-based soil. Excessive watering in winter when temperatures indoors are generally lower will cause brown streakmarks to appear in the centre of some leaves. Propagation is simply effected by pegging the small plantlets, that develop as perfect replicas of the parent in miniature, down in pots or boxes of soil and allowing them to root before severing the stalk that attaches the small plant to its parent. Plants that are starved of nourishment will develop brown tips to their leaves, which should be snipped off with scissors. However, little harm is done as new leaves are very quick to develop.

33

Cissus

[Kangaroo Vine; 10°C/50°F; Australia] The most important plant here is *C. antarctica* which has been popular for many years, but does not always do well indoors. Generally warm conditions, and particularly the dry conditions that prevail in centrally-heated rooms, can be disastrous as far as this plant is concerned. In excessive heat there is a tendency for the foliage to dehydrate so that it shrivels and dies. Cool, shaded and reasonably moist conditions at the roots are far the best way of getting the best from it. However, it often comes into its own when one is seeking a plant for the difficult positions in the hallway where it is often much too cool for most houseplants. The plant is a natural climber with attractive shiny green leaves that are tooth-edged. It needs a good loamy soil and a framework of canes or trellis on which to climb. Propagate from cuttings taken with a single leaf.

Codiaeum (Croton)

[Joseph's Coat; 16-18°C/61-64°F; South East Asia] Challenging plants that are available in many shades of orange, red and yellow, white, cream and purple-black, with some plants having all these colours in many shades present in a single leaf. In keeping with the majority of plants with highly-coloured leaves, Joseph's Coat is not at all easy to care for and will require the conditions that most tender plants demand and the skills of the experienced grower to maintain them in good order. In ideal greenhouse conditions plants will attain a height of 3m/10ft or more, by which time they are a truly magnificent sight; as a pot plant the usual height is 60cm/2ft. Maximum sunlight, though no scorching, is essential if they are to retain their exotic colouring, and it is also important that the soil should at no time be allowed to dry out. Liquid feeding of established plants once a week during summer must not be neglected, and it will be found that mature plants will require fertilizer at at least double the strength that the manufacturer recommends. When potting these plants, it is advisable to use a loam-based compost or a proprietary peat mix.

Propagate by means of cuttings about 13cm/5in in length taken from the top-most growth of the plant. Treat the severed end with rooting powder before inserting the cutting in a peat and sand mixture–the temperature in the propagator must be in the region of 20°C/70°F. Although conditions are not ideal, crotons will go on for a considerable time in a warm room that is well provided with windows, but draughts and sudden drops in temperature can prove fatal.

Coleus

[13°C/55°F; South East Asia] Of the less expensive foliage houseplants there are none that can compare with the Variegated Dead Nettles when it comes to leaf colouring. From a single packet of seed sown in the greenhouse in the spring come plants with colours and colour combinations of an almost infinite variety, including purple, red, bronze, yellow and white. Although seed-grown plants are not as good as named varieties that have been raised from cuttings (taken at any time when they are available provided there is a warm greenhouse or propagating case available for starting them off in) you can, nevertheless, get some very fine plants if the best colours are selected for growing on in larger pots. Pinch out the growing points regularly to promote bushy side growth. Coleus are generally greedy in respect of feeding, but need for feeding can be reduced by potting plants on into larger pots–it would be quite possible to have spring sown seedlings growing in 18cm/7in pots by the autumn. Use a loam-based mixture when potting and be sure to select only the best coloured plants, as there is no point in lavishing extra care on some of the more cabbage-like plants that one may find among the seedlings. All coleus do best in good light and reasonable warmth with a little tender care thrown in for good measure. Although seldom grown on for a second year, good forms can be overwintered for cuttings to be taken from them in spring.

Cordyline

[7-13°C/45-55°F; South East Asia] Much confusion exists concerning the naming of cordyline species and the similar dracaenas. Both are palm-like shrubs, grown for their ornamental foliage, and you will often find cordylines with dracaena name tags and vice versa. Some of the cordylines are hardy in mild districts, such as *C. indivisa*, with long narrow leaves, green with red or yellow midribs, all arising from a single unbranched trunk, up to 1.2m/4ft. It is a particularly durable plant that does very well in a pot in light airy rooms. More ornamental and also more tender is *C. terminalis*, often listed as *Dracaena terminalis*, of which there are a number of varieties. The species has swordshaped leaves that are deep green in young plants, but maturing to exotic shades of brilliant red, purple, cream, bronze and pink, according to variety. To retain the colouring it is important that the plants should be grown in good light. It is equally important to keep the growing mixture–a good loam or a proprietary peat mix–moist and to avoid extremes of wet and dry conditions. Soft rainwater is preferred for watering. *C. indivisa* will put up with cool temperatures, but *C.*

terminalis needs at least 13°C/55°F in winter. Propagation is effected in May or June by cutting up the thicker fleshy roots that develop on older plants into sections about 5cm/2in in length and inserting them in a peat and sand mixture in a heated propagating case.

Ctenanthe

[13-16°C/55-61°F; Brazil] Closely related to the calatheas which they resemble and with which they are often confused–possibly not without reason when one considers the difficulty of pronunciation. Both genera require similar treatment and conditions–plants should be kept moist, shaded and fairly warm if they are to do well. Wherever possible it will be an advantage if the plant pots can be plunged to their rims in moist peat. The best of the ctenanthes is *C. oppenheimiana* 'Tricolor', a compact tufted variety with narrow leaves that are banded in silver on the upper surfaces and a deep shade of maroon on the reverse. Propagate by dividing mature clumps at almost any time other than during colder winter months.

Cussonia spicata

[7-10°C/45-50°F; South Africa] A handsome tree with palmate leaves that are supported on strong stems; they are deeply divided on mature plants and of widely differing shapes. Glossy dark green, purple beneath. Even when roots are confined to large pots it will become a fairly substantial tree in a comparatively short space of time. Keep moist, well fed in a loam-

based soil and a light airy spot; pot on annually, but purchase only if there is ample space for the plant to develop, otherwise it could become an embarrassment. New plants are raised from seed.

Cyperus

[Umbrella Grass; 13°C/55°F; Africa] Never allow plants to remain wet in their pots for long periods, is almost standard advice when the experienced plantsman is asked for his, or her, advice on watering. However, there are a few exceptions to this rule, and the moisture-loving, rush-like cyperus is one of them. The loam mixture must be kept permanently wet, and it is usually advisable to allow the plant pot actually to stand in water (for most pot plants this would almost certainly mean a quick death). Cyperus develop grass-like growth at the top of slender stems which give an umbrella appearance, hence the common name. Stalks of *C. diffusus* are about 60cm/2ft tall and more numerous than those of *C. alternifolius* which attain a height of 1.8-2.4m/6-8ft even when plant roots are confined to pots. Dividing mature clumps is the best method of propagation.

Dieffenbachia

[Dumb Cane; 15°C/60°F; Tropical America] There are many exciting plants to be found in this genus of outstanding foliage plants, but only very few are suited to other than warm greenhouse conditions. Warm, moist and shaded conditions suit them best, protected from draughts. Use a rich loam-based soil. By far the best one for indoor use is *D.*

'Exotica', which has compact habit and superbly variegated cream, white and green leaves. As plants age, typical arum inflorescences are produced from the topmost leaf axils, but as these do nothing for the plant they should be removed. You should wash your hands after cutting any part of dieffenbachia plants, as the sap contains a poison that could render you speechless if enough of it gets onto your tongue. The variety 'Tropic Snow' is an even bolder plant attaining a height of some 1.5m/5ft with larger leaves and darker green colouring – a fine plant if space is not a problem. Dieffenbachias can be propagated by removing young plants from around the base of the stem of the parent, or the main stem of mature plants can be cut into 5cm/2in-long sections and partly buried in moist peat in a propagating case that is kept at around 20°C/70°F.

Dizygotheca elegantissima

[False Aralia; 15°C/60°F; New Hebrides] Formerly included in the genus Aralia, these graceful foliage plants will develop into small trees when cultivated in ideal surroundings. Plants are at their best when about 1.5m/5ft in height, thereafter the leaves begin to lose their fine, rich blue-black filigree appearance, and become much coarser and broader. But this is not likely to affect the grower of indoor plants unless he is particularly skilful in their care. Moist, lightly shaded and evenly warm conditions are most essential, as is a rich gritty soil and regular watering. Seed is the best method of raising plants, but it will be difficult to obtain.

Dracaena

[15°C/60°F; Tropical Africa] With the one exception of *D. godseffiana* 'Florida Beauty' (the best of this type) these are most erect plants of superb appearance that will add a new dimension to almost any plant collection. They will all do better in rich loam and in conditions that offer reasonable warmth, light shade and watering that errs on the side of dry rather than wet conditions. *D. marginata* has green, narrow and rigid leaves with a faint red margin and is one of the easiest to care for, while its variegated form, *D. marginata* 'Tricolor', has reddish-pink colouring and is one of the most exciting

Above left: A sunny dining room is enlivened by a *Ficus benjamina*, *Monstera deliciosa* and *Philodendron hastatum*.
Left: The furry purple leaves of *Gynura sarmentosa* give it its common name, Velvet Nettle.
Top: × *Fatshedera lizei* is a trailing or climbing plant perfect for staircases or balconies.
Above: One of the most exciting plants to be introduced recently, *Dracaena marginata* 'Tricolor'

plants to be introduced in recent years. There are many forms of *D. deremensis*, all of them with boldly striped leaves borne on stems that attain a height of some 2.4m/8ft when grown in ideal conditions. There are also several forms of *D. fragrans* – these have broader leaves that are longer and more curved as the plant develops. There are various methods of propagation, but the simplest is to cut stems into sections and partially bury them horizontally in a peat and sand mixture. *D. godseffiana* is done from top cuttings with three or four leaves attached inserted in peat and sand in warm conditions.

Euonymus

[Spindle Tree; 7-10°C/45-50°F; Japan] The golden form of this perfectly hardy garden plant will be fine as an indoor plant if placed in good soil on a light windowsill in a cool room. The amount of water given should not be excessive, and when feeding the plant moderation should be the watchword. To retain variegation green growth must be removed as it appears. The best variety is *E. japonica* 'Aurea', with golden-yellow glossy ovate leaves. To increase, use cuttings a few cm in length taken in spring or summer.

x Fatshedera

[7°C/45°F; Garden Origin] Attractive five-lobed green leaves are borne on erect stems that become woody with age – provision of a stake to support the plant is essential. There seems to be no limit to the amount of growth that a single stem will put on as you will frequently see them climbing and wandering along staircases and balconies with leading growth tied in to point them in the right direction. Reasonably easy to care for in cool, lightly shaded conditions. The plant is an interesting man-made cross between *Fatsia* (Aralia) *japonica* and *Hedera helix*, the green ivy. Grow in a rich loam-based mixture, potting on annually in March. New plants come from taking cuttings in July or August of either the top section of the plant or from single leaves with a piece of stem attached.

Fatsia (Aralia)

[4°C/39°F; Japan] Fine room plants for locations that are cool and light rather than stuffy and dark. Plants become quite large in time, up to 2.4m/8ft. Large palmate leaves are glossy, green in colour and form compact plants that are extremely useful when arranging groups of larger plants in a setting. A reasonably quick grower. New plants are raised from seed sown in the spring of the year.

Ficus

[7-18°C/45-64°F; Tropical Asia] The many species in this large genus are very varied and have different cultural requirements. Most frequently seen is the conventional Rubber Plant with its upright habit and glossy green leaves, the care of which may present some problems. The first of the conventional Rubber Plants was *F. elastica*, which gave way to the improved *F. elastica* 'Decora', which in turn has been superseded by the much stronger growing and greatly improved *F. elastica* 'Robusta'. Yet another variety, 'Black Prince', has much darker, almost black leaves and is gradually gaining in favour. All of these varieties are very tolerant of shady positions, and need a winter night temperature around 16°C/61°F. But, above all, it is most important that water should be given in moderation – the mixture should be well watered and allowed to dry out a little before the next application, as excessive watering will surely damage the root system which will in turn result in loss of leaves. Moderation really is the key word in most respects and also applies to feeding and potting the plant on into larger containers – the new pot should only be slightly larger than the old one and the need for potting on should only arise every second year unless plants are growing very vigorously. To improve the appearance of Rubber Plants they should have their leaves cleaned with a soft, damp cloth occasionally.

Most of the other ficus that one is likely to come across – *F. pumila*, *F. benjamina*, *F. lyrata*, *F. diversifolia* and *F. radicans* 'Variegata' – will all require to be kept a little moister, more shaded and some degrees cooler in winter in order to get best results from them. *F. pumila* is commonly named Creeping Fig on account of its prostrate habit and has small green oval-shaped leaves on thin, wiry, trailing stems. *F. radicans* 'Variegata' is similar in habit with slightly more pointed leaves that are attractively white and green variegated. If a graceful indoor tree is required than *F. benjamina*, the Weeping Fig, with its glossy green leaves would be an admirable choice. Also developing to tree size in time, *F. lyrata*, the Fiddle-back Fig, has glossy leaves that are roughly similar to the body of a violin. It is, however, one of the more difficult of the ficus tribe to care for. *F. diversifolia* is slower growing and takes many years to grow into a smallish bush – the most interesting feature of this plant is the way in which it seems to be constantly producing small berries that appear on even the smallest of plants. Some of the ficus may be raised from seed, but most of them are propagated from cuttings.

Fittonia

[Snakeskin Plant; 16°C/61°F; Peru] Both *F. verschaffeltii* with its red-veined oval leaves and creeping habit, and *F. argyroneura* with ivory-veined leaves of similar shape are difficult plants to care for regardless of the location. They must have constant warmth, fairly heavy shade and high humidity if they are to do well. However, in recent years a miniature form of the latter has appeared on the scene and is proving to be one of the most popular plant introductions. The leaves are small, congested and silvery and the plant has proved to be reasonably easy to care for, certainly much less of a problem than the parent from which it would seem to have sprung. It abhors direct sunlight and cold conditions, but otherwise seems very tolerant of room conditions. The simplest method of propagation is to place a small plant in the centre of a pot of moist peat and to allow the plant to grow over the peat and root into the medium. When rooted the pieces can be snipped off and potted up individually.

Gynura

[Velvet Nettle; 10°C/50°F; South East Asia] Very easily grown plants the gynuras should have a light situation to encourage their purple colouring. To prevent plants becoming too straggly the growing tips of shoots should be periodically removed. Feed regularly, avoid getting the loam- or peat-based soil too wet for long periods and they will give little bother. *G. aurantiaca* is larger and more vigorous than the better form *G. sarmentosa*, which eventually requires support, or it may be allowed to trail if grown in a hanging basket. Flowers have an unpleasant odour so should be removed as they appear. New plants are easily raised from cuttings taken at almost any time of the year.

Hedera

[Ivy; frost-free; Europe and Canary Islands]
The ivies are among the easiest of plants to care for given the right treatment and conditions, but they can be something of a problem if conditions are much too hot or much too wet. Hot and dry conditions can present a big problem in that plants will be very much more susceptible to attack from red spider mites, and these can reduce ivies to a dry and shrivelled mess in a very short space of time. There are no end of varieties to choose from, all of which will put up with cool and lightly shaded spots. *H. canariensis* 'Variegata', with its white and green variegation, the mottle-leaved 'Maculata' and 'Gold leaf', which has large green leaves with pale yellow centres.

Being natural trailing plants, the smaller-leaved ivies *H. helix* are always much in demand for use in mixed arrangements. There are any number of ivies with green leaves, many of them very similar, but others are very distinct in their appearance, quite a few being cristated. Among the variegated small-leaved ones there are many real gems. 'Little Diamond' and 'Adam', both with grey and white variegated leaves, are two of the best, but there are many more that one may chance to find in shop, garden centre or nursery. All of them root readily in peaty mixture, and best results will be obtained if several cuttings rather than one are put in each pot. Cuttings of smaller-leaved ones should be about 8cm/3in in length, while large-leaved ones will require a piece of stem with two leaves attached.

Helxine

[Mind Your Own Business or Baby's Tears; 7°C/45°F; Corsica] Everyone's plant, grows like the proverbial weed (which it is in outdoor situations) and forms neat mounds of minute green leaves. Enjoys all conditions other than those that are badly lit or are excessively hot. Keep moist and make new plants periodically. Dispose of old ones – minute pieces root like weeds.

Heptapleurum arboricola

[Green Rays; 15°C/60°F] The green palmate leaves look most effective when plants are growing on a single stem, but will also grow as a compact bush if the top of the plant is removed. Abhors radical changes in temperature or in amount of water that is given, and reacts by shedding leaves rather alarmingly, so keep the soil evenly moist throughout the year. However, in even temperature and in mixture that is kept evenly moist it becomes a most graceful plant. Does become quite large in time but can be pruned to shape whenever it may seem to be getting out of hand. New

plants raised from a single leaf with a piece of stem attached – a heated propagating case is essential.

Maranta

[Prayer Plant; 15°C/60°F; Tropical America] Mostly superb foliage plants the marantas need warm, moist and shaded locations. An interesting feature of this plant is the way in which leaves fold together as darkness descends. The most striking in this respect is *M. leuconeura* 'Kerchoveana' the leaves of which stand perfectly erect at nightfall – a greenhouse full of them can be an eerie sight when the lights are turned on during the night. This plant has pale grey-green leaves with distinctive dark

blotches that make the plant very interesting. When potting, all the marantas will require a peaty soil, also shallow pots which will be more in proportion with their squat appearance. They will all also do better if plant pots can be plunged to their rims in moist peat. Marantas are rapid growers and need potting on several times until they are in final 15cm/6in pots.

A more recent introduction is *M. leuconeura* 'Erythrophylla' which has reddish-brown colouring and intricately marked leaves in a herringbone pattern, and is an altogether bolder grower than the first mentioned. Despite the exotic colouring that would seem to suggest a delicate plant only suitable for the heated greenhouse, it is much more tolerant of room conditions than would seem possible. Growth that becomes untidy can be pruned to shape at any time, but is probably best done during the summer months when severed pieces can be cut up into sections and used for propagating new plants. A peat and sand mix should be used for inserting cuttings in and a warm propagator will greatly improve chances of success.

Monstera

[Swiss Cheese Plant; 10°C/50°F; Mexico] *Monstera deliciosa* possesses all the qualities that are required of a good houseplant subject. Leaves are a rich green in colour and have a

Left: *Hedera helix* 'Little Eva'.
Above: *Heptapleurum arboricola*.
Opposite: Large plants, such as *Howeia belmoreana* and *Monstera deliciosa*, are used effectively

natural gloss to them which is heightened when plants are cleaned with a proprietary leaf cleaner. White oil used at a strength of approximately one tablespoon to 3 litres/5 pints of water will improve the look of most plants with glossy leaves, but soft new leaves should never be cleaned. It will also help to keep pests under control. In ideal conditions the monstera will produce quite enormous leaves that, as well as being deeply serrated along their margins, will also become naturally perforated. Monstera plants will do better if the aerial roots that grow from the main stem can be directed into a container of water from which supplies will be drawn for the plant, thus reducing the need for too frequent watering of the mixture in the pot in which the roots of the plant are growing. Many questions are asked about whether or not these aerial roots should be removed from the plant, and the answer is that they should be directed into the mixture, or a container of water if such an arrangement does not present too many difficulties. However, it would not be too harmful to a large plant for some aerial roots to be taken off with a sharp knife. For best results monsteras should enjoy conditions that are fairly moist, shaded from the sun and reasonably warm.

When potting plants on into larger pots, a mix comprised of equal parts loam-based mixture and sphagnum peat or clean leafmould should be used. Mature plants produce exquisite creamy-white infloresences, the spathe part of which remains colourful for only a few days while the spadix in the centre develops into a rich-tasting fruit, which should be left until it is almost mushy ripe before it is eaten. New plants are raised by removing the growing tip with one mature leaf and inserting them in a peaty mix.

Pellionia

[15°C/60°F; South East Asia] Prostrate creeping plants that are ideal for covering the surface of the soil in containers that include other plants or for hanging baskets. Leaves are small and multi-coloured, and seem to take on ever more bright colours if plants are given only the minimum amount of fertilizer. Plants root readily into peat, gravel or any other loose surface that they may wander over–rooted pieces should be cut from the parent plant and potted up individually.

Peperomia

[13°C/55°F; Tropical America] The keen indoor plantsman may in time collect quite a number of peperomias, but not all of them are suitable as houseplants, or very attractive as potted plants for that matter. So a certain amount of selectivity is needed, and it will usually be found that those plants favoured by the commercial growers are, in fact, the better plants for room decoration. Possibly the most popular are varieties of *P. magnoliaefolia*, of compact habit and producing thick, fleshy leaves that are an attractive cream and green in colour in the variegated forms. Similar in colour is *P. glabella* 'Variegata' which has small light green and white leaves and is of trailing habit, so useful for many locations indoors where more erect plants would be out of place. These two will require a reasonably light position in the room and a watering programme that errs on the dry side. However, provide a humid atmosphere from April to September, syringing the leaves twice a day when hot. As peperomias go, a larger plant that may well suit the more selective purchaser is *P. obtusifolia*, of which there are a number of varieties. Leaves are a purplish green in colour and are about 10cm/4in in length–mature plants attain a height of some 30cm/1ft. All the foregoing may be propagated between April and August, either from top cuttings with two or three leaves attached, or they may be done with a single leaf with a piece of stem attached.

Peperomia caperata and *P. hederaefolia* are both propagated by using individual leaves with petiole attached and inserting far enough for the leaves to remain erect in a peat and sand mixture. The first mentioned has small dark green purple-tinted leaves that are crinkled and heart-shaped, while the latter has leaves of similar shape, a quilted texture and an overall metallic-grey colouring. All the peperomias do well in soilless, or very peaty mixture.

Philodendron

[15°C/60°F; Tropical America] Many and fine species are in this genus, some quite majestic and much too large for the average living room, while others like the Sweetheart Plant, *P. scandens*, with small heart-shaped leaves and habit, are ideal for room decoration. As one wishes, *P. scandens* can be encouraged to trail or climb depending on requirements. All of the philodendrons will appreciate the maximum amount of humidity that can be provided, and this will mean use of a larger container filled with peat for plunging plant pots, and regular spraying over of the foliage. *P. hastatum* has much larger green leaves that are arrow-shaped, and will develop into a plant of substantial size if a stout support can be provided. In fact, with all members of the aroid family it will considerably improve their performance if a thick layer of sphagnum moss can be wired to the supporting stake – this will encourage the aerial roots to work their way into the moss, so helping the plant to obtain additional moisture. The moss should be maintained in moist conditions by regular spraying, or by using a watering can to moisten the moss from the top of the support. When doing this, be careful not to get the soil in the pot too

Left: *Philodendron laciniatum* is supported by a sphagnum moss-covered stake.
Below: *Philodendron scandens* and *Rhoicissus rhomboidea* in a decorative container.
Opposite top: A large *Cissus antarctica*.
Opposite below: *Pilea cadierei*

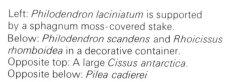

probably the easiest to care for. It has dark green, small oblong leaves with silvery markings. Plants need regular feeding if they are to retain their attractive silver-grey colouring. Also regular pinching out of leading shoots is necessary in order to keep plants compact.

Piper

[15°C/60°F; South East Asia] The plant you are most likely to come across here is *P. ornatum*, but even this may not be possible as they are all scarce. A climbing plant with most attractive waxy heart-shaped leaves that are pale green on the reverse, and a slightly deeper green on the surface with silver pink etched into the green. A most attractive plant, not easy to grow, so it is only recommended for those with well above average conditions. Warmth, light shade and evenly moist soil are necessary, also a free-draining peaty mixture. Propagate from cuttings kept in a warm propagator.

Pittosporum

[7°C/45°F; Australia/New Zealand] Hardy in milder areas, but suggested minimum temperature will give better results when plants are being grown in pots of good loam. Many types available, and *P. tenuifolium* is much used by florists for mixing in with cut flowers as pleasant glossy green foliage. There are variegated varieties and some with attractive undulating leaf margins. Propagate in July from 10cm/4in-long cuttings of half-ripe lateral shoots and insert in a propagating frame.

Rhoeo

[Three Men in a Boat; 10°C/50°F; Mexico] Boat-shaped purple and white flowers produced at base of lance-shaped and fleshy leaves that are a metallic-green on the upper surface and purple on the underside. Fairly compact growing plants of the tradescantia family that need reasonable warmth and light shade to do well. New plants made by removing suckers or offsets, and planting them up individually. Also easy from seed.

Rhoicissus rhomboidea

[Grape Ivy; 10°C/50°F; South Africa] A natural climbing plant growing to at least 120cm/4ft that will adapt to many different locations, but prefers reasonable warmth, light shade, moderate watering and regular feeding while in active growth. Stems are woody in older plants and leaves are tri-lobed and an attractive glossy green. Provide canes or a trellis for the tendrils to cling to. Pot on annually in April until they are in 23cm/9in pots. Cuttings are prepared in April or May from pieces of stem with two leaves attached – several cuttings should be put in each small pot to provide plants of full appearance.

Architecturally speaking, one of the finest of the lower-growing philodendrons is *P. wendlandii*, which produces leaves that radiate away from the centre of the plant in the shape of a shuttlecock – alas it is ever in short supply as most of the larger types of philodendron forever seem to be. Almost all the smaller-leaved plants may be propagated from individual leaves with a piece of stem attached, while the larger-leaved ones are, surprisingly enough, raised from seed.

Pilea

[Artillery Plant; 10-13°C/50-55°F; Tropical America] All of those offered for sale are compact plants that may be increased by means of cuttings with very little difficulty – quite a few will also seed themselves in every direction if, for example, they are growing on gravel on greenhouse staging. In fact, the ease of propagation should encourage you to adopt the practice of disposing of old and overgrown plants and replacing them with freshly-rooted new ones periodically. *P. muscosa* is a rather bushy little plant growing to a height of 28cm/11in, that is not unlike a fern at first sight. It has small pale to mid-green leaves and inconspicuous tufts of yellow-green flowers. The common name of Artillery Plant results from the manner in which seed pods explode when ripe and scatter seed in all directions. Of them all *P. cadierei* is by far the most popular, and

wet. Ideally you should endeavour to provide conditions that are warm, moist and shaded – in bright sunlight plants take on a very hard, less green appearance that is not so attractive.

Besides the upright growing types of philodendron there are numerous plants of much more squat habit that are more suitable for some locations. Many of the latter grow from short trunks that become most attractive as some of the lower leaves are naturally shed.

leaves that are seen to best effect when grown as individual specimens rather than in a group. Needs reasonable warmth, light shade in summer and moderate humidity, and must have a mixture with a loam base; keep the soil moist throughout the year. Give a dilute liquid feed once every month in summer. May be propagated either from seed in February or from cuttings of stem sections with leaves removed.

Scindapsus

[10-13°C/50-55°F; South East Asia] Natural climbers, these are akin to philodendrons but slightly more difficult. *S. aureus* has heart-shaped leaves that are attractively cream and green variegated. The variety 'Marble Queen' has almost entirely white leaves, and 'Golden Queen' is almost completely yellow. Warm, moist and shaded conditions are essential, although a well-lit spot is preferred in winter, also a mixture that is composed almost entirely of peat. A mossed support will also be beneficial for these climbers. New plants can be raised from individual leaves with a piece of stem attached.

Stenocarpus

[10°C/50°F; Australia] This becomes a tree of some 27.4m/90ft in height in nature, but makes a good foliage pot plant when young. Careful watering necessary if leaf margins are not to

Sansevieria

[Mother-in-law's Tongue; 10°C/50°F; West Africa] The erect sword-like leaves, dark green with mottled grey transverse bands of *S. trifasciata*, grow to 30-45cm/12-18in and make this species a popular feature of indoor plant gardens. The variety *S.t.* 'Laurentii', with creamy-yellow margins to the leaves, is the form usually seen. A loam-based soil mix is suitable for this semi-succulent, and like other succulents it should be allowed to dry out completely between waterings. Keep dry during the winter. A sunny or lightly shaded position will suit it well as it is a tough plant which will thrive in almost any light conditions. Feed established plants every three or four months during the growing season. Propagate by leaf cuttings or by dividing the rhizome. (*S.t.* 'Laurentii' cannot be propagated by leaf cuttings as the resulting plants will have lost the distinctive yellow stripes.)

Saxifraga stolonifera (S. sarmentosa)

[Mother of Thousands; 10°C/50°F; China] Ideal indoor hanging plants that are better in small pots with wire supports rather than in larger more conventional hanging baskets. Close inspection shows that the rounded leaves are multi-coloured, but the overall impression is a rather dull-grey colouring. Small starry flowers are produced in July and August. New plants are propagated from the perfectly shaped young plantlets that are produced on slender red stems by the parent plant – hence the common name.

Schefflera actinophylla

[Umbrella Plant; 10-13°C/50-55°F; Australia] Elegant plants with large palmate shiny green

become scorched – even moistness being better than extremes of wet and dry. A loam-based soil mix is preferable. Leaves are green, cut into lobes, smooth and glossy, and colour will vary from pale to dark green depending on available light; however, avoid direct sunlight in summer. Plants are in short supply – new ones are raised from seed.

Stromanthe

[15°C/60°F min; Brazil] These small plants are related to marantas and have the same cultural needs of warmth, shade and high humidity for best results. *S. amabilis* is the most popular, with rounded leaves that are delicately patterned and grey-green in colour. *S. sanguinea* has larger leaves, dark green and white above, maroon beneath. New plants are propagated from pieces of stem with two or three leaves attached taken from the top section of the plant.

Syngonium

[Goose Foot Plant; 15°C/60°F] In warm, humid conditions syngoniums (often sold as nephthytis) are very free growing plants that may be allowed to trail or be trained to grow on a support. They are similar in appearance, habit and cultural requirements to the climbing philodendrons. Less free in room conditions, but fine plants nevertheless. *S. podophyllum* 'Emerald Gem' is possibly the most popular. Leaves are glossy green and resemble the imprint of a goose foot. Its leaves change dramatically as it ages. Young plants have single 8cm/3in dark green leaves with silvery markings. Later, these develop into three unequal lobes and eventually up to 11 leaflets appear in the shape of an open fan and entirely green. They do best in bright indirect light and in barely moist loam-based soil. Easily increased in a warm propagator by using stem cuttings with two leaves attached.

Tetrastigma

[10-13°C/50-55°F; China] A large-leaved climber of extraordinary vigour, which has searching tendrils that will attach themselves to any available support. Needs a framework to climb onto, ample space to develop and large pots filled with a loam-based soil if it is to be seen at its best. Ample watering and good drainage also essential. The leaves, composed of three or five glossy green leaflets, resemble those of cissus. New plants from cuttings with a piece of stem and single leaf.

Tolmiea menziesii

[Pick-a-back Plant; Hardy; North America] A curiosity plant that produces perfectly-shaped young plants at the base of older parent leaves – young plants can be removed when large enough and propagated with little difficulty. Plants form into compact mounds of hairy green foliage and grow to a height of 15cm/6in. Pot between September and March, repot annually in March or April, and water freely in the growing period. You can expect few problems of care and attention.

Tradescantia

[Wandering Jew; 10°C/50°F; Tropical America] The vast majority of the great many tradescantias that are available are easy to care for, easy to propagate from almost any piece of stem, and are seen at their best when several plants are put into a hanging basket and given light and airy conditions in which they can develop.

The ovate leaves, closely set on the trailing stems, are striped in various colours. Flowers are three-petalled and basically triangular in outline. Avoid blazing sun, but in good light plants will have much more pleasingly coloured variegation. When propagating put several pieces in each small pot and remove the growing tips of young plants regularly to encourage more bushy appearance. After two or three growing seasons, plants should be disposed of and replaced with more vigorous young plants.

Zebrina pendula

[10°C/50°F; Mexico] This nice trailing plant often known by the same common name as the tradescantia, requires the same treatment and airy conditions; it is equally easy to manage.

Similarly, it is also a superb plant when seen in a hanging basket.

When given just a little more than the passing glance normally given to the tradescantia tribe, it will be found that the zebrina is a superbly-coloured plant with vivid purple to the undersides of leaves with rich green, purple and silver colouring to the upper surface. A perfectly grown plant in a hanging basket placed on a pedestal where it can be admired from all angles.

Opposite top: *Asplenium nidus*, sansevieria and maranta brighten an unused fireplace.
Opposite below: *Schefflera actinophylla* is an elegant plant.
Right: *Syngonium podophyllum*.
Far right: Several tradescantias potted together provide an attractive trailer for a bookcase

Palms

For elegant and majestic appearance there are few groups of foliage plants that can compete with the palms in their many forms. Some of them require to be mature plants before they are seen at their best – in the case of *Cycas revoluta* it is 10 years or more before the plant begins to develop its true character. By this time they have almost become heirlooms and are only to be seen in the rarified atmosphere of the botanic garden where the necessary time, cash and conditions are available to bring them to maturity. Commercially speaking, almost all the palms that are offered for sale are very costly on account of the time that is needed and the high heating costs involved in rearing plants. But as there are no satisfactory lower-cost substitutes, palms are still very popular plants in spite of expense.

Chamaedorea elegans (Neanthe bella)

[Parlour Palm; 13°C/55°F; Mexico] In common with all the palms, the best method of propagation is by means of seed. Seed is sown in shallow peat beds that are maintained at a temperature of not less than 20°C/70°F, and allowed to grow on in the bed until plants are several cm tall before potting them individually in small pots of open mixture. *Neanthe bella*, the more popular name for this plant, is grown in large quantities as they are very much smaller than most of the other palms and are sold in small pots. It is one of the easiest small palms to grow with light feathery foliage. It is, in fact, a natural miniature palm that is ideal for smaller rooms, for bottle gardens, and dish gardens. It is not unusual for plants little more than 46cm/18in tall to produce flowers and subsequently seed, which can be saved and sown in the manner described above.

Chrysalidocarpus (Areca) lutescens

[Butterfly Palm; 15°C/60°F; India] *Lutescens* means yellow, which refers to the yellow stems and leaves which results in a most attractive and desirable plant. At first sight these plants have the appearance of palms that are suffering as a result of some iron deficiency. However, the areca palm has much finer foliage and is altogether more delicate in appearance than *Kentia forsteriana*. An attractive feature of this plant is to witness the slow process of new leaves opening – leaves are delicately joined at their tips giving the leaf a skeletonized appearance prior to fully expanding.

Cocos nucifera

[Coconut Palm; 15°C/60°F; India] In their natural habitat the coconut palms attain a height of 27-30m/90-100ft, but can be restricted to reasonable size by growing in a container. They are also extremely slow-growing. Some nurserymen wishing to limit the upward growth go in for root pruning which, in a way, results in giant Bonsai-treated plants. In recent years a limited number of interesting Coconut Palms have been available in Europe – the giant coconut lies on its side in the pot like the biggest seed you have ever seen in your life, and from one end a typical Kentia-type palm growth seems to grow very freely. In its early stages the growth of this palm is very similar to that of *Kentia forsteriana* with dark green, arching leaves, silvery-grey beaneath.

Cocos (Syagrus) weddeliana

[15°C/60°F; Cocos Islands] One of the most delicate and compact of all the palms, the cocos has slender fronds that are dark green above, glaucous on the undersides. It retains a dwarf stature of about 30cm/1ft for several years and when established will go on for at least two years in the same pot. Some care is needed, such as a humid atmosphere, freely circulating air and good light out of direct sun. A loam-based soil mix is preferable, kept moist in summer.

Cycas revoluta

[Sago Palm; 15°C/60°F; China] One of the oldest and, surely, one of the most majestic plants in cultivation. In time the plant develops a substantial trunk, which adds considerably to the general appearance, to a height of at least 1.8m/6ft. Leaves are dark green and stiff and individual segments are narrow, bending slightly at their tips. Not a plant for the impatient gardener, as only a very few leaves are produced annually and growth rate is painfully slow. It needs plenty of moisture and water and you should use a loam-based mixture.

Howeia (Kentia)

[10-13°C/50-55°F; Lord Howe Islands] Kentia palms, now correctly known as Howeia, have remained in the forefront of popularity over the years in spite of ever-increasing cost. However, there remain few of the nurseries which, for most of this century, specialized in palms, especially *H. forsteriana* and *H. belmoreana*. We are faced with an almost permanent shortage of palms of all kinds with the result that they have a scarcity value that has meant much higher prices.

Howeia forsteriana has a more erect habit of growth than *H. belmoreana*, and for that reason is better suited to most indoor locations. Leaves are a rich, dark green in colour, but are surprisingly susceptible to damage if cleaned with chemical concoctions that seem to cause little or no harm to plants that would seem much more vulnerable. Given reasonable warmth, moisture and light shade (heavier shade in a greenhouse), palms in general can be very tolerant of room conditions.

When potting kentia palms on from one pot to another larger one it is very important that a good layer of crocks should be placed in the bottom of the new pot before introducing mixture, as this will ensure that drainage is sharp and that the mixture does not become waterlogged. The addition of coarse leafmould to standard potting mixture will be of considerable benefit in assisting plants to grow more freely indoors. When potting, the mixture should be made fairly firm. In a medium that is badly aerated there will be a tendency for the mixture to turn sour with the result that plants take on a generally hard, less green appearance, and in time will result in browning of tips of leaves and eventual loss of leaves.

Except for the fact that leaves are narrower it is difficult to detect the difference between *H. belmoreana* and *H. forsteriana* in the early stages of growth. However, as *belmoreana* ages, the midrib of the leaf arches and the plant adopts a more drooping appearance which is not unattractive in larger plants.

Below: *Chamaedorea elegans*.
Opposite left: *Chrysalidocarpus lutescens*.
Opposite right: *Howeia belmoreana*, and *Chamaedorea elegans* on the table.
Opposite bottom: *Cycas revoluta*

Phoenix

[10-13°C/50-55°F; South East Asia/Canary Islands] *P. dactylifera* is the commercial date palm of North Africa, but is seldom offered as a potted plant. Although in short supply, the two varieties that you are likely to come

across as potted plants are *P. canariensis* and *P. roebelenii*, the latter from South East Asia. Should there be a choice, the latter is much more graceful and is, therefore, a much more desirable plant for room decoration. Both are planted throughout the tropics as decorative trees, but they take many, many years to reach maturity when their roots are confined to plant pots. In many locations the slow growing plant of architectural merit, as these two are, is much more rewarding than plants that are forever in need of replacement. Both plants have stiff leaves and robust appearance, and are not difficult to care for in reasonable conditions—but avoid having the soil saturated for long periods.

45

How to grow Healthy Flowering and Foliage Houseplants

Providing the proper treatment and correct cultural conditions for a plant will take you three parts of the way along the road to successful growing. But all the proper treatment and conditions ever invented will be of no avail if the plant purchased is sub-standard. If a plant leaving a greenhouse, where it has had almost ideal growing conditions, is of poor quality, there is not much hope of it doing well in the home where conditions are likely to be much less agreeable. So look for healthy plants to buy and the end result will be very much more satisfactory.

Plants are very much like people in their requirements; they are much more likely to respond favourably to conditions and treatment that offer moderation rather than excess. Too much of almost everything will be detrimental to both flowering and foliage plants – too much water, too much heat, too much fertilizer, too much attention. By the same token almost all plants will suffer if there is too little water, fertilizers and such like. Moderation is the key word.

If the plant you purchase does not have a tag attached giving some advice concerning its particular needs, then refer to a book on the subject and follow the instructions given. An even amount of warmth throughout the 24 hours of the day is important, and if somewhere in the region of 13°C/55°F can be maintained it will suit the vast majority of foliage plants. Ivies, though, are an exception as they prefer cooler conditions in the region of 10°C/50°F. If grown in hot, dry rooms they quickly become dry and shrivelled.

Given reasonable warmth, the next most important need is for good light. Daylight is preferable, although many plants will do perfectly well if illuminated entirely by artificial light that is suitable for plant growth. Or use a mixture of artificial and natural daylight. Where the recommendation is that plants should be grown in the shade this does not mean that they ought to be relegated to the darkest corner of the room, although there are those plants, such as marantas and the aspidistra, that seem to do better in areas where the light is more restricted. On the whole, however, although many plants object to strong, direct sunlight, the majority will do little more than survive in poorly lit locations.

Some plants will do fine in full sunlight all the time and the two that really thrive in such positions are mother-in-law's tongue (*Sansevieria trifasciata* 'Laurentii') and the highly coloured crotons. The latter will quickly lose their brilliant colouring if adequate light and sun are not available. During the winter months, plants on the windowsill may suffer as a result of cold draughts, and it is advisable to move any from windows at night if these are not double-glazed. But plants should not come to any harm from the sun which is much less intense at that time. During the summer months, however, it may be necessary to remove plants from south-facing windows where they may become scorched, or where leaves will almost surely take on a harder appearance. Filtered sunlight, such as through net curtains or venetian blinds, will be adequate protection. Also, to prevent foliage becoming scorched by the sun, it is important when watering to ensure that the leaves of the plants do not become splashed.

Repotting and potting on

With all indoor plants it is necessary to pot them into slightly larger containers when they outgrow their present ones, or to renew the older, exhausted soil and to repot them in the same size container using fresh soil. The latter applies, for example, to cyclamen corms that are being grown on for a second year; the expended soil is completely removed and the corm planted in fresh mixture when the new growing season is begun. The golden rule when potting, as with feeding, is to ensure that only healthy plants are potted on because putting plants into fresh soil is a means to help them continue to grow healthy. Potting on will save pot-bound plants from an early demise. The best time to perform the operation is in the spring of the year when active growth commences, and it is essential for pot-bound subjects that the new container should be only a little larger than the one from which the plant is being removed. After potting the soil should be well watered, then kept on the dry side for about a week in order that roots become more active in the new fresh medium. If the soil is kept too wet immediately after potting, roots will penetrate the new soil much more slowly as there will be less need for them to go in search of moisture.

A moist atmosphere in their vicinity is one of the things that houseplants miss when they are introduced to the dry conditions that prevail in centrally heated rooms. Therefore, it is wise to provide plants with a moist gravel base on which to stand, or to provide a container packed with peat kept permanently moist into which the plant pots can be plunged to their rims. Overhead spraying with tepid water, except for plants with hairy leaves, also improves humidity.

Pot on rootbound plants when active growth commences

To repot, tip plant out of pot

Trim off old roots and soil

Add new potting mix to pot

Replace plant and tamp down soil

Feeding

It is sometimes thought that the feeding of plants is like giving medicine to someone lying sick in bed. Nothing could be further from the truth, as feeding plants is like feeding a healthy human being: it sustains and keeps the body in good condition, but is not necessarily a cure for illness. In fact, the feeding of sick plants could very well finish them off altogether. The plants to feed are those that are well-established in their pots and freely producing new growth, and the best time to feed is during the spring and summer months. In winter the majority of indoor plants are dormant, but should plants still be producing new growth it is advisable to feed with a weak fertilizer (follow the manufacturer's instructions). One important piece of advice that the houseplant grower should take note of when feeding his plants is the information on the package in which the fertilizer is supplied. The dose should only be increased if the plant being fed is an obviously strong growing subject.

Cleaning

Cleaning the leaves of many of the foliage plants will greatly improve their appearance, but at no time should plants with hairy leaves be cleaned, nor the new top leaves on any plant. Also one should use specially prepared leaf-cleaning agents with some care, and any new leaf cleaner should be tested before it is used indiscriminately on a collection of plants. Soft new leaves of plants such as *Monstera deliciosa* (Swiss cheese plant) should not at any time be handled and no attempt should be made to clean them until they have matured to deep glossy green. The glossy-leaved plants, *Ficus robusta* and such like, will be improved for cleaning periodically with a sponge moistened in water, but avoid too frequent use of chemical cleaners.

Watering

Watering is in all probability the most difficult operation for the inexperienced gardener to understand. More houseplants are killed by overwatering than by any other cause and most plants either get far too much or far too little. Excess in either direction will result in damage to the roots of the plant. Such damage will later be reflected when leaves lose their colour and take on a generally sick appearance.

When watering plants it is important that the entire rootball, this is all the soil and the roots, is thoroughly saturated. The best way of ascertaining this is to fill the space between the rim of the pot and the surface each time the plant is watered. Excess water should be seen to run through the hole in the bottom of the pot, and if water is not seen to do so reasonably soon after watering, then a further watering should be given. (Another point to watch when watering: if the water drains through very quickly, the plant could be pot-bound and require re-potting.) Plants growing in a group arrangement in a large container cannot be tested for sufficient watering by this method. You will have to use the old-fashioned 'finger into the soil' test. The soil should be allowed to dry out a little between waterings, but it should not be allowed to dry excessively unless the plant is in a dormant period, not requiring any water. Some plants need more thorough soaking and should have the plant pot plunged in a bucket of water until all the air in the pot has escaped. Although other plants may be watered by this method it is more essential for moisture-loving subjects like the indoor *Azalea indica* and the hydrangea. Allowing the hydrangea to dry out during its growing season, or the azalea to at any time, will result in general deterioration.

To some extent capillary watering containers take the hit-and-miss aspect out of watering as the fitted water level indicator clearly shows how much water is in the container reservoir, and how much is required. The important need with such containers, however, is to ensure that they dry out completely between each watering and to allow the reservoir to remain dry for four or five days before refilling. This will permit the soil to become aerated, which is essential for the plants to develop a healthy root system.

If a plant does become waterlogged, take it out of its pot (the entire rootball) and leave for a day so the air can dry the soil. After this you can return it to its pot – and water more carefully! It also helps to stir the crust on the top of the soil in the pot occasionally.

Hydroculture

Growing plants in water, entirely without soil, has been experimented with for many, many years, but never seemed to present a challenge to plants grown more conventionally in soil. In recent years, however, a marked change has occurred, so that hydroculture is now very much on the increase. Not all plants, such as the ivies, are suited to hydroculture and there are many experiments being carried out to see which plants are suited to conversion from soil-growing to water-growing. Fortunately the vast aeroid family, many of which are used for indoor decoration, seems to be especially adaptable to this method of growing.

Plants of almost any size can be converted. The procedure is first to wash off every vestige of soil from around the roots, then to place the plant roots in pots with open slotted sides. The area around the exposed roots is filled with clay granules, which absorb water and help to keep the plant upright. The pots are partially submerged in water and after about two months, the majority of plants produce sufficient water roots for them to be considered fully converted. They can then be planted up in more decorative containers and introduced to the living room.

In the decorative container there is a water level indicator to show when refilling is needed, and a tube through which fresh supplies of water can be poured. The same tube performs a dual purpose in that it is also used for syphoning water from the container when a complete change of water is necessary. This usually occurs every six months, but it may extend to 12 in some cases. A slow-release fertilizer is used for feeding hydroculture plants and, depending on the manufacturer's recommendations, need only be given every six or twelve months. Although plants grown by this method are more expensive than plants that are grown more conventionally in soil, there is no doubt that the general cleanliness and efficiency, not to say the improved standard of plant growth, has much to recommend it.

During the summer months many of the easier plants will benefit from being placed in

To prepare a plant for conversion to hydroculture, first wash off all the soil from the roots. Place the plant in a container with open slotted sides and pack in the clay granules. Put the 'basket' in a hydroculture container and cover with a plastic bag. (This maintains the humidity necessary to help the plant adjust to its new environment)

The closeup opposite shows the size of the clay granules and the dipstick-like water level indicator in the back of the container. Left: a *Monstera deliciosa*

a sheltered place out of doors where they will not be exposed to too much direct sunlight. The Calomondin orange (*Citrus mitis*) will, however, be very much improved by spending the summer months in as much sunlight as there is available provided the soil is never allowed to dry out.

The cutaway drawing, right, shows how thick, fleshy water roots have developed on the *Codiaeum variegatum*

Sow the seeds in a pot or pan containing a layer of crocks and a good seed potting mix, and moisten thoroughly. Cover individual pots with a plastic bag, suspended over wooden sticks, or group pots

Propagation

The simplest and cheapest way to increase your house plants is from seed (see left), either collected from the plants you already have or bought from a seed merchant. But by far the most common method

Softwood cuttings (right) are taken from plants such as pelargoniums and chrysanthemums. Ideally, select a side shoot, about 10cm/4in long. Cut cleanly just below a bud, then remove a few of the basal leaves. Insert the cutting, to one-third of its length, in a good potting mixture and keep in a warm place. Hardwood cuttings (far right), from shrubs, are treated in a similar way, except that as they take longer to root, they should be about 15cm/6in long

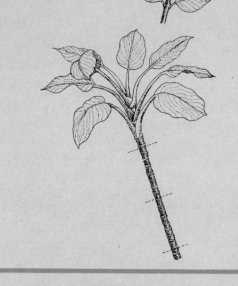

in a box and cover with glass. Wipe the glass every day or turn the bag inside-out to remove condensation. Water when necessary. Keep warm and dark until germination occurs, then remove the cover and place in full light. When seedlings have at least two leaves, prick out into other pots or pans, planting at least 5cm/2in apart

Propagation by leaf cutting is the method suitable for saintpaulias, gloxinias, begonias, etc. Take a mature leaf, with stem, from the parent plant and insert it in a pot in a mixture of peat and sand. Keep warm, in a propagating unit if possible. New plantlets will develop at the base of the leaf stalk. *Begonia rex* can be increased by vein cuttings. Remove a mature leaf from the parent plant and turn it upside-down. Make six or seven cuts through the larger veins, then lay the leaf, right side up, on moist sand in a pot. Secure the leaf with hairpins so that it will remain in contact with the sand. Cover the pot with a plastic bag and keep warm. New plantlets will appear at the cuts in the veins

of propagation is by cuttings, illustrated below, either leaf or stem. Other propagation methods shown here are leaf and vein cuttings (bottom left), air layering (bottom right) and soil layering (right).

Chlorophytum and *Saxifraga stolonifera* are two plants that multiply by sending out runners from which new plants grow. Propagation is, therefore, a simple operation. Place the parent plant, in its pot, in a tray containing potting mix and pin down the plantlets with hairpins. Alternatively, pin the plantlets down in separate pots. These new plants will soon take root

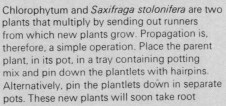

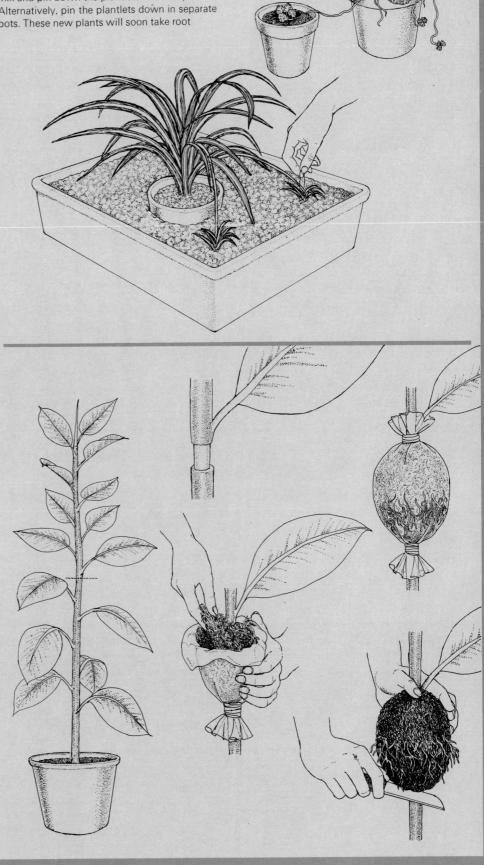

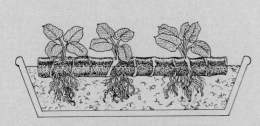

Divide a leafless stem into sections, each containing a bud. Make a cut above and below each bud and remove a small strip of bark from opposite the bud. Place the cut stem flat on the soil and keep warm. Small plants will form at each bud

Air layering, which can be used to increase camellias, hibiscus or *Ficus elastica*, is suitable for plants which have become very tall and lost their lower leaves. Slit the bark just below a leaf node, then remove the bark, as shown. Rub the area with rooting powder and pack moist sphagnum moss around it. Tie a piece of plastic around the moss. Small roots will grow from the plant through the moss and will be visible in about three weeks. When the moss is filled with roots, remove the plastic and cut the stem below the moss ball. This can then be planted up in a new pot. If this method has been used to produce a more attractive plant, rather than to propagate, the parent plant may be discarded

Bulbs

Few plants are easier to raise or give better returns for outlay than bulbs. Many bloom when little else is in flower, in rainbow shades and various heights and shapes. Additionally the fragrance of some – like hyacinths and lilies – is proverbial, providing a bonus on beauty.

A bulb is a thickened, generally underground bud having a flat basal stem with roots from its underside, and neatly packed layers of fleshy leaves which have been converted to non-green storage organs. When an onion is cut in half these details can be seen.

The term, however, is loosely applied to a number of plants which are not true bulbs, although they may have similar storage organs and periods of dormancy. Bulb growers find it convenient to group these together.

Gladioli and crocuses, for example, have corms, composed of swollen stems (not leaves) with membraneous coats; tubers and succulent stems or roots, usually (although not invariably) underground, with eyes or buds near their surfaces, like aconites. Crowns or pips are names applied to lily-of-the-valley roots, and rhizomes are underground stems which run horizontally like Solomon's seal, some irises and wood anemones.

Allium

[Ornamental Onion; Asia/Southern Europe] Although not all true bulbs, several varieties are suitable for alpine or cold greenhouses, or can be brought indoors for a short period when in flower. The flowers are in umbels and the foliage is strap-shaped; the characteristic family smell is only apparent when the bulbs are lifted or the leaves bruised. The whole family appreciate good drainage and full sun. Recommended kinds are *A. beesianum*, bright blue, 23-30cm/9-12in; *A. cyaneum*, brilliant turquoise blue, 23-30cm/9-12in; *A. flavum*, bright yellow, 30-39cm/12-15in; *A. moly*, golden-yellow, broad flat leaves, 15-30cm/6-12in; and *A. narcissiflorum*, pinkish-purple, flowers pendulous, 20-30cm/8-12in. All these are summer flowering but *A. neapolitanum*, white, 20-30cm/8-12in tall, flowers in spring. Propagate from seed or offsets from older bulbs.

Anemone

[Windflower; Greece] *A. blanda* can be grown under cold conditions in a frame or alpine house, when it will flower through late winter to mid-spring, with starry blue, mauve, pink or white flowers on 10-15cm/4-6in stems. The deeply cut leaves resemble those of a buttercup. The tubers should be planted 5cm/2in deep in rich soil and grown in full sun, or a light window. Propagation by division.

Babiana

[South Africa] Funnel-shaped flowers, sometimes fragrant, and tapering flat leaves make this an attractive houseplant. Insert four or five 2.5cm/1in deep in a 10cm/4in pot of sandy soil with a little well-rotted manure at the base. Blooms late winter to spring and then should be dried off gradually so as to ripen the corms. *B. stricta* is the best species with 15-30cm/6-12in stems carrying several flowers with six segments – three of which are white and three blue with darker blue blotches. Varieties have cream, crimson and brilliant blue flowers. Give a light situation indoors. Propagation by seed or offsets.

Brodiaea

[North and South America] Sun-loving Californians with grassy leaves which die away before the umbels of tubular flowers appear in summer. They thrive in a good light and rich loam soil, being particularly suitable for bright office windows or cool greenhouses. *B. californica* is lilac-pink, 60cm/2ft; *B. ida-maia* (syn. *Dichelostemma*), the floral firecracker, has umbels of long crimson flowers tipped with yellow and green on 46cm/18in stems and *B. laxa* (syn. *Triteleia*), the grass nut, has umbels of violet-blue or white flowers up to 30cm/1ft across on 60cm/2ft stems. Propagate by division.

Bulbocodium

[Meadow Saffron of the Spring; Europe] Also known as the red crocus, *B. vernum* has 8-10cm/3-4in crocus-like flowers of reddish-violet. These have no stems but seem to sit on the soil and are in character in early spring. The leaves are broadly strap-shaped. Suitable for pans in an alpine house. Frequent lifting and dividing is advisable.

Calochortus

[Mariposa Lily or Butterfly Tulip; North America] These beautiful bulbous plants have three 'petalled' tulip-shaped flowers, several to a stem in mid-summer. The segments are usually prominently blotched with other colours near the flower bases. Suitable for pan culture in a cool greenhouse or short sojourns indoors, calochortus must have sharp drainage, plenty of water in the growing season and a good baking when the flowers are done. *C. venustus* has white, yellow, purple or red flowers with contrasting blotches, 60cm/2ft; and *C. uniflorus* has lilac-pink flowers veined with crimson, 30-46cm/12-18in. Propagate by seed or division.

Chionodoxa

[Glory of the Snow; Asia Minor] A delightful early blooming bulb for window boxes, alpine pans or mixing with eranthis, tulips or narcissi in fancy bowls. Growing about 15cm/6in high, each stem carries several starry blue flowers with white centres. Plant the bulbs 3.75cm/1½in deep in any good well drained soil. *C. luciliae* is the most common species and has a pink form 'Pink Giant'. *C. sardensis* is brilliant blue with almost navy blue buds, 15-20cm/6-8in. Propagate by seed or division.

Clivia

[Kaffir Lily; Natal] *C. miniata* makes a splendid houseplant and can exist for years in the same pot if fed during the growing season. Broad, glossy, evergreen strap-shaped leaves are attractive at all times and in spring the plant produces its stout 60cm/2ft stems carrying umbels of large, funnel-shaped flowers with yellow throats. In the type they are light salmon-red but deeper red and yellow forms exist. Under good conditions these are succeeded by scarlet berries. Any good potting mix is suitable and the plants are propagated by division of the thick fleshy roots.

Colchicum

[Naked Boys; Europe/Asia Minor] These are mostly autumn-flowering, tuberous rooted plants with showy, goblet-shaped flowers like giant crocuses. They appear without the leaves (which follow on 30cm/1ft stems with the seedpods in spring) – hence the common name. They should be planted 5cm/2in deep in late summer, in good potting soil and deep pots. They can also be successfully flowered dry, without soil or water, but naturally deteriorate unless planted soon afterwards. *C. autumnale* has starry petalled, rosy-lilac or white flowers; *C. speciosus*, rosy-purple, has larger and more globular flowers. Good cultivars from the last include 'Album', white; 'Disraeli', deep mauve

Opposite: Sun-loving Californians, *Brodiaea ixioides* are particularly suitable for bright windowsills.
Above left: *Convallaria majalis* are usually sold in bundles of 25 and should be loosely planted in peat, light soil, or vermiculite.
Above: A brilliant blue flower, *Chionodoxa luciliae* is a delight in window boxes.
Left: 'Blue Pearl' is a cultivar of the winter-flowering *Crocus chrysanthus* group

with darker markings; 'Waterlily', fully double, rosy-mauve and 'The Giant', mauve-pink with a white base. The normal height is around 7.5-15cm/3-6in. *C. luteum*, with 2.5cm/1in yellow flowers, blooms in late winter. Propagation by seed or division.

Convallaria majalis

[Lily-of-the-Valley; Europe/Asia/North America] Lilies-of-the-Valley can be induced to flower out of season by forcing retarded crowns. These are usually sold in bundles of 25 and on arrival should be loosely planted together in peat, light soil or vermiculite. Keep them in a warm (24°C/75°F) dark place – such as a covered propagating frame or an airing cupboard – for about four days. They should then be brought into the light and a temperature of 10-13°C/50-55°F to flower. Some people plant them separately at this time. The whole operation takes approximately three weeks, from planting to flowering. 53

Crocus

[Asia Minor/Adriatic coast/Alps] Well-known plants for window boxes, bowls and pots. There are three main groups. Autumn-flowering crocuses need planting in late summer (July or August). *C. speciosus*, deep mauve-blue with violet veining and prominent orange stigmas, is one of the best, but the mauve-lilac *C. sativus* has special interest inasmuch as its stigmas are the source of saffron.

Winter-flowering crocuses are variable, particularly the *C. chrysanthus* group which has many cultivars like 'E. A. Bowles', yellow with bronze feathering, and 'Cream Beauty', cream and greyish-mauve with yellow throats. *C. tomasinianus* has long narrow flowers, varying from lilac-mauve to rich red-purple, usually with darker 'petal' tips. All these should be planted in early autumn.

The spring-flowering crocuses are the most useful for forcing purposes, especially the large flowered forms derived from *C. neapolitanus* (*C. vernus*) and commonly known as Dutch varieties. These come in a wide range of colours of which 'Kathleen Parlow', white;

'Yellow Giant' (sometimes called 'Dutch Yellow'), golden; 'Pickwick', pale lilac heavily striped and feathered with purple; 'Gladstone', deep purple, and 'Remembrance', violet-purple, are typical. These should be planted in autumn and like all crocuses require well-drained soil and good light. They will also grow in water, in a bulb glass, and can be propagated from seed or by growing on the young cormlets.

Eranthis

[Winter Aconite; Europe] A very easy, tuberous-rooted member of the buttercup family, with bright golden, chalice-shaped flowers set off by 'toby dog' ruffs of pale green, deeply cut, leafy bracts. They bloom in early winter and make delightful subjects for pans in an alpine house or tubs and window boxes. Damp soil is essential and the tubers should be set 5cm/2in deep. *E. hyemalis* is the easiest and when left undisturbed spreads by means of self-set seedlings. It grows 5-10cm/2-4in tall. *E. × tubergenii* has larger and deeper gold flowers on 7.5-12.5cm/3-5in stems but is sterile.

Erythronium

[Trout Lily; North America/Asia/Europe] Erythroniums can be planted 10cm/4in deep in pans of potting soil with extra peat added and must be kept cool and damp and in partial shade during the summer months. The roots must never dry out. *E. americanum* has pale to deep gold flowers with reflexed petals like a cyclamen, basally marked and flushed outside with red. The tongue-like leaves are beautifully blotched with chocolate. *E. dens-canis* is the dog's tooth violet (so called because of the shape of the tubers). It has purple blotched leaves and pink, crimson or purple flowers with reflexed petals and deeper basal markings. *E. tuolumnense* has plain green leaves and two or three large, deep yellow flowers on 15cm/6in stems. 'Pagoda' is a more vigorous form with larger flowers on 30cm/1ft stems and a fine cultivar of disputed origin is 'White Beauty' which is white with dark red basal markings. Erythroniums flower in spring and are not really suitable for house cultivation; they are better in a cold greenhouse or alpine house. Increase by offsets.

Left: *Hippeastrum* is an outstanding winter-flowering bulb with funnel-shaped flowers in striking colours.
Above: A member of the buttercup family, *Eranthis hyemalis* has golden, chalice-shaped flowers set off by leafy bracts.
Opposite above: Hyacinths are easy to grow and delightfully fragrant.
Opposite bottom: *Ipheion uniflorum*, produces lovely pale violet flowers in spring

a radiator or in a cupboard until they get going. They should then be placed in a good light to develop and flower. Little water should be given for the first two weeks and after that only a little on top of the soil. They must not be too wet. Propagate by seed or offsets.

Hyacinthus orientalis

[Hyacinth; West Asia/Eastern Europe] Hyacinths are easy to grow, the foliage is attractive, the flowers showy and in vivid colours and they are delightfully fragrant. Roman hyacinths are not a distinct species but a form of *H. orientalis* with slender stems and looser flower spikes. They come in pink, blue and white and usually bloom earlier than the sturdier Dutch hyacinths, which also have a wider colour range. Multiflora hyacinths are other derivatives, characterized by several graceful spikes from every bulb and there are also cynthella or miniature hyacinths only 14-15cm/5-6in tall – ideal for window boxes.

Hyacinths can be grown in ordinary potting soil, loamless mix, bulb fibre (best for fancy bowls with no drainage holes), newspaper and bulb glasses. Fertilizers are unnecessary but apply water regularly to keep the soil moist.

Representative of specially prepared forcing bulbs for Christmas and New Year flowering are: 'Carnegie' and 'L'Innocence', white; 'Yellow Hammer', yellow; 'Lady Derby' and 'Rosalie', pink; 'Jan Bos' and 'Amsterdam', red; 'Blue Giant', 'Delft Blue' and 'Ostara', blue.

Ipheion uniflorum

[Spring Flower; South America] Also known as *Brodiaea uniflora* and *Triteleia uniflora*, this is a pretty plant from Peru and Argentina with tufts of lax grassy leaves and many smooth 10-15cm/4-6in stems terminating in single, fragrant, pale violet flowers in spring. Suitable for growing indoors in pots and bowls like crocuses or in alpine houses and cold extensions.

Galanthus nivalis

[Snowdrop; Europe] Single and double snowdrops can be grown indoors or in pans in alpine houses but must not be subjected to much heat or the bulbs go blind. Grow them in good loam soil mix and keep them from strong sunlight through glass or direct heat. A north window and temperature around 10-13°C/50-55°F is ideal. Propagate by seed or bulb division.

Hippeastrum

[South America] Hippeastrum, frequently but erroneously known as amaryllis, are outstanding winter-flowering bulbs with funnel-shaped flowers of great substance and in striking colours – pink, rose, red, scarlet and white, frequently with narrow white petal streaks or

mottlings of other shades. Up to four blooms are borne at the tops of 60cm/2ft stems, each flower up to 12.5cm/5in long and 10cm/4in across when open. The flat strap-shaped leaves are more or less evergreen, although for convenience mature bulbs are usually dried off and rested in summer. Seedlings, however, should be kept going until the bulbs reach flowering size.

Prepared bulbs will flower around Christmas in the northern hemisphere. Start them by soaking the lower parts of the bulbs in tepid water for four to five days, then pot them singly in good loam, leafmould (equal parts) with enough silver sand to make the compost friable. Half the bulb should be left exposed. Bottom heat encourages vigorous growth so stand them on a warm mantelpiece, a shelf over

Iris

[Northern Hemisphere] Several dwarf irises are suitable for windowboxes or growing in pots in the home or alpine house, but they will not tolerate hard forcing so keep them cool (in a garden plunge, cellar or shed) for about eight weeks and then bring them into temperatures of around 10-13°C/50-55°F to flower. *I. danfordiae* has fragrant lemon-yellow flowers on 7.5cm/3in stems in winter (February). *I. reticulata*, in character a few weeks later, has violet-scented, dark purple-blue flowers with prominent gold markings on the falls on 10cm/5in stems.

Named varieties of this include 'Cantab', cornflower-blue; 'J. S. Dijt', reddish-purple; and 'Harmony', rich blue.

Lilium

[Lily; Japan/China] Mid-century hybrid lilies which bloom in late winter make welcome houseplants. The treated bulbs arrive in early winter (December) and should be immediately planted in leafmould, loam and coarse sand (equal parts) with a little crushed charcoal. Allow three bulbs to a 15cm/6in pot and cover them with 5-7.5cm/2-3in of soil. Keep them in full light and a temperature around 20°C/68°F. Varieties include 'Brandywine', apricot-yellow; 'Cinnabar', maroon-red; 'Enchantment', cherry-red; 'Paprika', deep crimson; and 'Prosperity', lemon-yellow.

Many other lilies make good pot plants for summer flowering especially *L. regale* and hybrids, *L. longiflorum* and *L. auratum*. All demand a rich soil mix consisting of equal parts loam, peat, leafmould and well decayed cow-manure with enough coarse sand to ensure good drainage. Use 15cm/6in pots, cover the bulbs with 3.75cm/1½in of soil mix and grow them along in a cool place, shaded from direct sun until the buds appear. They can then go into a warm room to flower.

Muscari

[Grape Hyacinth; Europe/Asia] These popular bulbs sometimes known as starch lilies because the mucilaginous bulb sap was once used for starching linen. Easiest to grow indoors are *M. botryoides* 'Album', which has compact cones of small grape-like, white, fragrant flowers on 15-25cm/6-10in stems and the brilliant blue *M. armeniacum*, also fragrant, and its double blue cultivar 'Blue Spire'.

Plant these 2.5cm/1in deep in pots of good soil mix and keep in a cool place (4.4°C/40°F) for six to eight weeks before bringing them into higher temperatures (10-13°C/50-55°F) to flower. They look particularly attractive when interplanted with daffodils, early tulips or primroses.

Narcissus

[Daffodil; Southern Europe] Daffodils may be grown in window boxes, bowls or pots of soil, soil mix or bulb fibre and additionally certain of the *Tazetta* varieties can be flowered on pebbles. All containers should be at least 12.5 cm/5in deep as narcissi make vigorous roots. Set them close together on a layer of soil mix, work more soil between them and leave with the noses of the bulbs just exposed, except in the case of window boxes when the bulbs must be completely covered. They require no fertilizers.

Prepared bulbs for Christmas flowering have to be planted in early autumn (October) and need eight or nine weeks in a plunge bed outdoors or a cool, dark but frost-free place inside (4.4°C/40°F). Unprepared or ordinary bulbs should go in earlier (September) for New Year flowers, or October for February blooms, and need 10 or 12 weeks in cold darkness. There is no other difference in cultivation except this one of timing. At the end of these periods take them into a good light and temperature of 10-13°C/50-55°F for flowering. Water freely.

Suitable kinds for Christmas flowering include 'Golden Harvest' and 'Unsurpassable', both yellow trumpets; 'Yellow Sun', a large-cupped; 'Barrett Browning', small-cupped; 'Texas', a double; 'Peeping Tom', a cyclamineus hybrid, and 'Cragford', 'Soleil d'Or' and

Above: A beautiful lily for forcing into bloom in late winter is 'Imperial Crimson'.
Below: *Muscari armeniacum* was once called the starch lily because its mucilaginous bulb sap was used for starching linen.
Opposite above: Narcissi make deep roots so set them in pots at least 12.5cm/5in deep.
They provide cheerful colour in winter.
Opposite below: Tulips need a long session in cold darkness before being brought into warmth

'Paper White', Tazetta hybrids. There are many others for later flowering, also certain dwarf narcissi like *N. bulbocodium*, the hoop petticoat daffodil, 15cm/6in; *N. asturiensis*, 7.5cm/3in; *N. minor* (*N. natius*), 10cm/4in; and *N. cyclamineus*, 15cm/6in.

Scilla

[Squill; Southern Europe/USSR/Iran] Several miniature scillas are suitable for window boxes and pot cultivation. *S. bifolia* has five to seven star-shaped flowers of turquoise blue, (or occasionally white or pink) on 20cm/8in stems; *S. sibirica* has brilliant prussian-blue bells about 2.5cm/1in across on 7.5-10cm/3-4in stems, and the 10cm/4in *S. mischtschenkoana* (*S. tubergeniana*) is very pale blue with a deep blue stripe down the centre of each petal. All associate pleasingly with snowdrops or miniature narcissi and can be grown in bulb fibre or bowls of light soil mix. Keep them cool (4.4°C/40°F) for six to eight weeks before bringing them into warm rooms to flower.

Sparaxis

[Harlequin Flower; South Africa] These variable members of the iris family are best grown in pots or in raised beds in a cool greenhouse. The flowers resemble freesias somewhat in white, yellow, orange, red or purple shades, always with yellow throats. They bloom in early summer and have grassy leaves. Plant the corms 7.5-10cm/3-4in deep and the same distance apart in light soil mix. After the foliage dies down, dry the corms and store them in a dry place until planting time comes round again in late autumn (November).

Tulipa

[Tulip; Europe] Tulips make good pot plants for indoor cultivation but only when the roots have had a long session (14-16 weeks) in cold darkness. Too often this procedure is scamped with inevitable and disappointing results. Ordinary unprepared bulbs should be planted in late summer (early September to mid-October) in good potting mix and kept in temperatures around 9°C/48°F for 10 to 12 weeks. A plunge bed out of doors is best but failing that a dark frost-free cellar, shed or room. They should then be brought into warm darkness (15.6°C/60°F) for two or three weeks and only after this taken into a light living room to flower. Specially prepared bulbs for Christmas flowering are planted before the middle of September, kept cool as before until the first week in December, then taken into temperatures of 18°C/65°F for a few days until growth is apparent. All this time they should be in darkness but may then go into light to flower.

Good forcing kinds are: early singles, 'Bellona', golden yellow, 46cm/18in; 'Brilliant Star', scarlet, 30cm/1ft; 'Doctor Plesman', orange-red, 36cm/14in; early doubles, 'Wilhelm Kordes', orange-yellow flushed red, 30cm/1ft; 'Orange Nassau', blood-red, 30cm/1ft; 'Electra', cherry-red, 30cm/1ft; 'Murillo Max', white flushed pink, 36cm/14in; and 'Mr Van der Hoef', golden-yellow, 30cm/1ft.

Vallota

[Scarborough Lily; South Africa] *V. speciosa*, a superb autumn-flowering amaryllid, does well in pots and bowls and looks most arresting in a fireplace with concealed lighting, on a pedestal stand or on a conservatory bench. Growing about 60cm/2ft tall, the 7.5cm/3in funnel-shaped blooms are vivid scarlet with prominent golden stamens. They are carried in umbels of four to ten on each stem. The leaves are long and narrow. Vallotas should be planted in loam, sand and leaf mould (equal parts) and are helped by an occasional feed during the growing season. They can be lifted, divided and repotted every three or four years.

How to grow Healthy Bulbs

Probably no plants give greater pleasure in the middle of winter than bowls of forced bulbs. Their message is clear; whatever the weather outside, spring is round the corner. No home too small, no situation too bleak for them, for with the aid of artificial lighting, both winter and summer bulbs can be grown in dim halls, stairways and landings as well as in light windows or greenhouses.

For table decorations they are unsurpassed; groups of bulbs can be arranged with other plants in empty fireplaces and in spring and summer they can be grown outside in windowboxes or on balconies. An ideal method for tiny bulbs which do not take kindly to forcing – like snowdrops, miniature narcissi and grape hyacinths – is to grow them in a cold alpine house or frame. The protection of the glass is enough to bring them to bloom several weeks earlier than outdoors and if raised on waist-high benches they can be seen and enjoyed in the bleakest months of the year and brought indoors when in bloom.

Cool (frost-free) greenhouses offer still greater scope: daffodils, tulips and hyacinths associate pleasantly with such plants as azaleas, cinerarias, primulas and ferns or, later in the season, vallotas and other exotics can be grown. No bulbs demand excessive heat so one or other of these situations suit most species.

The most rewarding bulbs for forcing are hyacinths, daffodils, tulips and hippeastrums, all of which are suitable for pot culture and specially treated by the growers for forcing.

Hyacinths can be grown in a variety of ways — in bulb fibre, soil mixture, newspaper and water. Fancy bowls without drainage holes prevent damage to furniture and are ideal for hyacinths in bulb fibre. This has a peat or moss fibre base with added crushed charcoal and oyster shell. It can be bought ready mixed from garden stores and only needs wetting before use, adding enough water to make it damp yet not so much that moisture is expressed when a handful is squeezed.

When the correct stage is reached, half fill the containers with fibre and place the bulbs in position so that they are close together without touching each other or the sides of the bowls. Add more fibre, working this between the bulbs with a wooden ladle or spoon handle until the bowls are filled to within 2.5cm/1in of their rims and only the noses of the hyacinths protrude. Wrap the containers in plastic sheeting or news-

paper and, if possible, stand them on a hard surface outdoors beneath 15cm/6in of sand, leaves or ashes. If they cannot go outside, even on a balcony, keep them in the coolest part of the house. Here they should remain for eight or nine weeks until the pots are full of roots and the white shoots are 2.5cm/1in high. A temperature of 5°C/40°F is ideal at this stage.

Normally those bulbs plunged outdoors need no attention during this period, but bulbs indoors should be looked at from time to time and watered if necessary. They should be kept moist but with no standing water; if dry at the roots they go blind (will not flower) or become stunted.

When the top growth is obvious bring the bulbs into moderate warmth (10°C/50°F) to draw out the foliage. The first white shoots should be gradually acclimatized to light in a darker part of the room and then go into a bright window. Pay regular attention to watering.

When the buds are prominent and the leaves well grown, the plants can go into warmth to flower. Give the pots a quarter turn every day so that they grow straight.

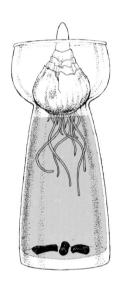

Hyacinths and crocuses can also be grown in bulb glasses. These come in the appropriate sizes and have hollowed-out necks to fit the bulbs. Keep these full of soft water almost, but not quite, up to the bulb bases, and stand them in a light window. Turn the glasses round daily, otherwise the stems pull over toward the light. A few pieces of charcoal in the water keeps it sweet.

Crocus and certain narcissus varieties will also grow and flower wedged on pebbles heaped in shallow dishes with a little water on the bottom. Here again the bulbs should not come in direct contact with the water. The best narcissi for the purpose are the tazetta or bunch-flowered types like 'Cragford', 'Paper White' and 'Soleil d'Or'.

Most narcissi do well in light soil mix as do many of the other bulbs mentioned in the alphabetical list. Narcissi should be planted with half of the bulbs protruding and stored in a cold place — as for hyacinths. Any good proprietary mix is suitable or a home mix composed of equal parts good sifted loam and leafmould with enough silver sand to keep the soil open is ideal. Fertilizers are rarely necessary.

Tulips also can be forced in soil mix, starting with the Christmas blooming prepared early singles and doubles. These are followed at appropriate intervals by the mid-season and darwin types. Other plants frequently forced for out of season flowers are hippeastrums, lilies, scillas and lilies-of-the-valley.

Some common causes of failure are:
1. Flowers failing to open, bud withering or yellow leaves — erratic watering; the roots are not functioning properly.
2. Stunted growth — poor root system, probably due to insufficient time in the dark, or too warm during that period; dry or waterlogged roots.
3. Yellow or limp foliage — draughts.
4. Failure to flower — dry roots or overheating.

As a rough temperature guide when forcing the more usual bulbs the following may be helpful:
For roots   – 5°C/40°F
For foliage and stems – 10°C/50°F
For flowers   – 16°C/60°F
21°C/70°F gives quick development, but 27°C/80°F will rush bulbs with loss of substance and risk of blindness (non-flowering).

5°C/40°F   10°C/50°F   15-21°C/60-70°F

The chart below shows
the varying heights
of popular bulbs:

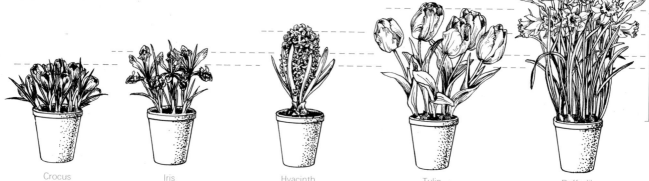

	35.5-45.5cm 14-18 in
	30.5-38 cm 12-15 in
	20.5-30.5cm 8-12 in
	15cm - 6 in
	4.5-10 cm 2-4 in

Crocus   Iris   Hyacinth   Tulip   Daffodil

Specially prepared forcing bulbs are naturally expensive; they have been grown along for perhaps 4 or 6 years and have been subjected to special heat or cold treatments to make them flower out of season — usually earlier but sometimes later than normal. You must expect to pay more for these.

For the rest, select large and solid, firm bulbs, free from bruise marks, mildew stains or any suspicion of flabbiness. They should not be damaged in any way and the outer coats should be intact. Sweating or rotting in storage or transit will spoil bulbs and so will premature lifting or improper curing or packing.

Attractive effects can be obtained by mixing bulbs in large containers, provided one selects varieties which come to flower around the same time. It is usually easier to grow the different sorts along separately, in boxes of loamless potting mix, then carefully lift them when they show bud and group them with others in bowls of similar compost.

Good companions are double pink tulips with blue grape hyacinths; scillas and blue hyacinths; white hyacinths and snowdrops; or golden bunch narcissi and crocuses.

Rye grass seed sown on the soil when bulbs come into the light will develop to an emerald green carpet by the time the bulbs are in flower. Small pieces of bark or tufts of moss also give an attractive finish to bulb bowls.

The mixed height arrangement of bulbs includes early tulips and *Muscari armeniacum*. Below, aconites, snowdrops and crocuses are grouped

Bulbs are not fussy houseplants. They require regular watering but no extra feeding when grown in bowls. A light airy situation is important and the recommended temperatures while growing. Never expose bulbs in the home to direct sunlight through glass, fires or other forms of direct heat.

Normally it does not pay to try and propagate bulbs where there is no garden. Occasionally, uncommon kinds may be reproduced from offsets at the bases of bulbs, cormlets found around adult corms or divisions in the case of clivias or lily-of-the-valley. These have to be grown on and may take several years to flower.

Forced bulbs cannot be brought to flowering indoors for a second year; they must be discarded after flowering or given to a friend with a garden. In the latter case, keep watering until the foliage turns yellow and then have the bulbs planted out in the garden. For indoor use, buy new bulbs for forcing every year — and fresh bulb fibre or soil mix.

Opposite: *Lilium regale*.

Cacti and other succulents

Plants which can be grown in the home are so varied now that there is no corner of it that will not suit some plant completely. Although there are many indoor plants which will not be happy in the extremely hot and sunny conditions of a south-facing window, there are a few exceptions such as the cacti and other succulents, which revel in this kind of environment and, indeed, without which they will not thrive or flower.

However, cacti and succulents cannot, as is so often thought, virtually do without water at all. They have certainly evolved plant forms which can store a great deal of water for long periods, but in their natural habitat they are subjected to torrential downpours of rain for short periods, at very infrequent intervals.

The cacti could be called the stem succulents, in which the stem has swollen, usually so that it is round and thus forms the main part of the plant. The other succulents are the leaf succulents – the leaves contain the water storage cells. Roots of both are developed so that they either spread great distances sideways though shallowly, or are deep rooting and tuberous, so that the maximum water can be absorbed.

A further distinction between the two is that the cacti, and only the true cacti, carry areoles, small woolly 'cushions', from which grow spines, bristles or hairs, flowers and occasionally leaves. The cacti come from the New World, that is North, Central and South America, and the West Indies, while the remaining succulents are from the Old World, particularly South Africa. All are found in such regions as semi-desert, prairies, steppes and scrub (the epiphytic cacti live in forests), where there is occasional rain, heavy dew or thick mist. Some grow in the shade of rocks and shrubs, or in thin grassland. All these areas can be quite cold at night in winter, but dry. They are not found in arid deserts, as these will not support any life.

Cacti are grown for their flowers and unusual shapes, succulents for their leaves. The cacti have very pretty, usually stemless flowers in spring and early summer in all colours except blue; many are easily flowered, especially the smaller cacti, and it is certainly not true that they only bloom once every seven years, at night. Some are fragrant. Succulents have highly ornamental leaves, both in colour and shape, and some also flower.

The cacti can be divided into two groups: the desert cacti, which contain most of the genera described, and which grow naturally in deserts, and the forest cacti, the epiphytic or branching types, which live on branches and in forks of trees. The latter include epiphyllums, rhipsalidopsis and schlumbergeras.

Forest cacti come from the tropical rain forests of Central and South America. They are subjected to filtered sunlight and a great deal of humidity. On the face of it, you would think that cacti would be the last plants to find in such conditions, but their roots are anchored in very shallow soil which dries out quickly, and they need to store water as much as any desert cactus. Their stems are flattened and leaf-like, the only cacti like this, apart from the Prickly Pear.

CACTI

Astrophytum

[Bishop's Cap Cactus or Star or Sea-urchin Cactus; 5°C/41°F min; Mexico] The easiest of these to grow is the Bishop's Cap Cactus, *A. myriostigma*, with five very pronounced ribs forming a roughly circular body when young, covered with white scales and topped by small yellow fragrant flowers in summer. *A. asterias* is the Star or Sea-urchin Cactus, a flattened ball with eight ribs and pale yellow, 2.5cm/1in wide, flowers. It grows to about 10cm/4in wide and 4cm/1½in high in pots, but specimens growing in the wild can be 20cm/8in and more in diameter. Astrophytums can be grown in the usual cactus potting mix and under normal cactus conditions.

Cephalocereus

[Old Man Cactus; Mexico] The Old Man Cactus, *C. senilis*, is well named, as it is a column-shaped plant covered in long white hair, and looks more like some species of animal than a plant. On a good plant the individual hairs can be 12cm/5in long. Plants can live to be very old – the 12m/40ft specimens found growing in Mexico are estimated to be 200 years old. Unfortunately it does not flower until 6m/20ft tall, and is extremely slow-growing, so when grown as an indoor plant, its chief attraction will be its hairiness. Some owners have been known to shampoo the hairs, to keep them a good light colour, but as the change from a clean creamy white to a rather dull beige is due to age, this is not very effective. It should be kept completely dry in winter.

Chamaecereus

[Peanut Cactus; 2°C/35°F min; Argentina] *C. silvestrii* is a very easily grown and commonly seen cactus, with finger-like curving stems 3-8cm/1-3in long lying flat on the soil, produced embarassingly freely. These are easily knocked off or can be taken off and will root readily without any particular treatment, beyond making sure that the base is firmly in contact with the soil mix. Bright red, open flowers about 2.5cm/1in in diameter come in

May, sitting directly on the stems. They will not set seed, however, because all the plants grown in cultivation have been vegetatively propagated. Provided you give it a good rest in winter, without water, and keep it quite cold – down to freezing will not kill it – it will flower all the more profusely.

Cleistocactus

[7°C/44°F min; South America] The name of this genus refers to the flowers; *cleisto* means closed and the flowers consist of a narrow, colourful tube, which never actually opens, though the stamens emerge from the end. *C. stransii* has erect columnar branches from the base, covered thickly with short white, rather prickly, spines, especially on the top of the column, which almost seems to have a top-knot. Flowers only appear on well-established

Opposite: The epiphyllum, or Orchid cactus, has beautiful flowers in spring and early summer.
Above: Echinocereus flowers last for two days.
Below: *Echinopsis eyriesii*

plants about 1.5m/5ft tall and are red; they come continuously all through the summer, from the sides of the plant. Offsets are readily produced. During the winter keep the soil mix just moist, not completely dry, unless the temperature goes down to freezing, and give them a slightly richer mixture than the usual.

Echinocactus

[5°C/41°F min; Mexico] A small genus of about nine species, echinocactus includes the Golden Barrel Cactus, *E. grusonii*, one of the easiest to grow, provided it has as much sun as possible. It is almost completely round, with numerous ribs, each densely set with bright yellow spines. On top is a tuft of yellow wool-like hair. The flowers, which are rarely produced in cultivation, occur in summer and are yellow tubes. It is slow to grow and takes many years to reach 15cm/6in, and will stand a drop in temperature at night, and also near freezing in winter, when it should be kept dry.

Echinocereus

[5°C/41°F min; Mexico/Southern United States] *E. pectinatus* has beautiful pink, tube-shaped flowers, the tube opening out at the end, and the whole flower being about 7.5cm/3in long. Flowering goes on intermittently for most of the summer, the flowers starting as small dark woolly buds. Each flower lasts about two days. The cactus body is a semi-prostrate column, with many ribs covered with small white spines. The soil needs to be specially well drained. Echinocereus are slow to grow, but produce offsets at the rate of about four or five to a plant. They can be kept quite dry all winter and will even take temperatures at frost level.

Echinopsis

[2°C/35°F min; Argentina] A very easily grown and flowered group of cactus, the echinopsis are small and round, flowering when about 7.5cm/3in in diameter, the flowers almost larger than the plants. *E. eyriesii* has fragrant, long funnel-shaped white flowers in summer; they open late in the day, and last through the next day. Echinopsis have been in cultivation for a long time, and most plants are hybrids, crossed with lobivias, with freely-produced flowers in shades of pink, salmon, orange and yellow. Offsets are produced readily and are easily rooted when still tiny, about 1-1½cm/½-¾in wide. No water is needed in winter, and they do not need much heat either.

Epiphyllum

[Orchid or Water-lily Cactus; 10°C/50°F min; Central and South America] The epiphyllums have the most beautiful flowers in late spring and early summer, and the recently produced hybrids have a second flush in autumn as well. The flowers can be 15cm/6in long and as much wide and are an open-trumpet shape, mostly in shades of red or pink, but with purple, magenta, white and yellow also included in the colour range. The centre consists of long cream-coloured stamens, and some flowers, especially the yellow and white hybrids, have the added attraction of fragrance. The stalkless flowerbuds are produced directly from the edges of the leaf-like stems (epiphyllum means 'on the leaf'), and start to develop two months or so before they actually unfold. Each flower lasts three or four days.

Epiphyllums can grow quite tall, 30-90cm/1-3ft, and need supporting; they are rather ungainly plants and without their flowers would be distinctly boring. The flattened stems are about 5cm/2in or more wide, with pronounced dark green segments or pads. Stems will carry flowerbuds when they are two years old, and these are generally produced from the upper parts of the plants. There are many hybrids. Some good ones are: the *E. × ackermannii* range, which includes all the red hybrids, and *E. cooperi* range, with the snow-white and yellow hybrids, fragrant and opening in the evening; 'London Sunshine', yellow; 'Midnight', purple and pink; 'Sunburst', salmon with red centre; 'Wanderlust', dark pink.

The resting period of epiphyllums is mainly winter, after the second flush, but they also have a short resting time in early summer, after the first flush of flowers.

Ferocactus

[5°C/41°F min; Central America/Southern United States] *Fero* means ferocious, and this describes the spines of these cacti exactly. They are long, stout and exceedingly pointed, and some are hooked as well. These cacti are grown for their spines, as flowers are rarely produced. The plant body is round and ribbed until the adult stage when it becomes more or less columnar. It slowly grows to a diameter of about 37cm/15in in the species–*F. latispinus*, whose small, red and scented flowers may be produced in late spring and summer on top of the plant. Some species can be 3m/9ft tall. *F. melocactiformis* has yellow spines and flowers in June and July, and grows to about 60cm/2ft. Give as much sun as possible, and let the plants dry out between waterings in summer.

Gymnocalycium

[5°C/41°F min; Northern South America] You sometimes see, at shows and in nurseries, some extraordinary-looking cacti with bright red scarlet balls on top of fleshy green columns. The red ball is the gymnocalycium which has been grafted on to a stock of *Myrtillocactus* or *Trichocereus*. This red gymnocalycium is a cultivar called 'Red Ball' from *G. mihanovichii friedrichii*; as it does not contain any chlorophyll, it has to be grafted to grow at all. The plant is cultivated because of its red colour and is unlikely to flower. There is also a yellow form and a red and green striped one.

The ordinary gymnocalyciums are mostly round plants about 5-15cm/2-6in in diameter with a few ribs and spines of varying size. Large flowers come from late spring through June and July; they last for four or five days, and are often bigger than the plant. Colours are in shades of pink or red, but sometimes white and yellow are also seen. No special care is needed beyond the normal cactus cultivation.

Lobivia

[2°C/35°F min; South America, particularly Peru] The main attraction of these cacti is their flowers, which are large, up to 10cm/4in across, and brightly coloured pink, red, purple, white, yellow or orange. They are funnel-shaped and occur in summer, and quite young plants of two or three years will flower; an added attraction is the ease with which they can be grown to flowering size. Although the flowers only last for a day, they come in quick succession and fresh buds are constantly appearing. The plant body is small and round, 5-15cm/2-6in in diameter. Some especially good species are *L. aurea*, bright golden flowers; *L. cinnabarina*, an almost luminous red; and *L. jajoiana*, deep red with a black throat. Lobivias will endure frost in winter, if kept completely dry at the

roots, which are tuberous and long – they need larger pots than other cacti of the same size.

Mammillaria

[5°C/41°F min; Central and South America/West Indies] Whole books have been written about mammillarias, and there is an entire society for mammillaria enthusiasts. It is a vast genus of over 200 species, very varied in plant forms and with species whose care ranges from easy to very difficult. The small flowers are produced in a ring round the top of the plant, which can be globular or cylindrical; flowering starts in early summer and can continue until autumn. Sometimes brightly coloured fruits follow and last until the new flowers the following season. On the whole, they are small plants, growing to, at the most, 20cm/8in tall, singly or in clusters. All have prominent spines, sometimes prickles, sometimes hair-like.

Some suitable species for a windowsill are: *M. wildii*, white flowers all through summer, clustered plant body; *M. zeilmanniana*, red-purple flowers on tiny plants, cylindrical but branching; *M. rhodantha*, red spines and magenta flowers in mid-summer, cylindrical; *M. microhelia*, golden spines and greenish yellow flowers, solitary body. *M. rhodantha* has a cristate or fasciated form, and so has *M. wildii*, which will also flower quite freely. Plenty of light is important for flower production, and the plants should be turned frequently to prevent them straining towards the source of light.

Notocactus

[5°C/41°F min; Central South America] A large group of vigorous, easily-grown cacti, the notocactus are easy to flower, mainly small (up to 18cm/7in) and round with flattened tops and many spines on the ribbed sides. Trumpet-shaped flowers, opening out wide, are usually yellow and large for the size of the plant, coming either singly or in a circle from the top. *N. haselbergii* is covered in white spines, so that it looks like a white ball, and has orange red flowers in early summer lasting for several weeks, though it does not start to flower until about five years old. *N. leninghausii* grows up to 90cm/3ft, has yellow spines and yellow flowers in summer, but these do not come until

it is a column about 17cm/7in tall. *N. apricus* is a name covering a group of plants (height 8cm/3in) whose flowers are large and yellow, appearing on even tiny plants; they have a dense covering of bristly brown and yellow spines. Notocactus need little heat in winter provided they are kept dry. They are easily grown from seed, the young plants flowering quite easily.

Opuntia

[Prickly Pear; 3°C/37°F min; North, Central and South America] The Prickly Pears have taken to Australia and warmer parts of Europe so readily since their introduction that they have been thought to be indigenous. The fruits of the opuntia can be eaten, and are grown in some areas of America for canning. The best known opuntias are those with flattened pads, but there are also tree-like types with cylindrical, branching stems. The smaller species, with pads, are the easiest to grow in the home. Opuntias are not difficult to grow, but flowers are rarely seen except under greenhouse conditions; the plants are usually grown for their shape and colourful spines with barbed bristles.

Above left: *Lobivia pseudocachensis*.
Top: *Opuntia microdasys*.
Above: *Mammillaria zeilmanniana*.
Opposite: A cactus garden

Rebutia

[5°C/41°F min; Mountains of South America] The rebutias are marvellous cacti for flowering; they are small globular plants, maximum height 12cm/5in, producing many offsets, and they bloom freely even when only a few years old. The trumpet-shaped flowers are produced near the base of the plants in great profusion, almost covering the plant in spring. Some species virtually flower themselves to death, but they are so easily rooted from offsets or grown from seed, that replacements are easy. Flower colour can be yellow, red, lilac, salmon, pink, orange and white. The rounded plant is not ribbed and has very few spines. Rebutias need good light in summer, but virtually no heat or water in winter. Some especially good species are: *R. minuscula*, red flowers and one of the earliest to bloom; *R. senilis*, red flowered from April onwards with long white spines; and *R. xanthocarpa salmonea*, salmon-pink.

Rhipsalidopsis

[Easter Cactus; 13°C/55°F min; Central and South America] The Easter Cactus, *R. gaertneri*, was formerly known as *Schlumbergera gaertneri*, and before that as *Zygocactus gaertneri* and it may be sold under any of these names. The Easter Cactus is one of the hanging types of cactus, with flattened leaf-like stems about 1-1.5cm/½-¾in wide, segmented into dull green pads. New growth appears from the tips of the end pad, as do the flower buds. A well grown plant may be 45cm/1½ft high and 45cm/1½ft wide, and when in full flower is extremely attractive. The flowers are trumpet-shaped and pendent with narrow, pointed, red and purple

These can become embedded in the skin and are difficult to remove. Suitable species, flowering occasionally, include *O. bergeriana*, dark red flowers in summer; *O. basilaris*, red flowers and purple-blue pads, to 90cm/3ft; *O. microdasys*, yellow-brown and spineless with yellow flowers occasionally, to 90cm/3ft; and *O. paraguayensis*, yellow flowers, the most easily flowered of this selection.

Parodia

[50°C/41°F min; Central South America] Globular cacti, small and slow growing to 6cm/2¼in, the parodias' main attraction is their spines. *P. chrysacanthion* has long, pale yellow spines covering it, and sometimes small yellow funnel-shaped flowers. *P. faustiana* has white spines and brown flowers, *P. sanguiniflora* has brown spines and numerous dark red flowers in summer, and *P. mairanana* has yellow spines and apricot flowers from summer until autumn. Be careful with watering, particularly in winter, as parodias are very prone to root rot.

petals, appearing in April and May, smaller but more numerous than those of the Christmas Cactus.

The Easter Cactus rests from autumn (September) to late winter, then begins to push out new flower buds; after flowering it grows new pads during summer, on which next year's flowers will come.

Schlumbergera

[Christmas Cactus; 13°C/55°F min; Brazil] Formerly called *Zygocactus truncatus*, this is now correctly known as *Schlumbergera × buckleyi* but may be sold under either name. Flowering can be between October and late January depending on variety and cultural care, but it will not form flowerbuds unless it is subjected to short days. The drooping, narrow trumpet-like flowers, up to 8cm/3in long, are magenta or rose-pink. If you keep it in the house in the autumn and early winter, it must not be given artificial light when it is naturally dark outdoors; the plant must still be kept in warmth, but in a dark place in the evening.

Habit of growth and flowers are very much like the Easter Cactus, but the larger and fewer flowers are more easily produced. It rests from late winter until late spring, then starts growing again, and in September the flowerbuds should begin to appear. If you delay giving it short days, it will take longer to form buds, and once you are experienced, you can manipulate flower production so that it coincides with Christmas. Warmth (18°C/65°F) also helps to encourage flowering.

Selenicereus

[10°C/50°F min; West Indies] Most of the species of this genus are night-flowering and are responsible for getting cacti in general a bad name for flowering once every seven years. *S. grandiflorus* (Queen of the Night) unfolds its beautiful blooms in the evening and they last all night, but they are produced much more frequently than every seven years. The white flowers are enormous, up to 30cm/1ft long, and very strongly scented, produced in June or July. The trailing or climbing stems can be 5m/17ft long in the wild, but in a container are less than half that length. The plant must have warmth in winter in order to produce buds.

Opposite top: *Parodia sanguiniflora* has numerous dark red flowers in summer.
Opposite bottom: Yellow, red, lilac, salmon pink, orange and white flowers are produced in great profusion by rebutias.
Above right: The fleshy leaves of *Aeonium arboreum* form in rosettes at the end of shoots

OTHER SUCCULENTS

Aeonium

[7°C/44°F min; Canary Islands/Azores/North Africa] The aeoniums are members of the crassula family, and can be small or shrubby, or tree-like with fleshy leaves either in rosettes at the end of shoots or flat and ground-hugging. The species are greatly varied in shape and colour; for instance *A. arboreum*, as it suggests, is like a miniature tree with brown branches bearing shiny green leaves and a main trunk to about 90cm/3ft tall. Its variety *A. a.* 'Atropurpureum' has slightly smaller leaves, flushed with purple, which will keep the colour provided it is kept in bright sun.

A. tabulaeforme naturally grows pressed against rocks and is quite flat, the leaves being light green and tightly compacted. *A. undulatum* has rather spoon-shaped leaves with wavy margins, in rosettes on top of and around the main stem; it produces starry yellow flowers in clusters in summer. Height is 60-90cm/2-3ft; winter temperature should be 10°C/50°F, unless kept dry, though they tend to lose their leaves if kept too dry. A little water during the winter improves their appearance, as well as their health.

Agave

[5°C/41°F min; Mexico] The form of all agaves is a rosette of fleshy, pointed leaves sitting close against the soil, from the centre of which is produced a flowering stem when the plant reaches maturity, sometimes at the age of 500.

The stem can be 7.8m/25ft tall, as in *A. americana*, the Century Plant, whose spiny leaves can be 1.8m/6ft long. In a container, however, it is very much smaller (up to 1.2m/4ft) and unlikely to flower. *A. victoriae-reginae* is more suitable for the home, slowly growing to 50cm/20in wide, height 15cm/6in, with white-edged dull green, very fleshy leaves. It needs a minimum winter temperature of 10°C/50°F. Agaves need more water than most succulents in summer, but need to be sparingly watered in winter.

Aloe

[5°C/41°F min; South Africa] The Partridge-breasted Aloe, *A. variegata*, is the most popular of the many species in this genus. It has a dark green rosette of leaves arranged in overlapping ranks, variegated with white horizontal bands. It is very handsome, about 10cm/4in wide, and with light red flowers in a loose spike 30cm/1ft tall in early spring. It does best if kept on the dry side in winter.

Ceropegia

[Hearts-entangled; 7°C/45°F min; Natal] It is difficult to believe that this genus is classed as a succulent. *C. woodii* belongs to the same family as *Hoya carnosa*, and has purple, long, hanging, thread-like stems, to 90cm/3ft, with small heart-shaped, fleshy leaves marbled white on green. From the axils of these grow greenish-white tubular flowers in summer. It grows from a tuber, and in winter can be kept quite cool and dry. The leaves will be fleshier the drier it is kept.

Conophytum

[Cone Plants; 5°C/41°F min; South West Africa] The conophytums are one of the 'living stones' group, seldom over 5cm/2in high and composed of fused lobes. One of the prettiest in flower is *C. ficiforme*, with violet-pink, daisy-like nocturnal flowers. It rests from April to August, in as much sun as possible, and should be kept quite dry at that time. Flowers and new plants appear in autumn, and the growing period is during winter and early spring. *C. truncatellum* is minute and has cream-white flowers which open during the day in October. (See also Lithops.)

Cotyledon

[7°C/45°F min; South Africa] One of the most popular species of this genus of succulents is *C. undulata*, a most attractive plant; the leaves are light green, thickly coated with silvery-white, and waved at the edges. Height is about 45cm/1½ft. It should never be watered or sprayed overhead, otherwise the coating on the leaves is spoilt. The summer flowers are narrow bell-shaped, pale yellow and red; the plant needs a little shade in summer, plenty of light in winter, and a moderate amount of water all year.

Crassula

[7°C/45°F min; South Africa] The crassula genus is a large and varied one, containing shrubs and herbaceous plants. The leaves of

some are extremely attractive, and others have good flowers as well. *C. falcata* has markedly grey-blue leaves in layers on a stem which can be 60cm/2ft tall, and a cluster of bright red flowers at the top in summer. *C. arborescens* is often seen looking rather dreary because it is not being given enough water or light; it grows at least 90cm/3ft tall, and has spoon-shaped fleshy grey-green leaves with a red margin; clusters of white starry flowers appear in May if the plant can be kept in a suitably hot and sunny place. *C. lactea* is also shrubby with dark green leaves and white flowers in mid-winter.

Echeveria

[5°C/41°F min; Central and Southern North America] All are rosette forming plants, with a single flower stem coming from the centre of the rosette, usually in winter or spring. *E. elegans* forms rosettes of almost white, translucent green leaves on stems eventually 30cm/1ft tall, with pink flowers. *E. gibbiflora* is shrubby with blue-green leaves, up to 20cm/8in long, in rosettes flushed with red or purple; red flowers in autumn. The variety *E. g. metallica* has pink-bronze leaves with a pink or red edge, and *E. g. cristata* has frilled leaf margins. *E. setosa* has a flat and silvery rosette, with red flowers throughout summer. Give these plants a richer potting mix than usual and keep cool. Give water all year, but keep it off the leaves.

Euphorbia

[10°C/50°F min; Madagascar] This genus is very large and extremely varied in its forms, from succulents through annual and perennial herbaceous plants to shrubs and trees. The sap is white and milky. The ferociously prickly spines of *E. milii* (Crown of Thorns) are rather off-putting, though the red flowers dotted all over it in spring and the fresh, light green

leaves are pretty enough to make up. The grey stems are thick, fleshy and gnarled, to 1.2m/4ft. Its resting time is winter in Britain, but elsewhere it can be in flower for many months. It needs to be kept slightly warmer and moister than other succulents, with some water all year.

Faucaria

[5°C/41°F min; South Africa] The leaves of these are tough and fleshy. *F. tigrina* (Tiger's Jaws) are armed with teeth along the edges, and their grey-green colour sets off the bright yellow flowers produced in autumn – they open in the afternoons. The plant is only about 7.5cm/3in high. Keep them in small pots to encourage flowering, and keep dry in the early spring and summer.

Fenestraria

[Window Plants; 2°C/35°F min; South Africa] Sometimes this is sold or listed under the name Mesembryanthemum, but it is quite different to those plants in its habit of growth, and looks very much more like the 'living stones'. Fenestrarias have attained their common name because the surface of each swollen pebble-like leaf is transparent. This allows just enough sun to reach the plant for it to live – the rest of it being buried – but not so much that it is burnt up. *F. rhopalophylla* forms clumps of cylindrical greenish-white leaves and has white flowers 3cm/1½in wide; the species, *F. aurantiaca* is similar but with yellow flowers. Plenty of sun, a wide shallow container and a little water throughout the year are advisable.

Left top: *Faucaria tigrina*.
Left bottom: *Fenestraria rhopalophylla*.
Below: *Crassula corymbulosa*.
Opposite left: *Kalanchoe blossfeldiana* 'Vulcan'
Opposite right: *Lithops salicola*

Haworthia

[5°C/41°F min; South Africa] These succulents of the lily family are small plants or shrublets, usually rosette-shaped. *H. margaritifera* has dark green, fleshy leaves, heavily marked with white, in a rosette up to 15cm/6in wide. *H. reinwardtii* forms a tall narrow rosette of fleshy, keeled leaves, up to a height of 15cm/6in. Haworthias like a good light but not full sun and a little water in winter.

Kalanchoe

[5°C/41°F min; South America/China/Madagascar] *K. blossfeldiana* 'Tom Thumb' is a small plant with rounded fleshy leaves and clusters of small, bright red flowers, often for sale at Christmas; there is a variety with yellow flowers. *K. tomentosa* is quite different, with thick, furry, silvery leaves, edged with chocolate brown hair, and silvery stems, to 75cm/2½ft; a very handsome plant seldom producing flowers. Other kalanchoes include those formerly known as *Bryophyllum*; they produce plantlets on the edges of the leaves in between the serrations, which drop off and root easily into the soil below. *K. diagremontiana* has pointed leaves, flat and arrow-shaped, and marked with purple-brown. The winter flowers are yellow and pink, and it grows up to 60cm/2ft tall. *K. fedtschenkoi* has blue-purple leaves fading to lilac-pink, with dark toothed edges, and yellow flowers in winter. Height is about 30cm/1ft. Kalanchoes are easily grown, needing slightly more water in summer and more food than most succulents; they also like humidity.

Lithops

[Living Stones; 5°C/41°F min; South Africa] These plants look exactly like the pebbles among which they grow. Only the surface of the plant can be seen; the rest is buried from the hot desert sun. Each plant consists of two extremely fleshy leaves, nearly completely joined, from the centre of which appear yellow or white daisy flowers in late summer and autumn. They rest between December and April, and need a potting mix consisting of almost half coarse sand or other drainage material. When they start to grow again, the dead outer skin will split, and each lobe bursts through it. Keep the plants dry while resting, and water only sparingly even when growing.

Rochea

[7°C/45°F min; South Africa] The French botanist La Roche (d. 1813) is commemorated in the name of this succulent. The best known species is *R. coccinea*, a shrubby plant which grows to about 60cm/2ft tall, with small fleshy leaves arranged in regular ranks up the stem, and a head of red fragrant flowers at the top from May or June onwards. *R. jasminea* has prostrate stems and white flowers in spring. Take off the dead flower stems to make room for new shoots, which will themselves flower later in the season. Like cotyledon, rochea needs water all year and a little shade in summer.

Sedum

[5°C/41°F min; Worldwide except Australia] This large genus also includes small succulent plants and there are many attractive species which grow well in the home. *S. sieboldii* 'Medio-variegatum' has fleshy blue-green leaves with a pale yellow or white stripe in the centre and red edges; in September it produces clusters of pink flowers, but then dies down completely for the winter. *S. pachyphyllum* (Jelly Beans) which grows to 30cm/1ft, has blue-green fleshy leaves, clubbed and red at the tips and red and yellow flowers in spring. *S. rubrotinctum* is a small plant (20cm/8in), and has small, thick, berry-like leaves which turn coppery red in the sun; the yellow flowers are seldom seen. Feeding is not required; shallow containers are best and keep the potting mix on the dry side.

Sempervivum

[Houseleek; 2°C/35°F min; Europe] These succulents are so well known as to hardly need description. Cultivation is easy in the extreme, as they seem able to exist virtually without any water – an occasional deluge every few months is sufficient. The Common Houseleek, *S. tectorum*, consists of rosettes 10cm/4in wide of fleshy pointed triangular leaves. *S. arachnoideum* is the Cobweb Houseleek, with tiny rosettes 2.5cm/1in wide covered in white webbing, from the centre of which come stems 7.5cm/3in or more tall, carrying pink starry flowers in June.

Stapelia

[5°C/41°F min; South and Tropical Africa] Stapelias are unlucky to have a reputation for smelling unpleasant, because it is only a few species which do so; the rest have no odour of any kind. The whole plant is fleshy including the flowers, which have bizarre and spectacular colouring. *S. grandiflora* has starfish-shaped blooms 15cm/6in wide, dark brown, with fringed and hairy petals. *S. revoluta* can reach a height of 37cm/15in and has purple flowers; the flowers of *S. verrucosa* are saucer-shaped, yellow with red spots – it is a small plant. The most well known one, *S. variegata* (10cm/4in) has pale yellow wrinkled petals with dark purple spots, but this is one of the evil-smelling species. All flower in summer and rest in winter; they need an ordinary potting mix with extra grit. A larger pot than usual is required as they need plenty of root room, as well as a little shade from sun in summer.

How to grow
Healthy
Cacti & Other
Succulents

The clues to the growing of healthy cacti
and other succulents can be found in the
description of their habitats: heat, plenty of
light, a dry atmosphere, occasional heavy
watering, and very well-drained potting
mix. The only exceptions to this are the
forest cacti.

Succulents can take any amount of heat
during their growing season, but while
resting (usually November–March in
Britain), the temperature can be allowed to
drop as low as 4°C/40°F, provided the
plants are not wet at the roots. There are
many cacti which inhabit the lower slopes
of the Andes, where it can be really cold in
winter. It is a combination of cold and
damp which rots the plant base and roots,
and indeed many need not be watered at all
during this time. If, however, they are being
kept in central heating, it is just as well to
give them a little water occasionally,
otherwise they shrivel.

On the whole, succulents like as much
sun as possible; in fact, it is not possible in
the home to give some of them the light
they need to flower. However, the majority
can be flowered on a south-facing windowsill. There is the occasional exception,
mentioned in individual descriptions, where
they grow in their natural habitat in the
shade of boulders, grass and small desert
shrubs, and such species will do best with
protection from midday sun, or in dappled
shade.

With this need for heat and light, a humid
atmosphere can be forgotten; dry air does
not damage them, so there is no need for
you to spray them, keep them in saucers of
water or in any way deliberately moisten
the air.

The epiphytic cacti from the forest will
need some shade and not such intense heat
as the desert cacti in summer. The potting
mix should be rich in humus. Rainwater or
soft water is best for watering, which will
be needed quite frequently while the plants
are growing. A little humidity is advisable.

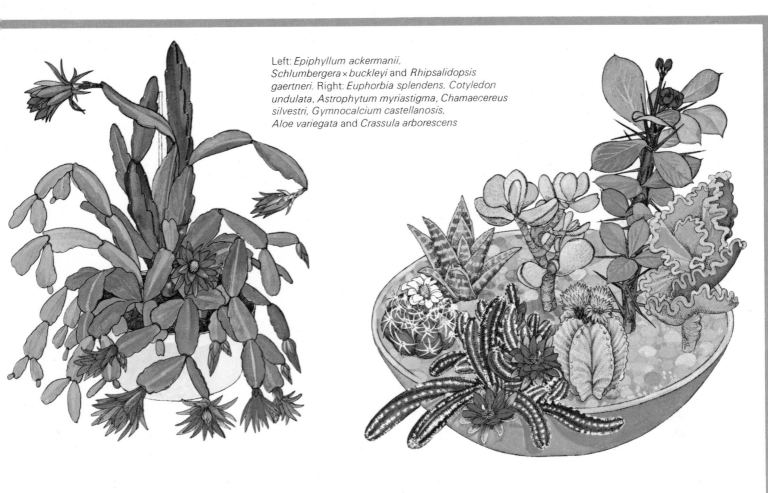

Left: *Epiphyllum ackermanii,*
Schlumbergera×buckleyi and *Rhipsalidopsis*
gaertneri. Right: *Euphorbia splendens, Cotyledon*
undulata, Astrophytum myriastigma, Chamaecereus
silvestri, Gymnocalcium castellanosis,
Aloe variegata and *Crassula arborescens*

Pots and repotting

Pots can be plastic or clay; pans can be used
instead of pots, and indeed some shallow-rooting
species do better in these. Repotting can be done
during spring or summer using a slightly larger
pot than the base of the plant. Use one large
piece of drainage material over the drainage hole
and remove some of the old potting mix carefully.
Cut off dead roots and set the root ball on a base
of the new mixture, filling in more round the
roots until the pot is full to within 1.2-2.5cm/
$\frac{1}{2}$-1in of the rim. Prickly cacti can be handled
with tongs (see right).

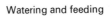

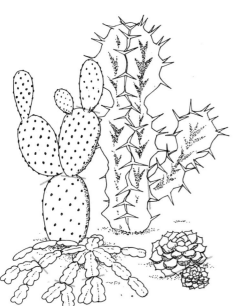

Propagation from seeds, offsets and cuttings

Cacti and other succulents can be easily increased
from seed if they can be kept at 21-27°C/70-
80°F while germinating. They are sown in early
spring in a seed mixture with extra grit. Allow up
to four weeks for germination. Offsets are also a
very easy method of propagation; simply remove
them and place them in the surface of the moist
potting mixture in a warm place. Leave offsets
which exude sap to dry for a few days before
potting up. Cuttings of cacti such as the Christmas Cactus and the Prickly Pears, and others
which do not produce offsets or sideshoots, are
taken just below a joint and should be allowed to
dry and form a callus at the cut end before
placing them in a damp, very sandy potting mix
to a depth of about 1.2cm/$\frac{1}{2}$in. The illustration,
left, shows where cuttings should be taken from
opuntia, zygocactus, euphorbia, and rosette-
forming succulents.

Watering and feeding

There is no plant which can live without any
water at all, and although the succulents have
adapted themselves to do without it for months
at a time, they must have some during the year.
Mostly the need is for water during spring and
summer, or whenever they are flowering and/or
producing new shoots. They should then be
watered normally, giving as much as you would
to an ordinary plant, whenever the potting mix
surface dries. When they are dormant, water only
once a month or so, or even not at all until
growth starts again. If you forget to water them
in summer, it won't matter as it would with other
plants, and they are ideal plants to grow from the
point of view of holidays.

Potting mixtures should, above all, be well
drained; you can use a good potting mix with
one-third extra part of a mixture of grit or coarse
sand, pieces of charcoal, broken brick or shingle.
With this mixture, which contains nutrient, there
is no need to feed during the resting period, but
an occasional potash feed from June to August
will help with flower production.

Bromeliads

The tropical jungles are the homes of some wonderful plants, such as the orchids, the forest climbers and the epiphytic cacti. The bromeliads are plants which grow cheek by jowl with the orchids, perched high up on branches or in the forks of trees. In general they are epiphytic, that is, they live on the branches, though not off them; some genera are terrestrial and live on the ground, though they are little different in their needs to the perchers.

The family *Bromeliaceae* is now thought to contain 1400 species in 44 genera, one of which is Bromelia, named after O. Bromel, a Swedish botanist of the seventeenth century. The habit of growth of the bromeliads is quite distinct from that of other plants: the greater majority form a rosette, sometimes flat, sometimes comparatively high, of leathery strap-shaped or pointed leaves in the centre of which is a tubular hollow called the 'vase' in which water collects.

The flower stem grows up through this water, the flower developing meanwhile, until the stem is 30cm/1ft or more tall, the flowerhead being in the shape of a cone, a spike, or a loose umbel. The overall appearance of a bromeliad is somewhat bizarre, even out of flower, though attractive. The family is not a difficult one to manage and although some bromeliads do best in warm greenhouses, many can be grown as houseplants.

Aechmea

[Urn Plant; 16°C/60°F min; Central and South America] The aechmea commonly grown as a houseplant is the epiphytic *A. fasciata*, and it is very handsome with narrow silvery grey-green leaves cross-banded in white, and a bright rose-pink cone-shaped flowerhead, whose flowers, blue at first, appear in summer (August). The flowerhead lasts for several months, though each flower dies after a few days. The plant may be 60cm/2ft high and at least 30cm/1ft wide.

Ananas

[Pineapple; 16°C/60°F min; Tropical America] *A. comosus*, the pineapple, is a terrestrial bromeliad which is bred to produce fruit for commercial cropping within two years. It makes an attractive foliage houseplant, but needs warm greenhouse conditions (33°C/90°F) to produce edible fruit. *A. comosus* 'Variegatus' has narrow, prickly-edged leaves in a rosette, longitudinally striped creamy white, flushed pink; the centre turns rose-pink at flowering time in summer. The whole plant is 90cm/3ft wide and the same height.

Above: The striking *Vriesia splendens*.
Below: *Billbergia × windii*

Opposite: In the centre of the table is an *Ananas comosus* 'Variegatus', the pineapple.
Opposite inset: *Aechmea fasciata*

Billbergia

[Queen's Tears; 16°C/60°F min; South America] This bromeliad was named after J. G. Billberg, a Swedish botanist of the late nineteenth century. *B. nutans* is a terrestrial bromeliad, very easy to grow and will tolerate short spells of quite low temperatures. It produces rosettes of narrow serrated leaves, dark green, with great speed. A fully grown rosette is about 45cm/1½ft tall. The unusual flowers hang in a graceful cluster from rose-pink bracts, and are coloured navy blue, green, yellow and pink. The flowering season is May and June, though they can be made to flower in winter if high temperatures can be provided.

Cryptanthus

[Earth Star or Starfish Bromeliad; 16°C/60°F min; South America] The cryptanthus are mostly rather flat growing, and the central vase is almost nonexistent. They are terrestrials, though there are some growing on trees. They make good foliage houseplants, the flowers being insignificant, and because of their dwarf habit are also suitable for bottle gardens. The colouring of their leaves alters according to the intensity of light in which they are being grown, for instance *C. bivittatus minor* has two cream-coloured longitudinal stripes on an olive green background; however, in strong light these stripes become flushed with deep pink. *C. fosterianus* (much larger to 45cm/1½ft wide but only 8cm/3in high) has succulent thick leaves banded horizontally with whitish-grey and copper brown in a good light, but again when the light diminishes, the leaves appear only dark and light green. *C. bromelioides* 'Tricolor' has light green leaves, broadly edged with cream, flushing to pink and is a little more upright than the other two, about 30cm/1ft wide and high.

Guzmania

[16°C/60°F min; Central and South America] The guzmanias have become popular as houseplants over the last 10 to 15 years, since hybrids have been widely introduced. The flowerhead is spearheaded in shape, though in some species it gradually opens out later into an almost waterlily-like shape. Apart from their rosette habit, guzmanias vary considerably in colouring, flower and leaf, but all are handsome. *G. lingulata* (height 30cm/1ft) has a brilliant red flowerhead, and small white flowers surrounded with orange to yellow smaller bracts. *G. zahnii* has olive green leaves striped with red, red bracts on the flower stem, and a yellow flowerhead with white flowers; height is about 60cm/2ft. *G. berteroniana* has a brilliant red flowerhead and yellow flowers; leaves are light green or wine red, and height is about 45cm/

1½ft. All guzmanias flower in the winter, and nearly all are epiphytes.

Neoregelia

[16°C/60°F min; Brazil] These epiphytic bromeliads are found in the rain forests, but because of the leathery nature of the leaves they will stand a dry atmosphere. *N. carolinae* 'Tricolor' is one of the most popular, with outer green leaves centred with yellow or white, the inner ones pinkish-red; the flowerhead is bright red, with violet flowers, but it stays within the rosette and does not grow on a stem. Flowering is in late spring and summer; the flat rosettes can be 40cm/16in wide. *N. concentrica* has broader leaves 10cm/4in wide and 30cm/1ft long; they are purple blotched. The bracts are purple and the blue flowers appear in the centre on a kind of pincushion.

Nidularium

[16°C/60°F min; Brazil] These epiphytic bromeliads are very like the neoregelias to look at, but their cultural treatment is different – they need more shade and humidity and higher temperatures to produce flowers. The name means a small nest, and refers to the flowerhead, which does not emerge from the rosette, but remains compact so that the flowers appear on a mound in the water in the vase. *N. innocentii* has dark red to almost purple-black leaves, and the tightly-packed flower bracts, in autumn, are orange to copper coloured with white flowers sitting on top; *paxianum* and *nana* are particularly attractive varieties of this.

Tillandsia

[16°C/60°F min; West Indies/Central America] The variation in habit of this genus is very great – it comes from tropical rain forests as well as deserts and steppes, and there are therefore both terrestrial and epiphytic forms. The Spanish Moss is an epiphytic species of tillandsia, *T. usneoides*, and if you wish to grow this, a bromeliad tree is ideal, so that the long trails can hang down from the branches. *T. lindeniana* is the Blue Bromeliad; it has large, brilliantly blue flowers emerging from a flattened spike of deep rose-pink bracts on a stem about 30cm/1ft long, and is altogether a very showy plant, flowering in summer. The leaves are narrow and pointed, dark green and purple.

Vriesea

[16°C/60°F min; Central and South America (esp. Brazil)] The leaves of these epiphytic and terrestrial bromeliads are thick and shiny green, often cross-banded in a darker colour. *V. splendens* (Flaming Sword) has a long flattened bright red flower spike about 60cm/2ft high with yellow flowers. The dark green leaves have purple bands. *V. gigantea* has 45cm/1½ft

long leaves with yellowish-green tessalated markings on the upper side, dark on the undersurface. The whole plant can be 1.8m/6ft tall. *V. psittacina* is small with yellowish-green leaves 20cm/8in long, and a feathery flowerhead with red bracts and yellow flowers which appears in July.

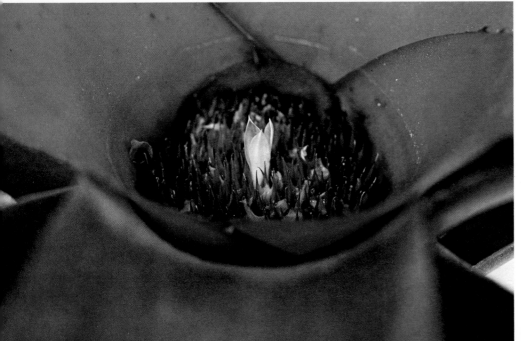

Above: The glossy green leaves of a neoregelia
look very elegant in a dining room.
Above left: *Neoregelia carolina* 'Tricolor'
has pinkish red inner leaves, surrounded by
attractive green leaves centred with yellow
or white stripes.
Bottom far left: *Aechmea fasciata*.
Bottom left: A closeup of the vase of a
Neoregelia concentrica, which has been drained
of water to show the flower head forming

75

The main thing to remember about bromeliads is that they grow in habitats where there is very little soil indeed, whether they are epiphytic or terrestrial. The epiphytes grow on trees, the terrestrials on the ground, in rocky and stony places in deserts and scrubland. Both kinds have tiny root systems, which serve mainly for anchorage, and will therefore grow in quite small pots. They absorb the food and water they need to a large extent through their leaves and the vase in the centre of the plant.

You can grow bromeliads singly, each in

How to grow Healthy Bromeliads

its own container, and mix them in with a group of other jungle plants, or you can experiment with a 'bromeliad tree'; in other words, you provide them with a branch or branches, real or artificial. This can be a piece of driftwood or an apple branch, or you can make a support with

pieces of cork-oak bark covering metal rods or canes on a stand. The plants are tucked into a little damp peat in the forks and hollows of the tree, and inconspicuously wired to the branches, using sphagnum moss to cover the mechanics. If you spray the branch with water before planting, from the top, you will see where the water collects naturally on its way down, and these will be the places to plant the bromeliads. On forest trees, they will always grow where the rain fills up hollows and crevices in bark and branch.

A Friendly Environment

Bromeliads need a good deal of heat (up to 30°C/85°F) in order to bring young plants to flowering, but they require less as foliage plants or to maintain a plant bought when in flower. In winter, temperatures can be allowed to drop to 10°C/50°F for short periods, provided the soil is kept just moist, but they survive better at 16°C/60°F.

Associated with warmth is the moisture in the atmosphere, in other words the humidity, which to most plants is vital to healthy growth. While most bromeliads appreciate the humid surroundings of the natural habitat, those described here will survive in centrally-heated conditions. There is no need for a daily overhead spraying with water in winter, though this should be done in the summer months, except for those with a mealy coating to the leaves. As well as moistening the leaves, this overhead spraying will help to keep the vase topped up, since the drops of water will run down the leaves into it, as rain would. However, it is advisable to add some water directly to the vase occasionally.

On the whole, direct sunlight is damaging. A position where the sun shines through other plants, or is filtered in some way, or a good light without the sun, will be preferred, heavily shaded positions are not recommended, especially for those bromeliads with striped and banded leaves. In a poor light they tend to lose these distinctive markings. Furthermore, some bromeliads may not flower if they do not receive enough light, so do not hide any away in a dark corner. They are pretty accommodating, but there are limits, even for them, and after all, you do want to grow the healthiest plant that you can, because that will be the most ornamental one.

Direct sunlight can be damaging, so choose a position where the light is filtered

Bromeliad troubles are not very many at all. Because they are amenable to various conditions they do not show the same cultural troubles that ordinary houseplants do, but they can be afflicted with pests such as scale insects and mealy bugs. Finger and thumb work will remove most of these; brushing the mealy bugs with methylated spirits or rubbing alcohol and spraying the scales with an insecticide will deal with the remainder. However, if the plants are badly afflicted, consider remedial care for them, because plants which are not growing very strongly always seem to be the first to fall victim to pest outbreaks.

Watering and Feeding

Bromeliads can be regarded as a kind of succulent from the watering point of view; most can retain water in the vase and so can go for long periods without being watered. As with any plant, more will be needed at flowering time and, although it may go against the grain to keep the vase filled with water as the flower stem pushes up through it, it is nevertheless the right thing to do.

The water should be tepid, preferably rainwater or, at any rate, not hard water. You will find that in the growing season, depending on temperature and the size of the plant, water will be required about every three or four weeks. If the soil mix becomes completely dry, it will not matter greatly, provided the vase still contains water, but it is better to keep it moist and to water it occasionally when filling the vase.

The amount of food that bromeliads require and the way in which they absorb it is also associated with the vase. Because they grow where there is virtually no soil, whether epiphytes or terrestrials, nutrient is taken in through the leaves and the vase. You may give a liquid nutrient solution, provided it is half strength, instead of plain water when topping up the vase, and you can also spray the leaves with a foliar feed, again with the exception of those with a mealy coating. Liquid feeding may be given once a month, when the plant is in active growth.

Propagation from Offsets

When bromeliads have flowered, the central rosette dies, but the offsets which will have been produced around it will continue to grow. They should be treated like the parent plant until they are ready for detaching. This will happen when they are at least 15cm/6in high, or they have been growing for several months. They are then removed, with roots, from the parent plant, and potted in a suitable mixture, being kept quite warm until they are established in a temperature of 21-27°C/70-80°F. When potting the offsets, sit the base of the plant on the potting mix surface, but cover the roots. The plant's crown should not be buried otherwise it will rot. The mixture should be moist. The vase should be kept topped up with water, particularly important when they have been taken away from the parent plant, and shade provided. Once the offsets are well established, they can be transferred to lighter, airier conditions, depending on the special needs of the genus.

After some months, the young plants will have a resting period, from November to March in most cases, when the temperature can be lowered a little, watering decreased, and feeding stopped altogether, until the spring.

Aechmea and billbergia, in particular, produce several offsets from each plant, and you can have four or five new plants from one parent. Although its leaves remain handsome for several more months, they will eventually deteriorate, and the plant should be discarded once the offsets have been taken.

The pineapple can be increased by slicing the tuft of leaves off the top of the fruit, so that there is one layer of pips, and placing this on the surface of a moist sandy potting mix. With warmth, and bottom heat (23°C/74°F), and a polyethelene bag over the pot, the tuft should root and grow into a new plant. Rooting is most likely if the tuft is as fresh as possible. When buying a pineapple, look for one with fresh, light green leaves on top, not dried greyish-green ones.

Soil Mixes

Bromeliads are not conventional plants, and when it comes to the kind of potting mix to use, this is also out of the ordinary in that it contains lots of humus in the form of peat or leafmould, but no soil. A good mixture would consist of equal parts of fibrous peat and leafmould with half a part of coarse sand. Equal parts of peat, sand and osmunda fibre would also be a good mix, or one of leafmould, sphagnum moss and peat, also in equal quantities.

If you are growing the plants on a bromeliad tree, the hollows and crevices can be filled with one of the above potting mixtures, and the plants set into it, and bound on with dark brown copper wire, if necessary. Spanish moss, *Tillandsia usneoides*, can be encouraged to root in these mixtures, or in osmunda fibre alone, or bound directly on to the bark which it will root into, provided it is moist, and the atmosphere humid.

Bromeliads will probably need potting once during the summer, but it is important not to overpot. Their small root system means that the pot need only be large enough to balance the top growth, and will be smaller than that required for a normal, broad-leaved plant of the same size. Occasional feeding during late summer will be advisable. Clay or plastic pots can be used, and for the larger bromeliads clay ones will probably be needed, so that their weight can counteract that of the plant and keep it upright.

Make a bromeliad tree with an apple branch

Ferns

The fern craze of the Victorian era reached a peak when Wardian cases allowed tender ferns to be grown in the home rather than in steamy stovehouses. Interest waned in the early part of this century and it is only now, 100 years later, that improved building methods and centrally heated homes have encouraged us to grow ferns in our homes once again.

Ferns differ from other plants in that they are non-flowering and so are unable to produce seed. Instead, dust-fine spores are formed in tiny sporangia, or spore sacks, on the underside of fertile pinnae.

Some fern species are readily available in florists, others need to be searched out. But no matter how they are obtained, the grower is sure to be rewarded by the varied appearance of these attractive plants.

Adiantum

[7°C/45°F min; Sub-tropical and temperate zones]

A. capillus-veneris (Venus'-hair or Maidenhair Fern) Many species of Maidenhair ferns are similar in appearance, having wiry black petioles (leaf stalks) growing out of a quickly spreading horizontal rhizome. This species grows to a height of 20-30cm/8-12in and the petioles carry many branched fronds of delicate fan-shaped pinnae which are pale green in colour. In mature plants the undersides of the pinnae are edged with brown sori (clusters of sporangia), giving extra colour to the fern. It is a fairly easy fern to grow when a humid atmosphere is provided around the pot to prevent shrivelling. A daily fine spray of tepid water is a help or the pot in a pot method should be used. Direct sunlight should be avoided; however, the plant should not be placed in a dark corner. A north or east-facing windowsill is ideal.

Asplenium nidus, the Bird's Nest Fern, has attractive glossy light green fronds which unfurl from the centre of the rosette

A. cuneatum (syn. *A. raddianum*) This Brazilian species is very similar in appearance to *A. capillus-veneris* although a little larger, growing to 50cm/1⅔ft in height. The pinnae are also coarser. However, it is not always easy to distinguish between the two as there are several cultivars of *A. cuneatum* which vary in size and also in colour from yellow-green to dark green.

A. hispidulum (Rosy Maidenhair) This species is different in appearance, the young foliage being reddish-brown in colour changing to medium green with age. The petioles are covered with dark brown scales and the plant grows to about 30cm/1ft in height. The frond blade looks more like the spread fingers of a hand, not branched nearly as much as in the other Maidenhair species, and pinnae are longer.

Maidenhair ferns are easily divided by cutting the rhizome into pieces, each with a few fronds and roots. Pot these into peaty potting mix in a smaller pot.

Left: A tolerant plant which can easily be grown in the dryer atmosphere of a home, *Davallia bullata* looks best in a tall container.
Above: The delicate beauty of *Adiantum tenerum* pinnae can be seen in close up.

Asplenium

[Spleenwort; 13°C/55°F min; Australia/New Zealand/Far East]

A. bulbiferum Deeply serrated pinnae spread out in a triangular shape from a black petiole and rachis to make a frond which can be up to 60cm/2ft in length and 23cm/9in wide. Fertile pinnae produce sporangia on narrow segments of the serrations while sterile pinnae have broader segments. Inter-mixing of fertile and sterile pinnae on the same frond gives added interest to the shape. The appearance of this fern can be rather bizarre for plantlets that are miniature editions of the parent plant grow from bulbils produced on the upper surface of the pinnae. Thus new plants are easily propagated by placing a pinna with bulbils onto moist peaty potting mix. Roots are quickly formed and the plantlets soon grow independently.

A. nidus (Bird's Nest Fern) This fern forms a definite rosette. The simple, entire blades are glossy, light green in colour and have a black rachis running the length of the frond. They unfurl from the centre of the rosette which is covered with a dark brown bristle-like scale. Depending upon growing conditions, the fronds can be anything from 30-120cm/1-4ft long and 5-20cm/2-8in wide. Warmer and more humid conditions give the larger plant. Sori forming a fishbone-like pattern on undersides of mature blades shower a mass of light brown spores on to lower fronds.

Cyrtomium falcatum

[Syn. *Polystichum falcatum*; Fish-tail Fern; 7°C/45°F min; South East Asia] The upright fronds can grow to 60cm/2ft long and they have silver furry scale covering their petioles. About 12 pairs of dark green glossy leathery pinnae form the blade, each pinna being similar in shape to a holly leaf. Sporangia are scattered irregularly over the underside of the pinnae and first appear as very small green spots changing to light brown with maturity. The cultivar 'Rochfordianum' (Holly Fern) is more compact growing, 30cm/1ft, with larger pinnae ideal in a living room. These ferns are said to be indestructible, but perhaps a better description would be that they are more tolerant to lower temperatures and humidity.

Davallia

[5°C/41°F min; Far East]

D. bullata (Squirrel's Foot Fern) The furry rhizomes, which give this fern its common name, spread quickly and a mass of dwarf fronds shoots up from them. The blade is triangular in outline, dark green and the pinnae are deeply cut. A rhizome tip when laid on moist potting mix will root quickly and then rapidly divide to cover a small hanging basket. It is a very tolerant plant, not objecting to the dryer atmosphere of a modern home and even liking a little sunlight.

D. canariensis (Hare's Foot Fern) A small popular species with thick rhizomes that are pale brown in colour. The leathery fronds are mid-green and finely cut.

D. fijiensis This species has a much freer habit of growth. The fronds are larger, lighter in colour and appear more delicate and finely cut.

Humata tyermannii

[Bear's-Foot Fern; 7°C/45°F min; West Africa] Small rhizomes covered with white furry scales divide frequently and a frond is sent up every 5-7.5cm/2-3in. When young the frond is rosy-green turning to very dark green with age. The blade shape is like a long pointed triangle 15-23cm/6-9in high and up to 12cm/5in wide at the base. The pinnae are finely cut. It is best to provide a fairly large potting mix surface for this fern as it is a quick grower under good conditions.

Lygodium japonicum

[Climbing Fern; 7°C/45°F min; Japan] The petiole and rachis are very long and wiry, climbing by twining round a trellis or pillar. Oppositely paired pinnae grow out from the rachis and are yellow-green to medium green in colour. Fertile pinnae are long and tapering with serrated edges, the lobes of which carry the sori; sterile pinnae are similar in form but with more and deeper serrations. When grown on a windowsill, a climbing fern is liable to twine through light curtains or venetian blinds unless precautions are taken.

Nephrolepis

[10°C/50°F min; tropics and sub-tropics]

N. cordifolia (Sword Fern) Very short petioles carry long narrow blades cut to the rachis, forming segments, the whole frond growing to a length of 60cm/2ft. The colour is light green. Large plants are best grown in hanging baskets or on pedestals, for the mixed upright and pendulous fronds show to advantage from a low angle. In the cultivar 'Plumosa' all the segment tips are fringed.

N. exaltata (Ladder Fern) Very similar to *N. cordifolia* but much larger and coarser, with pale green fronds growing up to 2m/6½ft long. The blade tapers at base and tip and looks somewhat like a ladder in silhouette. Many cultivars of *N. exaltata* have been produced by crossbreeding; most are of interest to indoor growers, the greatly divided blades giving cristate forms. *N. exaltata* 'Bostoniensis' (Boston Fern), with broad fronds and fast-growing, was a very early mutant and the many later mutations have provided us with modern cultivars that are easier to grow in present day living rooms. 'Rooseveltii Plumosa' has very wavy segments; 'Whitmanii' is commonly called the Lace Fern, a description in itself; 'Elegantissima' is similar to 'Whitmanii' but more upright. Occasionally a frond will revert to the original single segment form and it should be removed immediately. Often spores from these cultivars are infertile and then the form can only be propagated by runners.

Nephrolepis are propagated by runners growing from the top of a rhizome; the runners root quickly when in contact with moist potting mix.

Pellaea

[7°C/45°F min; New Zealand]

P. rotundifolia (Cliff-Brake or Button Fern) Brown hairy scales cover a wiry petiole and rachis which has about 20 pairs of alternately placed pinnae. The small roundish pinnae are dark green above, light green below and a little leathery. Fronds up to 50cm/2⅓ft long form a low spreading mat so that this fern is useful in temporary plant arrangements as ground cover for it is fairly tolerant as to conditions and able to utilize any humidity from surrounding potting mix. Sori form on the underside margins of a pinna but do not meet at the apex and are light brown in colour.

P. viridis Unlike the previous fern this African species is upright and bushy, has fronds growing up to 75cm/2½ft long; rachises are green when young turning shining black with age and blades of bright green spear-shaped pinnae. It is unusual for a fern to grow well in very bright light, but this species does well under the lower intensity of fluorescent lighting. It also needs a minimum winter temperature of 10°C/50°F.

Platycerium bifurcatum

[Syn. *P. alcicorne*; Stag Horn Fern; 10°C/50°F min; Australia] True epiphytes in that they grow on trees without taking food from them,

the Stag Horn ferns are unlike any other ferns in appearance. There is no mistaking sterile for fertile fronds. The former are wavy-edged, fan-shaped, pale green in colour and grow out from a very short rhizome. With age they enlarge and in nature grip a tree trunk or branch making a firm anchor for the fern, growing frond over frond so that the originals rot to provide food at the roots. The fertile fronds emerge from the centre and are antler-shaped, the older fern having more and larger 'tines'. These fronds are a darker green but appear greyish-green because they are covered by fine white hairs like velvet which are very easily removed by barely touching them. Sori form large brown patches on the underside of the antler tips. In the home a Stag Horn may be grown in a pot or attached to bark padded with sphagnum moss; either way, in time sterile fronds will cover the holder. It should be watered by immersing pot or bark periodically, preferably in rainwater. To keep its beautiful velvety appearance, inquisitive fingers should not be allowed to touch the fronds as once removed the 'velvet' will never return.

Polypodium aureum

[Syn. *Phlebodium aureum*; Hare's- or Rabbit's-foot Fern; 7°C/45°F min; West Indies] Good specimens will grow fronds 1m/3¼ft tall, although young plants of 40cm/16in are very decorative. The frond has a light green petiole turning brown with age, a blue- to yellow-green blade made of single and opposite pinnae each up to 12cm/5in long. In some cultivars the pinnae have wavy edges. Each frond arises

from a thick silver to brown furry rhizome that gives this fern its common name. The rhizome is surface-creeping and will follow the contour of a container. Dead fronds drop away leaving a scar on the rhizome rather like a small footprint.

Pteris

[10-13°C/50-55°F min; Mediterranean/Tropical Asia]

P. cretica (Ribbon Fern) A very short rhizome is common to all Pteris so that growth is in clumps with very many fronds arising from a crown. *P. cretica*, about 50cm/1⅔ft tall, has longish pointed pinnae with serrated edges that only show on the sterile pinnae because the sori are protected by the pinna edge curling back. It is medium green in colour and quite tough.

There are many cultivars, all more interesting in shape or colour. *P. c.* 'Albolineata',

Opposite: *Nephrolepis exaltata* is a graceful fern for a hanging basket.
Below: *Platycerium bifurcatum*.
Right: *Asparagus plumosus* hangs at a window.
Above: *Pteris ensiformis*

as the name implies, has a white central line running the length of each pinna; 'Rivertoniana' has pinnae with elongated segments growing irregularly from the margins; 'Wilsonii' and 'Wimsettii' both have heavily crested tips to their pinnae.

P. ensiformis The cultivar *P. e.* 'Victoriae' is grown much more often than the type. It is a most attractive plant with short bushy sterile fronds having pinnae with white central veins banded by dark green serrated margins. Fertile fronds are taller, up to 50cm/1⅔ft, with very slender long pinnae on which the serrations only show at the tips where the margins stop curling back over the sori.

P. tremula (Trembling Fern) This quickly-growing fern can reach over 1m/3ft if given the opportunity. However, young plants of 30-40cm/12-16in are useful for grouping with other pteris species, the yellow-green foliage making a perfect foil for the darker greens. The feathery blade is triangular when seen in silhouette, and the pinnae have very deeply cut serrations.

81

How to grow
Healthy Ferns

Most ferns grow well in cool to warm rooms (15-21°C/59-70°F) provided they also have good light, humidity around their fronds and moisture at their roots. The idea that being woodland plants ferns need a dark corner is wrong. Most indoor ferns are native to sub-tropical and tropical areas where light intensity is high even below trees. A windowsill facing east or north is, therefore, a good position for them, and some like fluorescent lighting.

High humidity is important for the dry atmosphere of modern homes makes for unhappy plants. A daily spraying will help or stand the plant on pebbles in a dish of water. The 'pot in a pot' method, whereby the potted fern is placed in a larger pot or container and moist peat packed around it, also raises humidity levels.

The potting mix needs to hold moisture yet at the same time be well drained. Two parts sterilized leaf-mould, one part sterilized loam and one part gritty sand plus small pieces of charcoal generally make a good fern soil mix. However, any peat-based mixture may be used.

Although not heavy feeders, ferns do need a regular weak liquid feed every two weeks during the growing season especially if growing in a peat-based medium which incorporates a limited amount of fertilizer. It is preferable to use a high nitrogen fertilizer as is usual for foliage plants.

There should always be moisture at the roots. Only if the root-ball has dried out should a fern stand in water and then only for a limited period before draining. Some ferns, such as Stag Horns, appreciate this treatment but the majority do not and quickly suffer root damage if dried out or saturated with water.

The increasing use of plastic pots means that fewer clay pots are made today. Porous clay pots have the advantage of producing a humid climate below the foliage but with plastic pots other humidity methods can be used. Ferns grow happily in either pot and some, such as Adiantums and Nephrolepsis, also grow well in hanging baskets. So it can be left to the grower's preference as to which type is used.

Ferns such as *Humata tyermanii* or *Davallia canariensis* can be trained to cover prewired shapes. One of the easiest is a round ball, made of wet sphagnum moss and kept symmetrical with florist wire ties. Put the plant in the centre, letting its long brown scaly rhizomes come to the outside. Tie these in place as they develop until the whole ball is covered with fern fronds.

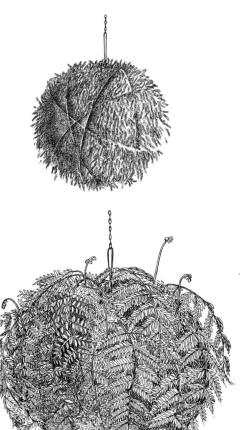

The fern ball can be hung up in a greenhouse or similar light place and is watered by dousing it for five minutes in a pail of lukewarm soft water. After draining it can go back on its hook.

The illustration above shows the parts of a fern frond, and below the life cycle of a fern

When the root-ball fills its pot the fern should be repotted and springtime, before new growth commences, is best for this. Judicious root pruning will allow a large fern to be replaced, with fresh potting mix, into the same or next size pot.

Many ferns may be propagated by division of the rhizome. Some, such as maidenhairs, may be broken apart and pieces of young rhizome with a few fronds and roots potted into small pots. Others, such as Humata, need longer pieces of rhizome with a growing tip to be rooted.

For more adventurous growers, propagation by spores is more interesting. The life-cycle of a fern is not as simple as it might appear for it is not a spore that grows into a fern. Given warmth, moisture and light a spore will produce a prothallus which has female and male organs on its underside. Male cells swim to fertilize female cells and from a fertilized cell a sporophyte grows.

To grow from spores a clean pot is filled with a well-moistered sterile medium such as peat. Fern spores are scattered onto the surface and a clear glass cover is placed on top. The covered pot should be put in a warm place. After a few weeks a green film will cover the growing medium and several months later the heart-shaped prothalli will be seen to have thin erect stems growing from them, the sporophytes. When large enough to handle, the baby ferns should be potted up and kept in a humid atmosphere.

Ferns have two major pests, scale and eelworm. Most pesticides are phytotoxic to ferns so scales should be picked off or brushed with methylated spirits or rubbing alcohol. Eelworm attack shows in blotched, stunted foliage and severely attacked ferns should be burned. Slight attack may be remedied by immersing the whole fern, washed clean of soil, in hot water (50-52°C/ 122-125°F) for five minutes.

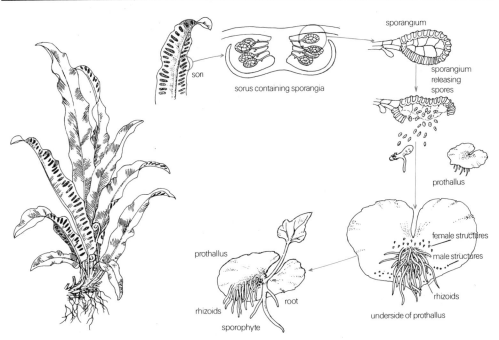

Roses

Many people get great pleasure from roses – evidence of this is readily found in song and story so it is hardly surprising that many amateur gardeners seek to increase their enjoyment by an extension of the rose season. Many more would do so if they were aware that roses can be grown under glass without any great difficulty. Blooms at least two months earlier are obtainable, untarnished by wind or rain, with clean foliage – indeed perfect roses whose exquisite scent is hardly believable.

Any type of greenhouse can be utilized; even an unheated one will produce blooms at least one month in advance of those growing in the open. A large house provides more scope, but where only a small one is available miniature roses in 13-15cm/5-6in pots may be grown.

Even without a greenhouse, roses can be grown in pots for indoor decoration, over short periods, provided they are given cool, airy conditions, adequate water and light. Garden rooms, screened porches and conservatories are suitable for hybrid tea, polyantha, and floribunda roses, as standards or bush grown in large pots. Climbers are not really suitable except for large conservatories, but miniature roses can be grown on sunny windowsills. However, roses will not thrive permanently indoors, but need a spell of several months in the open, usually after flowering, even if they are merely put out on a balcony. With correct maintenance and aftercare, roses can be grown indoors for a couple of seasons, but eventually flower production diminishes, and the plants must either be discarded or planted out in the garden.

Many roses, those seen as cut flowers in florists' shops, or the many thousands of blooms seen each year at flower shows, are grown planted under glass. But it is more advantageous to grow your greenhouse roses in pots because this enables you to move the pots out in June if you wish. You can also grow chrysanthemums, but these should be cleared by Christmas at the latest in order to house the roses again. Rose bushes may be purchased from any reputable grower and early delivery should be arranged so that the plants will be nicely settled before housing takes place. Many keen amateurs get extra pleasure from budding their own plants in which case they can be lifted from the garden. Plants with a good root system should be selected and it is necessary to trim some of the roots with a sharp knife so that they fit comfortably in a pot.

Clay pots still find favour with some growers, but good roses have also been grown in plastic pots. These do have an advantage; they are much lighter, are less liable to get broken and the plants do not dry out so quickly. Drainage is important and 2.5cm/1in of crocks or gravel in the bottom of the plastic pot will ensure this, especially if covered with some rougher pieces of turf. Grow climbers for conservatories in 25cm/10in pots or tubs; hybrid tea and floribunda roses need 20cm/8in pots, polyantha roses 15cm/6in, and most of the miniatures will fit into 13cm/5in pots.

Much is written about potting mixes these days, but the most satisfactory for roses is based on good loam, especially if it can be obtained from a good well-established pasture, cut and stacked for six months. Experienced growers frequently make up their own mixtures and may resort to using garden loam, preferably from the vegetable garden or where roses have not been grown. This can be improved by adding up to half its bulk of peat and a small amount of coarse sand. Bonfire or wood ash, if obtainable, may also be added, as can a fertilizer compounded for roses. Try 100g/4oz per bushel. All should be thoroughly mixed, sterilized and kept under cover until required for use.

Potting the plants requires a little care as once they are well-established the bulk of the soil will not be changed for some years. Before potting, examine bought rose plants, cut off any damaged roots and prune weak branches back to strong bud. Roughly fill the bottom third of the pot over the drainage with potting mix, making it reasonably firm. Place the plant in the centre, spreading out the roots and giving the plant a slight twirl around in the pot. Any roots not readily accommodated should be cut off with a sharp knife and some soil worked in among them with the fingers. Give the pot a few taps on the bench and firm with a stick. The point where the rose was budded should be kept 2.5cm/1in below the top of the pot and should be just covered with soil when potting has been completed. This will provide room for a good soaking when filled up with water. A good watering should be given to settle the soil properly and the pots should be stood outside on a firm surface where worms cannot enter the drainage holes and foul them up. Little attention should now be required until housing takes place in late autumn, according to your climate.

The newly potted roses must not be forced by the use of artificial heat the first year; it is essential that the plants become well rooted and established in their pots before doing so. Therefore, only sufficient heat must be used to encourage growth and prevent freezing conditions. A temperature of 5°C/40°F during the night will ensure this. Watering becomes necessary as growth commences; the roots must not be allowed to dry out, but over-watering must also be avoided. As the plants develop, an increased amount of water becomes necessary and growth will be assisted also by damping down the greenhouse floor and between the pots when days become warmer. In the home, give roses a daily overhead spray with tepid water and make sure there is adequate movement of air.

In spring, weather is often very changeable so a modern greenhouse with automatic ventilation is a boon. Generally a rise of 6°C/20°F during the day will be satisfactory, so if automatic ventilators are set to open at 10°C/50°F this will ensure adequate control and relieve the grower of any problem.

Hot sunny days in spring can be a hazard to roses under glass, scorching the blooms and sometimes foliage also. This can be overcome by spraying a shading material to filter the sunlight, or by the use of blinds unless mechanical means have been provided for. Indoors, filter the light in south-facing windows with venetian blinds or move miniature roses away from direct sunlight during the hottest part of the day.

Most rose lovers will wish to grow some hybrid tea varieties and to enjoy the perfection

Lovely roses in many shades can be grown in pots.
Opposite: Floribunda rose 'Dearest'.
Above: Climbing rose 'New Dawn'.
Right: Hybrid tea rose 'Super Star'

Pruning will be necessary and pot roses should be pruned hard leaving two buds or three at most, with the uppermost one pointing outwards. If only lightly pruned, tall spindly plants are likely to result. This operation can be carried out before bringing the roses in or after doing so, whichever suits the pruner best, depending on the weather. If weather is very wet it may be necessary to turn the pots on their sides to prevent waterlogging, an undesirable condition for most plants and certainly for roses. An exception to this pruning routine are climbing roses which should have all wood retained except dead or damaged growths, or very weak spindly tip growth. Some training is also necessary. A very good method is to place three bamboo canes around the inside edges of the pot and wind the growths around in a spiral framework. A large greenhouse is required for such plants.

Hybrid tea roses can be grown in pots in garden rooms, screened porches and conservatories. Two hybrid tea roses are 'Mullard's Jubilee' (top) and 'Grandpa Dickson'

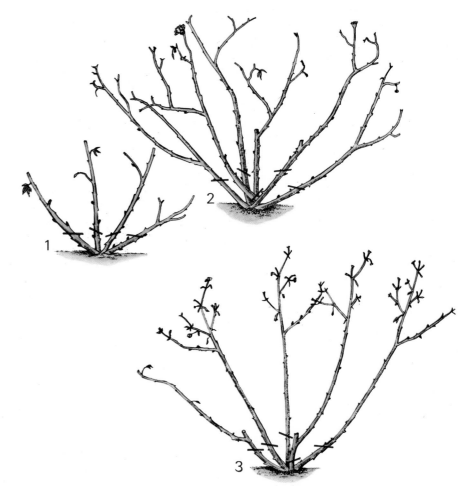

Roses grown in pots must be pruned rigorously after flowering. Illustration 1 shows where hybrid tea and floribunda roses should be cut back in their first spring to ensure ample new growth and good shape. In the second and subsequent years, the same hard pruning should be carried out for both hybrid tea (2) and floribunda (3) roses

of their full-petalled blooms. Where this is so disbudding is necessary and this is carried out by removing all side buds as soon as they can be handled, leaving only the larger more prominent main or crown bud which soon plumps up and opens in all its glory.

By early June the first and main flowering period will be over and the plants are hardened off for going outdoors by increasing ventilation and turning off heat if any is being used. The pots must now be placed outside for the summer months; this will depend on what space is available. Sinking the pots in an open piece of garden will lessen watering or risk of drying out. Plunging in a bed of ashes is ideal but not so readily attainable in these 'clean air' days, so it may be necessary to stand them on a hard surface somewhere. The plants must not be neglected at this time but kept growing steadily, removing any flowers or utilizing them for decoration as cut blooms, watering when necessary and feeding occasionally.

In late summer, preparations for the next season can begin by checking drainage. This is especially necessary where pots have been plunged in the open garden and worms may have entered through drainage holes. Removal of the worms and their casts is essential and for this the pot must be upturned and the plant knocked out by a sharp tap on a bench. When drainage has been cleared the top cm of soil should also be removed. After returning the ball of soil to the pot, top dressing with fresh potting mix to which a teaspoonful of a rose fertilizer has been added for each pot, can be carried out.

The pots will now be ready for bringing in again in December, or even later, depending on the weather, as before, but with this difference: as the plants will now be well-established and the pots full of roots more heat can be applied if desired. This, of course, depends on requirements and drastic changes are not desirable, but an increase of 3°C/5°F per week from March onwards until the end of April to a maximum of 16°C/60°F at night will consider-

ably advance blooms if light conditions are also good.

Feeding also will be necessary in the second and subsequent years when the plants are nicely in growth, usually around mid-March. Most growers have their own pet formula so until some experience has been gained the beginner would be well advised to use a feed especially compounded for roses.

The disease which affects roses most commonly when growing under glass is mildew, especially where wild fluctuations in temperature have prevailed or where draughts have been caused by the use of side ventilation. Several fungicides are obtainable. Of these, sprays or smoke bombs are most effective under glass. Aphis or greenfly is the most likely insect pest to give trouble on pot grown roses; they usually invade the young succulent tips of the new growths. Fortunately they are readily destroyed and many insecticides are available to do this. I must confess, however, I still like the old fashioned nicotine, especially under glass, either vaporized or in shred form. It can also be used as a spray.

VARIETIES

Suitable roses for growing in pots indoors include several of the hybrid teas, less vigorous floribunda roses and the smaller polyanthas which carry a profusion of small blooms. Miniature roses are available as bush, standards and climbers.

Hybrid Tea Roses (height .6-2m/2-4ft)

'Alec's Red' – cherry red, scented
'Blue Moon' – silvery lilac, scented
'Fragrant Cloud' – geranium red, exquisitely scented
'Grandpa Dickson' – creamy yellow fading to pink
'Medallion' – buff-pink, a fruity perfume
'Mister Lincoln' – red, strongly fragrant
'Mullard Jubilee' – deep rose pink, scented
'My Choice' – salmon pink and pale yellow, heavily scented
'Peace' – pale gold to ivory, flushed with pink
'Perfume Delight' – pure pink, spicy fragrance
'Pink Favourite' – clear rose pink, lovely shape
'Red Lion' – rosy red, scented
'Royal Highness' – pale pink, scented
'Super Star' ('Tropicana') – vermilion, scented, easily grown under glass but prone to diseases

Floribunda Roses (average height 90cm/3ft)

'Allgold' – bright buttercup yellow, slight scent
'Apricot Hectar' – pinkish apricot, scented
'Circus' – yellow suffused pink, salmon and scarlet, fragrant
'Dearest' – warm salmon pink, scented
'Elizabeth of Glamis' – salmon pink, scented
'Fashion' – soft coral to peach-pink, strongly fragrant
'Fire King' – fiery scarlet
'Saratoga' – pure white, old rose fragrance
'Spartan' – deep coral, extra good fragrance

Climbing Roses (grow as pillar roses in large greenhouses or conservatories)

'Golden Showers' – golden yellow to cream, scented
'New Dawn' – pale baby pink, scented
'Paul's Scarlet Climber' – bright crimson

Miniature Roses (20-30cm/8-12in)

'Baby Masquerade' – yellow changing to pink and crimson
'Crimson Gem' – non-fading deep red
'Gold Coin' – canary yellow
'Pink Cameo' – bright pink, climbing miniature
'Rosmarin' – soft light pink, slight fragrance
'Rosy-Gem' – light pink
'Scarlet Gem' – bright scarlet
'Starina' – vivid orange scarlet
'Sweet Fairy' – apple-blossom pink, very fragrant
'Toy Clown' – distinctive rosy pink, paler reverse

Polyantha Roses (up to 60cm/2ft)

'Cameo' – salmon pink, slightly fragrant
'Cameo Superior' – deep pink
'Captain Hayward' – light crimson, very fragrant
'China Doll' – bright pink
'Dick Koster' – deep pink
'Dick Koster Fulgens' – semi-double, light red
'Margo Koster' – salmon pink
'Mothersday' – deep red, popular in Scandinavia

Left: Hybrid tea rose 'Fragrant Cloud'.
Far left: Floribunda rose 'Elizabeth of Glamis'.
Bottom centre: Miniature roses.
Below: Hybrid tea rose 'Apricot Nectar'

Orchids

The tropical orchids which are cultivated in artificial conditions in greenhouses all over the world require, for their well-being, growing conditions approximate to those in their natural habitat. The three most important factors are heat, light and humidity. For nearly as long as orchids have been grown in greenhouses, since the beginning of the nineteenth century, many have also been successfully cultivated as houseplants. There were early Victorian growers all over the British Isles, and later many highly successful orchid growers in northern Europe, including Finland, Sweden and Germany and, of course, many more in the warmer parts of southern Europe and in the USA. All these enthusiasts had succeeded in producing growing conditions good enough to enable the orchid plants to thrive and to flower, in living rooms.

It was naturally found that some orchids were easier than others to grow in a living room, just as some are easier than others to grow in a greenhouse, and over the years the 'difficult' subjects have given way to the easy. The local climate has a great bearing on the types of orchids to grow; for instance, the varied and glamorous types cultivated in Singapore, with its high day and night temperatures and its very high humidity, could be grown in the temperate zones only at great cost but would be found easy in, say, Florida. The dice, however, are not entirely loaded in favour of Singapore and Florida, for there the orchid fans find it difficult to grow and flower some of the orchids so easy to grow in Europe and the northern part of the US.

With the coming into general use of central heating of the different types, the control of temperatures has become more precise. In addition to being able to adjust the day-time temperature by setting a thermostat, the night-time temperature can be, and usually is, lowered for the sake of economy.

This lower temperature during the hours of darkness is exactly what most orchid plants need to function properly. It was achieved automatically in the old days by the simple fact that solid fuel fires were allowed to die down or to go out altogether at night, to be re-lit in the morning. Heating during these days is the most expensive overhead of a greenhouse, but orchids grown in a living room cost nothing extra, for most orchids suitable for home growing like the same temperatures as are appreciated by humans. With a little ingenuity the question of humidity sufficient for the plants can be answered, and this humidity need not create mould on the fabrics, the curtains, carpets and upholstery or upset the fine tuning of a piano. The aim is to create a little local climate for the plants while at the same time allowing the rest of the air to be healthy and dry for the people living in the room.

The simplest method for a single plant, or two or three small plants, is to find a wide and fairly shallow container such as a bowl. Inside this is spread a layer of shingle (gravel), sand or some other substance which will retain moisture. The depth may be 2.5-5cm/1-2in and the material is thoroughly moistened. An inverted flower pot is then put on this, the orchid is set on the inverted pot and the bowl is then sited in a convenient place, near, for instance, a radiator. The effect of the warm air from the radiator on the moist shingle in the bowl is to vaporize it slowly. This vapour moves upwards past and through the plant's leaves thus providing the essential humidity for the plant. Radiators are frequently situated under a window and a windowsill would be a good place for the plants, provided precautions are taken to ensure that the sunshine in summer is diffused before it strikes the plants. A north-facing window in summer and a south-facing one in winter would be ideal. On cold winter

Tropical orchids will thrive and flower in the living room, if the necessary heat, light and humidity are provided. Suitable orchids include cattleyas, a hybrid of which is shown left, and cymbidiums, above. Both are exotic and beautifully coloured

nights, move the bowls from the windowsill into the room if there is any risk of frosty draughts coming through the window.

In the tropics, where the orchid plants now grown commercially originated, the hours of daylight are about 12 a day with an equal number of dark hours. For indoor growing in temperate zones this is not so necessary and provided at least 10 hours of daylight can be given, this will be enough. During the winter, of course, the few daylight hours can be extended by a mixture of fluorescent tubes and incandescent bulbs, in the relation of nine watts of fluorescent to every one of incandescent.

When choosing the kinds of orchids with which to start one or two things must be considered. Firstly, of course, the plants should be easily cultivated and obtained at a price within easy range, and the space or spaces available and the necessary height should be taken into account. Some orchids are too tall except for the largest kind of window alcove or for siting in a corner to give them room. Then there is the question of colours. Practically every colour except blue is to be found somewhere in the orchid family, and even blue is found in *Vanda caerulea*, one of the plants which grows very well in Singapore and Florida but is not so easy in northern conditions.

Further points to be considered are the period in the year of flowering and re-potting. The plants should be chosen for flowering when the family is at home to enjoy them, and not while they are on holiday, and the re-potting will depend on the availability of potting material. It is best to obtain special orchid soil mix from the supplier of the plants; very few commercial suppliers really appreciate being asked to supply it for one or two plants purchased from somebody else. Orchid nurseries usually supply the special type of soil mix needed for orchids. Epiphytic orchids are grown in an open soil mix of two parts osmunda fibre and one part sphagnum moss, but terrestrial species should be grown in a more loamy soil mix of equal parts peat or leafmould, loam, sand and moss.

The price to be paid for beginner's plants depends mostly on whether they are hybrids or species. Hybrids, if raised by the supplier, have cost him higher and higher overheads for five to ten years, which is roughly the time it takes to flower a cattleya or many other genera from the moment of sowing the seed. Even the seed pod requires a year to ripen. Fortunately, however, the growing use of the new meristematic method of propagation is bringing the price of orchid hybrids down by greatly shortening the time needed to produce them in large quantities.

Species are imported direct from the jungles of the world, and although some are very expensive because of rarity, on the whole they are less expensive than hybrids, having been bought 'ready-made' from a dealer who has only collecting and transport charges to pay for. These plants require careful treatment on being received and some take a long while to recover. There are, however, many commercial orchid growers who import species of various kinds, and who retail them to the public only when the plants are well established. These are to be preferred by the beginner, but they are a little more expensive than those brought direct from the jungle.

It seems very likely that species previously inexpensive will become less easy to import because of recent legislation. The UK and the US are among the nearly 60 signatories to the 1973 Convention on Trade in Endangered Species of Wild Fauna and Flora. A few orchids are on the 'endangered' list and all others on the 'vulnerable' list. The endangered cannot be imported for trade; the others must have an export permit from the country of origin and the importing country must have an import permit.

A brief description of the life of an orchid hybrid may be of interest. Firstly the hybridizer selects two plants for parents of the new hybrid, removes the pollen from each and transfers it from one to the other. At the end of a year, more or less, the seed pods have matured. They are then taken from the two plants and sown on the surface of an 'agar slope' in flasks or test-tubes in hygienic conditions in a laboratory. After a few months the seed, which is very fine, has germinated and is ready to be taken from the flasks to be pricked off on to the surface of a small pot containing the appropriate soil, 20 or 30 plants to a community pot. After a further few months these tiny plants have increased in size sufficiently to be transferred to another pot, but this time only four or five of the young plants to a pot.

They remain here for a year or so by which time they are now really growing up, although only about half way to maturity. A further move or two will take them to the large pot in which they will flower. Some will flower after five or six years, others during the following year or two, but there will always be some which will not flower for eight to ten or so years after sowing. These frequently turn out to be the finest varieties.

Some orchids go through a resting period after flowering when they make no active growth and often lose their leaves and stems. During this period, very little water or humidity should be supplied.

89

ORCHIDS FOR THE LIVING ROOM

The two criteria for home growing are: is it easy and is it available? Among the over 20,000 species of wild orchids and 100,000 hybrids it would seem there are plenty from which to choose. The following, however, although only a tiny fraction of this huge number, meet both criteria. There are many others equally suitable for growing indoors, but to mention them all would be impossible and would result in only a catalogue.

Cattleya

[10°C/50°F min; Mexico to Southern Brazil] The most striking of all orchids for size and colour is by general consent the cattleyas. This group contains other genera very similar in appearance to the cattleyas but which are botanically different and which have been interbred with each other to make multi-generic hybrids.

There are a great number of cattleya species and a vast number of cattleya hybrids. Depending upon the pedigree, the hybrids show a great variation in colour, from pure white to deep purple, most having several different colours in their various segments and also, depending on their genetic background, a great difference in size, an important consideration for home orchid-growers. Recommended species of cattleyas are *C. labiata*, which gave its name to a whole group of unifoliate species and which has a single thick leaf and 23cm/9in stem bearing large rose-coloured blooms with a frilled crimson lip and yellow throat in autumn; *C. bowringiana*, at 60cm/2ft rather too large except for a room with exceptional height, has several rose-purple, yellow-throated blooms from September to December; *C. aurantiaca*, a multi-flowered small plant, orange-red in summer. Allied genera include *Laelia anceps* (lilac-rose blooms), *L. gouldiana* (rose-purple) and *L. purpurata* (white and deep purple with veined yellow throat), a favourite among Brazilian growers. *Sophronitis uniflora* (syn. *S. grandiflora*), a small brilliant red orchid, was intercrossed many generations ago to produce warmer colours in multigeneric cattleyas. *Brassavola digbyana* is another orchid in the cattleya family, noted for its magnificent fringed lip.

Cattleyas generally are lovers of light, but in common with most orchids do not appreciate full summer sun through glass, and so must be either shaded or removed to a situation away from direct sunlight. They also prefer plenty of humidity and water while they are growing and should be repotted when they become crowded in the pot. Propagate by division.

Cymbidium

[7-10°C/45-50°F min; Ceylon to India and Japan/Malaysia to Australia] This is probably the most popular cool-house orchid and is grown outside in such favoured climates as those of California and New South Wales. For living room conditions, however, most species are probably a little too large, but miniature hybrids, a comparatively recent trend, are suitable. They originate from *C. devonianum* from the Himalayas and *C. pumilum* from China and Japan and have erect or arching flower sprays in almost any shade, self-coloured or flushed, in spring and early summer. Shade from strong sunlight in summer. Repot every year after flowering. Propagation is by division.

Miltonia

[Tansy Orchid; 10°C/50°F min; Tropical America/Brazil] There are two main kinds, those originating in Colombia, the more popular at present, and those from Brazil. The Colombian hybrid miltonias are derived from *M. vexillaria* and *M. roezlii*, the last of which is difficult to obtain. There are many hybrids

Orchids vary from the more familiar shapes and colours to striking and unusual forms. Below is a hybrid derived from *Miltonia regnellii* and at the bottom *Paphiopedilum praestans*. Opposite above: A paphiopedilum hybrid. Opposite below: A cattleya hybrid, 'Nellie Roberts'

with narrow leaves and pansy-like flowers, in brilliant colours, ranging from white, through rose to deep red. There are several blooms 9cm/3½in wide on each 45cm/18in spike. They require shade during the summer, when they flower, and good winter light. Keep the soil moist and repot every two or three years. Propagate by division of the pseudobulbs. There are also now quite a number of Brazilian hybrids, different in general appearance from the Colombian types, and some attractive species, best of which are *M. spectabilis* 'Moreliana', a dramatic bloom, and *M. regnellii* with rose-pink and yellow flowers.

Odontoglossum

[10°C/50°F min; Central and South America] Cool-growing, shade-loving and having long-lasting flowers, this is a most attractive genus. Many species are still easily obtainable and there are great numbers of odontoglossum hybrids, mostly from *O. crispum*. There are about 300 species found in higher altitudes in Central and South America, and in particular Colombia. In a living room they require a cool, moist, buoyant atmosphere; consequently they will do best in some form of container near a ventilator and lightly shaded. *O. crispum* is the best known, with its 60cm/2ft long flowering stem of numerous white and pink blooms in spring; others are *O. bictoniense* (brown and pale rose), *O. cervantesii* (white or pink with chocolate-brown lip), *O. insleayi* and *O. grande*, the largest flowered of all odontoglossums, being yellow-striped brown. Propagate by division.

Oncidium

[10°C/50°F min; Central and South America] There are more than 700 oncidium species, many of which have been used in hybridizing. Although most oncidium species have leaves about 30cm/1ft long, the flower spikes are usually even longer, often .9-1.2m/3-4ft. One rather more modest species is *O. ornithorynchum* whose flower spike is 60cm/2ft high and sometimes even smaller. The branched flower spikes arch or droop with numerous small blooms, yellow or brown, and usually appearing in autumn. Treat oncidiums as odontoglossums.

Paphiopedilum

[Slipper Orchid; 13°C/55°F min; Tropical Asia] For many reasons this genus is the odd man out, but as far as cultivation is concerned the most significant differences are that it is usually a terrestrial orchid, most others being epiphytic, and that it has no pseudobulbs. These two points are probably co-related because, growing on the ground, it has access to nutrients in the soil and so does not need the pseudobulbs common to most epiphytes. This is the orchid which also goes contrary to the general rule that orchids should not be watered except when dry, for paphiopedilums need to be pleasantly moist at all times, with plenty of humidity and shade during summer, and fertilizer from May to September. The 40 species are widely distributed over the Far East, and the hybrids run into thousands as this was a genus much used very early on in hybridization. The hybrids are almost invariably shade-loving; they are very tidy-growing and the blooms are long-lasting. These are conspicuous by a large slipper-shaped lip rising above two petals and a dorsal sepal. Colours vary from yellow through green and brown to purple, and the slipper is often veined or striped. Flowering time is throughout the year, depending on the type. Propagate by division in the spring.

Herbs, fruit and vegetables

Why grow outdoor crops in the home? There is a simple answer – no garden. Many homes do not possess a garden or any place where crops can be grown except on windowsills, in pots, or in a makeshift greenhouse such as a sun lounge or porch. Fruit, vegetables and herbs can be grown on balconies and patios in tubs, window boxes, and raised beds, but certain crops can also be grown successfully in the living room or kitchen.

Before choosing anything for indoor cultivation, certain factors must be studied. Plants require light, moisture, an adequate rootrun, and nutrients, but the most critical item to consider is space. Although one room can be converted into a 'growing chamber', with fans and lighting installed, such a plan is impractical in most homes where room space is always at a premium. In any case, large vegetables such as potatoes, Brussels sprouts and leeks, or fruit crops such as raspberries or blackcurrants, are not really feasible. The answer is to use troughs and large pots in the living room to grow the less usual crops, and pots on the windowsills in the bathroom and kitchen.

Light plays a vital part in the production of healthy plants, so either grow in positions near the windows or use ample artificial light.

If a bank of lights is provided and leakproof trays are used, almost any crop can be grown indoors. Only 6.7sq.m/8sq.yd is needed for an 'A' frame with supplementary lights. Sufficient light for most plants can be provided by six 125 watt tubes or by using high pressure mercury, or low pressure sodium lamps, but the cost of electricity may be prohibitive!

As with other plants in the home, avoid excessive draughts and sudden temperature changes. Never let your indoor fruit and vegetable garden dry out or overwater it, but keep it moist and humid.

Various seed firms offer special seed collections of herbs and tomatoes for growing indoors, as well as packs for growing peanuts. These are particularly attractive to children, and any indoor gardening will stimulate their interest in living material.

CROPS TO GROW

Strawberries are probably the easiest of the soft fruits to grow indoors; it is unwise to attempt growing cane fruits such as raspberries or bush fruits such as blackcurrants in the home, although these can be grown on patios. Top fruit (apples, pears, plums and cherries) should only be attempted indoors if there is ample space for development; if they are grown a small crop, if any, will result. A mature pot-grown tree is about 1.8m/6ft or more in height with fruit developing about 1.2m/4ft from pot level.

Although they make more growth and require more attention, more exotic fruit crops to grow are peaches, nectarines or apricots. These are also more interesting to the householder.

The choice of vegetables is limited by rootrun and space. It seems rather pointless to grow cabbages which are rather mundane and may have a somewhat distinctive odour while growing, as well as being inexpensive to buy fresh. The simplest crops to grow are aubergines or eggplants, peppers, tomatoes, mustard and cress, and possibly dwarf beans, carrots and lettuce.

Aubergines or eggplants, peppers and tomatoes are greenhouse crops and recent plant breeding has resulted in a wide range of cultivars – some suitable for cultivation in the home. Mustard and cress have been a favourite with children for many years and their cultivation is very easy. With some adaptation of the room and careful selection of cultivars certain outdoor vegetables can be tried, such as carrots, choosing early stump-rooted cultivars like Early Gem, Short'n Sweet or Goldinhart, and avoiding cultivars with roots of over 15cm/6in.

With herbs, the larger, shrubby species cannot be grown but some annuals and the more dwarf perennials like chives, marjoram, mint, parsley and thyme make good indoor pot plants that are easy to grow.

Amusing, and attractive, plants can be grown from vegetables, such as this sweet potato (*Ipomoea*) above

A fruit and vegetable garden in your kitchen windowsill: runner beans, tomatoes, lettuces, peppers, plants from citrus pips, *Citrus mitis* in the front row, and bay, mustard and cress, an avocado stone, pineapple, herbs (parsley, chives, rosemary and sage) and strawberries behind

Peaches, Nectarines and Apricots

Peaches, nectarines and apricots can be grown from a stone, although some skill and attention is required. There is a risk of failure if the stone is planted in autumn months due to the stone rotting so start your tree in warm weather. Crack the stone carefully with nutcrackers to aid germination and plant it 8-10cm/3-4in deep in a 9cm/3½in pot. Cover and keep in a warm, dark place until the shoots appear.

The more usual method of growing peach, nectarine or apricot trees is by purchasing a two-year-old of a known cultivar from a garden centre or nurseryman. They should be potted up in a good rich soil, firming the young tree thoroughly and staking it. The pot size should be at least 25cm/10in, and may be up to 38cm/15in or more. Such pots are in short supply, so a wooden tub can be used. Incorporate plenty of peat and a general-purpose fertilizer into the mix (about 125g/4oz fertilizer per 25cm/10in pot), since the peat will assist moisture retention and the fertilizer will boost the nutrient supply. All three fruit trees are self-fertile (do not need another tree for pollination), but it is wise to hand-pollinate the flowers. The pollen is transferred from the male floral parts, or stamens, to the female parts, or style, by brushing the centre of the fully open flowers gently, using a fine camel hair brush.

When pruning pot-grown trees, remove some of the older harder wood and leave younger wood in its place – this forms the fruiting wood. The fruit should be thinned when it is about 3cm/1¼in in diameter, leaving the fruits about 23cm/9in apart. It should, however, be noted that after the first year no pruning is done, but after the second year all branches should be cut back by half since this will encourage the production of numerous young laterals. Because the tree has a restricted rootrun, regular feeding is necessary. Work in about 125g/4oz of dried blood into the top cm in the early spring and feed with a well-balanced liquid fertilizer throughout the growing season.

The Peregrine Peach and the genetic dwarf Bonanza are probably the best cultivars to grow, alternatives being Bellegarde, Rochester or a dwarfed Hale Haven. Before growing a peach, nectarine or apricot tree in the living room, please remember that it is normally an outdoor commercial crop and may grow fairly large unless regular selective pruning is carried out as well as feeding to keep the tree healthy.

Strawberries

The best crop to grow indoors is strawberries. The continental cultivars such as Gento and Remont or Fairfax and Catshill should be grown since they have a real strawberry flavour.

A 20-23cm/8-9in pot is used and each plant should be grown singly in a pot. A rich soil is required. When potting up the young plants, fill up the pots until the plants can be placed with the crown about 2.5cm/1in below the top, then hold the plant in one hand, placing mixture around the roots, firming gently with the fingers until the crown of the plant is half

covered. Keep the plants moist and remove any yellowing leaves. Runners will be produced and these can be allowed to fall down from the pot. After the fruiting season the plants should be tidied up, removing dead leaves, and repotting if necessary. Young plants can be potted up from the runners.

Other cultivars worth growing include Frapendula and the everbearing Ozark Beauty, freely fruiting cultivars, ideally suited to this work, which start fruiting in June with their peak in September.

Vegetables

The choice of vegetables that can be grown indoors may seem rather limited, but if you are lucky enough to have space on balconies or patios, the range can be vastly widened to include almost every type of vegetable.

Tomatoes

Tomatoes are the easiest of the fruiting vegetables to grow indoors and can be grown with ease in large pots or in specially prepared bags, often known as growing bags (not used in the United States). Temperature and humidity are vitally important. The minimum temperature should be 15°C/60°F when raising the plants, and 10°C/50°F for the growing plants, though preferably 15°C/60°F.

Growing bags contain a peat-based mixture, and because peat dries out rather quickly in dry warm temperatures, problems such as Blossom End Rot may arise. Careful watering must be carried out and the bags kept moist.

In pots it is best to use a loam-based mixture. Always buy fresh material each season as this will reduce the chance of attacks by soil-borne diseases, e.g. Verticillium Wilt. Peat-based mixture can be used, but if it dries out serious problems can arise, and watering can be tricky. The size of pot required eventually will be 25cm/10in and plastic, polyethylene or clay pots are equally good. Commercial growers use bitumen-covered paper pots, but these are not recommended for the amateur since they are unsightly and start to rot after a few months.

There is an open choice between buying plants from a garden centre or nurseryman, or raising them from seed. By buying plants there is little choice of cultivar, but at least the plants have had a good start and should be healthy. By growing them from seed the cultivar choice is open and some pleasure is always derived from choosing and examining different ones. Sow the seed from January onwards in small pots or pans, e.g. margarine cartons, with about 12 seeds per pot, and use a seed or potting mixture. A temperature of 15°C/60°F is required for germination, as well as sufficient water, and germination will take about 10 days.

When the first seed leaves have fully formed and there are signs of the first true leaves, prick out into individual 10cm/4in pots containing a loam-based mixture, and keep the young plants moist. When the first flower truss is showing, plant them in a 25cm/10in pot or container, firming well with the fingers, and give them a good watering to settle the mixture and roots. The seed leaves should be level with the ground. Each plant will need a cane to support it, so fasten the stem with string, wool, thread or twist tie to a cane – this should not be too tight but just act as a means of support. Remove the side shoots except on bush culti-

vars, and restrict the plants to five trusses. This means removing the growing tip when five trusses are visible.

Tomatoes must have water, or several nutritional and cultural problems will arise. One of these is Blossom End Rot, which as the name suggests, affects the end of the fruit, with a black-grey ring developing which makes the fruit inedible. It is caused by a lack of water and a high concentration of nutrients in the growing medium. The solution is to keep the plant well watered – but never saturated. One idea is to place the pot in a saucer containing gravel, and keep the gravel wet. To achieve a good

Your kitchen garden can be made even more attractive by combining foliage houseplants with fruit and vegetables. Lettuces, pineapple, *Citrus mitis*, tomatoes, mint (in the kettle), and parsley (on the windowsill) combine with ferns to brighten up the window opposite.
Below: 'Sub-Arctic Plenty' tomatoes grow in a small pot. Sideshoots on cane-supported tomatoes should be pinched out, so when each plant has five trusses, remove any other growing tips, as shown in the illustration.
The hot peppers, right, are easy to grow indoors

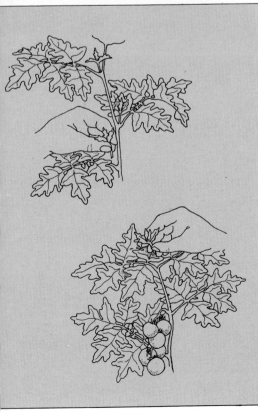

fruit set, pollinate each flower with a camel hair brush, or spray the plants overhead.

From experience Pixie is probably the best cultivar. It is very early in ripening and ideal for indoor cultivation. The fruits have a sweet flavour. Big Early and Golden Amateur are also early, producing a heavy crop of good flavoured yellow fruit. Tiny Tim and Sugarplum produce large quantities of small tomatoes with a sweet flavour. Of the commercial cultivars, Marglobe and Dobies Champion are good fool-proof cultivars with a good-sized fruit, early in ripening and easy to set.

Peppers

Sweet and hot peppers are also easy to grow in pots and containers indoors. Hot peppers require more heat than sweet peppers. (Spice peppers are a different plant.)

Sow the seed from January onwards, as for tomatoes. Germination is slower, and may take up to a month. After germination and the full development of the seed leaves, prick out into 10cm/4in pots and keep warm: if the temperature falls below 12°C/55°F, the plants will turn yellow and stop growing. During flowering the blossoms may drop if the temperature falls below 15°C/60°F. Over 24°C/75°F the fruit is less likely to set. Although this may sound tricky, it is simple – minimum temperature is 15°C/60°F and maximum is 24°C/75°F.

Repot into the final containers, such as 25cm/10in pots, about eight weeks after germination, and throughout the growing season keep well watered but not saturated. A gravel-filled saucer is a good base.

Harvest the peppers when they start to turn from green to red. (Green-fruiting cultivars will not turn red, but just mature and then rot.) There is no harm in harvesting peppers too early. A useful guide is that a mature pepper is about the size of an orange.

A good cultivar is Canape, which matures early, with sweet mild flesh and deep green fruits turning red on maturing. California Horder and New Ace are other good heavy croppers which have green fruits when matured.

Aubergines or Eggplants

Aubergines or eggplants are increasing in popularity and can be grown without a greenhouse. Sow the seed from February onwards in small pans or pots containing a seed mixture, and on the expansion of the seed leaves prick out in 10cm/4in pots. Nip out the growing point when the plants are about 15cm/6in high to encourage bushy growth. When the plants are about 20cm/8in high, repot in 25cm/10in pots. To achieve a fruit set either pollinate with a camel hair brush or spray overhead. At no stage should the plants lack water or the fruits will crack. The crop takes 80 days to reach maturity, and the fruits should be picked when the skin is glossy and they are about the size of a large pear or small cantaloupe.

Suitable cultivars, for all purposes, include Black Beauty, an early cropper with oval to round shiny, almost black fruits, and Jersey King, a late cropper with round dark purple fruits.

All these fruiting vegetables profit from a regular feeding once every 10 days with a liquid fertilizer, and in early May a top dressing of a high potash fertilizer should be gently applied.

Mustard, Cress and Lettuce

Mustard and cress are easy to grow, but if they are to be ready at the same time, sow the cress four days before the mustard. In both cases use thick, wet kitchen paper or muslin flannel or cheesecloth, For germination, keep them dark and moist, but after they germinate, place in a well-lit position. About two weeks later they can be cut.

Although large hearting lettuce are impractical to grow in pots, the cultivar Salad Bowl can be grown in a 13cm/5in pot. As it is non-hearting, just remove enough for a salad or sandwich.

Dwarf French or Green Beans

Dwarf beans can be grown in a large pot. Sow three seeds in an 18cm/7in pot containing a seed mixture in March. On germination, place in a well-lit position and stake the young plants with split canes or small thin bamboos. To aid pollination an overhead spray with water will be necessary. Top dress with 50g/2oz of a general-purpose fertilizer per pot about six weeks after sowing.

Plants from Pips and Stones

Tropical fruits such as pineapples, oranges, lemons, dates and mangoes can be grown easily from stones or other simple means – even peaches can be grown this way.

Pineapples

Cut the top off a pineapple below its leaves, and insert it in a 13cm/5in pot to a depth of 10cm/4in, using a 50% peat/sand potting mixture. Cover the 'plant' with a polyethelene or plastic bag to keep the young plant humid, turning the bag inside out daily to avoid damping off. Within a few months some roots and new leaves will form. ('Damping off' is a fungal disease encouraged by lack of air, and excessive damp.)

Avocados

The stone of the avocado pear when propagated will produce an attractive small tree. Since darkness is helpful for germination, use a darkened glass tumbler or cover an ordinary tumbler with kitchen foil. Remove the hard stone from the middle of the avocado and fix it, pointed end upwards, in a cardboard collar. Suspend it in a tumbler half-full of water so that half the stone is submerged. Keep the water supply up, and if the stone and glass become covered with a green slime, rinse them under a running tap. After a month or so the stone will start to split at the top, with the root and shoot appearing. When the root/shoot is about 2.5cm/1in in length, pot up the plant into a 10cm/4in pot using a loam-based mixture, which should come to within 2.5cm/1in of the top of the stone. After potting, place the avocado plant in a warm shady place and keep the mixture moist. Once the shoot starts to grow

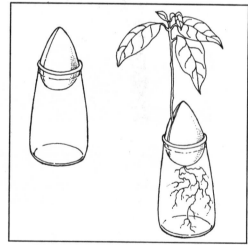

away, move the plant to a well-lit position, repotting when pot-bound and staking the shoot to keep it straight. Eventually the avocado tree will require a 30cm/12in pot and be over 1.8m/6ft tall. Plenty of light is required, but avoid draughts.

Citrus Fruit

Growing citrus trees (similar to *Citrus mitis*) is easy and they will eventually fruit after six years or more. Never mix the seeds of different fruits in one pot, since they germinate at different speeds. After removing the seeds from any citrus fruit – orange, lemon, grapefruit, etc. – press three into a 9cm/3½in pot containing a loam-based mixture and place the pot in a warm dark place. Do not wash the seeds as this will remove some of the enzymes required for germination. After germination, which takes about six weeks, place the pot in a light position. When they are about 10cm/4in high, pot up the young plants, taking care not to break the roots. Repotting will be necessary about every two years or when pot-bound. (A useful guide to judge when a plant is pot-bound is that the top portion should be not more than three times the diameter of the pot, although in pots of over 15cm/6in this rule does not hold.)

Dates

Although date palms can be hard to grow, they are a challenge. Dates require a lot of heat and humidity, but with care and attention a date palm will result. Plant three stones in a 9cm/3½in pot and cover it with a polyethylene or plastic bag to assist germination until the shoots appear. Turn the bag inside-out daily to avoid mould and stand the pot near a radiator or warm air vent. When the plants are about 8cm/3in in height, repot into individual 9cm/3½in pots.

Mangoes and Lychees

More exotic to grow are mangoes and lychees, and their cultivation is the same as avocados. Mangoes at first have fantastic stem contortions and then settle down, giving a jungle-like appearance to any home with their long green leaves. Since they are semi-tropical, keep them moist and warm. On occasion a fruit will form.

Sprouting Seeds

Growing 'sprouting seeds' is a gimmick, but the food value in a sprouting seed is 600% more than in a dry seed. Seeds that are commonly 'sprouted' are mung bean, oats, fenugreek, pumpkin and alfalfa. All that is required is a jam jar, or cotton wool, plus water and a dark warm corner, and the almost instant vegetable will be ready within a few days.

It is important to buy seeds that are meant for 'sprouting' since many commercial seed firms dress their seeds with fungicides; such seeds should never be used for sprouting.

The same method is used for all varieties. Two tablespoonfuls of seed are enough for three people. Soak the seeds overnight in cold water and rinse in the morning. If a jam jar is to be used for growing, the sides of the jar must be blacked out with black polyethelene or plastic or kitchen foil in order to stop the light from getting in. (Darkness is necessary so the seeds remain white, tasty and nutritious.) Put the moist seeds in the jar and cover with a lid. Place the jar in a dark warm place – the warmer the place the quicker the shoots will develop (temperatures of over 34°C/90°F are too high). Rinse out the beans daily by swirling a little water around in the jar and tipping water and beans into a strainer through which the water is flushed. Frequent washing is important as it keeps the beans fresh; otherwise they are likely to go mouldy.

After about six days the beans will have increased in size by 500% and will be ready for eating. Before cooking, remove any seed coats that are still attached to the shoots.

An alternative method, which is also successful, is to grow them on cotton wool, placed in a foil or plastic tray. Cover with foil or black polyethelene or plastic and keep the cotton wool moist. After several days the seedlings will be ready. They are at their most nutritious when they are about 5cm/2in in height.

Herbs

Some of the smaller herbs can be grown with ease in a well-lit spot in the home. Treat them like any other pot plant and give them plenty of light and sufficient water. A loam-based potting mixture should be used. The herbs that can be grown include chives, mint, parsley, rosemary, sage and thyme.

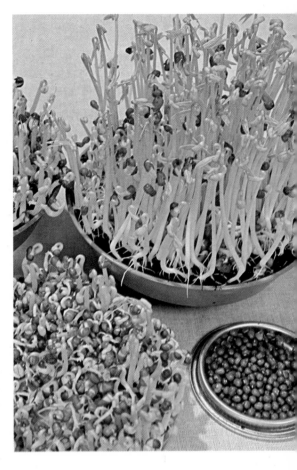

Avocado stones will produce an attractive small tree (opposite above): suspend the stone in a tumbler half-full of water. After about a month, roots will have appeared and a shoot at the top, as in the illustration. Plants from other fruit include the pineapple (opposite below), which can be grown from the pineapple crown. Above, sprouted mung beans. Fresh herbs can easily be grown in the kitchen; the box below contains tarragon, chives, sage and thyme

Physiological disorders

Although you might imagine that pests and diseases are the cause of so many plant problems, it is, in fact, the physiological disorders or cultural faults which claim the largest toll of indoor plant failures.

Physiological disorders or cultural faults are by definition problems that affect the plant due to where it is grown, how it is grown and what we may do to the plant. This includes over-watering, under-watering, sun scald, cold water scald, physical damage, draughts, temperature fluctuation, low humidity and misuse of aerosols.

Over-watering, Under-watering?

Probably more plants die, or at the least suffer, from over-watering than from any other problem, and indeed it can be a little difficult to identify immediately whether the plant has been over- or under-watered.

The obvious symptoms of both are that the plant wilts, followed by leaf dehydration and thereafter rapid leaf drop. In both cases this is due to the fact that the plant is not absorbing water. In the dry plant there is obviously little or no water left in the mixture, but with an excessively wet plant, although there is a super-abundance of water, there are usually no active roots.

The cause of an under-watered plant is obvious but with an over-watered plant the problem is a little more complex. Most people think that to keep a plant healthy, the addition of water to a pot is quite sufficient, with the occasional drop of liquid fertilizer, but the truth is that air is also required. Therefore, with the majority of plants frequent addition of water to an already moist soil mixture quickly displaces any surplus air and an araerobic or airless soil mix results.

The roots then suffocate, die and break down, and the plant above, ironically, dies from dehydration.

A plant that is over-watered and is showing primary signs of stress may be saved by removing it from its pot and letting it dry out. This should take 24-48 hours, after which it can be replaced in the pot and watered. It does help at this stage to water the plant with a 'Benomyl' solution as this fungicide applied to the soil kills parasitic fungi which may inhibit the growth of fresh roots.

Sun Scald

When certain plants are exposed to high light intensities, sun scald may result. The damage may take the appearance of dehydrated areas on the leaf surface, for large irregular patches on the leaves usually mean that the plant has been exposed directly to the sun's rays.

Cold Water Scorch

This more usually affects plants such as Saintpaulias and Gloxinias and occurs when a plant is watered with cold instead of tepid water, the water droplets being allowed to remain on the leaves. An unusual marbling effect results looking somewhat similar to the tracks left by the leaf miner in chrysanthemums and cineraria. It is better, therefore, to water these plants from below.

Physical Damage

It is surprising how much damage can be caused to a plant, the resultant effect not becoming apparent for some time. The actual visible result is extremely variable, but tears and splits in the leaf are most common, caused by rough handling.

Probably the most unusual effect of physical damage occurs when the growing point is damaged. Even if the damage to the terminal bud appears slight, as the leaf grows the damage looks more severe and subsequent leaves invisible in the terminal bud at the time of damage may also show some signs of marking if the effect was more than one leaf deep. Eventually the plant will grow through this although it may take a little while.

Draughts

The more delicate plants are susceptible to draughts and the usual effect is sudden and rapid leaf drop. On certain plants, however, the effect may be nothing more than drooping of the leaves. Quite obviously if the plant is reacting either way it is in a bad position and should be moved immediately.

Temperature Fluctuation

This is more of a problem in winter than at any other time as temperatures are more liable to sudden changes. The most usual effect of temperature fluctuation is rapid leaf drop: as much as one-third of the leaves may drop overnight if the fluctuation is great enough.

During the day the room tends to be warmer while it is occupied, but at night the heating is usually lower and the temperature drops. It is not the low temperature which is the causal factor but the temperature difference, i.e. relatively high to low temperature in a short time.

Plants allowed to stand on windowsills are more susceptible than those placed in the body of the room. It is more important to aim at a stable temperature of approximately 13-15°C/ 55-59°F constant than to aim at a high temperature of 24°C/75°F which will drop as soon as the heating is lowered.

Low Humidity

Plants that originate in warm humid conditions are particularly susceptible to dry arid conditions. Leaf tips and edges are the first to suffer, turning brown and dehydrating.

Plants continually lose water from their leaves by the process of transpiration in an

1. leaf drop due to over- or under-watering, draughts or temperature fluctuation
2. marbling of the leaves due to cold water scorch
3. dehydrated patches on leaves due to sun scald, and an infestation of scale insects
4. leaf tips turning brown due to low humidity
5. white specks on leaves caused by aerosols
6. tears or splits in leaves caused by physical damage

2

1

effort to stop the leaf tissue from over-heating. If the atmosphere is excessively dry, the plant continues losing water, often at a higher level than it can compensate for by absorbing water through the roots in the process of osmosis. The result is that the last part of the plant to receive water is the first to lose it and thus dehydration occurs.

The brown tips and edges can be trimmed back but this does not solve the problem, only masks the effect.

In order to obviate the problem an attempt must be made to raise the humidity around the plant by plunging the pot into a tray of a moist medium such as peat or sphagnum moss. The micro-climate thus produced helps the plant to retain water within its tissue.

One other problem thought to be caused by excessively dry conditions is the loss of perforations and slits in the leaves of monstera – the Mexican Breadfruit Plant. In its natural habitat holes are produced in order to accelerate trans-piration under excessively humid conditions. However, in a dry arid condition the plant no longer has to adapt to lose water and so reverts, it is believed, to a simple leaf which is not as efficient as a perforated one.

Aerosols

Certain aerosols can damage plants, producing minute flecks on the leaf, sometimes with a silvery appearance. Avoid spraying aerosols such as hair lacquer, polish, etc. near plants.

Pests

Whereas physiological disorders can be prevented by better culture, the occurrence of pests is a problem which is difficult to avoid.

Certain pests, such as aphids, white-fly, thrips and fungus gnats, may fly in at any time, whereas others such as mealy bug and scale insects are more endemic to certain plants. As far as spread of infestation is concerned, aphids, etc. can colonize many plants in a wide area in a short time. Mealy bugs, etc. tend only to spread to those plants in the near vicinity. These are important points to note when treating a plant which is infested by one of these 'beasties'. For example, if one plant is infected with aphids it would be advantageous to treat all others or at least check all of the others carefully. Infestations of mealy bugs and scale insects are usually more localized and as such plants can be treated individually.

Aphids
Aphids attack the young growth of plants — young leaves, buds and flowers — where they feed by stabbing the tissue with a long pointed 'beak'. These punctures cause leaf deformation which spoils the appearance of the plant as well as inhibiting active growth. Honeydew, a sticky material excreted by the aphids, also poses a problem as it cultures sooty mould, a black fungus.

(Honeydew and sooty mould are also often seen when there is an insect infestation caused by other pests.)

Control of Aphids — Pyrethum or Pirimicarb: Spray once a week for two weeks.

Control of Aphids and Sooty Mould — Gently wipe leaves with a very mild detergent solution. Rinse or wipe with fresh water.

◀ White-fly
Although the adult white-fly presents a nuisance by flying up when the foliage is disturbed, it is the larvae, not the adults, which cause damage to the plant. Adhering to the undersides of the leaves, the oval-shaped larvae suck the plant's sap. The adults can often be seen on the undersides of the leaves where the eggs are laid. This pest tends to be difficult to control because of its life cycle with five stages, one of egg, three of larval and one of adult.

Control — Pyrethrum and/or Resmethrin: Spray two to three times a week for four weeks.

◀ Red Spider Mites
The red spider is actually a straw-coloured minute creature which causes severe mottling and deformation of growth. It has biting mouth-parts and chews the leaf undersides. In severe infestations the mites produce a mass of webs. Infestations become increasingly severe the hotter and drier the conditions.

Control — Liquid Derris: Spray twice a week for three weeks.

Sciarid-fly
The adult insect is more of a nuisance pest than anything else as it flies up from the planting mix of infected plants once the surface is disturbed. The larvae, however, may be a problem at times as they live on decaying organic matter and sometimes nibble the occasional root. The larvae are white with a black head and although small can be seen with the naked eye.

Control — Malathion: Water the mixture once a week for two weeks.

Thrips
This is a minor pest of pot plants, the small black insects causing flecking of the leaves and sometimes marking or abortion of the flower buds.

Control — Malathion: Spray once a week for two weeks.

Diseases

Mealy bug
Mealy bugs as adults look like small white woodlice which tend to feed on or around leaf axils and under the leaves near the veins. The young are incubated in the white wooly areas.
Control — Malathion: Spray once a week for three weeks. Methylated Spirit or Alcohol: Dab with cotton wool soaked in the liquid on the end of a matchstick.

Root mealy bug
Located on the roots they inhibit the plant's growth and may cause leaf yellowing.
Control — Malathion: Water the growing medium once a week for three weeks.

Many diseases are in fact the result of poor culture, the disease getting its primary foothold by living off decaying leaves and then infecting the plant. Poor growing conditions may also encourage the growth of many pathogenic fungi. It must be remembered that prevention is always better than cure.

Root Diseases and Damping off
Providing the soil mix is sterile, these diseases should not be a problem unless the soil is kept too moist under cool conditions. The symptoms are wilting of the plant while the soil is still moist, the effects being that of either rotting of the roots or stem.
Prevention — Sterile mixture and good cultural conditions.
Cure — Water mixture with Benomyl or Orthocide Solution once every ten days for three weeks.

Botrytis
This fungus may originally secure its position by living on old leaves and flowers which the plant has discarded. Under moist conditions the fungus thrives and may then attack the living plant. Plants susceptible to this are cyclamen, saintpaulia and gloxinia. The fungus appears as a fluffy greyish mould on the tissue and once disturbed, clouds of spores are released.
Prevention — Clean away dead and dying parts of plants as soon as possible.
Cure — Benomyl: Spray once a week for three weeks.

Scale insects
Almost looking like part of the plant, the blister shaped scale insects feed usually on the undersides of leaves and on the stems, but in severe infestations may be found on the upper leaf surfaces. The young straw-coloured insects can be killed with an insecticide, but once the insect has turned into a dark brown egg case, the young are protected by the dead adult's tough-shelled body.
Control — (Young feeding insects) Malathion, Dimethoate: Spray once a week for three weeks. (Egg cases) — Physically wipe off to remove.

Fungal Spots
Under humid conditions certain plants may suffer from fungal spot. Dracaenas, hederas, dieffenbachias and others also may become infected by these. The spot or spots take the appearance of soft brown roughly circular areas. This is not a major problem and is usually an uncommon one and as such prevention is often not thought necessary.
Cure — Benomyl: Spray once a week for three weeks. If possible remove infected leaves, although this is not essential, if the leaf is only slightly affected.

Rust
Apparent as reddish or brownish areas on the leaves, rust fungi affect only a few indoor plants such as fuchsia and pelargoniums. Once infected it is difficult to control.
Prevention — Spray once every week with Thiram or Zineb.
Cure — Spray twice a week with Thiram or Zineb.

Mildew
There are two main types of mildew — powdery and downy. Powdery mildew appears as white dusty areas on the leaves, whereas downy mildew has a fluffy appearance. Poor air circulation can often encourage the growth of these fungi.
Prevention — Dust lightly once every two weeks with Sulphur or Thiram.
Cure — Dust twice a week with Sulphur, Thiram or Karathan, or spray once a week with Karathan, or Benomyl.

CHAPTER 2
BEAUTIFUL PLANTS
FOR AN EFFECT

The most important requirement of
any display of plants is that
it should be seen, so for maximum
effect choose a prominent
position; plants are too beautiful
to be hidden away in a dark
corner, although they can be used
to hide an ugly feature or
create a new dimension for a dull
spot. The setting should not
be too permanent as seeing the
same plants month after month
looking exactly the same may be
dull. Make provision for
some of the plants, particularly the
flowering subjects, to be of a
more temporary nature. And feel
free to experiment: choose
plants to show each other off
in habit, texture, colour and shape,
and to blend with or highlight
the colours of the room.

Plants as room dividers

As room dividers, potted plants offer an excellent alternative to the sort of furniture that is specifically manufactured for this purpose. When plants are used to divide large interiors into sections as, for instance, the living-dining areas, they offer some flexibility, as well as providing privacy without a solid wall.

To facilitate movement of plants, many of the containers that are manufactured specifically as planters have easy running castors fitted to the base of them. Containers of this type, besides being useful for the time when re-arrangement of plants is necessary, will also make cleaning a much simpler task.

Containers are available in a wide variety of shapes and sizes, but as room dividers the square or oblong trough types are best, as they can be more easily butted together to form a barrier between one part of the room and the other. Some of the containers are fitted with capillary watering devices which greatly reduce the need for visiting the planters with the watering can, as it is only necessary to top up the water reservoir in the bottom of the container about once every two weeks. Capillary containers have indicators fitted which will show exactly how much water is required by the plants. However, it must be stressed that the reservoir should be allowed to dry out completely and remain dry for about five days between each topping up operation – this will permit the soil in the container to become aerated, which would be impossible if it remained wet all the time.

Although containers used as room dividers are essentially oblong in shape, there is no reason why the feature should not be made up as a combination of smaller containers. The advantage here is that if several plants are used they can each be planted in their individual boxes, so that any problems that may occur with the soil in the box at a later date will be confined to one container and will not affect all the plants. If preferred, a layer of gravel can be placed in the bottom of the container and the plants, in their pots, placed on this.

Above: A planter containing pteris,
ficus, aechmea, asparagus ferns and a kentia palm
divides the entrance hall from the living room.
Right: A *Cissus antarctica*
gives the illusion of dividing the library
from a glass-enclosed porch

Four ways of using plants to divide a room:
1. Easily assembled units show off plants and ornaments. On the top shelf are a croton, *Anthurium scherzerianum* and *Ficus radicans*.

Below, *Ficus pumila* and *Begonia masoniana*.
2. A modern planter uses different levels and contains *Dracaena terminalis*, *Ficus elastica*, a hedera, sansevieria and *Ficus benjamina*.

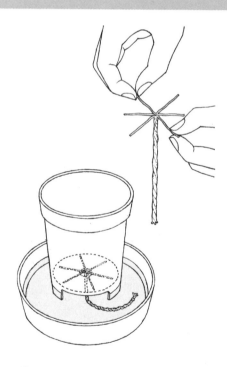

A capillary watering device can be made very simply using a glass-fibre wick.
Unravel one end, insert it through the drainage hole of the pot, and spread it out on the bottom before adding the soil mix. Stand the pot in a holder and add just enough water to cover the wick without touching the pot

In many instances indoors there is often the need for providing a container for a given location and it may then be necessary for one of the correct size to be made. When making such containers it is important that they should not be too unwieldy, so if a very long trough type container is wanted, it may be necessary to build it in two or more sections.

Width and depth are important factors to consider if large plants that are intended to climb to the ceiling are envisaged. Tall plants of 1.8m/6ft or more in height will have to have a considerable bulk of soil around their roots to keep them going. Therefore it means providing containers large enough to accept pots that may be as much as 25cm/10in in diameter; the trough that is made must be at least that much across. The depth of the pot will be in the region of 30cm/1ft, but it would be wiser to allow for at least 38cm/15in in order that a layer of gravel may be placed in the bottom of the trough on which the plant pots can be placed. The container must also have a liner of metal or plastic, so that any surplus moisture gathers in the bottom of the container rather than running out onto the carpet.

Climbing Plants

Having prepared the trough for accommodating the roots of the plant, or the pot, there is then need for providing some form of support on which the chosen plants may be allowed to climb. A simple trellis is probably the best way of overcoming the problem, and it can either have diamond- or square-shaped sections – the latter being my preference. Most trellis sections that are purchased ready-made for the job are almost invariably a dull brown in colour and not very interesting as features in the home. But the same trellis can be made to look very different simply by painting it white (or a colour that blends with the room's colour scheme) rather than brown, and leaves will be set off much more effectively against the white.

The cheapest method of providing some form of support is to screw a 5 × 2.5cm/2 × 1in slat into the ceiling immediately above the trough, and to insert stout screw eyelets into the slat. It will then be a simple task to tie thick nylon string from the eyelets in the ceiling to similar eyelets screwed into the trough. Screws can be inserted into either side of the trough so that the string can be traced up and down to form an open tent shape up which plant growth can either be trained or allowed to grow naturally. Done in this fashion the growth of the plant will be much less congested and will grow very much better.

By fixing a similar slat to the ceiling, you can employ slender lathes of wood for plants to grow against, the lathes to be pinned to the ceiling slat at one end and to a centre bar of

3. Pleomele, *Cissus antarctica* and *Rhoicissus rhomboidea* are planted in a homemade trough. Nylon string, run between the trough and a slat fixed to the ceiling, provides support.

4. A simple trellis is the easiest method of providing a frame on which plants can climb. Illustrated here are *Scindapsus* 'Marble Queen', *Philodendron scandens, P.* 'Burgundy' and a hedera

wood running through the length of the trough at the bottom.

Although all manner of elaborate and expensive materials may be used for making the upper sections of room dividers, the simple and natural materials are very much more effective, as it is the plants themselves that should be the feature and not the framework.

Although flexibility could be claimed to be an advantage here, it will usually be found that the climbing plants normally used as room dividers will quickly become intertwined and a more or less permanent feature of the room.

Possibly the best plant of climbing habit that is intended for a location offering poor light is the grape ivy, *Rhoicissus rhomboidea*, with *Philodendron scandens* running a close second. If rapid growth is an important need in the climbing plant used as a room divider there can be no better choice than *Tetrastigma voinieriana* – a vine that will grow at almost frightening pace if the prevailing conditions are to its liking.

Light

Room dividers are usually some distance from the natural light source of the window, so highly coloured plants such as crotons and variegated plants such as *Hedera canariensis* are comparatively unsuitable as they need ample light to keep them in good condition. Although crotons are not of climbing habit and would not be suitable if a trellis or other framework were used, they could well be included in plant boxes that are raised on a waist-high wall near a window. The advantage of the latter method is that the plants are more easily seen in respect of their watering and other requirements and can be dealt with without need for too much bending.

If plants are some distance from the natural light source they will benefit from having artificial lighting placed above them, especially during the evening when they will not only benefit growthwise from the additional light but they will also be considerably improved in appearance.

From the foregoing it may seem that climbing plants against a framework are the only subjects that are suitable as room dividers, but this is not so as there is no reason why a row of stately dracaenas or ficus plants should not do an equally good job of segregating one part of the room from the other. But it must be remembered that only mature plants will be suitable for this purpose and, in any event, that mature plants will give the desired effect immediately. Also larger plants that are well established in their pots will settle to room conditions very much more readily than young plants. They would almost be scared out of their pots at the prospect of climbing a 2.4m/ 8ft bamboo, or lathe attached to the ceiling!

Large houseplants, such as monsteras and *Ficus elastica* (rubber plants), placed on a long unit will effectively divide a room

Plants to brighten dull spots

It is often supposed that plants are the perfect choice when it comes to selecting something to lighten up that darker corner of the living room, but nothing could be further from the truth. The only foliage plants that are likely to brighten the dark corners are those with highly coloured or variegated foliage, and these are the very plants that will require more than the average amount of light if they are to retain their colouring and prosper.

But this is not to say that there are no plants that are suited to less well-lit conditions, as there are many purely green foliage plants that will fare better in the darker, shaded corner or unused fireplace than they will if placed on the sunny windowsill. Among these you may choose from almost any of the many green-leaved philodendrons, which have either small leaves, in the case of *P. scandens*, or larger leaves, in the case of *P. hastatum*. Most of the bolder types of ferns will also be better if placed out of the sun's rays, and the larger types, such as *Nephrolepis*, will fill the space in almost any corner location. The latter, as well as most palms, are at their best when placed on top of one of those superb Victorian-style pedestals, or on top of a wrought iron pedestal if antique designs are out of the question. Mention of Victoriana immediately brings to mind the dear old aspidistra which was so much a part of the Victorian interior. *A. lurida*, the cast iron plant, is one of the most durable of potted plants provided a reasonable temperature is maintained. For proper decoration value, however, it depends on a handsome container.

Plants for Corners

If one must have a colourful plant in the darker corner it will be essential to augment the available daylight with an electric lamp of some kind adjacent to the plant. It would be an expensive business to have a plant in each corner of the room with its own electric lamp providing the essential additional amount of light, but for the owner of a number of plants the problem can be solved by grouping the plants together in one corner with one light source catering for all their needs. A group of plants growing together in this way with a light over them will be much more effective,

and the plants will grow very much better than if they were scattered about the room because plants thrive better in company than singly.

You can purchase or have made wrought iron or bamboo stands that are fitted with a series of rings in which plant pots of varying size can be placed. These rings are set at varying heights on the metal or bamboo stand and can be most effective when a variety of plants are placed in them. A selection of plants placed on a tall stand of this kind will also solve many

problems for the householder who has far too many plants in living accommodation that is restricted in respect of space.

When arranging a plant stand of this kind it is essential that plant pot covers should first be placed in the rings into which plant pots are then placed – this will ensure that surplus moisture draining through the soil collects in the bottom of the pot holder and not on the carpet! A further small precaution will be to tip away any water regularly that has accumulated in

the outer pot as it is important that plants should not stand in water for any length of time.

Another method of utilizing a corner location, dark or otherwise, is to fit a series of triangular shelves in the corner supported by wall brackets or by firmly fixing the actual shelves to the wall. Such shelves will require waterproof trays lined with absorbent felt pads in which surplus moisture will collect – the more conventional sand or gravel base would be

Left: Ferns add a refreshing air to an entrance hall; tulips in a planter lighten the foyer behind.
Below: *Rhoicissus capensis* in a wall-niche.

Above: *Howeia forsteriana* and *Ficus benjamina* bring a corner spot to life: the contrast of leaf shape and height is attractive, and is set off by the plain containers

much too heavy for wall-fitted shelving. Shelves of this sort should be fitted about 45cm/ 18in apart, and plants will benefit considerably if the undersides of shelves incorporate a small fluorescent tube that is concealed behind the front edge of the shelf. For shelving of this type the smaller and more compact houseplants will be more suitable as the taller growing ones will too quickly outgrow their available headroom. A few to choose from would be the smaller-leaved ferns, the peperomias with darker green foliage, *Ficus pumila*, *Philodendron scandens*, the small-leaved *Fittonia argyroneura nana* and saintpaulias, provided additional light has been incorporated.

Wall-hanging plant supports, made of wrought iron or bamboo, and wall supports of bark are another good way to utilize space. The latter are ideal for some ferns, particularly *Platycerium bifurcatum*, and some orchids. 109

Left: Pelargoniums and *Ficus pumila* in hanging baskets are used imaginatively in the area above a spiral staircase. The hanging container, above, is planted with ivy, *Philodendron hastatum* and a parlour palm. *Opposite:* A stairwell is brightened by *Ficus pumila*.

Hanging Baskets

You may be keen to grow plants in the house, but feel you cannot because there is insufficient space to accommodate them. The surprising thing is that you often have much more room than you had ever imagined – it's above your head. In every building the largest area of free and unused space is above your head, and it is quite amazing the number of plants and other accessories that the inventive person can suspend from his ceilings. You can even use the open area under stairs, provided it isn't too dark. The fashion for hanging plants and baskets has had a strong grip on the American side of the Atlantic for a number of years and if fashion is to take its usual course it cannot be long before the vogue becomes more popular on the other continents.

To suspend the more conventional moss-lined hanging basket from the ceiling indoors would result in an almost continual shower bath, as it is the intention with moss-lined baskets that all surplus moisture should drain through the moss on to the floor below. Out of doors, where such baskets are mostly put to use, such an arrangement is fine, but continual drips do very little for the living room carpet! Therefore, you should seek out baskets that are designed with a drip tray attached to the base.

Such baskets are usually made of plastic and on the small side compared to the more conventional wire basket that is moss-lined before soil is inserted. Being much smaller they are obviously not going to hold the same amount of soil, so do not expect the same sort of results. The larger outdoor, or greenhouse-type, basket when filled with soil is quite capable

of sustaining a collection of six or more plants for an entire flowering season if feeding is not neglected.

For indoor baskets use a soil that contains a high proportion of peat and restrict the choice of plants to foliage ones rather than flowering types, such as fuchsias and hanging geraniums, both of which require very good light if they are to prosper and retain their flowers. This is not to say, however, that flowering plants are completely taboo, as excellent results can be achieved with baskets filled with columneas or aeschyanthus, provided a reasonable temperature can be maintained. With the smaller indoor basket the best effect will be had by planting with three or four plants of the same variety, rather than by grouping a collection of different species together. The plants will also be much easier to look after if they all need the same amount of water and fertilizer.

Green foliage plants can have a pleasingly cool appearance when seen suspended from the ceiling, and a fine choice for an individual planting is *Philodendron scandens* with its attractive heart-shaped glossy green leaves, allowed to trail rather than climb. Another that is suitable, provided it is never allowed to dry out, is the creeping fig, *Ficus pumila*. Keep it out of sunny windows and away from the drying heat of radiators. For cooler rooms that are well lit there is a wide selection of ivies with both green and variegated foliage, green-leaved ivies will tolerate dark situations and those with smaller leaves are best suited to planting in baskets. Another good subject for cool, well-lit conditions is the tradescantia of which there are many different forms and colours. Periodic pinching-out of leading shoots will ensure that your basket full of tradescantia plants will retain a pleasing rather than untidy shape. Trailing ferns, such as nephrolepis and *Asparagus sprengerii*, as well as trailing peperomias and chlorophytums are also suitable for hanging baskets.

A final word on baskets: the hook securing the basket to the ceiling must be firm enough to support the basket when the soil is wet and the basket is heaviest. And the basket should never be so high on the ceiling that maintainance becomes a problem – suspended just above head height is about right.

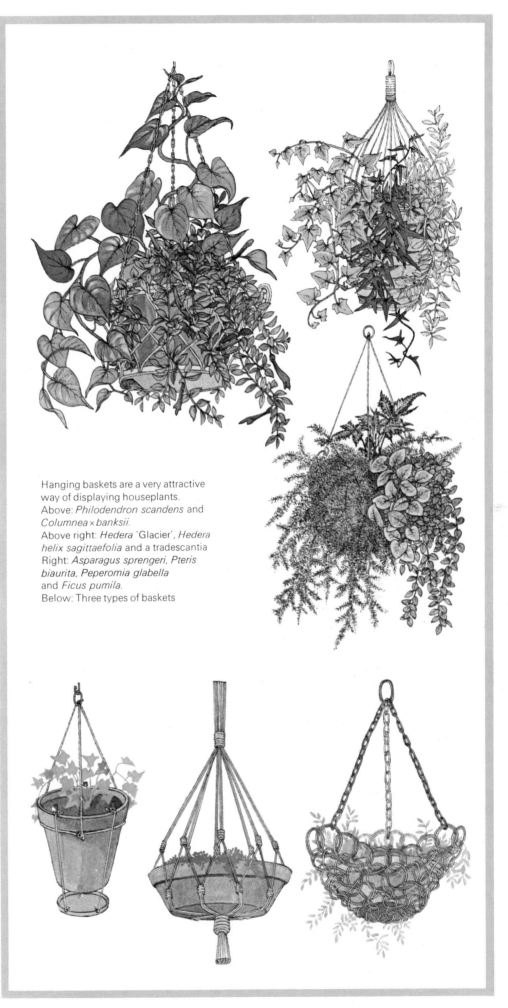

Hanging baskets are a very attractive way of displaying houseplants.
Above: *Philodendron scandens* and *Columnea × banksii*.
Above right: *Hedera* 'Glacier', *Hedera helix sagittaefolia* and a tradescantia
Right: *Asparagus sprengeri, Pteris biaurita, Peperomia glabella* and *Ficus pumila*.
Below: Three types of baskets

Perhaps the most difficult time for indoor plants is the settling in period immediately after they have been purchased, when they are introduced to room conditions. Therefore it is important in the beginning that they should enjoy the best possible location in the home, for the first few weeks at least. The average greenhouse for flowering plants offers light and airy conditions that are ideal for cyclamen, cinerarias and such like, and for the more delicate foliage plants warm, shaded and moist conditions are the order of the day. So it is important to check the requirements of plants being purchased in order that conditions as near the ideal as possible can be provided when plants are introduced to their new home. Over a period of three to four weeks most plants will adapt to the new environment and can then be moved to less suitable areas. But to place plants immediately after purchase in rooms that are totally alien to their needs will almost certainly result in them doing much less well than might be expected.

For foliage plants that have enjoyed the warm, moist and shaded conditions mentioned earlier, the warm, steamy bathroom is one of the best places to keep them during their initial few weeks indoors. It is, however, important that the temperature in the room should be maintained in the region of 18°C/65°F with reasonable consistency throughout the 24 hours of the day, as fluctuating temperatures can be particularly harmful to newly introduced plants.

Besides being an ideal home for new plants of a delicate nature, and a convalescent home for flagging plants, the bathroom with its warm and moist conditions is far and away the best permanent home for many of the more temperamental plants. In this respect almost all the plants in the vast aeroid family would be suitable and some of the exotic ferns from tropical forests, although care would have to be exercised when selecting plants to ensure that aeroids with potential growth suited to the size of the bathroom are chosen. The king of philodendrons, *P. eichleri*, produces its large leaves from a stout central stem and develops into a plant some 3m/10ft in height, with a spread of leaves taking in an area of similar diameter. With such a plant most bathrooms would be filled to capacity, and this is not quite what you are looking for when considering the

possibility of using plants to enhance the beauty of the homestead! Fortunately the foregoing plant is one of the exceptions and, for those with smaller bathrooms, should not put you off the possibility of growing plants of the aeroid family indoors.

There are a great many others of more modest dimension that are among the finest of indoor plants. And what better choice could there be than the bathroom plant, or sweetheart plant, *Philodendron scandens*, with its glossy green leaves that are heart-shaped in appearance. This plant, like the scindapsus and other aeroids with smaller leaves, can be adapted either to climb or trail, depending on what is required.

With aeroids you need not be restricted to purely foliage plants as the anthuriums with their long-lasting spathe flowers, mostly in shades of red, will give a fine display and need only a warm, moist and shaded situation in order to succeed. Where space is limited the best choice will be *A. scherzerianum*. Also with spathe flowers there is *Spathiphyllum wallisii*, the white spathes of which are produced almost throughout the year, and will surely be more numerous if the plants are grown in the steamy warmth of the bathroom.

If you are fortunate enough to have a say in the design of your house, persuade the architect to allow for recessed shelving in the bathroom. This is an excellent solution to finding shelf space for plants.

The only limiting factor concerning which plants can and cannot be used is the size of the bathroom, as almost all the foliage plants needing warm conditions will be suitable. However, there is one very important precaution that you should take, and that is to ensure that all plants are kept well out of harm's way when aersol sprays are being used, unless these are specifically intended for treating plants. Also, with the clouds of talcum powder that are usually prevalent in the bathroom it is necessary to clean the foliage of bathroom plants more frequently than those in other rooms. In most instances this can be done by placing the plant in the bathtub and spraying it over. The extra moisture will usually be to the benefit of the plant.

If the bathroom is the ideal place for the more tender, warm-loving plants, then the kitchen windowsill is the perfect spot for the

plants that prefer cooler locations. This applies in particular to the spring-flowering subjects, which seem to favour this location, not least the often problematical saintpaulia and the pelargoniums.

The fact that the kitchen has few, if any, heavy curtaining around its windows plays an important part in getting the best out of your plants. And, provided water is kept off leaves and flowers, the majority of our indoor plants will tolerate much more direct sunlight than you would believe possible. Exposing plants to very strong sunlight for long periods is, however, not advisable, and it will be better to remove plants that are likely to be harmed from the windowledge during the hottest part of the day.

To make the movement of plants a less tedious business it will help if they are all grown in a container of some kind so that the complete collection of plants may be transferred at one go. Windowledge troughs will give the windowledge a neat appearance, and plants will almost invariably do better when they are grouped together rather than when they are dotted about the room.

Troughs for plants can be utilized in several different ways, and there is no reason why they should not simply be put to use as pot holders with a selection of plants placed in them. An improvement on this is to place a 5cm/2in layer of gravel in the bottom of the container before setting in the plant pots. Thereafter the gravel should be kept moist, but the plant pots must at no time be allowed actually to stand in water. An alternative to gravel would be to fill the trough with moist peat, packing it up to the rims of the pots in which the plants are growing. Both methods will help to maintain a reasonable level of humidity around the plants, which is one of the most important requirements of all plants that are growing in relatively dry atmospheric conditions. Leaves should be sponged frequently to remove coatings of grease.

By leaving plants in their individual pots they may all be attended to as individuals when it comes to watering and feeding. However, if plants that are reasonably compatible in their watering and feeding needs are grouped together there is no reason why they should not be removed from their pots and planted individually in the trough. When planting in this way a soil containing a reasonably high proportion of peat should be used. Following planting, water must be given sparingly until plants are obviously established in the new medium, and at no time should water be given excessively as few of the troughs will have holes from which excess moisture may drain.

The average-size kitchen is seldom suited to the growing of larger plants, yet there is often the need for using plants to divide the working part of the kitchen from the small dining recess that is part of the kitchen area. Although there may be little chance of using large plants there is ample scope for using smaller plants placed on tiered shelving. In this respect, smaller plants in decorative pots placed among other small ornaments can be most effective, and the entire scene will be enhanced if some of the plants trail over the edges of the shelves.

Most of the plant pot holders offered for sale are more costly than the plants that are placed in them, but there are also the more reasonable plastic items. Some are attractive while others are not so appealing to the eye. For narrow kitchen shelves, however, there are some excellent plastic plant trays that are shallow enough not to be obtrusive.

Left: The feathery fronds of a fern provide a pleasing focal point. Here in the dining-room is an adiantum on the table and a *Nephrolepis* hanging above.

Left above: Ferns look attractive in a bathroom and thrive in the humid atmosphere.

Above: Hanging baskets containing foliage plants are a decorative and unusual way of dividing the kitchen from the eating area.

Right: Succulents on a bathroom windowsill.

Far right: *Howeia forsteriana*, tulips, calatheas, ferns and primula surround a bathtub

There is nothing less pleasing than the sight of dust-laden plants fighting a losing battle to survive in a corner of a room that is badly lighted and devoid of windows. Plants are attractive features in themselves, and their attraction will be heightened if they are given an important position in which to grow and light to show off their beauty.

By going to some expense and fitting special cabinets with built-in lighting, it is possible for many plants to be grown entirely under artificial light conditions, with no help whatsoever from natural daylight. Alternatively, plants may be grown on shelves placed one above the other and spaced about 60cm/2ft apart with lighting on the undersides of the upper shelves. For such situations, Grolux tubes will give the best results as the light from these will both improve the appearance of the plants as well as improve their growth. But it must be remembered that the further the light source is from the plant the less effective it will become. By trial and error you will find that a great many plants are suited to this form of culture. The saintpaulia (African Violet) does especially well and may be had in flower throughout the year, with a collection of different varieties.

In larger rooms where bolder plants are in use, the standard warm white fluorescent tube will be satisfactory provided it is not attached

Lighting plants for effect

Plant collections are often seen at their best when darkness descends and lights are switched on above them – unsightly pots and plant stems are lost in the darker, lower area of the plants, and flowers and foliage are highlighted. It is worth the trouble being taken to ensure that indoor plants are provided with artificial lighting that will set them off to best advantage.

Should adaptability be an important advantage as far as lighting is concerned it is advisable to use spotlights that can be adjusted much more readily than fixed light fittings. Spotlights can be used to augment the more permanent lighting, and may be used to highlight particular plants in a collection. But it is important that such lights should not be placed too close to the plants as there is every possibility that foliage will be damaged by the heat that is generated.

It almost goes without saying that almost anywhere that plants may be indoors there will also be moisture about, and any light installations that are provided in the vicinity of plants should be undertaken with the problem of dampness in mind. It may be necessary, for example, to have the electrical wiring concealed in the peat in which the plant pots are plunged, which will entail use of heavy duty cable that is impervious to moisture, such as that sold for outdoor use.

to a high ceiling that is too far away from the plants to be effective. Where the natural light source is very poor and plants are more dependent on artificial, it will be necessary for the lighting to be switched on for at least 12 hours each day. Although coloured lights may improve the appearance of some plants it is really very much better to avoid strong colours as they can have very odd effects on the appearance of some plants.

Even the humble and solitary plant on the windowsill can have its appearance and performance enhanced by placing it under a wall or table lamp during the evening. But bear in mind when lighting plants for effect for a particular occasion, it is better to err on the side of too little light rather than too much. Harsh lighting that is overdone is much less effective than softer lighting that gives the plants in a collection an air of mystery.

Grouping plants

Besides being more appealing to the eye, plants that are grown together in a group will almost invariably be much more satisfactory in respect of growth.

All sorts of containers may be used for this purpose, from the very cheap plastic one holding a few small plants to the more ambitious affair where plants may be grown to quite majestic proportions. The smaller container is the sort of thing that you receive as a gift and enjoy for 12 months or so, by which time the plants will either have died off, or they will have begun to outgrow the container. Plants dying off is usually the result of too much water. The roots rot and die, soon to be followed by leaves turning yellow and falling off. When plants become overgrown in smaller containers the obvious remedy is to remove them from the pot and to plant them up individually in appropriate-sized pots. Alternatively they may be removed from the container and the roots teased apart to form individual plants which can be planted up with a little more space in a larger decorative plant bowl.

Although few of the plant bowls purchased ready-filled with plants will have drainage holes in the bottom, it is, nevertheless, of the utmost importance that all such containers should be placed on a protective mat of some kind and not directly onto tables or other furniture. From almost all such containers there will be a certain amount of moisture seepage that will damage most wood surfaces on which they are placed.

If you are planting your own container with plants the best beginning will be to acquire an attractive container of reasonable depth, and of a size that will accommodate a reasonable number of plants without undue crowding. The depth of the container should be able to take the rootball of the plants without need for it to be reduced in size by removing surplus soil. Any mutilation of the root system of growing plants will cause them to have a setback from which they may not recover.

Prior to planting the container should be filled with a drainage layer of coarse gravel and peaty soil mix and the plants should then be individually planted into it, each plant being firmed into position before the next is introduced. At all costs the temptation to overcrowd plants should be resisted, as a container filled with too many plants seldom looks attractive, and the plants themselves will do less well as a result of overcrowding. When planting, keep in mind the appearance of the planted bowl some weeks after planting and not the immediate effect that has been created.

The first requirement in choosing the plants is to select those which have the same cultural needs in respect of soil, humidity, light and watering. The plants should form a pleasing mixture of green and variegated or colourful foliage, with contrast in leaf shapes, and the arrangement show a balance of tall, medium and shorter plants. Use of the odd one or two flowering plants will naturally give the planting a more colourful appearance, but flowering subjects should be used sparingly as their life is much more limited than the majority of foliage plants and their continual replacement can be a costly business.

Below: A Kentia palm and chlorophytum complement the green and white decor of this room.
Opposite Chlorophytum and *Cissus antarctica* are grouped in a beautiful oriental urn

To facilitate the replacement of flowering plants it is often advisable to leave them in their growing pots and to plunge the pots to their rims in the surrounding medium. Treated in this way the flowering plants can be individually watered. This is a help as many may require more frequent watering than the other plants in the arrangement.

On slightly grander scale there are many plastic and fibreglass containers available that range from 45-90cm/1½-3ft in diameter, many of which have built-in capillary watering systems. The capillary watering container has an internal platform near the base of the container on which the soil is placed, and below which there is a water reservoir. One end of a water-conducting wick lies in the water while the other end is in contact with the soil. As the soil dries out water is drawn from the reservoir in the bottom of the container, so making the job of watering comparatively simple and much less hit-and-miss than it normally is. For topping up the water supply, a tube runs through the soil and directly into the reservoir. Another tube which runs through the soil into the reservoir has a level indicator and allows you to check the water level.

In spite of all these apparent refinements, however, many indoor plant growers have very little success with capillary watering units. The main reason for failure is overwatering which is caused by allowing the reservoir to remain permanently topped up with water. It is very much more satisfactory to allow the soil to dry out completely and to remain dry for at least four days before replenishing the reservoir. Allowing the reservoir to dry out will help aerate the soil and prevent it becoming waterlogged.

When planting the large containers it is again important to ensure that the plants are not overcrowded, and possibly more important to ensure that reasonably mature plants are used. A large container with a hotch-potch of small plants has much less appeal than the same container filled with a selection of fewer plants of reasonable size. Also, filling the container with

Below: *Philodendron scandens, Cordyline terminalis* and *Rhoicissus rhomboidea*. Right: *Ficus* 'Black Prince', *F. benjamina, F. pumila* and *F. radicans*. Illustration left: *Aglaonema* 'Silver King', *Monstera deliciosa, Ficus elastica* and *Ananas comus* 'Variegatus'. Illustration right: tradescantia, *Maranta leuconeura massangeana, Begonia rex* and *Peperomia magnoliaefolia*

several plants of one variety will present a more pleasing picture, in some locations, than the same container filled with a general mixture. In this respect *Sansevieria trifasciata* 'Laurentii' is especially fine, as is *Schefflera actinophylla* with its large green-fingered leaves. The last mentioned, the taller-growing ficus varieties and *Philodendron hastatum* are particularly suitable if attaining height with the plant arrangement is an important factor.

Capillary watering containers and the use of larger plants in them will inevitably involve a considerable cash outlay, so the well-being of the plants is of particular importance. Consequently they must enjoy the best possible conditions. Plants need good light in which to grow and agreeable warmth that is kept at a fairly constant level. In all new ventures with indoor plants it is wise not to be too ambitious in the use of delicate plants until you have acquired some knowledge of how they are likely to do. Learn with the easier ones before becoming too adventurous is the best policy.

Where space is available indoors you could well be more ambitious with the grouping of plants as there will be scope for larger groups in containers that can be an integral part of the architectural design of the house. Such features can be let into the floor, or they may run the length of the edge of the upper level in a split-level room, possibly with plants trailing over the edge to form a feature in both parts of the room. In large containers you might like to concentrate on one family of plants. In this respect the bromeliad family could be considered as they are easy to manage, with foliage of a fascinating range of both colour and shape. Also, the colourful bracts can be expected at any time of the year. To give added height to the grouping make up a bromeliad tree by using an old tree trunk of pleasing shape and, with moss and wire, attach the plants to the tree. Simply by spraying the plant and moss with water regularly the bromeliad tree will be an intriguing feature indoors.

Window displays

One of the difficulties with window displays often is the problem of deciding for whom the display is intended – the owner or the man in the street looking in. But however the display is arranged, the looker-in is likely to get the best from it, as almost all plants will quite quickly turn their leaves to the natural light source. The occasional twist of the pot will, of course, help to improve the internal appearance of the window arrangement. Twisting the pot in this way will also keep the more rounded type of plant, such as *Peperomia caperata*, looking less lop-sided.

Before arranging a window display, take into account the light requirements of the plant you intend to use, as there is nothing to be gained from putting shade-loving marantas in window locations that will expose them to the full, albeit filtered, rays of the sun. Similarly, there would be little point in putting sun-loving crotons in windows that face due north. Also, if there is nothing more than a simple windowledge for placing plants on, ensure that radiators immediately below the windowledge are not going to damage plants placed immediately above them. Hot air ascending from room heaters will be harmful to almost all potted plants, and the hot, dry conditions created will be a perfect breeding place for such pests as red spider. One way of overcoming the problem is to place a shelf on top of the radiator which will deflect hot air from the plants.

Where shelf space around the window is limited, a great deal can be done to increase the potential plant area by putting plants in hanging pots. Hanging baskets have been mentioned elsewhere, but in most instances these would be much too large for the smaller window. However, there is no reason why conventional plant pot covers should not be

Opposite: Begonias, chlorophytum, pelargoniums, saintpaulias and tradescantia in an unusual three-tiered window display case, specially built for a bay window.
Below left: *Cissus antarctica* in a recessed window.
Above: Impatiens provides colour on a windowsill

adapted to become hanging planters. This is done by drilling three holes spaced at equal distance around the rim of the pot cover just below the lip, and fitting three slender chains or nylon string from which the plant in its pot can be suspended in the pot cover. Not having holes in the bottom, the pot cover will collect any surplus water that drains through the growing pot after watering. There are any number of attractive indoor plants that are well suited to this sort of treatment; almost all the ivies, *Philodendron scandens*, *Rhoicissus rhomboidea* and columneas.

Many of the trailing green-foliaged plants grow equally well when climbing a supporting stake or trellis, and the majority are sold as climbing plants. They are sold in this way simply because it is more practical for the producer of the plant to control them when they are neatly tied in to a support of some kind. Fortunately for the householder, the majority of the smaller-leaved plants can be carefully removed from their supports and allowed to trail down more naturally. Following removal from the support the plant leaves will have an unnatural appearance, but will quickly adjust to the new position as they turn their leaves to the light source.

Two trailing plants that are not too bulky, so not so demanding in respect of space, are *Saxifraga stolonifera* (Mother of Thousands) and *Ceropegia woodii* (Hearts Entangled), both of which will trail very effectively. The ceropegia has small heart-shaped leaves that are attached to very slender stems that hang straight downwards from the pot and may be several metres in length. Trailing *Sedum sieboldii* is another good choice.

For the narrow windowledge, trough-type containers are excellent as they blend more naturally and you can get many more plants into them, certainly more than if the container had a circular shape. Also with trough-type containers it is possible to butt them one to the other so that a continual display along the windowsill is possible. Having several smaller troughs is often better than one very long one, as you can give the plants in the smaller containers more individual treatment. If there should be a major disaster then only a small section of the plant collection is affected. Also, with a number of small containers rather than one very large one their removal will be a much simpler task when such essential operations as window-cleaning become necessary. A further advantage with a collection of containers is that a range of plants needing very different treatment in respect of soil, watering and feeding could be grown alongside one another; for example, one of the troughs on the windowsill could be devoted to growing cacti or other succulents.

Often enough the houseplant grower wishing to make the window area a special feature of the room will need a selection of larger plants at either side, to frame the picture as it were. The size of such plants will, to some extent, be dictated by the area and the height of the window area. But whatever the size of the plant, it is important that any framework to which they may be attached (trellis, for example) should be free-standing and not attached to the wall of the room, as plants will then in effect become part of the room. While the plant is growing trouble-free this sort of situation may be all very well, but if pests, for example, become a problem plants should be mobile enough to be moved outside and thoroughly sprayed over.

There is no doubt whatsoever that the best indoor plants are grown in the rooms that have the largest window area in relation to the size of the room, and that the best plants in such rooms will be growing in the vicinity of the window. Bay windows that are glassed to the floor are probably best of all as there is reasonable scope with such windows for the artistic plant grower to create a really eye-catching array of plants. In such window areas there is an environment that is as near to that of a greenhouse as is ever likely to be in the home. And with a little extra effort the floor area of such windows can be waterproofed so that plants in the window recess can be watered more freely.

Besides the bolder display on the floor there is also the possibility of fixing shelves across the window on which a wide selection of both foliage and flowering plants may be grown. Also, to keep the area surrounding plants cleaner and more agreeable for the plants themselves a metal container fitting exactly into the window recess can be made. If the container is filled with moist peat into which the plant pots can be plunged the resultant plant growth could just possibly prove to be a tiny bit astonishing.

If the job is to be done properly it will also be necessary to fit blinds to the window. These can be drawn to protect more tender plants from the full effect of the sun's rays on warmer days.

Drawing blinds in the evening will protect plants from cold draughts. The same applies on colder days as the leaves of plants should not touch the glass. Keeping plant leaves away from the glass on very sunny days is an equally important precaution, as they can very easily be scorched. When the curtains are drawn in the evening the plants should be taken from the window area, or draw the curtains between the plants and the glass. This will ensure that the plant collection is not unduly exposed to colder conditions.

Make your view more exciting. In the photograph, right, cinerarias and *Philodendron scandens* are on the shelf, while *Rhoicissus rhomboidea* and *Hedera helix* 'Chicago' are on the windowsill. Far right, an adiantum grows in the hanging basket and *Hedera helix canariensis* and an azalea lend colour and texture

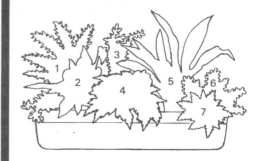

For a north-facing window, try an arrangement such as that below (key above): 1. *Nephrolepis cordifolia*, 2. anthurium, 3. *Ficus pumila*, 4. begonia, 5. *Aspidistra elatior*, 6. *Adiantum cuneatum*. 7. *Begonia rex*. For a south-facing window, below right, you could include (key below): 1. sansevieria, 2. impatiens, 3. tulips, 4. *Jasminum polyanthum*, 5. *Primula vulgaris*, 6. cyclamen, 7. *Primula denticulata*, 8. hedera

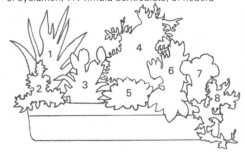

CHAPTER 3
INDOOR PLANT GARDENS

Growing plants indoors can be just
as adventurous as cultivating
them in the garden, the
main differences being in the size of
individual features. The
possibilities, however, are wide.
With proper care and attention,
you can grow such things as
rock plants, rose trees, orchids, bulbs,
small conifers, indoor fruits
and a wide range of flowering and
foliage houseplants. Do not be afraid
to experiment—any container
which will hold a little soil is a
possible garden for plants.

B

Bottle gardens

Bottle gardens are an interesting variant on the terrarium and as long as the plants inside have the right soil and moisture content, with sufficient overhead light, they are foolproof.

Almost any type of bottle can be used provided the glass is clear. Dark brown glass is not suitable. The range includes sweet jars, magnum champagne bottles, cider jars, chemist's bottles and carboys. The last two, being larger, give plenty of scope and when fitted with a lamp holder and shade (instead of a cork or stopper) make excellent hall lamps. The light (a 60 watt lamp) should be on 6-7 hours daily for best effects. The gardens inside remain attractive – without need for watering – about three years, when the growth of some plants will have become too rampant. They should then be emptied, washed out and replanted.

The Tools

Since one cannot normally get a hand inside a carboy, special planting tools are required. These can be made at home. Lash a dessert-spoon firmly to a bamboo cane of sufficient length to extend 15-23cm/6-9in above the neck of the bottle. Prepare another using a dinner fork and a third having one end firmly wedged into the hole running through an empty spool of thread.

Other requirements are some good potting mixture such as loam/sand/peat in equal quantities, plus a little crushed charcoal, some small pieces of moss or bark (for ornamental effect

Tools for planting a bottle garden can be made at home: a spoon and a fork tied on to bamboo canes and an empty thread spool on the end of a third cane. As shown in the illustration, use the thread spool to tamp down the soil mixture in the bottle. Drop in small rooted plants and plant them with the spoon and fork

but not obligatory), a small watering can or a length of narrow plastic tubing and a number of small rooted plants.

Planting

Make sure the carboy is clean and dry and then, using a funnel, pour enough dryish soil through the opening to come a third of the way up the carboy.

Next, using the cane as a handle, tamp the mixture firm and even with the thread spool.

Small rooted plants, washed free of soil, may then be dropped inside and planted with the aid of the spoon and fork. Firm round the roots with the spoon. Pieces of bark or moss may be added to enhance the general effect. Add a little water, from a can or via a piece of rubber tubing so that it trickles down the sides but slowly so that the soil does not splash up on to the sides of the bottle. This moistens the soil and cleans the glass at the same time. Stopper the jar and leave until next day.

The following morning will probably find the carboy misted over inside, so remove the stopper but replace it when the glass has cleared. It will probably be necessary to repeat the procedure for several days, but eventually the stopper can be left in place permanently. Temperature changes early morning and evening may cause temporary misting but if this persists less than an hour it can be ignored.

Stand the carboy in a light sunless position – sun mists the glass immediately – such as a north window; or else treat it as a lamp standard for use in a less favourable position.

Other Containers

Sweet jars made of glass can be planted and used in an upright position but look more attractive when laid on their sides. This also allows greater scope for planting although the choice of material is naturally narrowed. Anything more than 8-10cm/3-4in high is too tall.

A glass goldfish bowl or a bell jar – like those used by gardeners for raising small quantities of cuttings – can be inverted over a dish garden made up as suggested on p. 134-9 (Miniature Gardens). Or the goldfish bowl could hold an African violet when used the right way up. Either way attractive table pieces can be made with such containers with the plants inside well protected from draughts.

The Plants

Plants most likely to succeed within the confines of a stoppered bottle are those found naturally in moist or shady situations. There are more of these than is generally realized, including the seaweed-like selaginellas (which soon perish in dry air), mosses, baby ferns, small-leaved ivies, the trailing *Pellionia pulchra* which has round silvery leaves with green vein markings, tradescantias (as long as these are kept in check), the gold-speckled *Dracaena godseffiana* or a small red-foliaged variety of dracaena for a central position, the squat *Sansevieria hahnii* and any of the handsomely leaf-patterned fittonias.

Such low growing bromeliads as *Cryptanthus bivittatus minor* or *C. fosterianus* make useful front row plants, forming flat rosettes of crinkly, variously striated and patterned leaves.

Few flowering plants, however, are likely to succeed, although African violets may continue in bloom for a time and most peperomias will produce their not very spectacular mouse-tail, brown spikes.

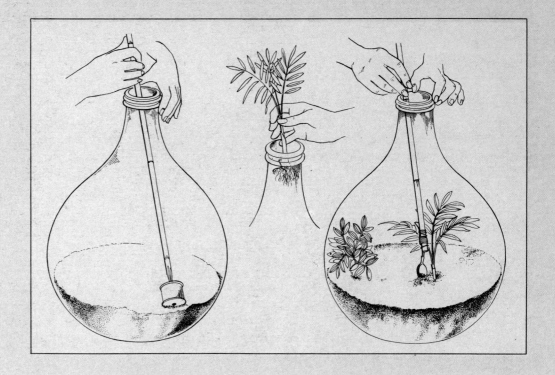

Terrariums and vivariums

In 1829, Nathaniel Ward, a London physician, accidentally discovered that plants could be successfully grown in a closed glass case. Water evaporated from the leaves during transpiration, condensed on the glass and trickled down its sides to be reabsorbed by the roots. It was his belief that mosses and ferns so imprisoned might exist for a century without extra watering.

The idea was soon developed by Victorian gardeners. Wardian cases became the 'in' thing and were produced in various shapes and sizes – often large and extremely elaborate. Sometimes they were built onto the house, usually on the north side with a communicating window 'peep-through', and had heating and elaborate rock work containing pockets to take ferns and similar plants. Simple, sealed box-like glass cases were also extensively used by plant collectors for the transportation of tender specimens.

The principle is highly suitable for the growing of ferns, mosses, selaginellas and similar plants requiring a humid atmosphere and moist growing conditions. The size of the container is immaterial as long as it is transparent, although obviously more interesting effects can be obtained in the larger sizes.

It is also possible to use closed glass cases for plants which have to be kept dry for most or part of the year, such as cacti and succulents, and the naturalist may like to introduce a few small lizards and other reptiles which like dry conditions. Be sure to safeguard these against escape, however, with a perforated lid or top on the vivarium.

Their Place in the Home

Elaborate effects can be created in homes and offices by installing large plant cases as permanent fixtures. These should have sliding glass doors in front and if provided with heat and lighting they will even succeed in dark recesses or corridors. They can also be fixed above TV sets (heat from the latter seems to benefit plants) or made into free-standing pedestal containers. It is also possible to purchase ready-made portable frames of clear plastic, light to handle and with adjustable side vents. These may be round, square or oblong and are ideal for broad window sills or tables. Some are of sufficient height to take quite tall flowering plants.

On a simpler scale old aquaria can be used as containers, or inverted bell jars, a brandy snifter for tiny specimens, the glass top of an old gas street lamp, an open goldfish bowl, bottles (see p. 132) or indeed practically any transparent container.

Planting

Terrariums can be planted up in a variety of ways. A 'dry wall' at the back of an aquarium or similar oblong container, for example, makes a pleasing background for African violets (Saintpaulia). Use flat pieces of stone, setting these in lines one above another – like courses of bricks – with an inch of soil mixture between each layer. A plant (turned from its pot) should be inserted sideways here and there between the stones – so that it faces front – as the work proceeds, and to ensure stability let each stone tip very slightly towards the back of the container. Keep the front of the tank clear, except for a layer of sand or granite chippings, with perhaps one African violet or a small fern to break its flatness.

Houseplants with different shaped leaves and textures and variously coloured can be planted in a peat/sand/loam mixture (equal parts) to suggest a jungle effect. Keep the tallest specimens towards the back and very small ones in the foreground. Here again, open spaces should be left to suggest forest glades. Suitable plants for such compositions are calatheas, the aquatic grasslike *Acorus gramineus pusillus* (sweet flag) with stiff green and white leaves

(8cm/3in) and the slightly taller, but also grasslike, *Carex morrowii*, tiny red-leaved dracaenas, *Helxine soleirolii*, selaginella and small ferns.

Flowering Plants

The taller clear plastic containers can be used to accommodate larger house plants like *Begonia rex*, codiaeums, and similar leafy subjects, with flowering plants like azaleas, primulas and solanums in season. These can be kept in pots, plunged in peat or hidden by rocks and mixture. Protected from draughts and sudden chills they grow luxuriantly, needing only careful watering, the removal of old leaves and occasional feeding with water soluble fertilizer pills or liquid fertilizer.

Cactus Gardens

Cactus gardens look best against a background of blue sky and desert, so cut a picture out of a book or paint such a scene and stick it along the back of an aquarium. Put a generous layer of sand over the bottom with a few pieces of rock and plant small desert cacti, turned from their pots, in the sand. Cacti gardens require a fair amount of water during the growing season but little or none in winter.

Bottle gardens, which provide a humid atmosphere
and moist growing conditions, can be any shape
or size. Those shown here contain saintpaulias,
cymbidium orchids, bromeliads, ferns,
codiaeum, pileas, hederas, marantas and
tradescantias

Unusual containers

Hanging Bottles

This is a method which can be adopted for growing plants of a semi-woody nature like dwarf fuchsias, pelargoniums, plectranthus, coleus and heliotrope in confined areas. As the plants are hanging they do not take valuable sill space. It is also suitable for growing mint, thyme and sage in a kitchen window.

The best bottles for the purpose are those which have held wine and have thick rims and inward-pointed domed bases. Start by making a hole about 2.5cm/1in across with a diamond or similar instrument in the centre of the dome. Thread a stout piece of wire right through the bottle and hook one end securely over the base. There should be sufficient wire left to run through to the top and be twisted into a curved handle for hanging – like a coat hanger.

Turn the bottle upside-down and half fill it with peat, sand and sifted loam in equal proportions. Wedge two or three rooted cuttings into the base opening and then turn the bottle the right way up so that the soil drops and anchors the plants. Water through the neck opening and hang the bottle in a light window. Although the plants hang down at first they soon turn and start to grow upwards. In a few months the bottle will be completely masked.

Parsley and Herb Pots

Parsley is a herb continually in demand and since it is not always possible to purchase fresh supplies, those without gardens should grow some in their kitchens.

The odd plant can be kept in a flower pot, but for larger quantities a more interesting method is to install a parsley pot. These are made of terracotta and shaped like a chimney, with a solid base and lots of 1.25cm/½in holes all round the sides. They arrive with a large saucer which is kept with a little water in the bottom, which saves trouble.

The seed is sown in a seed tray or pan of soil mixture and when the seedlings are large enough to handle they are carefully transplanted. Fill the parsley pot with a good potting mixture or use equal parts of coarse sand, peat and sifted loam and gently insert a plantlet through each hole plus three or four in the top. Stand in a light place. Water regularly (via the saucer) and the plants grow rapidly.

Another method is to plant the seedlings in tower pots – the kind sold for strawberries and houseplants. These come in 23cm/9in sections with two lipped openings about 5cm/2in across and are made of white or black plastic. Fill them with soil and fit one inside another to a con-

venient height, twisting them round so that one set of lipped openings alternates with those of the section above. They take up very little space but hold a surprising number of parsley plants. Alternatively grow a different kind of herb in each opening, except mint which is too rampant and will soon swamp all others.

Small mixed herb gardens can also be made up in old casserole or vegetable dishes and kept on a windowsill for ornament and picking. In light basement wells, strawberry jars – which are like parsley pots but with fewer and larger holes – are suitable for mixed herbs.

Hyacinths on Newspaper

Hyacinths grown on newspaper are invariably successful for the paper does not readily dry out and is easy for roots to penetrate. The papers should be soaked and then squeezed to remove surplus water, after which the pulp should be broken up into small pieces, about the size of a walnut.

Half fill a bulb bowl with these, plus a few pieces of lump charcoal and stand the bulbs closely on top without touching. Work more paper pieces between them until only the noses of the bulbs show. The paper must not be pressed down hard or it will form a hard layer like papier mâché which the roots cannot penetrate.

Wrap the bowls in black polyethylene or plastic and keep them in a cool place (about 4.4°C/40°F) for nine weeks. Then take them

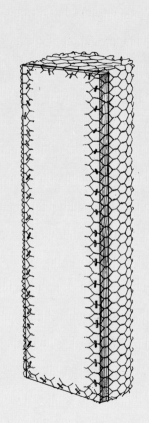

A log garden can be made using a plank of wood. Cover one side of the log with damp sphagnum moss, doming it up to make a semi-circle and secure it with wire netting. Staple the wire at the back of the plank to hold the moss firmly. Insert small plants such as achimenes (as here) small bromeliads and dwarf begonias in the front. Fix a hook in the top to hang the log garden. To water immerse the log in tepid water for 10 to 20 minutes. Another unusual container can be made very simply by inverting a glass fish bowl over a pan of peat or soil. African Violets, as here, grow well under this dome

out, topdress the paper with moist peat, sow some grass seed on top and place them in a light but cool place (10°C/50°F) until the leaves are well out of the bulbs and the flower buds show. They can then go into warmer rooms to flower.

Gardens on Bricks

Builder's bricks with holes through them (for taking cables etc.) make suitable containers for houseleeks (sempervivums) and sedums. Stand them on a flat surface, fill the holes with a suit-able soil mixture, insert a plant in each hole and water by spraying over the foliage as required.

Indoor Standards

With a little patience and by constantly nip-ping out unwanted shoots, attractive little evergreen standards can be grown in large pots. Such plants as rosemary and santolina as well as bay (*Laurus nobilis*) and box react well to cutting and can be trained to globes, pyramids and spirals by careful nipping.

A parsley pot, as above, made of terracotta and shaped like a chimney, will ensure there is a lot of parsley on hand for cooking. The seed is sown in a seed tray and then transplanted to the pot. Right: a basket full of ivy makes a green display in a dull corner

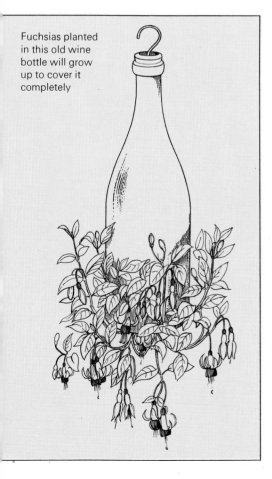

Fuchsias planted in this old wine bottle will grow up to cover it completely

Miniature gardens

Collecting small objects appeals to many people – things like tiny animals, car models, dolls' house furniture or, for gardeners, lilliputian plants and miniature gardens. The latter have special appeal because they are alive and consequently always changing.

Few containers are too small to accommodate at least one or two plants and I have seen charming compositions in teacups and brandy snifters. Greater variety and more artistic effects, however, require something larger, such as a vegetable dish or an old sink.

SINK GARDENS

The first miniature garden made in a sink was exhibited at the Chelsea Flower Show in 1923. It caused a sensation and suddenly everybody contracted sink mania. In the Twenties, thousands of natural stone sinks were broken up and discarded in favour of the then fashionable yellow glaze or deep white butler's sinks. Builders at that time were only too glad to give away objects which are now scarce and valuable. It is, however, possible to make something similar of concrete; or, as the yellow and white types are now being ousted in their turn by stainless steel or moulded units, maybe pick up one of these for a song.

To give them a more attractive appearance, the outsides of the sinks should be camouflaged so that they look old and matured. This is the method.

Paint the sides, tops and 2.5cm/1in down inside with strong industrial glue. Allow this to dry to a tacky consistency, which should take about 20 minutes. Meantime, mix together equal parts of coarse builder's sand, peat and cement and then add a *little* water so that the mixture is just moist. If it is too wet it will seep down without adhering to the sides.

Spread this mixture thinly all over the gummed areas, starting at the bottom and working upwards, also overlapping the top and 2.5cm/1in down inside. If the layer is too thick it will slip down from the sink. Knead it to leave a rugged appearance.

When the material has set, paint it over with cow-manure and water, or sour milk, or a seaweed fertilizer to encourage moss and algae to grow and thus give it a mature appearance.

Any spare mixture can be moulded into small artificial rocks, making holes here and there in these with the thumb to take such plants as house-leeks (sempervivums) and sedums.

Siting

Heavy containers like sinks and troughs should be stood on a firm base, either at ground level or raised on piers of brick or stone. Keep them in a light place such as a window or glass roofed extension. The plug hole at the base is an insurance against overwatering but not essential indoors if care is taken. If you decide to leave it, cover the hole with wire mesh and stones or crocks and let the sink tilt very slightly towards this outlet. A plant pot or dish stood underneath will catch any drips.

Smaller containers fashioned from wood, terracotta, porcelain, glassfibre and the like can be stood on windowsills, small tables or special plant stands – always in a good light or where artificial illumination can be provided.

Planting

Start by covering the base of the container with 1.25–2cm/$\frac{1}{2}$–$\frac{3}{4}$in of drainage material, such as broken crocks or pebbles. Over this spread some sort of roughage, e.g. dry leaves, rough peat, skimmings of old turf and similar debris. Its purpose is to form a barrier between the mixture above and the drainage crocks below.

Naturally, soil composition varies according to the type of plants grown, but for general purposes a good mix can be made using the following ingredients: 1 part by bulk good quality sifted loam; 1 part by bulk silver sand; 1 part by bulk decayed leaf soil (oak or beech for preference) or moist peat; 1 part by bulk gritty material like small granite chippings or crushed brick.

The last ingredient keeps the soil open and assists drainage. When thoroughly mixed the mixture should feel springy and be just moist.

A porous mixture well supplied with humus is suitable for many plants including lime lovers but those which prefer acid conditions like

Succulent gardens, left and above, planted in shallow decorative bowls, are interesting and unusual

Plant each specimen firmly, preferably from pots so that there is little root disturbance. Some will go in sideways between rocks – like sempervivums or the mauve-flowered *Ramonda myconi* (also known as *R. pyrenaica*). Others, such as aubrieta and alpine phlox, can be planted near the edges of the sink so that the flowers trail over its sides. When all is complete water gently and sprinkle granite chippings on the bare soil between limestone rocks or use tiny pebbles amongst sandstone rocks. Besides giving the sink a finishing touch, stones keep the soil cool, inhibit weeds and lessen moisture losses.

Formal Gardens

Formal gardens in miniature can be copies of larger ones outdoors. A good craftsman can copy almost any feature, making paths, fences, fountains, furniture and the like to make them more realistic. Rose gardens are particularly popular with flagged paths, sundials, pergolas and summerhouses, and there are real miniature roses available from growers, both as bush and standard types. Another idea is to make a water garden complete with tiny pool (a glass salt cellar will do or it can be moulded from concrete) surrounded by grass and flowers and even a cottage at one end. There are no water-

Left: A bottle garden creates a miniature world, here planted with a small trailing plant, palm and bromeliad.
Below: An open seed propagator can be used to make a miniature garden, possibly containing tradescantia, zebrina and ferns

heathers, pernettyias, gentians and dwarf rhododendrons need two parts of peat (instead of one) in the general mixture. Succulents, on the other hand, require two parts sand and one part broken lump charcoal added to the basic mixture.

Fill the sink with the mixture to within 2.5cm/1in below the rim, inserting pieces of rock as the work proceeds. Some rocks may extend well above the height of the container with soil packed between to provide extra depth and more planting areas. Informal gardens should be left at different levels, to suggest a range of mountain peaks. Rocks with stratification lines should be laid correctly, flat or nearly so as in nature.

Informal Gardens

A dwarf conifer should set the scale for an informal miniature garden and, generally speaking, will be the tallest plant it contains. Real pygmies are the aim, not small specimens of what will become large shrubs in a few years time. Similarly with the plants – they must be naturally miniature, not tiny sprigs of fairly large alpines.

lilies small enough for the pool but the little white-flowered frogbit (*Hydrocharis morsusranae*) or a scrap of floating Fairy Moss (*Azolla*) make good substitutes.

Grass sown in the normal way will soon germinate in a sink garden and can be kept short with scissors. Clever fingers can make archways, well heads, steps and fences (matches can act as palings). Plan the garden on one or several levels or it can be given over entirely to one kind of plant, such as gentians or sempervivums.

Aftercare All miniature gardens need careful watering and they should be regularly weeded. Cut back excessive growth, particularly on trailing plants, also dead flowers and leaves. Occasional feeding is beneficial in summer, using a mild proprietary fertilizer.

DISH GARDENS

The general principles of making and planting these are similiar to those of sink gardens except that those destined to stand on polished surfaces should not be made of porous material or have drainage holes unless stood on a drip tray.

All kinds of containers are permissable – porcelain bowls, baking tins, bulb bowls, vegetable or meat dishes, basins, alpine pans, even a large flower pot cut in half lengthwise could be used.

The plants used must be miniatures yet even so will probably outgrow the container in a few years. When they seem overcrowded empty the bowl, break them up and start again.

Aftercare Miniature gardens need good light at all times and careful watering. If you overdo the last, turn the container on its side for a time to allow surplus moisture to drain away. In summer the gardens benefit from a sojurn outdoors or should be sprayed over frequently with soft water at room temperature. Most require cool growing conditions with temperatures between 4-15°C/40-60°F.

Above: Plant a bonsai juniper in a shallow tray and add a few rocks and ground cover. Keep the arrangement simple to set off the graceful miniature tree.
Left: Good drainage is essential, so cover the base of the container with broken crocks or pebbles, then with dry leaves or rough peat, and finally a good soil mix. The bonsai cypress in the centre of this garden is surrounded by aubrieta, miniature pelargoniums, sempervivums, draba and asperula, and phlox 'Blue Eyes' is trailing over the side

137

AND NOW THE PLANTS

Conifers

Chamaecyparis obtusa 'Caespitosa' makes a rounded bun-shaped bush, with its light green foliage sprays arranged in seashell-shapes. It is one of the smallest conifers known and always miniature. Others in this group are *C.o.* 'Flabelliformis', also globular and extremely slow growing and green; *C.o.* 'Intermedia' has loose sprays but is similar; *C.o.* 'Minima' with tightly packed, moss-like sprays is considered to be the smallest conifer of its kind (8cm/3in at 10 years); and *C.o.* 'Snow' has blue-grey foliage tipped with white and is bun-shaped. Most of these only grow to about 25cm/10in in 10 years.

Cryptomeria japonica 'Bandai-sugi' has a compact habit, becoming lighter and more spreading with age. Clusters of pendulous leafy branches and leaves which are pale green in spring but bronzy-red in winter. Height 25cm/10in.

Juniperus communis 'Compressa' is a delightful little juniper with upright, blue-grey columns of evergreen foliage, growing barely 2.5cm/1in a year. This is an excellent kind to start with as it gives a semblance of height. Height 25cm/10in.

J. sabina 'Arcadia' is a prostrate growing juniper useful for drooping over the side of a sink. It is very slow growing and grey-green in colour.

Picea glauca 'Albertiana Conica' is a popular spruce with short, closely set branches covered with grass green leaves. In spring the tips of the branches are fringed with the soft gold of the new growth. It will eventually outgrow the sink but can be kept for several years and then be potted or put out in the garden.

Thuja orientalis 'Rosedalis' grows erect with fine, soft to the touch foliage which is soft yellow when young, passing to pale green and plum-purple as the summer advances. Height 25cm/10in after several years.

Sprouting acorns, beech seedlings and horse chestnuts remain small enough to be retained for several years.

Bulbs

Most small bulbs are suitable for miniature gardens provided they are grown cool. They soon fade in a hot atmosphere. Chionodoxas, miniature narcissi, particularly the elfin *N. asturiensis* which only grows about 5cm/2in high, and the slightly larger hoop-petticoat daffodil *N. bulbocodium* are delightful. Snowdrops, scillas, grape hyacinths (muscari) and dwarf cyclamen are others to try, and for autumn *Sternbergia lutea* (which looks like a large yellow crocus), *Cyclamen neapolitanum* and the September and October flowering mauve *Crocus speciosus* are lovely. One of the longest in bloom is *Rhodohypoxis baurii*, with grassy leaves and wide, pink, rose or white flowers on 5cm/2in stems.

Shrubs

Few flowering shrubs are true miniatures so the choice is fairly limited. Roses are an exception. The species rose, *Rosa chinensis* has countless varieties including 'Minima' (syn. Roulettii), a real dwarf at 10-13cm/4-5in. Even the most robust only grow around 30cm/12in tall. Colours vary from pink, rose, crimson, scarlet, white and yellow and the flowers may be single or double. Among the most interesting are 'Elf', 10cm/4in dark crimson and single; 'Pixie', 10-13cm/4-5in double pale pink; 'Oakington Ruby', 23-25cm/9-10in double crimson and 'Josephine Wheatcroft', 25cm/10in golden-yellow. Miniature roses need little pruning except for removal of dead flowers, damaged or weak branches and the shortening back of unduly long shoots.

Cassiope lycopodioides is a small heath-like shrubby lime-hater with minute leaves and pendant white, lily-of-the-valley-like flowers on 8cm/3in stems; *Alyssum spinosum*, 15cm/6in high and prickly has silvery leaves and white flowers; *Salix repens* is a dwarf willow; and *Corokia cotoneaster* has fragrant, star-like yellow flowers and twiggy contorted shoots with small green leaves, silver underneath.

Other Plants

Here there is more choice to select plants which will extend the flowering season.

Trailers include the spring blooming aubrietas in various shades of blue, mauve, purple and red, also one with variegated foliage; alpine phlox (*Phlox subulata*) which has pink, red, white or mauve flowers; golden *Alyssum saxatile*; the pink-flowered soapwort (*Saponaria ocymoides*); *Arabis caucasica* (syn. *A. albida*) 'Flore Pleno' with double white flowers like miniature stocks; and rock roses (*Helianthemum nummularium*) with white, pink, rose, red, orange, yellow and bronze single or double flowers. All these need hard cutting back after flowering to keep them in bounds and healthy.

For summer flowering in sunny positions few plants surpass the bitterroots (Lewisia hybrids). The large and spectacular single flowers are in 15cm/6in umbels and may be cream, apricot, pink or red, often with contrasting stripes of other colours. The oblong leaves are arranged in rosettes. Some of the smaller pinks (dianthus) like 'Mars' and 'Little Jock' are also suitable and *Erinus alpinus*, which has 8-10cm/3-4in spikes of mauve

Right: *Narcissus asturiensis*.
Far right: Lewisia.
Centre: Saxifraga 'Cranbourne'.
Bottom right: *Armeria juniperifolia*.
Bottom centre: *Juniperus.
horizontalis* 'Glauca'.
Bottom left: *Phlox subulata*

or white flowers. There are also dwarf campanulas like *C. carpatica* with blue or white flowers; *Thymus serpyllum*, another carpeter is evergreen with pungent-smelling leaves and white, rose or red flowers and there are countless sedums, sempervivums and saxifrages – particularly the Kabschia group.

Others to note are *Oxalis enneaphylla* and *O. adenophylla*, both about 8cm/3in high with pink flowers and shamrock leaves; *Raoulia australis* (syn. *R. hookeri*), a creeping plant with tiny silver leaves and white flowers; *Mentha requienii*, tiny mauve flowers and leaves with a strong smell of peppermint; a small blue iris called *I. cristata*, 5cm/2in tall and the miniature (5cm/2in) thrift – *Armeria caespitosa*, with pink flowers.

Bonsai

Bonsai is the ancient oriental art of dwarfing trees by skilful branch and root pruning. The aim is to reproduce in miniature a forest giant or glade of trees without malformation or any indication of restriction. The results must look natural – and to achieve this calls for ingenuity and infinite patience.

The origin of the art is lost in the mists of time, although bonsai in ceramic containers are portrayed in Japanese picture scrolls of the Twelfth and Thirteenth centuries. They were also written about, although not everyone appreciated their charm as is indicated by the carping of Kenko Yoshida (1283-1350) in his famous Tsurezure-gusa: 'To appreciate and find pleasure in curiously curved potted trees is to love deformity.' True bonsai, of course, is not deformity.

However, even earlier in time the Chinese collected naturally dwarfed pines and other trees from mountain tops and rock crevices, growing these in containers for home decoration. Probably the Japanese saw some of these in their regular forays into China and elaborated the technique. They are now masters of a craft which has spread to the western world.

Today most countries are interested in bonsai, which are more and more frequently exhibited at British and European horticultural shows. In the United States regular instruction is given in dwarfing techniques by exponents of the art and many Americans build special slatted greenhouses to house their collections.

Bonsai Styles

Many different styles of bonsai are recognized by the Japanese and these are named according to their shape and the angle of the trunks in the pots. An upright tree for example is called *chokkan*; one with a slanting trunk *shakan*, or semi-cascade in the west; a true cascade (*kengai* in Japanese) has a drooping trunk and all its growth spills downwards, which makes it ideal for tall stands. There are also trees with gnarled and twisted trunks suggesting a plant growing on a windswept cliff (*hankan*).

Group plantings, or bonsai with two or more trunks growing from one stump, are particularly attractive as they suggest landscapes in miniature. *Ishi-tsuki*, literally tree with a stone, refers to a tree growing out of a stone, such as may sometimes be seen on a cliff top. Here small trees are either planted in a depression in a suitable stone or the roots are trained to grow over a stone. One difficulty of group planting is keeping all the specimens equally healthy, so that enthusiasts usually graduate to rather than commence with this style of bonsai.

The styles of bonsai trees are named by the Japanese according to their shape and the angle of the trunks in the pots. Illustrated below are a *shakan* maple (slanting trunk), top left; a *hornbeam* group (suggesting a miniature landscape), bottom left; a *kengai* pine (true cascade with a drooping trunk), centre; a *chokkan* beech (upright), top right; and a *hankan* juniper (gnarled and twisted trunk to suggest a windswept cliff), bottom right. Opposite is a beautiful bonsai maple

Containers

Bonsai means 'plant in a tray', a reminder that these little trees are often grown in shallow dishes – frequently only 3.75cm/1½in deep.

Shapes vary but usually conform to some geometrical design, such as a square or circle, and shallow oblongs are particularly favoured for group plantings. These may be rimless or have protruding outer or inner rims. Taller containers are used for cascading specimens which need extra support, and moderately deep round or oval dishes for individual trees, especially those grown primarily for their fruits or foliage.

While glazed pots are usual for shallow containers, the deeper kinds are best left unglazed as they are more susceptible to water-logging. Colours are plain – blue, grey, black, cinnabar, dark brown or green – and there should be no ornamentation. It is the trees which matter, not the pots. Drainage holes are also essential – the Japanese call these 'eyes' – and to protect blockage from soil must be protected with mesh or crocks or the special unglazed, earthenware covers studded with holes (which the Japanese call 'eyelids') before the mixture is put in place.

For display purposes bonsai trees can be raised to eye level on a table or bench, or stood on plant stands (essential for the cascading types). Contrary to popular belief they are not real houseplants and must only be brought inside for limited periods. The rest of the year they should stand in the dappled light of an open slatted house or on a shaded balcony. Although very hardy they can be damaged by sustained hard frosts so may need protection at such times. Similarly an overheated room, or sun shining on them through glass may cause damage. Plants growing indoors need spraying over with soft water several times daily (especially in centrally heated houses) and regularly watered.

Mixture

The mixture for bonsai trees should be rich enough to sustain healthy growth yet very well drained and aerated. Volcanic soil has these qualities and is often used in Japan, but elsewhere loam, sand and leafmould are the main ingredients.

The sand must be sharp and coarse but not salt (so seashore sand is out), the leafmould well rotted and from deciduous trees, preferably oak, and the loam of a sandy nature, although heavier loams are occasionally used for flowering trees like wistaria, Japanese quince (*Chaenomeles speciosa*) and crabapples.

Kan Yashiroda, a most experienced grower at the Brooklyn Botanic Garden in New York, suggests three basic mixes for various tree types. These can be amended to suit individual species. Thus for conifers, which need a very free draining mixture, nine parts sand are mixed with one part leafmould; deciduous trees have three parts sand to one of leafmould and fruiting trees two parts sand to one of leafmould. Good quality porous loam can replace the leafmould for deciduous trees if desired.

Cultivation

Most bonsai trees are acquired originally from a shop or nursery. They can be expensive so it behooves the buyer to examine them carefully before purchase. The tree should be shapely and not show tell-tale cuts where branches or roots have been crudely removed to reduce its stature. The leaves should be bright and green without brown tips or spotting and dormant buds plump and healthy. The soil should feel damp but not sodden and the tree stand firmly – without rocking – in its container. The presence of moss on the trunk is a good sign as it denotes age and careful cultivation. There should be at least one drainage hole in the container.

After purchase keep the plant outdoors for several weeks (except in very severe weather), before taking it indoors to nullify the effects of what may have been a long shoplife. This sojourn outdoors should be repeated from time to time. Once inside, give the tree a light place, but away from radiators, fires, or strong sunlight through glass. Spray over the foliage and water the plant regularly – twice daily if necessary – using soft water, and feed the trees in summer at 10-14 day intervals with weak liquid manure. Keep a good lookout for pests and use a weak insecticide at the first sign of attack.

Dedicated bonsai enthusiasts – realizing that it takes years to make and minutes to spoil – never leave their trees to chance when going on holiday. One American lady of my acquaintance takes them – lock, stock and barrel – to her bonsai teacher, the only person she trusts to look after her valuable collection. Bearing in mind that these little trees can live for centuries and that good specimens in Japan are treated as heirlooms, such concern is under-

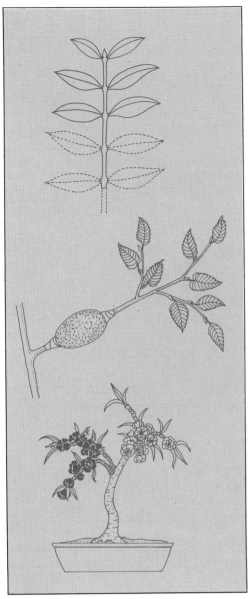

Illustrated above are three methods of propagating bonsai. 1. Cuttings are taken from plants such as ginkgos, tamarisks, willows and tree ivies. The bottom leaves are removed and the cutting inserted in potting mixture in a propagating frame. 2. Air-layering is most satisfactorily done on an existing tree in spring. First bind the branch where it should root tightly with a piece of wire. Remove some or all of the bark in the area, then cover with damp sphagnum moss and a plastic bag. When roots appear, detach and pot up. 3. Grafting a male or female branch on to a bonsai tree of the opposite sex will produce different coloured blossoms on the same tree. Left: a bonsai *Juniperus sargentiana*. Above right: a bonsai *Picea pungens kosteriana*

standable. Lacking a suitable 'nurse' the trees should be grouped outdoors in light shade and have moist peat packed between and over the pots, to keep them damp until the owner returns. Nothing, however, equals the regular attention of a sympathetic gardener.

Propagation

The usual methods of obtaining bonsai material are as follows.

(1) Starting with plants already stunted, twisted or deformed collected from cliffsides, mountains or wooded districts. The larger roots are removed, leaving the smaller to feed and establish the newly potted plant. Training takes on from there.

(2) By cuttings. A number of plants respond satisfactorily to this method, particularly ginkgos, tamarisks, *Picea jezoensis* and willows. Some – like weeping willows (*Salix babylonica*), tree ivies and *Ilex serrata* (a twiggy, slowgrowing, deciduous holly) – can be rooted from quite fat stems (up to 2.5cm/1in across), which is useful when stout trunked trees are required. They should be rooted in a propagating frame. Later the cuttings are separately potted.

(3) By layers. Air layering on an existing tree in spring is the most satisfactory form of this, as one can select a well-proportioned stem or branch. The upper part of the shoot is induced to root and when this takes place the rooted segment is cut off. The first process is to arrest the flow of sap downwards by binding the branch tightly with a piece of wire at the place where it should root. To stimulate the latter the section is sometimes ring-barked, by taking out a narrow strip of bark between two parallel rings cut round the stem with a sharp knife. Very weak branches should only have a partial

ring of bark removed. The wounded area is then bound round with damp sphagnum moss, secured in its turn by a polyethylene or plastic wrap tightly fastened above and below the moss with binding tape. It then looks like a white sausage. Centuries ago clay was used to seal the wounded tissue or a section of bamboo was sliced down its centre and clamped either side of the moss covered area.

When rooting takes place (usually visible through the polyethylene or plastic) the rooted part is detached, potted and kept in a close atmosphere until it becomes established.

(4) By grafting. Grafting is practised by professionals more particularly with monaecious trees like the maidenhair (*Ginkgo biloba*). By grafting a male or female branch on to a bonsai tree of the opposite sex it is possible to produce fruits on the specimen. The Japanese also graft different varieties of cherry or crabapple on the same tree, which thus simultaneously produces both white and red blossoms. Such specimens are frequently offered for sale by Japanese growers in spring.

(5) From seed. Seed represents the slowest method of obtaining bonsai material but is also the cheapest. A wide range of plants can be used including pyracantha, hawthorn, beech, cotoneaster, yew, junipers, cherries, peaches, horse chestnuts, oaks, zelkovias, spruces, pines, larch, hemlock and crabapples. The berried kinds should first be stratified as this hastens germination. Spread the berries out thinly on flat boxes of damp sand and place these outside in an exposed position so that they receive the full effects of the weather – alternate soaking and drying, freezing and thawing. This rapidly breaks down the soft flesh after which the seeds will come away easily when rinsed through a strainer. Sow the seeds in light sandy mixture 143

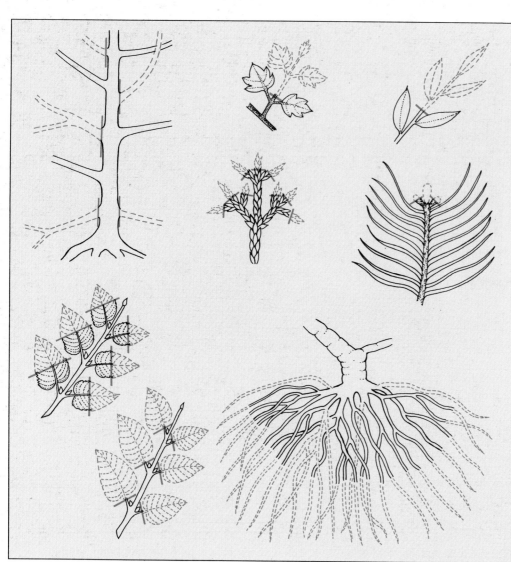

Pruning is necessary to remove dead, diseased or misplaced branches. Illustrated left:
1. In the dormant season prune branches growing opposite another or too low in the container;
2. Pinch out leaves on deciduous trees such as maples; 3, 4, 5. Pinch out growing shoots and tips throughout the growing season; 6. Remove some or all of the leaves in early summer to encourage the tree to make new foliage – the new leaves will be smaller and finer;
7. Cut back old or dead roots when the plant has to be repotted, and prune the remaining roots by one- or two-thirds.

and they soon germinate. To protect the berries from vermin while in the garden, cover the boxes with perforated zinc or foil mesh.

Seeds which do not require stratifying are the fleshless types like hemlocks (*Tsuga*), pines, spruce and larch. These should be kept dry until sowing time in spring.

Training

Bonsai trees need regular training right through their lives. The aim is not only to restrict growth but to give them an appearance of age and maturity. Pruning and wiring are the chief means adopted, the former to check over vigorous growth and the latter to produce interesting shapes.

When a seedling pine tree, for example, develops it is pinched back hard to a point just above the two cotyledon (seed) leaves. This encourages the formation of two lesser shoots rather than one vigorous central stem. Later only the weaker of the two will be retained. Growth is slow in small containers but as soon as the shoots are long enough they are twisted into an 'S' shape or bent in various designs. This operation checks development and produces unusual growth formation at the crowns.

When branches develop those which are retained are twisted or wired to make them take on irregular forms – horizontal, weeping, sinuous, zigzag according to the desired effect.

Copper wire is better than galvanized, which soon rusts. Electrically treated copper wire is suitable (sizes 10-20 are best), or if ordinary wire is burnt it loses its offensive, give-away brightness. Tough barked trees will not suffer from direct contact with the wire but more delicate branches should be protected by wrapping the wire round beforehand, using with tape the same colour as the tree.

Older trees which are to be wired should be well manured the previous season, to build up their stamina for this testing operation. If the branches are tough, withholding water for a day or two often softens them up and makes them more flexible. The usual method of bending a stem or branch is to wind the wire around it in spirals. It is the spiral which keeps it in place, all without marking, and 6-12 months later when it is removed the branch will keep its shape. Never wire or bend branches in unnatural or impossible shapes and never leave evidence where tops of branches or trunks have been removed.

Miniature trees, dwarfed by skilful branch and root pruning, must look natural and these are perfect examples of forest giants reproduced in miniature:
Left: bonsai *Gingkgo biloba*
Above: bonsai *Zelkova serrata* in autumn
Right: bonsai *Acer* in spring
Below: bonsai *Acer* in autumn

Pruning

Leaves, branches and roots all need to be cut back from time to time. Dead, diseased or misplaced branches for example have to be carefully taken out, using a very sharp pruning knife so that the wound soon callouses and disappears. This is normally carried out in the dormant season, but other objectives are to remove any low branches or opposite or crossing branches.

Leaf pinching, an early summer operation, is practised on such deciduous trees as maples. Some or all of the leaves are removed, a process which impels the tree to make new foliage. These new leaves will be smaller and finer.

Growing shoots are also checked as necessary throughout the growing season, simply by pinching out the shoots to two or three buds or leaves. Root pruning occurs when plants have to be repotted, normally every two or three years. After they have been turned from their containers and the soil removed, cut back old or dead roots and reduce the remainder by one-third or two-thirds according to the age of the specimen. Repot in the same sized or very slightly larger dish, using a fresh mixture.

One to Try

A good plant to practise on is the fast-growing weeping willow, *Salix babylonica* which normally grows to more than 6m/20ft. Strike a cutting from an adult tree, using a branch about 2.5cm/1in thick and 45-60cm/1½-2ft long. Insert this for a third of its length in sandy soil (a propagating frame hastens rooting) at an angle of 45°. After it roots, shoots will develop and any of these which run upright – and so lose their weeping habit – should be tied down to a bamboo cane inserted at an angle in the soil mixture. The following spring, pot the plant separately in a small container–still keeping the trunk at an angle–and cut back all shoots to two or three buds. Eventually the pot will become rootbound and when this occurs take the tree out, shake off the soil and severely prune the roots before repotting. At the same time take the shoots back again to two or three buds.

By repeating this procedure the tree will adopt a most interesting shape with long trailing branches. The angle of the trunk will enable these to droop over the edge of a plant stand or similar raised support.

Indoor water gardens

A recent innovation which is becoming increasingly popular is indoor water gardening. Both in the United States and Britain the use of indoor pools is spreading, not only in the lobbies of large business houses and apartment blocks, but also in private homes. A garden room or glass extension unit makes the project fairly simple, since these ensure good lighting which is most important for water plants.

In warm countries like Spain, Colombia and Brazil, indoor pools are often installed with fountains to convey a sense of coolness. In colder climates they are more likely to be still water ponds, their main functions the growing of tropical aquatics which will not live outdoors and providing a home for exotic fish.

Construction

Any watertight container more than 20cm/ 8in deep is a potential water garden, so that large bowls, cisterns, aquaria, troughs and tubs are all suitable. The smallest of these will only hold one or two plants, so for a more comprehensive range a larger pool is necessary. Ideally this should be of concrete built down into the floor and connected to drains for easy emptying. It should also have raised sides, built with a wide ledge to provide a standing area for houseplants at the back and a seat in front. A slab of marble or other stone is ideal for the purpose. Raised sides also prevent dust and small objects from rolling into the water.

Heating can be provided by means of thermostatic immersion heaters, and extra illumination, if required, by underwater lighting or suspended neon lights. Concrete pools should be 30-40cm/12-15in deep.

Many garden centres sell prefabricated resin-bonded glassfibre pools. Although designed for gardens these are rigid enough to make free-standing pools when supported by timber frames. A simple shape is easier to set up than a complicated design.

Planting

There are four categories of aquatic plants used in water gardening: (a) those with submerged roots but floating leaves and flowers; (b) entirely submerged; (c) floating; and (d) with submerged roots but emergent leaves, stems and flowers.

The first group (a) includes water-lilies and lotus – plants requiring rich mixture and plenty of light. Hardy water-lilies, which have floating flowers of pink, red, white, yellow or apricot should be planted in aquatic pots (which have holes bored round the sides), in good sifted but fibrefree loam with a little bonemeal (about an eggcup full per pot). Plant them firmly, topdress the soil with clean pea-sized gravel (to prevent fish rooting in the soil and making the water muddy) and stand the pots in the pool. Spring is the best time for this operation.

Tropical water-lilies have stellate flowers standing above the water on long stems. They are variously coloured – white, blue, purple, pink and red, each bloom with an inner mass of golden stamens, tipped the same colour as the petals. Most are highly fragrant and there are also night bloomers with broader petals (the lotus types) which open their red or white flowers at dusk and close them soon after dawn. Tropical water-lilies have small bulb-like

tubers so can go into smaller 8-13cm/3-5in pots and should have some sand in the soil mixture.

Hindu lotuses (*Nelumbo nucifera*) have spectacular flowers like huge red, pink or white roses standing well above the water, and large round parasol like leaves – all from a creeping banana-like rhizome. These can be grown in tubs or near the back of a concrete pool.

Group (b), the submerged plants, are vitally important since they keep the water clear and

An indoor water garden, like the one left, will provide a sense of coolness and an unusual feature in a home. The illustration above shows how planting may be done. Submerged plants, such as *Lagarosiphon major*, are weighted with a narrow metal strip pressed around the base

also provide nurseries for fish ova and fry. They have practically no roots so must be weighted to get them to sink. Gather two or three stems together and gently press a narrow strip of lead round the bases, then drop them into the water. Submerged aquatics oxygenate the water and absorb the carbon-dioxide emitted by fish, so that the two together keep the pool balanced. Some are more efficient oxygenators than others, but for indoor pools any of the milfoils (*Myriophyllum*; *Tillaea* (*Crassula*) *recurva*; *Anacharis canadensis* or *Lagarosiphon major* – both of which resemble giant white-flowered elodeas – are suitable. They can be introduced at any season.

Floating aquatics, (c), shade the water, thus providing cool resting areas for fish in warm weather, and they starve out (and thus keep down) algae. Many are highly decorative.

The water poppy (*Hydrocleys nymphoides*) creeps across the water surface supported by small oval leaves and has three-petalled, golden, poppy-like flowers; fairy moss, *Azolla caroliniana* is another creeper, with light green, red-tinted tiny leaves; salvinias are fern allies with small crinkled floating leaves, and the water lettuce (*Pistia stratiotes*) is well named on account of the shape of its silky green floating leaf-rosettes. The frogbit, *Hydrocharis morsus-ranae*, has small, white, three-petalled flowers above the round leaves. Floating plants are simply placed on the water surface.

Section (d) contains many ornamental aquatics, rising to various heights. One of the most exotic is the Egyptian papyrus (*Papyrus antiquorum*), a tall 1.8-2.5m/6-8ft reed with triangular stems and mop-like heads of grassy inflorescence. Elephant's ears (*Xanthosoma*) have large yellow arum-like flowers and purple-veined, ear-shaped leaves on purple stems. Other plants worth growing are the golden-flowered jussiaeas (60-90cm/2-3ft) which look like elegant evening primroses; parrot's feather (*Myriophyllum proserpinacoides*) with green, feathery, leafy stems which turn reddish at the tips and grow out of the water to trail over the pool edges; and the true water

Caltha palustris, or marsh marigolds (above) and *Iris laevigata* (below) are aquatics for indoor water gardens. A fountain can be added for a special effect (right). An aquarium, as illustrated above right, provides another method of cultivating water plants as well as keeping fish. Growing here are *Cryptocoryne beckettii*, *Aponogeton crispus*, *Echinodorus tenellus*, *Najas microdon*, *Echinodorus horizontalis*, *Alternanthera lilacina* and *Vallisneria asiatica*

irises (*Iris laevigata*) with blue, purple, white or rose pink flowers. Most of these can be planted in pots of plain loam and then stood in the pool with containers hidden beneath the water.

Livestock

According to the water temperature all kinds of fish – hardy and exotic – can be kept in indoor pools. Fancy goldfish breeds like veiltails, moors, shubunkins and comets as well as golden orfe are reliable but becoming popular are the brilliantly coloured koi carp – with several colours, white, blue, black, red or mauve on the same fish. These are easily tamed and will then feed from the fingers. Various tropical fishes are suitable for warm water.

Not only are fish attractive to watch but they keep down mosquito larvae and their excreta nourish the water plants.

Aquaria

Aquaria provide another method of cultivating water plants and keeping fish indoors. They can be free standing on metal supports or (if

there is room to tend them behind) let into walls or used as room dividers. Treated thus they make pleasant wall pictures, especially near a fireplace. They will also go under a TV set. Small strip lights above the tank, but hidden from view by a metal hood, give sufficient illumination to watch the fish and also keep the plants actively growing.

Aquaria mixture is usually washed coarse sand, spread over the base of the aquarium but slightly higher towards the back. Pieces of rock can be inserted to make a pleasant composition and plants pushed into the sand behind the rocks and towards the back and sides. Keep the front fairly clear in order to see the fish. Submerged plants like milfoils, *Lagarosiphon major*, and cryptocorynes are all suitable and show variation in leaf shape, colour and texture. Plant these with the tank half full of water (you get a better idea of the effect) and fill it when the operation is complete.

A few small floaters like azolla and salvinias can then go on top and the fish put in soon afterwards.

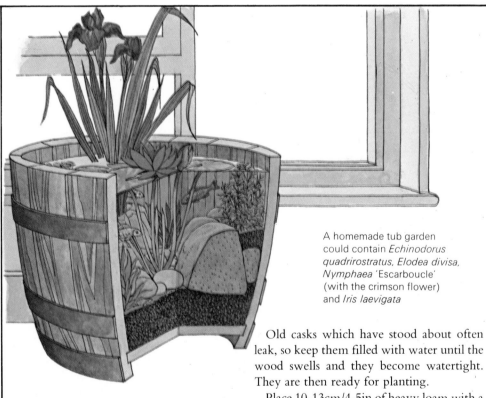

A homemade tub garden could contain *Echinodorus quadrirostratus, Elodea divisa, Nymphaea* 'Escarboucle' (with the crimson flower) and *Iris laevigata*

Old casks which have stood about often leak, so keep them filled with water until the wood swells and they become watertight. They are then ready for planting.

Place 10-13cm/4-5in of heavy loam with a little bonemeal over the base and build up one or two side pockets with pieces of stone to take shallow water plants. Alternatively these can be grown in pots and stood on bricks. Plant a water-lily in the centre, with about six submerged aquatics and three or four marginals – like kingcups or marsh marigolds (*Caltha palustris*), water forget-me-nots (*Myosotis palustris*), both 23cm/9in high, and irises – around. Fill with water and add two or three small goldfish.

A Tub Garden

An old sawn-down beer or wine cask is easily turned into a small water garden. Cut these down to about 50cm/20in from the ground and wash them thoroughly. Tubs which have held oily substances are difficult to clean unless they can be burnt over inside (stuff them with hay or straw, set fire to this and then turn upside-down before the wood catches fire).

CHAPTER 4
CONTAINER GARDENING OUTDOORS

Lacking the traditional garden –
or one of adequate size – a
gardener must use whatever is to
hand. He will be anxious not
to wait too long before achieving at
least something like the
desired effect, so he will not be
particularly drawn to propagating
plants from the start (either
by seed or small tip cuttings) if it then
will take several years before any
recognizable plant or shrub
of the type chosen is produced.
And because space is limited on
a patio, balcony, rooftop or other
small paved area, tubs, raised
troughs and pots must be used.
Choosing the right plants
for the right containers, then,
is the answer.

Creating a container garden

A small greenhouse – preferably one that is heated – is the best possible adjunct to a container garden. Plants for use in the containers can be begun in the structure, and the more delicate plants can be housed there during the worst winter months.

With or without a greenhouse, one of the great advantages of container gardening is that it need never be monotonous. Plants can be moved around to suit the grower. The grower without a greenhouse need not feel disheartened by the lack of one as he can buy a wide selection of suitable plants, often in an early stage of growth when they quickly acclimatize to the growing conditions available.

Containers for plants grown out of doors can range in scope from raised beds, such as might be appropriate as the main feature in a tiny paved garden, to a shallow dish in which Bonsai trees are grown. The link is that the plants are not growing in the open ground – they do not have a free rootrun.

Container gardening is most appropriate to small spaces such as town gardens, flat roofs, patios, balconies, courtyards, flights of steps and window boxes, but a well-placed container can look exactly right in a large garden and there are many such gardens which have gained an extra dimension by the use of a well-sited urn, tub or vase. Most great gardens use containers quite freely.

The uses to which plants in containers can be put are endless; when carefully planted and well placed they can make a dull outlook, such as a flight of steps, a thing of beauty. Many such plantings not only give considerable pleasure to their owners but also great joy to passers-by who chance to see them. Some of the most successful plant groupings are those which can be seen at close quarters. Much of the joy of container gardening is obtained from the close proximity of the plants and many of these should be viewed close up. Sink gardens, for instance, enable the grower to examine the fine detail of a plant's delicate leaves or tiny flowers – points perhaps passing quite unnoticed in the long border or large group planting.

Too many pots, tubs and urns can look a mess. Often it is better to do some multiple planting rather than have too many single containers. Positioning is often half the battle; try a tub on either side of an entrance door, or a few placed with care at the top of a low wall or one on either side of a flight of steps. Train a climbing plant along a balcony railing or up the bannisters of a stairway and against a house wall; use window ledges and roof tops to bring life to paving, concrete or tarmac.

Too many containers can spoil an effect, but containers themselves usually look best if they are overflowing with plants. One or two plants strikingly placed to complement or vie with neighbouring ones and a number tumbling over the edges and down the sides can create this effect. The opulence of a still life by a Dutch Master might be the target. Conversely, one of the best ways of showing off a plant is to isolate it. I know of one house where outside each window is a perfectly grown, perfectly proportioned, evergreen Bonsai – beautifully displayed in an attractive and appropriate container.

WHAT TO PLANT AND WHERE

Small trees and shrubs are usually used to form a backbone to a garden. This can also be the case with containers. They offer height and substance to the plan but they should not be too numerous. They also need quite substantial root space. The small shrubby plants (including naturally dwarf trees, especially conifers) form the main body of the layout. They are more easily replaced than their big brothers. Climbers and trailers can also provide height to the composition or break up sharp edges and hard lines. The small stuff is for filling in corners, covering expanses of bare soil and for spots where the diminutive is appropriate and will not be overlooked.

A degree of compatibility is essential when mixing plants together. It is pointless to attempt to grow plants in the same container if they have opposing likes and dislikes of soil conditions, sun, shade and water. Nor is it possible to allow a shy grower to be smothered by a rampant one.

Sinks

One of the shallowest containers in use is the sink. These first came into general use when old houses were being stripped of a very pleasant-looking, but totally inadequate for its purpose, shallow stoneware kitchen sink. It was already provided with drainage having a bottom that sloped to the plughole; all that was needed was for it to be raised on a pedestal, for gravel or crocks to be placed at the bottom of the sink to assist drainage and for soil, plants and rocks to be set in place. These old sinks are, however, becoming a rarity, and simulated sinks can be purchased in a number of different and lighter materials, such as asbestos cement and glass fibre. Any shallow type of container can be given a stone sink appearance by coating it with cement and leaving it rough.

A container garden can be a cool patio with a riot of exotic plants, such as the one left with lilies, fuchsias, ferns and roses, or a simple bricked area highlighted with a single unusual urn, above. A trough filled with pelargoniums, petunias, lobelia and alyssum brings colour to an outside wall, below left. Pelargoniums and petunias growing on a balcony railing, below, provide a cheerful outlook

CONTAINERS

Plants can be grown in virtually anything that holds soil – even discarded tin-cans such as the garden centres tend to use and which are standard containers along practically the length of the Mediterranean coast. An attractive holder does, however, add a great deal to the appearance of the whole and as the container is often half the picture, care should be taken to see that the choice fits the plants to be used and the situation and conditions available.

Containers need not be the traditional clay or plastic pot; all types of everyday objects can be brought into service. Such things as old glazed earthenware – or unglazed – bread or egg-preserving crocks, tall casseroles and stew-pots are often seen in markets and can add interest to the grouping. There are lovely large khaki-green pottery tubs to be had from Chinese shops which have been emptied of the ancient pickled eggs that come from Hong Kong and China and decorative jars from all

masonry bit or the chore can be passed on to a semi-professional.

A number of wooden tubs and baskets that have been used for packing fresh fruit, vegetables and fish can look charming when properly matched with the right plants and situation. Most of these will not last forever but they will last for several years for such things as annual climbing plants, which are finished when the worst weather begins, and as planters. Paint them all with a wood preservative before use and take indoors during the winter when they are empty.

Planters outdoors range from the very beautiful lead urns into which flowering plants are dropped for the few weeks when they are in their heyday to rather open wicker baskets used to hide such unsightly containers as tin-cans and plastic pots the grower happens to dislike.

Unglazed clay flower pots are the most popular and usually the most suitable containers for use out of doors. They are heavy

sorts of places. A lot of these distinctive containers provide a different shape and additionally can be picked up for a song. All such containers must, however, be provided with drainage holes (and plenty of them) – unless they are to be used as planters, which merely hide the actual growing pots. Drainage can easily be provided by using a hand drill and

enough when filled with soil not to be blown over easily in wind; they are tough enough to stand up to normal handling and quite severe frosts; they are absorbent and well drained. They are, however, rapidly being replaced by plastic pots, and will often have to be sought out at markets and bric-a-brac shops. Glazed pots are on the market and, while more expensive, do have the advantage that they do not dry out so quickly.

Plastic pots are the most commonly-seen containers for indoor plants and in that field have all the advantages – lightness, ease of cleaning and cheapness. Outdoors the thinner plastic pots cannot give much protection to the roots of the plants during severe weather, do not have the stability of their heavier brothers and in strong sunlight can get quite hot. Some of the larger plastic tubs are made of sturdier material and thereby overcome some of the snags of the smaller ones.

Wooden tubs, both small circular ones like fire-buckets and square shaped ones, can be very useful when large containers are called for. Fewer wooden barrels are being produced than previously but barrels cut in half can still be had and these have an attractive shape and good capacity, especially when a mixture of different plants is contemplated. If not already present, drainage holes must be provided and the wood treated to stand up to outdoor conditions.

good containers for use when wishing to grow some of the smaller plants. Shallow pans of sempervivums (the name means 'live forever'), commonly called Houseleeks, can be very attractive. Although supposed to live forever, the individual rosette of leaves sending up the inflorescence dies when it does so, but there are a mass of other rosettes to take its place.

In some cases a container is needed to fit a particular position and the best solution is to have something in wood or another material made to measure. With timber this need not be so difficult and can be attempted in the home. Many timber merchants are prepared to cut any number of pieces of wood to exact sizes – particularly if they are given a list in advance of the number and size of pieces required. The grower then only needs to prepare the timber and assemble the box, tub or bucket – it is not necessary to be the complete carpenter and joiner to make simple containers.

Alternatively, containers can be cast in concrete. The walls of these need be no more than

Like everything else that is made of wood they are subject to decay, but if properly treated with preservative and raised off the ground by blocks or bricks to allow a free flow of air beneath them they will last tolerably well. Wood does not heat up in sun like terra-cotta and is more suitable in sunny spots.

Square and circular seed-pans also make

2.5cm/1in thick if they are reinforced with wires or wire-mesh and are not man-handled too much. If the concrete used is mixed with very coarse sand it becomes much more porous and weathers beautifully. Inexpensive timber is used to knock up the mould and a number of 'pots' can be taken from the same mould over a period.

155

Window Boxes

Window boxes are popular. They are practically obligatory for the country cottage, are seen all over towns, are invaluable to the apartment dweller who is without a garden and are an attractive feature of some office buildings. They can be stocked in a seasonal way, first with spring flowers and bulbs, then filled with summer bedding plants, and finally with such plants as chrysanthemums or solanums and ivies. Some are stocked pretty permanently with dwarf conifers, ivies and hard-wearing green plants. Window boxes must be completely secure and additionally should not constitute a nuisance to other people down below who naturally might object if they are deluged each time the plants are watered.

Courtyards, Patios and Terraces

These three situations are possibly slight variations on the same thing. The word patio evokes sun-drenched, wall-locked southern gardens for some. Terraces can be raised or sunk or level with the areas outside the French windows of large country houses, and courtyards are enclosed by walls on all sides and usually refer to the small back areas of old houses in built-up sections. All are, as far as we are concerned, places in which to sit and places in which to garden. Perhaps the exotic-looking plants should be chosen for the patio, the classical lead urns for the terrace, and a mass of lovely cool green plants for the courtyard.

Small Paved Areas

These are perhaps most common in towns and cities. They are paved because they are too small to support the formal lawn, however small, flower borders and the usual garden features. With containers, otherwise completely daunting areas can be transformed into oases; they can provide sitting areas in either sun or shade (or luckily both) and a place in which to potter. Many small paved areas are blessed with the finest backcloth – old brick walls. When these can be clothed with interesting climbers as a permanent feature it is often sufficient if a few plants can be grouped together in one area allowing the owners the rest of the space as a sitting area or a place in which a small number of guests can saunter.

Roof Gardens and Balconies

These, too, are places that should allow the owner to potter; they can provide that break from the house and balconies can supply that view from the rooms they serve. The weight of the filled containers, gardener, guests, etc., must be considered in all instances and also the ease of access to a water supply and disposal of garden rubbish.

Opposite above: A roof garden, with hydrangeas, impatiens and pelargoniums, brings a country feeling to a city apartment.
Opposite below left: Hanging baskets and a trough filled with pelargoniums, petunias and chlorophytum, make good use of a small paved area.
Opposite below centre: A bowl overflowing with pelargoniums, petunias and lobelia is colourful.
Opposite below right: A courtyard with cool green plants, such as ferns and ivy, is a lovely place to sit on a warm day.
Above: A sunny balcony garden.
Right: Large glass windows, with plants on either side, enlarge a room

157

Trouble Spots

In northern climates it is hard to believe that there are some places where they get too much sun or that it is too hot – but that can be the case.

Containers which stand in full sun, particularly if they are heat absorbent, can dry out at an alarmingly fast rate. Strong winds also cause drying out and some multi-storey blocks, while apparently calm, have a regular current of air. Plants for sunny spots should be chosen because they revel in sunlight – such plants as pelargoniums, Ipomoea (Morning Glory) and *Agapanthus africanus* will do well. Brittle-stemmed plants must be avoided in windy situations and in such situations tall plants will need to be staked or perhaps given a miss. In heavy shade don't attempt the sun-worshippers and in sun avoid the woodland plants. Soil alkalinity is no problem – if peat-loving plants are wanted, grow them in that; if chalk or lime is preferred give it to them.

Overwintering

Most trees and shrubs listed here are either completely frost hardy or hardy in all but the most exposed situations couped with a severe winter. In some cases winter hardiness is dependent on some cultural detail. One of these is that many plants are capable of surviving quite cold spells provided they are not unduly wet. Another is that some plants will come through a winter unscathed if they are planted a little deeper than would be normal. Fuchsias are an instance of the latter. If they are planted 5-8cm/2-3in deeper than the original soil line they will shoot from below ground even if all top growth is killed by frost and bitterly cold winds.

Shelter afforded by neighbouring buildings gives some degree of protection to most container-grown plants, and particularly exposed situations should be avoided whenever possible.

The thinness of the walls of some containers tends to expose a plant's roots to cold which they would not suffer if planted in the open soil. Exceptionally, and it is appreciated that this will detract from the appearance of the plants, sacking or some similar material can be wrapped around the containers when severe weather is expected. Over-wetness should be avoided even if this means having to divert some rainwater from entering the containers by means of a piece of slate or polythene or plastic.

When comparatively expensive pots are used, it may be advisable to move them to the shelter of an existing building or to erect some form of temporary shelter for them. For this reason large containers should be equipped with castors to make them easily movable.

Hanging Containers

Apart from the rather open wire baskets there are other hanging containers, but, to deal with this simple type first, it is basically just a painted or plastic-covered frame shaped like half a globe. It is lined with sphagnum moss or osmunda fibre and filled to about 4-5cm/1½-2in of the brim with peaty soil. The sides of the basket can be planted as well as the upper surface provided the planting is done as the basket is being filled. The disadvantages are that, when filled with plants which are flourishing, it needs very regular watering preferably by immersing the whole thing in a bucket of water about once a day and that for some long time after this the basket will tend to drip. There are half baskets which are a quarter of a globe and which hang with their flat side against a wall. Green plastic sheeting has been used very successfully recently instead of the sphagnum moss and this helps considerably to reduce the frequency of watering by retaining some water and preventing evaporation. The plastic sheeting should have some holes pierced in it. Another aid is a deep plastic saucer in the bottom of the basket.

A rigid but quite lightweight plastic basket with a drainage hole built in and with a fixed saucer attachment can be obtained. Additionally there are the wooden slatted baskets favoured by orchid growers – but the last are only suitable for plants needing the very best of drainage. A few ceramic hanging containers are seen but these tend to be quite expensive and are usually fairly shallow.

Hanging baskets are best suspended from porches, patio rafters, wall brackets and arches; they should be held securely in place with chains and hooks, ideally a chain that allows the basket to be raised and lowered without dismantling the whole contraption.

Spring plantings can be made using wallflowers and forget-me-nots, but baskets really come into their own when they are used during the summer months brimming over with such plants as trailing fuchsias, pendulous begonias, ivies, pelargoniums, ferns, nasturtiums and trailing and dwarf lobelias.

Flourishing baskets should be fed at least weekly from about July through to frosts.

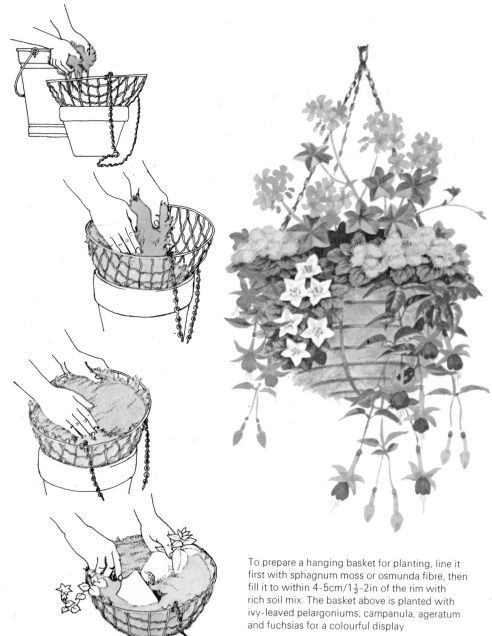

To prepare a hanging basket for planting, line it first with sphagnum moss or osmunda fibre, then fill it to within 4-5cm/1½-2in of the rim with rich soil mix. The basket above is planted with ivy-leaved pelargoniums, campanula, ageratum and fuchsias for a colourful display

Window boxes

Window boxes of wood or asbestos are comparatively light and inexpensive. Terracotta ones are around and, subject to accident, will last forever but they are expensive. Boxes should fit window recesses within 2.5-5cm/1-2in. They should sit firmly on window ledges and should be absolutely safe. Wooden boxes can additionally be fixed to wooden window frames by hooks when this is possible thus providing an extra safeguard against collapse.

Generally speaking, it is a good idea to line wooden window boxes with heavy-duty polythene or plastic as this not only helps to retain moisture but also delays the wood rotting. The usual depth of a window box is 15-20cm/6-8in and this is normally needed for the types of plants commonly used in such positions. Some of the very small alpine plants, and for that matter some dwarf trees also, are happy to grow in only 5-8cm/2-3in of soil—the shallower the container the more water will be needed.

For those who wish to make their own wooden boxes, the choice of timber is wide, but hardwood should be chosen for durability (a box made of a softwood such as deal will not last more than a few years whereas one of teak will last a lifetime). The hardwood is, however, harder and more difficult to work in. Plywood can be useful as it is quite tough and light but edges must be protected and it does tend to split into its sections and to warp.

Window boxes, when being tailor-made, should be as deep as they can be and still look right, not become too heavy nor obstruct the window too much. Drainage holes can be made with a drill or a red hot poker. Brass screws will not rust and are preferable to nails. It is good practice to lift window boxes off the window recess to allow aeration, and when the recesses are sloping this can be done by using sloped wooden wedges.

The grain of the wood used should run the length of the box and not vertically. A good wood preservative and paint should be used to extend the life of wood as long as possible and ideally each window box should be lined with a lightweight metal box, which not only prevents rotting of the wood but also makes it easier to renew the display by simply lifting out the metal box and replacing it with another.

Hardwood is the best choice if you make your own windowbox, as it is very durable. A good wood preservative and paint should be used

Drainage and aeration of the soil are vital, so use wooden wedges to lift the box off the window recess, or sloping ledge

The window box above contains Red Riding Hood tulips, hyacinths, polyanthus and narcissi.
Left: Make the most of a confined space, such as the steps area in an apartment building, by training clematis around the railing, adding a pot of agapanthus and an urn containing pelargoniums, alyssum and lobelia

Shrubs and small trees

Acer

[Maple; Japan] The majority of maples are sizeable deciduous trees and of little value where space is at a premium. However, the Japanese maple, *A. palmatum* 'Dissectum Atropurpureum' (apart from labouring under an uncommonly long name), is slow growing and does not reach more than about 2.4m/8ft in a container after many years. The purple leaves of this tree turn a vivid dark scarlet in the autumn before they fall. There are a number of cultivated garden varieties of *A. palmatum* with a wide range of leaf size, shape and colour; they all have dissected leaves, sometimes very feathery and some almost fern-like.

Japanese maples strongly dislike winds and can suffer damage from them. Their young growth in the spring can occasionally be nipped by a late frost. They should, therefore, be placed in situations offering them shelter from both winds and early morning sunshine as the latter when striking slightly frozen new growth can cause burning which would not occur if the frost melted slowly in shade. Propagation is by grafting, a difficult process for the amateur.

Arundinaria

[Bamboo; Japan] Provided that the invasive nature of the evergreen bamboos is appreciated and an attempt is not made to grow them together with other plants, they can be very useful as focal points. Many of the family are quite tall growing and unsuitable for growing in containers – unless they be extremely large. There are, however, a few which, if grown alone in sizeable tubs, will thrive in either sun or some shade. None of the species like wind and despite the idea that they are often associated with water, none of them like their feet wet and do prefer a dry soil. *A. variegata* (*Sasa fortunei*), which grows up to 1.2m/4ft, has pale green canes and dark green leaves striped with white. *A. viridistriata*, which needs more light and grows 1-2m/3-6ft, has purplish-green canes and dark green leaves with rich yellow heavy stripes. The latter plant can be cut down to the ground each spring to encourage the growth of and display the attractive new foliage. Overgrown plants may be divided and replanted in spring.

Aucuba japonica variegata

[Variegated Laurel or Gold-dust Tree; Japan] This shrub from Japan was terribly overdone in the Victorian era when it was used in parlours, greenhouses, shrubberies and practically every other situation. It is, however, a very tough and tolerant small female, evergreen shrub which provides cheer during winter months in window boxes in mild climates. Being able to stand shady conditions, which little else would, a polluted atmosphere and a good deal of neglect, it is a useful plant for really difficult situations.

The aucuba will certainly repay, being given reasonably good conditions, by producing large glossy leaves with spots and splashes of gold and, occasionally, bright red berries in autumn. Only female shrubs of this genus produce berries as they are dioecious (separate sexes). If several shrubs are used there is likely to be a male in the collection – or there could be one in the area which the bees will use. Cuttings, about 20cm/8in long, root quite easily in the spring.

Azalea

[Asia] The botanists have recently moved all the plants that used to be called azaleas to the rhododendron group where they belong botanically, but it is still very convenient to use this category for the fragrant deciduous shrubs like the Ghent hybrids, with long tubular flowers – all of which have some of the characteristics of the yellow parent *A. pontica* (syn. *Rhododendron flavum*) and flower in May-June and *A. mollis* (syn. *Rhododendron sinense*) which are not usually scented but flower early in May. Colours range from cream, yellow and buff to pink, scarlet or orange. These are quite tall growing (up to 1.5m/5ft) but not necessarily quick growing and will in time need some pruning. Faded flowers should be removed before seed pods begin to form. The Kurume hybrids are evergreen, very dwarf growing and smother themselves in flowers during April and May. Most varieties have Japanese names and come in a wide range of colours. All azaleas need an acid soil and some shade, although the evergreens will take sun and need shelter from stormy winds. Propagation is by cuttings or layering.

Berberis

[Barberry; Asia/South America] There are well over 400 different species of berberis known and they have deservedly rocketed into popularity in recent years. Starting with the deciduous kinds, *B. thunbergii* is fairly compact and comparatively upright. It is usually less than 1.2m/4ft tall, has pale yellow flowers, red berries and colours beautifully in the autumn when the small holly-like leaves turn red. The variety *B. thunbergii* 'Atropurpurea' has foliage which is the colour of copper beech and colours beautifully too. There is also a dwarf form, 'Nana', of this.

Charles Darwin discovered *B. darwinii* in Chile in 1835. It is a spendid evergreen berberis which will eventually reach 1.8m/6ft tall. The flowers are yellowish-orange and are borne in

heavy clusters during May, almost smothering the small shiny leaves. The berries are dark purple. *B. × stenophylla* is an evergreen hybrid with delicate arching stems with dark green leaves which are hidden by small golden-coloured flowers at the end of April. It is capable of becoming quite tall but there are several dwarf forms, including 'Corallina Compacta' and *B. × stenophylla* (syn. *irwinii*) 'Nana' which rarely grows taller than 46cm/18in and bears rich yellow flowers in May. Cuttings 8-10cm/3-4in long taken in August and September should root by the next spring.

Buxus

[Box; Europe/West Asia/North Africa] *B. sempervirens* is the small-leaved dark glossy evergreen shrub used for edging borders and for clipping into topiary. Small already shaped plants are occasionally available; they are slow growing and much time has been devoted to training them to the particular shape. They end up by being fairly expensive and should be looked after. Small mound shapes are useful in window boxes in mild climates where that shade of dark green is appropriate, and small plants can look very attractive spilling over the edge of mixed plantings. They are reasonably happy in any situation – they just ask to be watered when they need it. In the autumn and in some positions they take on a rusty hue. Propagation is by cuttings in late summer.

Calluna

[Ling or Heather; Northwestern Europe/Eastern United States] The evergreen Lings, which vary in height from 8cm/3in to 60cm/2ft, like a lime-free soil which is not over-rich and a dry open position. They can be grown quite successfully in hanging baskets providing that the soil mix is right and that it is not shaded. Flowers of pink shades and occasionally white are produced in the autumn and there are double varieties like 'Alba Plena' – double white – and 'Alportii' – a tall crimson single and 'H. E. Beale' a rose-pink double. Increase by cuttings after flowering.

Camellia

[China/Japan/Korea] For years camellias were regarded as tender when all the time they were quite hardy. Opening buds and flowers are, however, subject to damage by morning sun after night frost, but many problems can be overcome if these plants are situated other than in a position facing east. They are ideal for growing in tubs and large pots. The species *C. japonica* and the hybrid *C. × williamsii* are the most commonly seen and new hybrids from each of these two parents are recommended. *C. japonica*, with characteristically polished leaves, is capable of growing into a large shrub (2-4m/6-12ft). Most of the named hybrids are of medium size but growing them in con-

Opposite: Arundaria, one of the evergreen bamboos, do best if grown alone and, despite being associated with water, prefer a dry soil.
Left: *Skimmia japonica* is a tough shrub which will tolerate shady conditions, a polluted atmosphere and a good deal of neglect.
Above: *Camellia × williamsii* 'Shocking Pink' will flower from November to May

tainers tends to reduce the ultimate size of the plants. The handsome large flowers are usually produced between January and early May and may be a wide range of sizes and forms. There are single, semi-double, double, anemone, paeony and imbricated. Recommended varieties include 'Adolphe Audusson', large blood-red semi-double, 'Alba Plena', large white double, and 'Pink Perfection', small shell-pink double. *C. × williamsii* and its progeny are very free flowering over a period extending from November to May. 'Donation', large semi-double orchid-pink, and 'J. C. Williams', medium single blush-pink, are two of the best.

Camellias are not tender, as said before, but equally they are not plants to be neglected. Keep moist at all times, grow in acid soil, avoid early morning sun when in bud and flower and top dress annually with well-rotted leafmould. Propagation is by cuttings or leaf-bud cuttings in summer.

Cassiope

[Northern Hemisphere] Small evergreen shrub resembling heathers, *C. lycopodioides* is only 4-8cm/2-3in high with minute dark green leaves. The white bell-shaped flowers appear in April and May. Cassiopes, being native to Arctic regions, need cool growing conditions in a shady north-facing position and a peat-based soil mix. Propagation is by cuttings.

Chaenomeles or Cydonia

[Japanese Quince; Asia] The plant *C. speciosa*, usually called simply japonica, has laboured under several different names for several decades. It has at last come to be accepted as *C. speciosa*. This flowering deciduous shrub is not a bit difficult to grow. Its best display in early spring is particularly beautiful. Given its head it is really quite a large shrub capable of reaching the house guttering, but by careful training and pruning it can be kept within bounds.

It is perfectly hardy and in sheltered positions often begins to flower in December with apple-like saucer-shaped red blossoms about 4cm/1½in across on the naked branches. These can continue for several weeks. Named varieties include hybrids such as 'Apple Blossom', white, pink-flushed flowers; 'Crimson and Gold', red and yellow; 'Rowallane', deep red; and 'Nivalis', large pure white.

C. japonica

[Maulès Quince; Asia] This deciduous shrub is much smaller growing–up to 90cm/3ft–but inclined to sprawl. The flowers, bright orange flame in colour, are freely produced but do not appear until April or May. Outstanding hybrids are 'Knap Hill Scarlet',

orange scarlet, and 'Pink Lady', clear rose-pink. These are the flowering quinces which produce odd-shaped fruit that can be made into preserves. They all like sun and a good rich potting soil. If possible, buy plants which have been pot-grown as they take a little time to settle down again after being lifted from the open ground. Seeds will germinate freely, but named varieties must be increased from cuttings.

Cistus

[Rock Rose or Sun Rose; Mediterranean] Cistus are evergreen shrubs, rather on the borderline of hardiness, but cuttings root easily and some small reserve plants should ideally be taken which will survive even in the worst winter in a cold frame. More than the cold they dislike the wet – or really a combination of the two. *C. × corbariensis* is a bushy shrub 45-90cm/1½-3ft in height having 4cm/1½in single rose-like flowers of white with a yellow base. Less hardy but with one of the best flowers – purple-red with a dark blotch on each petal – is *C. × purpureus* which grows to about 90cm/3ft. *C.* 'Silver Pink' is an exceptionally pretty almost hardy hybrid. A number of named hybrids are offered by some nurserymen in mild climates. A light sandy soil suits them best and they love the sun, sheltered from winds.

Clematis

[Asia/North America] Clematis are some of the most beautiful climbing plants obtainable. They provide height and with their large and vivid flowers add splashes of colour over a long period. Given long canes or a background framework they will attach themselves and require no tying to their supports. Good sized tubs are best, affording an extensive and cool root run. Some shade for the roots must be given and this is best done either by planting some dense but shallow-rooting plants in the tub or by placing tiles (or a collection of attractive pebbles from the beach) over their feet. The top growth, however, loves the sun. The most suitable for containers are those deciduous types which flower on the extremities of new growth as this allows their being pruned almost to the ground each year. With young plants this pruning is best done in February but more mature specimens can be doctored in December. *C. jackmanii* (deep-purple) and the many other named sorts offer a very wide choice of colour, from May to September. Without doubt the best way to choose the colour and form of flower that appeals most is, in the months of July to September, to visit a garden with a good collection of clematis. Propagate by stem cuttings in July.

Conifers

Conifers are valuable for their permanent appearance, for the year-round colour, foliage texture and unusual shapes. Beautiful pyramid piles of green, gold, blue-green or grey-green can be had and can look superb either on their own or when associated with plants of contrasting foliage. The colour range is tremendous.

The best way to choose a few conifers is to visit a good nursery and taking a little advice from the nurseryman, to come home with those that appeal most and those which are likely to best suit the position chosen for them. Perhaps a pair of Irish yews (*Taxus baccata*) are needed, one on either side of an entrance door, or some really small trees for a trough or sink garden, or maybe some evergreens that will not too soon outgrow a small paved area.

Generally speaking, an average soil suits conifers best. In such a mix they will most probably continue to grow true to type – neither too swiftly and lose their desirable shape or habit nor will they be so starved that they will hardly grow at all. The naturally very tiny trees (as opposed to the ones which are just slow growing) should perhaps be encouraged to go ahead by being given a good soil mixture and a small amount of slow-acting fertilizer.

All newly planted trees require particularly careful attention during their first year in their new positions and it is essential with conifers. Firm planting is also a must. It is a mistake to surround a conifer with a few handsful of loose peat in the belief that you are doing it a favour; such light-weight material inhibits firm planting and it is a really secure contact with the surrounding soil that is required.

The following conifers are merely a sample of what might be tried and for convenience they have been divided into those that are dwarf, compact and bushy, followed by the pencil-slim types.

Cedrus libani 'Nana' is a very dwarf dark green cedar of Lebanon. Instead of being the large tree of biblical fame that can top 24m/80ft without difficulty, this type will not exceed 60cm/2ft in a container. *C. brevifolia*, the Cyprus Cedar, can in the open ground grow to 15m/60ft but usually in a container it will stay small.

Chamaecyparis obtusa 'Caespitosa' is a slow-growing, light green, dense little bush and one of the smallest ever of the conifers. It is ideal for trough or sink gardens.

Picea abies 'Nidiformis' is a thoroughly miniature form (13cm/5in) of the Norway spruce. It has rather spreading branches but very even and dense growth. *P. glauca* 'Albertiana Conica' is deservedly one of the most popular dwarf trees (25cm/10in) with its conical shape and a flush of short bright green foliage in the spring.

Pinus mugo, the mountain pine, is itself too sprawling, but individually named dwarf forms, 'Mops' being one, are well worth seeking out.

Thuja orientalis 'Aurea Nana' is a miniature of the Western Red Cedar, seldom reaching more than 25cm/10in in 10 years, and dense with yellow-green needles.

The tall, slim look of some of the conifers can give height to containers and a new shape to mixed plantings. Naturally the very slow growing sorts are fairly expensive as they have taken a long time and a lot of effort to produce and until they get well established they will need special care to see that they do not dry out nor are swamped by some of the more vigorous growers.

Quite a mouthful but a splendid small tree is *Taxus baccata* 'Fastigiata Aureo-Marginata', the golden Irish yew. Complaints are sometimes made that it is unusually slow-growing but this is not necessarily so provided that it is given good soil and some attention while becoming established. It is completely upright growing and provides a column of fine gold-edged needle foliage.

Also columnar, very slow-growing and eminently suitable for window boxes, the blue-grey foliaged *Juniper communis* 'Compressa' is unlikely to grow more than about 30cm/1ft in a dozen years. The slightly coarser but very easy Lawson's cypress, the grey-green *Chamaecyparis lawsoniana* 'Ellwoodii' is quite commonly seen and is usually comparatively cheap.

There are much taller growing conifers, some with a pencil-like look, and a cultivar *Juniperus virginiana* 'Skyrocket' of a blue-grey colour and reaching 3-3.6m/10-12ft high is one of the best. They can reach up to 30cm/12in in diameter and look spectacular.

Left: A bonsai chamaecyparis is an attractive focal point in a decorative container.
Above: *Taxus baccata*, the yew.
Top: *Chamaecyparis obtusa*.

Cordyline

[Cabbage Palm; Australia/New Zealand] A group of evergreen palm-like shrubs, these are not fully hardy and are often grown as houseplants. In sheltered areas, *C. australis* is the perfect plant for adding a touch of the exotic to a courtyard. It looks best and seems happiest when growing in a large container filled with rich potting soil. Its strap-shaped leaves are arranged in a great tuft at the top of a short stout trunk. Plants will take copious watering during the growing season and benefit from regular feeding. They seem quite unaffected by pests and are perfectly able to grow well in either full sun or fairly average shade. As they grow, some of the older leaves tend to shrivel and brown and should be removed for appearance's sake. Keep frost-free in winter. There is a very attractive bronze form *C. a.* 'Purpurea'. Some florists still name this plant *Dracaena indivisa*, which is no longer correct.

Corokia

[New Zealand] These evergreen shrubs are not really hardy, but they will usually grow well if they can be protected against a south or west wall, in full sun. They like light and well-drained, even poor soil. *C. cotoneaster* is a curious little shrub, with twisted tortuous branches. It is covered with masses of small yellow flowers in late spring and early summer and also has small orange-yellow berries later in the year. Propagation is by cuttings in summer.

Cytisus

[Broom; Europe] Small pot-grown plants of brooms should be obtained as they do not transplant well when they get older. Some varieties get very tall and need more rootrun than the container gardener can normally afford, but there are a number of deciduous brooms which will fit into large tubs and pots. The hybrid *C. × beanii* is a small and trailing sort not much more than 30cm/1ft high and 90cm/3ft across. It flowers in spring with golden-yellow blooms. *C. nigricans* is much later flowering (in July to September) and should be pruned hard back, but not into very old wood, in late spring. *C. × praecox* ('Warminster Broom') is useful as it is arching and very free flowering in a pale primrose colour in April and May. There is also a white form, 'Albus', and a cultivar 'Allgold' with long-lasting, rich yellow blossoms. If plants have a tendency to get over-large they can with safety be pruned back hard. They all like a sunny position and rather dry conditions. Seeds germinate freely, but the offspring are not necessarily true to type. Named varieties are better increased by cuttings of lateral shoots in late summer.

Elaeagnus pungens

[Japan] This elaeagnus has handsome evergreen foliage and the variegated forms are well worth growing. The best and most popular variety is perhaps 'Maculata' with each leaf heavily splashed with an irregular golden patch. 'Argentea Variegata' is similar but with silver markings. Both have rather insignificant fragrant flowers in late autumn. These beautiful shrubs, which if anything look better in the winter, will grow in ordinary soil in either sun or shade, although the leaf colour is better in the sun. They do not need much pruning and should be allowed to develop freely if room is available. Propagation is by cuttings in late summer.

Eucalyptus

[Gum Tree; Australia] Two eucalypts are valuable in container gardening: they are the widely grown blue gum, *E. globulus*, and the near hardy *E. gunnii*, the cedar-gum. Both can be grown from seed sown in heat in February/March or be bought growing in pots as 46cm/18in high miniatures. Each is capable of developing into a very large tree but the containers tend to restrain overenthusiastic growth and it is possible to prune them hard back every year in spring or remove new growth when 23cm/9in long in early summer. Propagate by seeds.

Gums have beautiful glaucous-grey foliage and add quite a distinctive change of leaf colour to gardens. They should be given adequate root room and frequent watering. Sheltered positions, in full sun, suit them best. Juvenile foliage is quite different from the mature growth and usually more attractive than adult leaves.

Fatsia

[Japan/Formosa] The single species in this genus *F. japonica* (Castor-oil Plant) is commonly used as a houseplant; however, it is passably hardy and adds a sub-tropical look to a courtyard or small paved garden. The large leaves, averaging 30cm/1ft across, are deeply fingered and of a shiny dark green. Milky white filaments of flowers form during the late autumn and early winter. Small plants are occasionally used in large window boxes but they grow eventually to over 1.8m/6ft tall and are more suited in the long term to a shady position in a large container.

This plant was one of the parents of a bi-generic cross (a cross between two plants of different genera) – the other being the Irish ivy, *Hedera helix* 'Hibernica'. The product is *× Fatshedera lizei* (produced in 1910; this is slightly shorter (1.2m/4ft) with leathery deep green and glossy palmate leaves. It is equally hardy, although also grown as a houseplant. Both plants have variegated forms with cream-white edges; they are a little more delicate, but all have good sculptural quality worth cultivating. Outdoors they grow in ordinary soil and are increased by removing rooted suckers.

Fuchsia

[Central and South America/New Zealand] Fuchsias were very fashionable in Victorian times and then went out of fashion. They are now back in and it is difficult to see why they ever ceased to be popular. Fuchsias should be in every garden; they are deciduous, and grow well in either sun or partial shade; they have a long flowering period; can easily be propagated from cuttings; come in a wide range of

shapes and sizes, and offer a great diversity of flower form and colour. The fuchsia flower is composed of a tube which ends in four sepals and four petals which are in a bell shape and often in a contrasting colour to the tube. Most nurserymen offer hundreds of named hybrids. They grow exceptionally well in containers.

Dwarf types (up to 60cm/2ft) such as 'Alice Hoffman', carmine and white, and 'Tom Thumb', cherry-red and mauve, can be used in window boxes and small containers. Trailers such as 'Golden Marinka', red flowers, 'Cascade', red and white, and 'Red Spider', all red, are particularly suitable for hanging baskets and for planting at the edge of raised containers when their growth spills over the edge and is seen to best advantage from below. These trailing varieties are not fully hardy and should be taken indoors for the winter. The taller growing varieties are legion and a number of them are suitable for growing as standards or half-standards.

Standard fuchsias are very attractive and are easy to train, but a greenhouse is helpful. The idea is to produce a straight stem to the required height and then to allow side shoots to branch out only at the top to produce a head. To do this a cutting is made about 10cm/4in long in August/September and is taken straight up – rubbing out any side shoots that are produced. When the required height is achieved – usually .9-1.2m/3-4ft for a full standard and 45-60cm/1½-2ft for a half-standard – the tip is pinched out and the resulting shoots at the top of the stem are encouraged to form a bushy head. A cane is needed to keep the young 'whip' straight and later a stout stake will be needed to prevent the head of the plant from blowing around or even snapping off.

The majority of fuchsias will live out of doors through the winter in mild climates provided they are planted a little deeper than normal and banked with soil. The standard and hanging plants will, however, need some cover as all of their growth is at the top of the standard stem. If both standards and other plants can be lifted, cut back hard and placed in a cool place under cover, they will, given a little heat in the spring, come into bloom much earlier and will give better value. They will, in fact, bloom weeks earlier than those which have to stay out of doors. If small cuttings can be taken in August and grown on in a greenhouse kept

at around 10°C/50°F they will continue growing through the winter and will have made nice flowering sized plants by April. Some growers do this each year enabling them to clear the containers for other plants during the winter and early spring. The young plants should be hardened off by gradually acclimatizing them to outdoor conditions before they are put into their summer positions.

Fuchsias enjoy rich soil, full sun or light shade, regular watering and periodic feeding. As the flowering season approaches do not stop the new growths unnecessarily as a pinched outshoot takes 8 to 12 weeks thereafter to flower.

Griselinia

[New Zealand] These evergreen shrubs are often grown at the seaside where they certainly thrive. G. littoralis is, however, a lot hardier than is commonly supposed. The leaves are very leathery, glossy and of a lovely apple-

green colour. A good fertile soil is best and a position affording some shelter from the east and north, especially for young plants. It will grow quite tall (up to 3m/10ft) but only slowly. Propagate by heel cuttings in summer.

Hebes

[Australasia/South America] Although said not to be reliably hardy except in favoured districts, the hebes will succeed in seaside districts, in most industrial areas and where they are in well-drained positions. These small evergreen flowering shrubs are often erroneously called Veronicas, a related genus of herbaceous plants. The smaller growing types are often used in window boxes where they prove long lasting if not able to continue indefinitely. Most have dark green evergreen foliage; some additionally have wine or purple colouring under the leaves and a few are variegated.

H. glaucophylla 'Variegata' is a small neat shrub with greyish-green leaves margined with creamy white. 'Marjorie' is hardier than most and grows to about 90cm/3ft high, flowering in July to September with white and light violet blooms. H. pinguifolia 'Pagei' (15-23cm/6-9in high) has small blue-grey leaves which are an attraction all the year round and small white flowers in May.

H. 'Autumn Glory' is a small shrub of rather loose habit growing to no more than 46cm/18in tall and has deep blue flowers on short spikes during late summer and the autumn. It is sometimes used for autumn and winter window boxes where winters are very gentle. Remove faded flowers. Propagate by cuttings.

Opposite left: *Cytisus praecox*.
Opposite right: *Elaeagnus pungens* 'Maculata'.
Above: Fuchsia 'Marinka'.
Above right: Fuchsia 'Cascade'

165

Hedera

[Ivy; Europe/Canary Islands] Few plants are more valuable for container gardening than the ivies. These evergreen climbers and trailers are excellent in cities where they stand up to pollution and have no objection to shade. *H. canariensis* and its variegated form *H. c.* 'Variegata' are colourful tall-growing, large-leaved plants which can be trained around canes and allowed to splay out from the ties or to clamber up a wall. The heart-shaped leaves are bright green, marked with silver and white in the variegated form. *H. helix*, the common or English ivy has many handsome and adaptable forms. For trailing there is 'Glacier', small leaves, edged with white, 'Sagittaefolia', with arrow-shaped leaves, 'Tricolor', pale green, white-edged leaves turning red in autumn, 'Gold Heart' (also called 'Jubilee'), dark green, gold-centred leaves and 'Hibernica' (Irish ivy), large dark green leaves; the lovely golden 'Buttercup' is one of the finest. Ivies are happy in either sun or shade. In bright sun they will tend to colour up better with shorter spaces between the leaves; in dense shade they will lose some of their variegation (if variegated) and be lusher. Pieces root with ease, even in water.

Many of the varieties grown in the home can be put out of doors but when doing so, see that they are hardened off for outdoor life before moving them outside permanently in May.

They should be gradually accustomed to the harder conditions, otherwise soft, lush growth produced indoors may be seriously burnt if put out in full sun or scorched with cold or wind during the harsher months.

Hibiscus

[Syria] This genus includes deciduous and ever-green plants, some of which are grown in the greenhouse or as houseplants. *H. syriacus* (1.8-3m/6-10ft) is a hardy deciduous shrub which makes an excellent tub plant if it can be placed out of biting cold winds and in a sunny position.

The leaves are deep shining green and wide flowers make a fine display from July to October although the individual flowers are short-lived. The variety 'Blue Bird', with single blossoms of a violet-blue, and an old hybrid 'Hamabo', with soft pink flowers and a crimson eye, are perhaps two of the best, although there are a number of double-flowered varieties in beautiful shades of white, pink, red and purple.

Hibiscus do well in fertile soil, given shelter. Long shoots may be cut hard back after flowering, and new plants can be obtained from cuttings of non-flowering shoots in July.

Hydrangea

[North America/Japan] Hydrangeas, when well grown, can be most effective in containers. They will not, however, look after themselves – they have to be cared for. The splendid shrub *H. macrophylla* or *H. hortensia* is sold by florists as a pot plant when it is smothered with large flower heads. The plant itself is quite winter hardy, but its young leaves should be protected from frost. However, they soon grow again if damaged. The plants respond dramatically in flower colouring to the acidity of the soil in which they are grown and thereby the grower who can regulate the acidity can grow plants which have flowers from deep blue, vivid purple, red to soft pink or blue or even white. A small collection of deciduous hydrangeas growing in large pots (at least 38cm/15in) or tubs filled with varying soils can provide a good range of flower colouring.

Acid soil produces blue flowers but it can be improved upon by adding alum to the soil or a proprietary blueing powder. Limy soil produces pink to red flowers and slightly acid soil – possibly one inducing pale blue flowers – could be turned into a slightly limy one by nothing more than tap water that is too hard.

The flower heads of hydrangeas are made up of male and female (sterile or fertile) florets and are borne on the same mop-head of bloom; happily, the more decorative sterile flowers predominate. In the best florists' varieties it is difficult to see the insignificant seed-bearing fertile flowers.

Pots should have a large drainage hole, and a good layer of crocks and well-rotted leaves at the bottom of the pot will help to conserve moisture. An all-purpose potting soil (with or without lime) is satisfactory, but leave plenty of space at the top of the pots for copious watering. If possible, allow the pots to begin to dry out before watering, but do not allow the plants to become so dry that they wilt.

Hydrangeas, provided they do not get too big, need very little routine pruning; it is sufficient if weaker shoots are removed in April; the dead flower heads, often attractive in themselves and used for dried flower arrangements, may be left on the plants during winter and removed at the time of pruning. Cuttings root easily in August and September.

H. arborescens 'Grandiflora' (height 1.2m/4ft) is a less decorative but frost-hardy American species. It has 15-20cm/6-8in heads of completely sterile flowers of creamy-white which can cause the rather weak stems to bend downwards. This shrub flowers in August and September on the new wood produced during the spring and summer and should be pruned back hard in April. The *H. macrophylla* Lacecap

varieties (height up to 1.2m/4ft) have flat flower heads of small fertile florets in the centre and a ring of large sterile florets on the outer edge. They have flowers in much softer colours and are strong growing and hardy. 'Blue Wave' and 'White Wave' are two attractive varieties.

H. macrophylla Hortensia varieties have round mop heads of nearly all sterile florets. They are larger than the lacecaps and according to soil type, are pink, red or blue. 'Ami Pasquier', deep red, 'Goliath', pink or purple blue, and 'Lovely', carmine or deep blue, are recommended.

Hydrangeas need regular but timely watering and feeding when in strong active growth. If a definite colour of flower is sought, attention must be paid to the hardness of the water and the make-up of the fertilizer used with the florist type. Semi-shade certainly suits them – they can get scorched and collapse if too dry and too hot. Despite these likes and dislikes, hydrangeas are very popular and when completely happy are very rewarding shrubs.

Hibiscus syriacus 'Dorothy Crane'.
Opposite: A popular houseplant, *Fatsia japonica* can add a sub-tropical look to a courtyard

Laurus

[Green Bay or Sweet Bay; Southern Europe] This evergreen shrub is the laurel of the classics, used for making crowning wreaths for victors. It is both a culinary herb and a very decorative shrub with glossy green lance-shaped leaves. A pair of aromatic bay trees, clipped either into a pyramid shape or as mop-headed standards, often look exactly right in tubs near entrances. Bay is a very tolerant shrub that will stand up well to clipping, cramped root conditions, pollution and short periods of neglect. It will thrive with plenty of sunshine and survive quite well if it does not get as much as it would like – the form merely gets a little looser. The small containers they are usually grown in tend to restrict growth and such plants should never be allowed to dry out completely. When given a bigger rootrun they will grow quite fast and then need snipping back periodically. They are subject to frost damage in cold districts and should be given a sheltered position. Trim tub plants, grown as standards or pyramids, to shape during summer. Propagation is by cuttings.

Lavandula

[Lavender; India] Lavender is an evergreen aromatic shrub for those who can give it a position in full sun. They give a happy welcome in a south-facing porch. *L. spica* 'Hidcote' has violet flowers in dense spikes which open fully in June and early July and can be picked for drying for use in pot-pourris and lavender bags. Growth is compact. The leaves are grey-green and the growth can be kept compact by hand pruning in spring. *L. vera* 'Nana Alba' is very dwarf with white flowers. Bushes should be trimmed back after the flowers have faded and need renewing periodically as they tend to grow leggy with age. Cuttings will root easily in autumn in a sheltered position.

Mahonia

[Hollygrapes; Asia/North and Central America] The genus Mahonia represents one of the most important groups of hardy evergreen shrubs for use in shady places. They do, however, much prefer the good things in life such as rich well-rotted leafmould and positions which shelter them from boisterous chilly winds.

Most grow best in some shade, the exceptions being the not quite so hardy white-veined and grey-leaved types such as *M. trifoliolata*. The best known are *M. aquifolium* (Oregon grape) which is used as ground cover, and two taller growers, *M. japonica* and *M. lomariifolia*, both of which are ideal for restricted areas such as courtyards. A beautiful hybrid arising from the last two is called 'Charity' with spiny deep green leaves and long spikes of scented yellow flowers throughout winter.

M. japonica is the hardiest of the Asiatic species. It flowers in the depth of winter in mild climates with racemes (which may be 30cm/1ft in length) of palest lemon-yellow flowers and a lily-of-the-valley fragrance. It has large, beautifully-split sculptural leaves of up to 60cm/2ft in length and is a very impressive shrub.

M. lomariifolia is less hardy and has many (up to 20 pairs) small leaflets – a distinctive feature. The fragrant deep yellow flowers appear from January to March. The specific name implies a resemblance to a fern. It is quite tall-growing and capable of reaching 1.8-3m/6-10ft.

Like all large evergreen shrubs mahonias must receive adequate water, and a regular spray overhead during the growing season helps to freshen them up. Mahonias are best bought as small shrubs in 13-18cm/5-7in pots in September/October or late April/early May. Cuttings of *M. japonica* and 'Charity', which should be of well-ripened wood, will root easily in a mixture of peat and sharp sand in a close, shaded frame.

Myrtus

[Myrtle; Southern Europe/West Africa] The common or true Myrtle, *M. communis*, is hardy in most districts – particularly by the sea. It has been cultivated in Britain since the sixteenth century. It is an aromatic evergreen shrub, as a pot plant reaching a height of 60cm/2ft, with white flowers from June to August followed by blue-black berries; the stems are densely covered with deep green leaves. It needs full sun, some protection from cold winds and well drained soil. The form 'Variegata' is a great improvement on the type and is no more delicate. Increase by cuttings taken in early summer.

Palms

[China/Canary Islands] Most palms come from sub-tropical or tropical regions and are grown as house or conservatory plants, but one palm is hardier than most and that is *Trachycarpus fortunei*. This is the Chinese, Chusan or Fan palm developing into a small tree (2m/6ft) with a single trunk, heavily fibred. The green pleated leaves can reach 60-90cm/2-3ft across and will last for many years. *Phoenix canariensis*, related to the date palm, *P. dactylifera*, is seen grown in tubs and while tolerant of inclement weather, is only suitable for sheltered areas and should not be put to the test of too hard cold. Both palms enjoy good drainage and a rich potting mixture. Strong winds can damage the large leaves and some sheltered position should be chosen for them.

Perovskia

[Afghanistan] These hardy shrubby perennials come from Afghanistan. *P. atriplicifolia* is a deciduous semi-woody shrub (90cm/3ft) with a sage scent, finely cut grey-green leaves and 25cm/10in long flower spikes of violet blue in August and September. It loves the sun and a well-drained soil. Cuttings root very easily. This relative of the salvia is unusual and well worth growing.

Phormium

[New Zealand] *P. tenax*, the New Zealand flax, is a strong-growing plant with evergreen sword-shaped leaves, a handsome evergreen perennial. It resembles a very large flag iris in leaf shape but with leaves from .9-2.7m/3-9ft long. The decorative leaves are very useful for creating a feel of the waterside or of a sub-tropical rain forest. They are tolerant of pollution, practically any aspect and a variety of soils but do appreciate plenty of moisture at the roots. A bronze purple variety, *P. t.* 'purpureum', with bronze-purple leaves, is sometimes seen. Propagation is best by division.

Pieris

[Flame of the Forest; Asia] Pieris require very much the same conditions as rhododendrons and they are often grown together. They need a lime-free soil and dislike drying out. The young tender growth is liable to be nipped by late frosts unless precautions are taken to keep the plants protected from the north and east and grown in light shade. All the pieris are evergreen, with brilliantly coloured new foliage in the spring at the same time as the lovely racemes of flowers resembling lily-of-the-valley. The leaves change slowly to dark green. *P. japonica* has coppery-red leaves in spring and is comparatively small growing (1.2-2m/4-6ft). *P. formosa* 'Forrestii' has most striking red young leaves maintained for a long time. There are a number of named hybrids and forms, including variegated forms. Late in the autumn, all produce flower buds which remain attractive throughout the winter and open into the characteristic sprays of waxy white flowers in April and May. Large pots or tubs should be used for these truly beautiful, arresting shrubs.

Opposite: *Cordyline indivisa*, pelargoniums, fuchsias and impatiens in a courtyard.
Below: *Chamaecyparis lawsoniana* 'Fletcheri', aucuba and coleus in a shallow container.
Right above: *Rhododendron* 'Blue Diamond'.
Right below: *Pieris formosa* 'Forrestii' has beautifully coloured leaves

Potentilla

[Cinquefoil; Northern Hemisphere] The potentillas include medium-sized deciduous shrubs of tidy habit that will thrive practically anywhere, in any soil and in sun or shade, but they do best in a sunny position. *P. fruticosa* is the most popular with small dissected light green leaves and flowers like single wild roses (or strawberries) in shades of yellow and white over a long period from May to September. Many named forms are available, flowering from June to October, including 'Farrer's White', small and compact with white flowers, and 'Vilmoriniana', with silver-grey leaves and creamy-white flowers. Increase by bud cuttings in early autumn.

Rhododendron

[Asia] In confined spaces it is essential to see that shrubs that are selected are as attractive for as long as possible throughout the year. During the flowering season all rhododendrons look handsome but the majority of evergreen rhododendrons have very sombre leaves and when this obstacle can be overcome by using types which have the more attractive foliage so much the better. A number of rhododendrons are very tall-growing and would quickly outgrow the space they occupy. The following varieties have different leaf shapes and colouring and will not quickly outgrow their welcome. The hybrid *R.* 'Praecox' (1.2m/4ft) often starts to flower in mid-January in mild areas and has rose-purple flowers on a bushy shrub. It dislikes frost. A red hybrid, *R.* 'Elizabeth' (60cm/2ft), has attractive foliage and trumpet-shaped blooms in April and May. *R. williamsianum* (height 1.2m/4ft) with unfolding bronze leaves changing to green and blue-grey and reddish-pink flowers in April, and its hybrids – particularly 'Mystic' which is pale pink and will not exceed 1.2m/4ft in 25 years – should be tried. Other recommended hybrids are the two small-growing blues *R.* 'Blue Diamond' (90cm/3ft), very free flowering and intense violet-blue in April, and *R.* 'Blue Tit', smaller-growing and of a paler lavender-blue shade.

Rhododendrons must have an acid, or at least a neutral, soil but this need prove no hardship to the container gardener. He may have to buy soil for his containers and in this case it must be free from lime. Top-dressings of well-rotted leafmould or peat will keep the kinds mentioned happy for a number of years. Overhead watering will help in the development of flowerbuds and a constantly moist soil will also prove beneficial. Semi-shade is the best position. Remove the flowers as they fade by twisting, not cutting them off. Propagation is by layering or cuttings.

Rhus

[Sumach; North America] Distinguished from *Cotinus* by having pinnate leaves. *R. typhinius* (Stag's Horn Sumach) is a hardy deciduous tree grown for its distinctive leaf shape and fine autumn colouring. It is a small tree but is often slightly reduced in scale, say to 2.4m/8ft, when its roots are confined. It has thick succulent-looking branches and large pinnate leaves which turn to orange, red and purple in autumn. There are several named varieties with even more outstanding autumn tints. It should have plenty of root room and can easily be trained into a shape of a bare trunk capped with flat-topped branches. Ordinary garden soil and sun suit these small trees; they should not be allowed to dry out, and avoid heavy fertilizing which impairs the autumn colours. Propagate by layering or cuttings in August.

Ribes

[Flowering Currant; Europe/North America] The flowering currants are some of the most welcome of spring shrubs. Some of the varieties start blooming as early as February where winters are mild, while others are at their best in late May. *R. sanguineum* 'Atrorubens' can grow to 1.8m/6ft and has deep crimson flowers March to May. A lovely cultivar, which is considerably shorter and has flowers in April of a slightly paler hue, is 'King Edward VII'. Totally different is a dwarf with practically yellow leaves, *R. alpinum* 'Aureum'. All are very tolerant of some hardship but will repay better attention. They have a characteristic, rather pungent smell – not approved of by all. *R. speciosum* is generally small-growing but not fully hardy although the most attractive of the species with red flowers appearing from April to June.

Good drainage and the shelter of a south-facing wall is an asset. Pruning of the species should be undertaken in spring when necessary to trim the shrubs back into the desired shape. Cuttings root with ease in the autumn.

Rosa

[Rose; Northern Hemisphere] Roses are grown in pots and tubs in greenhouses for providing perfect, unblemished florists' blooms and for the production of earlier flowers. To grow them in containers out of doors involves a different technique but when they are successfully grown few plants can give so much pleasure. Strong growing kinds – hybrid tea or floribunda – are the most popular. Pots of at least 20cm/8in diameter must be provided, and it may be necessary to move them on into 25cm/10in pots after one year's growth. Any all-purpose potting soil rich in fertilizer is suit-

able and planting may be done at any time from October to April. The pots should be well-crocked and, if it is available, a 5cm/2in layer of leafmould should be put over the crocks. When planting fill in the soil gradually around the roots, firming well. Some pruning of the roots and shortening of the top growth can be done at the time of planting. Regular watering and some mild feeding throughout the growing season will ensure healthy growth and a quantity of blooms. Established shrubs should be top-dressed with fresh soil early in the year when hard pruning should normally be undertaken. Watch out for suckers (growth from below ground rising from the briar on which the rose is grafted) and remove these right back to the main stem by twisting them off. Some sun is essential to rose growing but it is possible to grow good roses in partly shaded situations. They need frequent watering, removal of faded blooms and careful attention to attack of pests (greenfly) and diseases such as mildew. Avoid at all costs trying to grow hybrid teas and floribundas under the shade of trees – they hate it.

Rosmarinus

[Rosemary; Europe/Asia Minor] Apart from being the perfect herb flavouring for roast lamb, *R. officinalis* is a very attractive evergreen shrub with fine grey-green pinnate leaves of a strong fragrance and pleasant pale violet flowers. It is comparatively slow growing and slightly tender in its first years; it can be trained into the position it is needed to occupy. It loves sun, and even more a maritime home, and is propagated from 15cm/6in cuttings. These can, if necessary, be rooted in water and when potted up quickly establish themselves. The variety 'Jessop's Upright' is more erect and perhaps tidier. If regular use of rosemary is made in the kitchen, regular pinching out of soft tip cuttings will be all the pruning that is needed. The soil mixture used should be light and quick draining.

Ruta

[Rue; Southern Europe] These hardy evergreen shrubs have blue-green foliage with a pungent scent. *R. graveolens* 'Jackman's Blue' is a slow-growing dense form of the species. The aromatic foliage is a vivid glaucous-blue, fernlike and invaluable when that colour is needed. The terminal clusters of bloom are small and of a mustard-yellow colour (rather unpleasantly scented) and are produced from June to August. They like a well-drained soil and plenty of sun. No pruning is necessary, although they may be cut back to old wood in spring to keep them within bounds. They can be propagated easily by cuttings taken in August.

Salix

[Willow; Europe/Asia Minor] These handsome deciduous trees grow in moist soil and are generally too large for container growing. *S. repens* (Creeping Willow), however, is suitable for a large tub as it seldom grows above 1m/3ft, and if it can be kept in dry and stony soil, in full sun, growth is further restricted. The grey-green leaves are covered in silky hairs and there are long grey catkins in late spring. The variety *S. repens argentea* can be grown as a miniature creeping standard.

Salvia

[Sage; Southern Europe] This is a large group of plants, including the culinary herb, *S. officinalis*. For garden planting there is a very decorative cultivar, 'Purpurascens', the purple-leaf sage in which stems and young foliage are suffused purple. There is also a three coloured form, 'Tricolor' with grey-green, white and purple-pink leaves. The sages like a warm, dry position in full sun. Spikes of purple flowers are produced in summer.

Above: *Rhus typhina*, the Staghorn Sumach, is beautifully coloured in autumn with orange, red and purple pinnate leaves.
Left: Floribunda roses can successfully be grown in containers outdoors, if carefully attended to with some sun and frequent watering. The rose here is Elizabeth of Glamis.
Below: *Salvia officinalis* 'Tricolor' has grey-green, white and purple-pink leaves

Santolina

[Cotton Lavender; Mediterranean] Santolinas are low-growing grey or silvery foliaged evergreen aromatic shrubs. *S. chamaecyparissus* (45cm/18in) has woolly silver foliage and bright yellow daisy-like flowers in July. Old plants become rather untidy and cuttings should be taken to replace old and straggly stock: Pruning after flowering helps to keep these shrubs in shape. *S. c. corsica* is a dwarf variety. Avoid rich soil and do not overwater; these wiry shrubs prefer sandy soil and sun. Propagate by cuttings during summer.

Senecio

[New Zealand] This large complex genus includes *S. laxifolius*, a low-spreading evergreen shrub with silvery foliage; it thrives in the poorest and driest of soils and produces its yellow daisy-like flowers during most of the summer. In rich soils it tends to get unduly leggy and some of the silver is lost from the leaves. A related species, *S. monroi*, has many edges to the white-felted leaves. Keep tidy by thinning out old and overgrown shoots after flowering. Increase by cuttings in August.

Viburnum

[Europe/Asia] Viburnums are a large genus of evergreen and deciduous shrubs of very varied appearance and quite a number would not be easily recognized as relatives of the others. All are quite hardy and most are very tolerant of a wide range of soil and situation. *V. tinus* (laurustinus) (up to 2m/7ft) is evergreen and flowers through the winter, often to April, with 8-10cm/3-4in heads of small pink and white flowers. It should not be pruned if this can be avoided as it usually develops into a nice shape if left alone. *V. plicatum* (previously *V. tomentosum*) is deciduous and is commonly known as the Japanese Snowball tree. This medium-sized shrub (2.4m/8ft) has globular white flowers in pairs, each about the size of a tennis ball, in late May and early June. Both plants thrive in moist soil, protected from north and east winds; a position in full sun is best, although *V. tinus* will tolerate some shade. Propagation is by cuttings in early summer or layering in September.

Vitis

[Vines or The Grapes; Europe/Japan] The ornamental vines are useful for giving height, a canopy of foliage, gorgeous autumn colours and grapes or grape-like fruit even where the truss is far removed from the luscious bunches at the fruit stand. They are excellent for clothing walls and fences. *V. × 'Brandt'* is a chance seedling of very mixed parentage which does fruit with sweet aromatic bunches of purple black grapes and has attractive three to five lobed leaves which turn a deep red or purple with lighter veining in the autumn. *V. coignetiae* is not only very strong growing but also impressive. The leaves are roughly rounded and turn crimson in the autumn. Small black inedible berries are produced. An ornamental variety, *V. vinifera* 'Purpurea', has red leaves turning to purple in autumn.

All grapes love the sun and a plentiful supply of moisture, regular top-dressings of bonemeal and, when flowers have set, small doses of fertilizer high in nitrogen to produce fruits. Propagation is by cuttings or layering.

Bulbs for containers

When most bulbs are bought they already have within them perfectly formed embryo flowers. All the grower needs to do that first year is to bring the embryo out of the neck of the bulb and up to the flowering stage without set-back. To get them to flower again the next year depends to a large extent on how nearly the conditions they are grown under correspond to natural garden conditions. If large bulbs such as daffodils, hyacinths and tulips are grown in rather shallow window boxes they are unlikely to put on as good a show in their second year, always assuming that their wants after flowering are supplied. The build-up of the flower for the second year depends on the foliage being retained until such time as it dies down naturally and on the bulb being thoroughly ripened. Bulbs planted in beds in very shady gardens do not usually give of their best in successive years and often cease to bloom adequately even a second year; this is always due to the bulb not receiving enough sunshine to ripen it. The best destination for most of the larger bulbs once they have finished flowering is some country friend's garden.

Except for tulips, spring-flowering bulbs should be planted as early in autumn as is practicable at the indicated depth. Most bulbs will start to put down roots within a week or two of planting although there may be no sign of growth above ground until February, March or April. Establishing a good root system is essential. The only other needs this side of the flowering stage are adequate water and, with the taller growers, some form of light staking to prevent possible wind damage. The staking is best done with slim canes and garden twine or raffia. Once flowering finishes, carefully lift bulbs and heel them in a sunny, sheltered place or get them to a friend's garden as soon as possible.

Plants with other types of bulky rootstock, such as tubers and corms, are included here.

SPRING-FLOWERING BULBS

Anemone

[Windflower; Mediterranean] Two types of hardy perennial anemones are of interest for use in containers; the first is the windflower *A. blanda*, a low-growing plant (up to 15cm/6in) from Greece which flowers in February and March in shades of pink and blue. The other is *A. coronaria* (about 23cm/9in), the florist's flower with poppy-like blooms. Good strains of the latter are De Caen (single) and St Brigid (semi-double). Spring-flowering anemones grow from corms which should be planted about 7.5cm/3in deep in full sun or partial shade. They enjoy rich soil and regular watering. Anemones are not very long lived, particularly *A. coronaria*, but in a sunny place they could flower for two or three successive years and their foliage does not occupy much space so little is lost by leaving them in the container. Increase by division or offsets in late summer.

Crocus

[Mediterranean] The true species of the perennial crocus can be very charming and usually flowers in winter and early spring, but the large-flowered garden hybrids, many of Dutch origin, will create the most effect. 'Dutch Yellow' is one of the first to flower, followed by varieties in bronze, rich purple, white, blue lavender, self-coloured and striped. They like ordinary well-drained soil and full sun and show to best advantage in a sunny sheltered spot. Early autumn planting of the small corms is advisable. Propagate by offsets.

Hyacinthus

[Hyacinth; Eastern Mediterranean] Hardy bulbs, most are hybrids of *H. orientalis*. Medium-sized bulbs will usually produce one good flower spike each about 30cm/1ft high; the huge bulbs sometimes produce two spikes which are not so large and more prone to wind damage in window boxes. 'City of Haarlem', yellow; 'Jan Bos', red; 'L'Innocence', white; 'Pink Pearl', clear pink; and 'Bismarck', clear blue; are all excellent. They love sun and may need staking, if grown too warm; do this in the early stages. May be increased from seeds, but named varieties do not come true.

Muscari

[Grape Hyacinth; Asia Minor/Southern Europe] The grape hyacinths are hardy, long-lasting spring bulbs with small flask-shaped flowers in dense spikes and dark green pointed leaves. The leaves usually appear above ground in the autumn, survive the winter without damage and provide a background for the brilliant azure-blue flowers in April. Good species include *M. armeniacum* up to 25cm/10in, and its varieties, 'Cantab', pale blue, and 'Heavenly Blue', bright blue, and the dwarfer species, *M. botryoides*, 15-20cm/6-8in with sky-blue flowers. There is also a white variety. All love the sun and are happy in any average well-drained soil. New bulbs should be planted 8cm/3in deep early in the autumn; established clumps should be divided every three years.

Narcissus

[Daffodil; Europe, mainly Spain and Portugal] The hardy garden varieties of daffodils are probably the most widely grown of all bulbs. With their prominent, often scented trumpet flowers they are the most beloved of all spring flowers. There are several thousands of registered narcissi varieties and their number is increasing each year. The strong-growing older varieties are best for containers. The deep yellow 'Golden Harvest' and 'Carlton' with soft yellow frilled flowers are recommended, as well as the cream-white 'Mount Hood', the pure white 'Glacier' and 'Cantatrice', the white-petalled 'La Riante' with orange-red cup, and the jonquil hybrids, scented and with several blooms on each stem. Some of the miniature varieties, such as the tiny yellow *N. asturiensis*, the hoop petticoats, *N. bulbocodium*, the cyclamen-like *N. cyclamineus* and the pendant cream-white *N. triandrus albus* (Angel's

Tears) are excellent in small window boxes and trough gardens. They flower from February on.

Narcissus are tolerant of a wide variety of soils, kept moist, and are content with either sun and an open situation or semi-shade. Early planting in autumn is beneficial and the bulbs should be set with their tips at least 8cm/3in below the surface of the soil. Propagation is by offsets at the time of lifting.

Tulipa

[Tulip; Eastern Europe/Asia Minor] Tulips are some of the best and hardiest bulbs for containers as they are reasonably happy to be lifted soon after flowering. They were at one time always dried off in the sun after lifting. The early (March and April) singles and doubles (25-30cm/10-12in) are good for window boxes and higher positions as they are practically unaffected by wind. 'Peach Blossom', a rosy pink, and 'Marechal Niel', a bright canary yellow with an orange flush, are but two doubles. Recommended singles include 'Brilliant Star', red, and 'Van der Neer', deep mauve. The taller and later cottage and parrot tulips (up to 60cm/2ft) are more suitable for tubs and deep containers. 'President Hoover', orange-red, and 'Mrs John T. Scheepers', bright yellow, are among the best cottage tulips. The parrot types include the mauve 'Blue Parrot' and 'White Parrot'. For raised beds, some of the dwarf tulip species make a good choice, such as named varieties of *T. greigii* (23cm/9in), with handsome purple-marked leaves, and *T. kaufmanniana*, also known as the water-lily tulip. Both flower in April.

Plant 15cm/6in deep in October and November in rich soil and in some sun, preferably sheltered from wind. Propagation is by division of the bulbils.

Opposite above: Charming crocuses.
Opposite below: Hyacinths.
Above: Narcissus 'Edward Buxton' and Tulip 'Red Emperor'. Right: Tulip 'Brilliant Star' and hyacinth 'Delft Blue'.
Below: Anemone 'de Caen'.

173

SUMMER-FLOWERING BULBS

Canna hybrida

[Indian Shot; Central and Southern America] Cannas are half-hardy tuberous plants and must be lifted and stored on the dryish side in peat for the winter. They make splendid container plants with their wide leaves, some of which are tinted mahogany-red, and all have large impressive tubular summer and autumn flowers. These range in colour from deep red, through orange (some are orange-speckled red), to the palest yellow. The fleshy rhizomes should be planted, possibly best on their own, in March, April or May in 25cm/10in or larger pots, setting the strangely shaped tubers 15cm/6in deep. Care should be taken over watering until they have made a good root system when they can be watered freely and fed every two weeks. Cannas like the sun but should not be allowed to dry out completely. Dwarf varieties like 'Alberich', a lovely salmon-pink with dark-green foliage, will not grow over 45cm/18in tall, but stronger growing sorts will eventually reach 1-1.2m/3-4 ft.

Convallaria

[Lily of the Valley; Europe/Asia] This popular perennial increases readily by spreading rhizomes if it is given the right cool and shady conditions. There is only one species, *C. majalis*, which lifts its graceful arching stems above a pair of deep green leaves in April to display the sweetly scented, pure white and bell-like flowers. Shade and rich moist soil are essential for Lilies of the Valley; plant in early autumn, just covering the crowns with soil.

Dahlia

Some small-growing dahlias are suitable for container gardening; the bigger ones are deep rooting and a problem to grow in comparatively little soil. They are all half-hardy perennials of garden origin. The miniature and dwarf sorts (45-60cm/1½-2ft) include the cactus-flowered, pompon, decorative dahlias and those known as Lilliput dahlias (30cm/1ft) in single colours or with different stripes or shading. Some new hybrids start flowering when surprisingly young and it is claimed that these may be raised from seed sown in a greenhouse in March, planted out in May and flowered in July. Such plants would need to be particularly well grown and well fed for dahlias are thirsty and greedy. These plants will put up a continuous show provided that they have their wants supplied and faded flowers removed. The tuberous roots should be lifted after the first frost blackens the foliage. Tubers

can be stored in boxes of peat and used again the following year, but young plants bought annually in May are less trouble.

Fritillaria

[Europe/Himalayas] These hardy bulbous plants can sometimes be difficult; the stately *F. imperialis* (Crown Imperial) is most handsome, with its cluster of flowers on top of a tall stem. Named varieties embrace shades of yellow, orange and red. The smaller *F. meleagris* (Snake's Head) is more suited to containers, being only about 30cm/1ft high; each flower stem usually terminates in a drooping, bell-shaped flower that is basically white but heavily marked with purple in a chequered pattern. 'Alba' is white with green markings. Fritillaria bulbs must be handled with care; never buy any that are bruised or have been left in the open air for long. Plant them fresh in early autumn, about 10cm/4in deep, and in a good sandy loam, in sun or light shade. Propagate by seeds or by offsets.

Galtonia candicans

[Summer Hyacinth; South Africa] This relative of the hyacinth from South Africa is easily obtained, is cheap to buy and simple to grow. It is best planted in a sunny position, burying the bulb at least 15cm/6in deep whenever practicable. Soon after planting, the bulb will send up strap-shaped blue-green leaves and a tall (to 1.2m/4ft) flowering stem which is capped with a loose raceme of large drooping white bells. There is often a suggestion of green colour in the flowers. These should open around August/September. Bulbs should not be allowed to dry out and should be left undisturbed. Propagation is by offsets, which are not frequently produced, or by seeds which are easy.

Gladiolus

[South Africa/Eastern Mediterranean] Most people think only of the large-flowered hybrids of gladiolus but there are a number of attractive species of these half-hardy peren-

Opposite: *Canna hybrida* produces impressive flowers that range from deep red through orange and orange-speckled red to pale yellow.
Above: Miniature and dwarf dahlias, such as 'Ormerod', are suitable for container gardening.
Right: Lilies are a challenge to grow but are worth a try for their exotic flowers

nials. The best is *G. byzantinus* (60cm/2ft) from Asia Minor which is fully hardy. The flower colour is a very strong magenta-crimson and blooms appear early in June. This corm when happy in a sunny position and well-drained soil, will spread freely and should not be disturbed.

The popular gladiolus hybrids include the large flowered butterfly, primulinus and miniature groups, the latter two being suitable for large containers. The primulinus and miniature hybrids have a wide colour range, often with contrasting centres, available in normal forms or in mixtures. The miniature 'Bo Peep', like most others in this group, has frilled flowers.

Corms are normally planted in April, about 10cm/4in deep, in a sunny position. In windy situations it is advisable to stake the corms when planting; this not only eventually provides support for the comparatively large flower spike but also marks the planting position until growth appears. Some bonemeal applied at the time of planting will help to provide good flower spikes and it is important to see that the corms do not dry out completely. After flowering the corms should be lifted (about November), dried off and the new corm (situated above the old) separated from the old. The new corms should be stored dry until the following spring.

Iris

[Northern Hemisphere] This large genus includes rhizomatous and bulbous species, the latter being most suitable for container gardening. The most popular are the hybrids which fall into three groups – the Dutch, Spanish and English. The Dutch irises (38-60cm/15-24in) flower first in May and June, followed by the Spanish (30-45cm/12-18in) and lastly the English (30-60cm/1-2ft) in July. All come in a variety of colours, except the English which have no yellow forms. The English irises have the largest flowers, 13cm/5in wide, and the Spanish the smallest (9cm/3½in). All should be planted in October, 10-15cm/4-6in deep, in full sun and light soil for the Dutch and Spanish types. These should be lifted after flowering for the bulbs to dry off before replanting in October. The English irises do not need lifting, and they do best in a richer, more moist soil. Propagation is by division.

Lilium

[Lily; Europe/Northern Asia/North America] Many lilies are quite a challenge to grow but a number can be grown very successfully in pots. The pots or tubs must be fairly deep and rich leafy soil mixture should be used. Large containers will enable them to be left undisturbed for several years, merely being top-dressed with fresh soil. Lilies grown in smaller containers will need repotting each year. All containers should be free-draining. Most lilies used are stem-rooting, i.e. roots are produced on the growing stems; bulbs, therefore, need planting deeply and space should be left at the top of the containers for subsequent topping

up with new soil once the growth has emerged above soil level. They should be watered only moderately until growth is well established and can be allowed almost to dry out before re-watering during the growing season. Some winter protection from excess rain may be necessary. The oriental lilies are very exotic, with large bowl-shaped deeply-fragrant flowers, and happily there are many bulbs of various colours from which to choose. *L. auratum*, the golden-rayed lily of Japan, and the oriental hybrids as they are called, developed from crosses made between *L. auratum* and *L. speciosum*. A cool greenhouse is very helpful to start them into growth.

L. regale from Western China makes a fine show when grown in tubs. It carries huge white trumpet-shaped scented flowers with light purple markings on the outside of the petals. A well-grown clump will certainly reach 1.2m/4ft high in July when the blooms begin opening. Whenever possible they should be planted about 20cm/8in deep. A layer of coarse sand

just below the bases of the bulbs helps prevent rot. Give plenty of sunshine and plant as soon as received, avoiding specimens that have dried out.

Ranunculus

[Far East] *R. asiaticus* (up to 30cm/1ft) is not hardy, and the tuberous roots are easily killed by frost; the plants should be lifted in autumn and stored for the winter. But their showy flowers add so much colour to the late spring scene that they are worth a little extra trouble. They are usually offered as a mixture of semi-double flowers in all colour tones from white to deep red. Plant the tubers, claws downwards and 5cm/2in deep, in March and April after the worst frosts, in sun and shelter and in fertile soil enriched with peat. Propagation is by division of the tubers in spring.

AUTUMN-FLOWERING BULBS

The colchicums are beautiful autumn-flowering bulbs but unfortunately after their flowers they produce large leaves which turn brown as they fade. They are ideal for growing in short grass where the pastel crocus-like flowers add welcome splashes of colour. Pure white, rose-pink and lilac colours are available from *C. autumnale*. The genuine autumn crocus (*Crocus speciosus* and its varieties) from Eastern Europe and Asia Minor are, however, different and are useful for planting under shrubs. Rose, lilac and white forms are available and should be planted about 5cm/2in deep from mid-August when they will flower in September and October. They are best left undisturbed from year to year.

Many other bulbs add welcome autumn colour, such as *Amaryllis belladonna* (popular name Belladonna Lily). Huge, trumpet-shaped flowers appear on naked stems in autumn, usually pale pink and sweetly fragrant, but there is also a pure white and a deeper pink form. They are half-hardy, and need some protection against wind and frost. Pot the bulbs in pots, 15-20cm/6-8in deep, in June, using a good, well-drained soil. Set the plants in a sunny, sheltered position. Propagation is by division after the leaves die down in summer.

Nerine bowdenii from South Africa is hardier than generally assumed and will flower for years at the foot of a south-facing wall. The delicate large flower heads are composed of small pink flowers on leafless 60cm/2ft high stems through the autumn. Plant the bulbs 10cm/4in deep in April or summer, in any type of good soil, preferably in full sun. Leave undisturbed for several years, then lift, divide and replant.

Sternbergia lutea (20cm/8in) has yellow crocus-like flowers in October, but unlike crocus the grass-like leaves appear at the same time as the flowers. Plant the hardy bulbs 15cm/6in deep in ordinary soil and full sun. Leave alone until the clumps become crowded, then lift, divide and replant.

Another cheerful little autumn-flowering bulb is the snowflake, *Leucojum autumnale*, whose white drooping flowers resemble snowdrops although the petals are shorter and more rounded and usually have a pink flush. Grow in sun and well-drained soil, setting the bulbs 5cm/2in deep in early summer. Propagation is by division.

WINTER-FLOWERING BULBS

Early crocus species, such as *C. ancyrensis* 'Golden Bunch', appear in February, at the same time as the attractive bronze-coloured *C. chrysanthus* and the white, pointed *C. biflorus*, several weeks before the more popular and large-flowered hybrids. The attractive little winter aconite, *Eranthis hyemalis*, appears now too. It seldom reaches more than 10cm/4in in height, and the small, bright yellow flowers surrounded by a frill of pale green, deeply divided leaves, poke their heads up over snow and frost. The small tubers should be planted as soon as available in early autumn, 3cm/1in deep, in well-drained moist soil, preferably loamy. They do very well in light shade and associate marvellously with snowdrops. Lack of water during the spring season may curtail flowering the following year unless the soil can be kept moist.

The dwarf bulbous irises, such as *I. danfordiae*, bright yellow, *I. histrioides major*, blue, and *I. reticulata*, scented and almost purple-blue, are perfect winter-flowering plants for raised beds and pans, in sheltered positions. They are perfectly hardy.

Chionodoxa luciliae

[Glory of the Snow; Crete and Turkey] These small blue and white star-shaped flowers are often evident after snow has melted, hence the common name. These hardy bulbous perennials (15-20cm/6-8in) are exceptionally easy to grow and will last for years – where they are completely happy they will multiply annually. The small bulbs should be planted 5-7.5cm/2-3in deep in early autumn. Pink and white forms are available but may take some tracking down. Propagate by seeds in spring.

Cyclamen neapolitanum

[Italy/Greece] These are perfectly hardy miniature perennial cyclamens with small rose-pink or mauve flowers blotched with a deep crim-

Below left: Galanthus, or snowdrops.
Above: *Iris reticulata* 'Harmony'.
Opposite: *Bellis perennis* 'Monstrosa'.

son eye. They flower when leafless from September to November and the corms, which should be planted as soon as they are received, should be only half buried. The attractive leaves, which persist until the spring, are deep green with silvery markings. They must be planted in good leafy loam and left undisturbed for years if sheltered from wind and sun. One route to success is to plant them in rather deep clay pans on their own. The tubers should be set with the slight indentation on top as it is from that surface that the roots emerge.

Galanthus

[Snowdrop; Europe] The hardy bulbs of single and double flowered snowdrops may be planted in September or October about 5-8cm/2-3in deep. Ideally they should only be moved immediately after they have flowered when in full leaf but to do so, for instance, to a window box would be a little unsightly. Dry bulbs do, however, flower even if they take some time to become established. They do not demand sun and show their pure white drooping flowers as early as January.

Scilla sibirica 'Spring Beauty'

[Squill; Siberia] These scillas are an enchanting blue and are so cheap to buy and so easy to cater for. The hardy bulbs are happy in either sun or partial shade and will seed themselves freely. They show flower colour – an intense blue – within a day or two of coming through the soil and open up fully from February onwards. Plant 8cm/3in deep.

Flowering plants and their seasons

It is impracticable, other than in a very rough manner, to allocate plants to particular seasons. One of the reasons for this is that a late spring flower in a favoured southern region may not bloom until early summer in a northern, less clement district. Another is that many annuals can be had in flower in different seasons (the flowering period being dependent upon when the seed was sown). A third is that some plants have a long flowering season and if placed in one group could just as appropriately be placed in another. However, an attempt at allocation to seasons has been made.

The plants for each sub-section have been chosen either because of their long flowering period or on account of the long-term effect of their foliage, petunias and pelargoniums being examples of the former and hostas of the latter. Some, like nemesia, have been included because they provide a brief but dazzling burst of colour and others because they offer flowers at a difficult season. An indication of the life span of flowering plants has been included, showing it to be annual, biennial or perennial; a temperature tolerance is suggested by the words 'hardy' or 'half-hardy'. Plants which are hardy will tolerate cold, but half-hardy plants will not survive frost and must not be planted out until all danger of it is past. They must also be hardened off, e.g. gradually acclimatized to outdoor conditions before planting out.

Tender plants, with the exception of a few, have not been included.

SPRING-FLOWERING PLANTS

Alyssum saxatile

[Gold Dust; Southern Europe] This hardy perennial, up to 30cm/1ft tall, flowers from April onwards when its tiny yellow flowers, which are produced in great frothing clusters, practically obscure the greyish foliage. It fits in well with other plants providing a foil for green-leaved plants when not in flower and is useful in containers because of the brilliance of its flowers in early summer. It is inclined to sprawl but can be tidied up by clipping it back immediately after flowering. *A. s.* 'Compactum' is about half the size, reaching about 15cm/6in. Any soil and full sun suit the plant. Propagation is by cuttings or seeds sown in mid-summer.

Arabis

[Snow-in-Summer; Southern Europe/Asia Minor] The perennial species, *A. albida* (syn. *A. caucasica*) is very invasive but is valued for its grey-green leaves and small white flowers in great masses throughout the spring months. The varieties 'Flore Pleno' and 'Snowflake' have large white blooms and are less apt to spread. Grow in ordinary soil and light shade; propagation is by division.

Armeria

[Thrift; Europe] These are small neat perennials, good for edging and in paving cracks and raised beds. The grey-green leaves are grassy, and small round flower heads show in May above the evergreen hummocks. *A. caespitosa* (5cm/2in high) has pink flowers, and so has *A. maritima* (height 15cm/6in); there is a white variety 'Alba', and 'Vindictive' is deep red. Any soil and full sun will suit armerias, and they can be increased by division in spring.

Aubrieta

[Mediterranean/Asia Minor] Thankful evergreen, low and spreading perennials, these are suitable for edging beds and for trailing in window boxes. They are easily grown from seeds, most being varieties of *A. deltoidea*, and they are just as easily propagated by division in spring or autumn. The small flowers appear from March to June and again later if they are trimmed right back after the spring display. 'Barker's Double' is purple-red, while 'Dr Mules' has violet-purple blooms. Plant in ordinary soil, ideally with some lime, and in sun.

Bellis perennis

[Double or English Daisy; Europe/Central America] The double daisies, about 13cm/5in high, are basically 'sports' of the common lawn daisy (which incidentally is native only to Europe and Central America). The double daisies, usually offered as the *B. p.* 'Monstrosa' strain, are also perennial; they are very valuable as they flower practically all the year round in mild climates, are extremely easy to cater for and have long-lasting flowers. A miniature daisy with deep carmine, button-shaped flowers, 'Red Buttons', looks good in window boxes and small containers. All of the sorts available do not demand large pots nor much attention. Mixed doubles can sometimes be had in most shades of red and pink and in white. Double daisies should be planted in the autumn or in February and grown in sun or light shade for the main spring and summer display. Propagation is from seeds sown in May, but named varieties are better increased by division in early spring.

Cheiranthus

[Wallflower; Europe] Although hardy perennials, wallflowers are usually treated as biennials as they are short-lived. They get too leggy and sparse-flowering if kept over from one flowering to the next. They are excellent as container plants, in mixed schemes with tulips and Forget-me-nots. Seed is sown in May. The resulting seedlings are grown on in a nursery bed where they develop into sturdy plants for setting in their flowering positions in the autumn.

Varieties of *C. cheiri* (the cottage type) with the heavy scent come in blood-red, gold, orange, primrose-yellow, mahogany-brown and in mixed shades, such as the 'Tom Thumb' strain, and bloom from February to May. The taller varieties vary from 38-45cm/15-18in and dwarf types, suitable for window boxes, 23-30cm/9-12in. The hybrid Siberian Wallflower *C.×allionii* has bright orange or apricot flowers held on flatter heads during May. They are usually about 30cm/1ft in height.

Young transplanted stock can sometimes be bought in the autumn for those who do not have the opportunity (or desire) to raise their own from seed. Keep plants well watered until they are well-established and avoid planting out in windy or frosty weather. After flowering, the plants should be pulled up and destroyed before they seed.

Try not to use the same soil a second year because wallflowers exhaust whatever soil they are grown in. Any soil and full sun suit these plants.

Iberis

[Candytuft; Southern Europe] These small plants are excellent for town gardens as they do not mind pollution. *I. sempervirens* is a hardy evergreen perennial, best in the variety 'Little Gem' (10cm/4in), a mass of tiny white blooms in May. There is also a double-flowered form. Even in poor soil iberis will flourish, and best in sun; pick off the dead blooms to extend the flowering period. Propagation is by cuttings in summer.

Myosotis

[Forget-me-not; Europe] The hybrid Forget-me-nots are invaluable in the spring for there is hardly a truer blue flower and they are so accommodating that they will grow practically anywhere. They relish a certain amount of shade and moist soil. They are grown as biennial plants, but seed themselves freely throughout the summer. The varieties 'Blue Ball' (15cm/6in), 'Royal Blue' (20cm/8in) and the variant 'White Ball' are excellent types. Plant in good, preferably moist, soil and in light shade.

Phlox

[United States] The perennial *P. paniculata* is not really suitable for container gardening, but the dwarf species *P. subulata* (5-10cm/2-4in) grows well in paving and as edging. It has purple or pink flowers in April, and among many named varieties are the blue 'Bonita' and the pale pink 'Apple Blossom'. Good soil and a sunny position will suit these plants; they are best increased by cuttings in summer.

Polygonatum hybridum

[Solomon's Seal; Europe/North America/Asia] Polygonatum are perfect perennial plants for shady positions. They have thick creeping rhizomatous rootstocks from which arise 60cm/2ft long arching stems, bearing blue-green leaves and rather small but attractive bell-shaped greenish-white flowers. Solomon's Seal is sometimes listed as *P. multiflorum*. There is a variegated form 'Striatum' which also manages to grow in shade where its paler flecking shows to advantage. Flowers are produced in the late spring and dark berries appear in the autumn. Polygonatums enjoy rich moist soil when they will make stately and elegant plants. Top growth should be cut down when it begins to fade in late autumn and the plants should be given a top-dressing of leafmould in spring. Propagation is by division of the spreading rhizomes in spring or autumn.

Primula

[Primrose, Auricula, Polyanthus, Cowslip; Europe/Asia] The primrose family is a very large one and includes many types of diverse shape, hardiness and flower arrangement. The early flowering perennial primrose of the woods, *P. vulgaris*, and the cowslip, *P. veris*, with its delicate pale-yellow flowers are both well known in the wild. Modern cultivars of both types are well worth growing in containers for the early spring display. The auriculas, which have been derived from *P. auricula*

are beautiful plants (15cm/6in) perfectly suited to the specialist who fancies the unusual in the way of colouring. The 'Dusty Miller' ranges have flowers in soft, often bizarre colours, usually beautifully muted shades of purple, yellow, mahogany and greenish-yellow. A number have soft green foliage covered with or at least margined by a mealy white powder or farina. Dozens of named and un-named hybrids are available which give year-round interest with their foliage appeal and unusually coloured spring flowers. The fleshy rootstocks of these plants are inclined to ride out of the soil, and for really good plants full of bloom they should have rich soil shaken over their exposed roots or should be lifted every two or so years, divided and be set deeper down.

P. denticulata is the Himalayan drumstick primula with dense circular heads of lilac or purple blooms held on 15-23cm/6-9in flower stalks above the neat foliage from March to May. 'Alba' is a white form and 'Ruby' is deep-purple. *P. japonica* is usually known as the candelabra primula and has 45cm/18in stems bearing whorls of white, pink, purple or crimson flowers during May and early June started indoors. The fabulous range of polyanthus is a cross between the primrose and the cowslip; they are available in shades of blue and purple, yellow, red, pink, apricot, white with yellow throats and the bicolours, usually in the Pacific strain.

All primulas enjoy some shade and a regularly moist soil; some will stand quite wet conditions but none will tolerate a really dry state for long. Good rich soil suits them best with plenty of leafmould worked in and some regular liquid feeding during the growing

Opposite left: *Primula* × 'Wanda'.
Centre: The true blue flowers of *Myosotis alpestris*, the Forget-me-not.
Above left: *Saxifraga umbrosa*.
Above: Violas in an ornate container.
Left: *Primula auricula* 'Blairside Yellow'

months. If they can be used just for their flowering season so much the better, but if they have to be left in situ all the summer their leaves have a pleasant cool quality that is not objectionable. Increase by division after flowering.

Saxifraga × urbium

[London Pride; Europe] This is a very long-lived but charming plant usually listed in catalogues as *S. umbrosa*. Between May and July it produces many fine 30cm/12in high flower stems bearing minute but perfectly formed star-shaped flowers of white and pink, each tiny petal being spotted with red. The leaves are arranged in a close-growing rosette and it is happy practically anywhere in sun or light shade. There is a very beautiful variegated form with its leaves splashed with gold known as 'Variegata' or 'Aurea', which does better in full sun. Increase by division after flowering.

Viola

[Viola and Pansy; Europe] The big floppy pansies *V.* × *wittrockiana* are generally treated as biennials because although perennial they tend to be rather short-lived. *V. cornuta*, with lavender blue flowers, lives for years and can be raised from cuttings although they also come partially true to type from seed. *V. cornuta* 'Alba' is a white form and like 'Jersey Gem' comes practically 100 per cent the right colour from seed. A good mixture with flowers of a smaller size but of a single colour is 'Bambini'. *V. lutea splendens* is a glorious yellow.

Some of the larger pansies (15cm/6in) have huge scented and velvety flowers with 'faces' of a different colour, the shades usually being rich ones. Swiss Giants is a popular group, the flowers being self-coloured or mixed in a wide range of colours. Most can be encouraged to flower late by delaying sowing until mid-summer and some of these are capable of producing a few flowers during the milder days of winter in addition to the spring bloom. 'Ullswater Blue' is one that is often listed as winter-flowering. Seed of most will germinate out of doors in May/June but earlier sowings under glass will produce earlier flowers and span a longer season. Young plantlets, provided they are not tiny, will normally over-winter successfully and cuttings taken in August will usually root quite swiftly. Good rich soil and some sun suits them best.

Summer flowering plants

Agapanthus

[African Lily; South Africa] Agapanthus are among the few perennial plants which do better in large pots and tubs than when planted directly in the garden. They are generally half-hardy and like cramped root conditions and flower profusely when this is provided. They need top dressing annually and feeding when in active growth but once they are flowering well in large containers they should not be moved on. A rich soil with a high proportion of loam is recommended. Although usually classified as bulbous plants these South Africans do in fact have a short fleshy rootstock with thick fleshy roots. *A. africanus* has evergreen strap-shaped arching leaves and long flower scapes – perhaps to 60cm/2ft – and umbels of 20 to 30 deep violet blue flowers in August. They should ideally be given the protection of some frost-free shelter during the winter when they can be kept practically dry. *A. campanulatus* (syn. *A. mooreanus*) is much hardier and has narrower leaves. They can scarcely be given too much water during the summer; in fact some municipal parks actually stand the tubs in ornamental pools so that the base just touches the water.

Some very much improved hybrids have been raised which are considerably hardier than anything seen before – they do, however, lose their leaves in winter. These are known as 'Headbourne Hybrids' and in Britain can be bought in shades of blue from indigo to very pale and in white. Sun suits them all best as one would expect of plants from South Africa.

Propagation is by division in spring or from seed – the latter a rather slow business.

Alchemilla mollis

[Lady's Mantle; Asia Minor] The leaves of this hardy perennial are perfectly round, deeply incised and with the attractive addition of scalloped edges. They are also a pleasant soft green colour and much sought after by flower-arrangers. Clusters of tiny sulphur-green flowers are produced in June and July. They are perfect town plants (30-45cm/1-1½ft), forming ground-covering clumps able to thrive in either sun or shade and in most soil mixes, preferably moist. Left alone the clumps will seed freely and extend the plantings or they can prove useful as gift plants. Crowded clumps can be divided in autumn or spring.

Althaea rosea

[Hollyhock; Asia] Hollyhocks are normally grown as biennial or annual plants, the seed being sown in June or July and the plantlets being well cared for until October or November when they may be planted in their permanent flowering positions. The species may grow up to 1.8m/6ft or even more, but some of the newer hybrids are less vigorous. A wide selection of colours can be had and some of the double-flowered strains are particularly attractive. 'Summer Carnival' and the Chater Doubles are recent outstanding strains with double flowers and some annual types with double flowers, such as 'Double Triumph Mixed' are valuable provided that seed can be raised early in the year. All hollyhocks need a good deep root-run and average soil, frequent watering, and it is advisable to stake the flower spikes as soon as they begin to appear.

Alyssum maritimum

[Sweet Alyssum; Southern Europe] *A. maritimum*, the low-growing (8-15cm/3-6in), sweetly-scented, carpet-bedding annual has been renamed *Lobularia maritima* but it is included here as an alyssum as it is so well known under its old name. Although so often associated with the blue lobelia it is a very valuable plant in its own right. 'Little Dorrit', white, 'Pink Heather', 'Tiny Tim', 'Carpet of Snow' and 'Violet Queen' are a few very attractive hybrids which are commonly grown. The foliage is tiny and has a grey appearance. This alyssum is a very easy and undemanding plant that will flourish in virtually any soil or position, flowering practically nonstop over the whole summer and autumn. It is invaluable for tucking into small spaces where a touch of white is needed. Seed can be scattered where required or tiny plants can be individually planted in April.

Antirrhinum

[Snapdragons; Southern Europe] We now have a whole range of new F.1 hybrid snapdragons which are vigorous and rust resistant (this used to be a tiresome virulent disease). Colours and flower shapes have all been improved and extended so that there are now ruffled and double flowered sorts and individual colours can be raised from seed. Snapdragons are best treated as half-hardy annuals, raising (or buying in) new plants each year for planting outdoors in April. The dwarf forms are particularly valuable for window boxes and when space is restricted. Some cultivars have recently won medals in both British and American Trials. A mixture 'Little Darling', growing between 23-30cm/9-12in tall, is compact and has a wide colour range. The mixtures 'Floral Carpet' and 'Magic Carpet' are also miniature. These plants will not need staking. All need a good fertile soil, full sun and regular feeding during most of the summer months. Once the main flower spikes have faded they should be cut back to shoots lower down which will usually continue the show.

Top: A terracotta pot contains-flowering begonias and tradescantia.
Above: *Calendula officinalis* 'Happy Talk'.
Opposite top: Alyssum and begonias grow in a stone trough.
Opposite centre: *Begonia* × *tuberhybrida* Pendula.
Opposite below: Agapanthus

Begonia

[South America] Few bedding plants can equal *B. semperflorens* (15-23cm/6-9in) for providing a continuous display. Cuttings can be taken from these half-hardy perennials (if this is done those from low down on the plant should be used as these produce bushy plants) but they really are best when grown from seed. The seed is as fine as snuff and when sown should be sprinkled on the surface of well-sieved soil and not covered. It can be mixed with fine sand to help get an even distribution. Pans of sown seed should be covered with a sheet of glass or with a plastic lid and left undisturbed to germinate. A greenhouse is an advantage, although they may, with luck, be raised on a sunny window ledge. Many different strains are available, with white, pink or red flowers and some with bronze foliage. Old plants can be cut hard back in the autumn when they will shoot afresh provided that there is a frost free greenhouse available in which to overwinter them. *B. semperflorens* are particularly valuable in window boxes, hanging baskets and for spots which receive quite a lot of sun. The name means 'always flowering' and this they certainly do.

B. tuberhybrida Pendula is the botanical name for a strain of pendulous begonias. They make ideal plants for hanging baskets when their large double flowers and foliage are seen to best advantage. They are tender tuberous plants, both named and unnamed varieties, but in distinct colours of yellows, pinks and reds. They should be planted in peat early in the year to induce them to make some root growth. They should be potted on and kept in good light under cover until all fear of frost is past. Harden off before setting outdoors in early June and take indoors before the first frost.

The Multiflora begonias are also tuberous rooted and form compact plants with a bushy habit. They are the nearest thing to *B. semperflorens* for continuous flowers, but the individual blooms are double or semi-double and sometimes quite rosebud-like in form. Named varieties are available.

The huge double-flowered begonias *B. × tuberhybrida* can be magnificent. The tender tubers for bedding or outdoor pot plants are available from specialist growers and garden stores in both unnamed and named varieties, colours ranging from white to yellow and red, many with frilled petals. Both these and the multifloras should be rooted in trays of peat in February and March and treated like the Pendulas. Care should be taken to see that the tubers are planted the right way up – the concave side is usually the top. In the initial stages of growth care should be taken when watering to see that no water lodges in the depression at the top of the tuber as this can cause rot. The pendular sorts should not be staked – they should be allowed to sprawl – but the tuberous doubles will need small stakes and regular tying in.

All begonias will take some shade but most prefer to have a few hours of sunshine, the tuberous sorts standing shade the best. The semperflorens will enjoy sun and not object unduly if the soil begins to dry out a little. The others should be kept moist at all times. The tubers should be lifted in the autumn before they are caught by the frost. Their top growth should be allowed to dry off naturally and when this has fallen they should be stored (preferably in rather dry peat) until the next spring when they can be started into growth again.

Calendula officinalis

[Pot Marigold; Southern Europe] This hardy annual has given rise to many beautiful hybrids (60cm/2ft) quite unlike the rather weedy single-flowered sorts that used to plague cottage gardens. The plants, with daisy-like flowers, will flower most of the year from successive sowings in the open and will be content with only light soil and little attention. Sun really helps to produce short sturdy plants, as does pinching out of the top shoot, but they will grow in some shade. The lovely double-flowered hybrid 'Geisha Girl', which is pure orange with incurved petals like a show chrysanthemum, 'Orange King' and 'Lemon Queen' are just a selection. Give them plenty of room to develop allowing at least 30cm/1ft between plants and feed at least every two weeks.

Campanula

[Bellflower; Europe/Asia Minor] Campanulas in nature are very widely distributed and about 300 species and hybrids of annuals and perennials are known. Some, like *C. isophylla* from Northern Italy, are suitable for hanging baskets and for trailing over the edges of containers. The predominant flower colour is blue although there are a number of lovely whites and both tend to show up to advantage in town gardens. *C. isophylla*, a dwarf perennial, is lilac-blue, but it has two varieties, 'Alba' (white) and 'Mayii' (mauve, with furry grey foliage). It is perhaps best considered as not quite hardy and one that should have cuttings taken from it in autumn to be overwintered indoors or in a

greenhouse. A hanging basket of one sort or of the two colours planted together can look splendid in July/August when they begin flowering. They look good in window boxes too.

C. cochlearifolia is the common campanula of the Alps and is a tough little perennial with harebell-like flowers, sometimes called Fairies' Thimbles, forming dense mats of fine foliage, wiry stems and pale blue flowers. Named varieties are available including 'Miss Willmott' and a white form 'Alba'. *C. poscharskyana* is a strong perennial grower (30cm/1ft) from Dalmatia with lavender-blue flowers. *C. pyramidalis*, the Chimney Bellflower, is upright growing and superb for use in pots. It grows easily from seed but needs care and shelter from winds as it can top 1.5m/5ft in height under very favourable conditions. It is best treated as a biennial. There are blue and white forms. All

campanulas will be happy either in sun or shade and prefer a rich soil mixture incorporating some leafmould. A regular feeding programme will ensure a continuous display.

Chrysanthemum frutescens

[Paris Daisy or Marguerite; Canary Islands] The Paris Daisy or Marguerite is not a completely hardy perennial, but is grown all over the Mediterranean, parts of America and Australasia and deserves to be grown much more extensively. This is the single white daisy with the golden eye that is sold in pots in bud or full bloom in the spring and as cut flowers. It continues flowering all the way through the summer and when it finishes can be cut back to bloom again in the autumn. *C. frutescens* does not need a great deal of heat but it must be overwintered under cover. Cuttings root easily in peat and sand in August/September and can be made bushy by pinching out the growing points to build up the required shape or trained like a fuchsia into a standard. They flower profusely in pots and tubs, need regular watering and feeding and like all daisies love sun. 'Etoile d'Or' is a lemon-coloured form.

Clarkia

[North America] Clarkias come in a very wide colour range with tall flower spikes and are extremely easy to grow. Most of the double-flowered hybrids now available have been developed from one of the original species, *C. elegans*. These half-hardy annuals do not transplant very well and are best sown where they are to flower, thinning out the seedlings to around 23cm/9in apart. Some thin twigs for support are necessary as clarkias are very inclined to snap off at soil level in any degree of wind. Most hybrids reach about 45cm/18in high and some of the salmon-coloured sorts like 'Salmon Bouquet' are particularly beautiful. Other shades include white, lavender, purple, scarlet and orange. Average soil and any position other than heavy shade suit them.

Coleus blumei

[Painted Leaf; Java] These perennials, usually grown as annuals, are popular houseplants and also used in outdoor bedding schemes. The new hybrid coleus offer a great wealth of leaf colour and should be included in as many plantings as possible. They are tender and should not be attempted out of doors until all danger of frost is past. May is a good month for planting and most will still be attractive in October. The flowers are insignificant and should be pinched out; this also helps to make the plants bushy. Tiny plantlets are usually offered for sale early in the year, already showing their leaf colouring, and a selection can prove quite a feature. Sun or shade is suitable to them although leaf colouring will normally be stronger in sun. They must not be allowed to dry out completely as this causes collapse and while they recover, some of the lower leaves are usually shed when this happens. Good rich soil and a weekly feed will produce splendid plants up to 45cm/1½ft. Treat as an-

Left: A riot of colour can be obtained from a container of mixed *Clarkia pulchella*.
Below: *Dianthus barbatus*. Opposite: *Fuchsia* 'Marinka' and *Campanula isophylla*.

nuals and discard when past their best; new plants are easily raised from tip cuttings, taken during the summer and overwintered indoors as a houseplant.

Delphinium

[Larkspur; Europe] The tall perennial delphiniums take up much room, but the annual species and hybrids can be sown in the autumn or the spring, in positions where it is to flower (although they can be slow to germinate) or small plants can be set out in the spring. The larkspurs have finely divided foliage and the Rocket type (springing from *D. ajacis*), usually with single stems of loose flowers, can be had in both tall and dwarf sorts. The hyacinth-flowered larkspurs have also been developed from *D. ajacis* and can be bought in separate colours or mixed. The colours available are blues or pinks of all shades and white. The branching larkspurs have stock-like double flowers in the same colour range. These originated from a different species, *D. consolida*, and are usually considerably taller (up to 90cm/3ft) with fewer and more scattered flowers. Larkspurs prefer a sunny position and to be supported by thin twigs. They enjoy rich soil and a regular liquid feeding.

Dianthus

[Pinks; Southern Europe] This group includes the well-known carnations, the pinks and the sweet williams. Dealing just with pinks, there are a number of perennial sorts which mature quickly from seed and produce a wide range of double and single flowers of colours extending from white to deep crimson. Most are scented and neat and low-growing (about 25cm/10in). *D. × allwoodii* is normally dwarf and free flowering in a wide range of colours. It is the parent of the modern hybrid pinks. They flower practically continuously and as a result are understandably rather short-lived. *D. deltoides* (Maiden Pink) is a small (15cm/6in tall) species which lives for years and seeds itself freely in cracks and chinks.

'Mrs Sinkins' is an old-fashioned fully-double, heavily-scented white perennial that grows easily from slips (pipings as they are called in some places). It flowers in July only. Dianthus provide nice frontage for containers with their neat blue-grey foliage. They all love the sun and some rough rubble in the soil mix for quick drainage. Named varieties are best propagated by cuttings in summer.

Dicentra spectabilis

[Bleeding Heart and Dutchman's Breeches; Asia] This graceful spring- and summer-flowering plant is a hardy perennial. It has finely divided, fern-like foliage, and rose-crimson heart-shaped flowers 2.5cm/1in long

on arching racemes. Old clumps should be divided periodically ensuring that some fibrous roots are left on each gnarled-looking piece of root. They really don't care whether they have sun or shade, rich or poor soil, although they prefer shelter from strong winds.

Digitalis purpurea

[Foxglove; Europe] In nature the hardy biennial foxgloves are found growing wild in some shade on the edge of woodland and they have colonized such sites as well-drained railway embankments. This has happened because they seed so profusely and will easily set up home if the soil is left undisturbed long enough for them to germinate. As the Latin name suggests, the best-known species is purple-flowered, the individual slightly drooping florets being borne in a tall erect spike, but they vary through mauve shades to white with purple spots. They can be grown from seed sown in April/May, or small plants can be bought in September to November when they should be planted in their flowering positions. The species is quite tall growing – up to 1.5m/5ft – but there is a lower-growing pure white form ('Alba') and selected primrose-yellow types which are almost dwarf for a foxglove – around 1m/3ft. Among new introductions is the 'Foxy' strain which can be grown as an annual and will usually flower in five months from sowing; it comes in a wide colour range.

All foxgloves do quite well in full sun provided they are kept well watered and have plenty of soil worked in around them.

Hosta

[Funkia or Plantain Lily; East Asia] Hostas have all the necessary good points for first-class container plants. They have a very pleasant habit (average 60cm/2ft high) and appearance, are perfectly hardy and adaptable and additionally have outstanding perfect foliage. They enjoy moist conditions in good fertile soil, and some shade but, provided that they do not dry out and that they get adequate food, will grow well in sun. The nodding flowers on tall racemes are short-lived but are produced in succession. Species with particularly attractive foliage include *H. fortunei*, grey-green, heavily veined leaves, and its variegated form *H. f.* 'Marginata Alba' with white edges to the leaves. Other variegated kinds are *H. crispula* with creamy white edges and *H. undulata* with a broad cream or silvery centre and waved edges. A strong grower is *H. sieboldiana* 'Elegans' with bluish-grey foliage and very pale lilac, trumpet-like flowers. There has been considerable confusion over hosta's names and this can in part be put down to the remarkable way in which a hitherto little considered plant suddenly shot into popularity.

Propagation is by division of the clumps in early spring.

Impatiens

[Busy Lizzie, Patient Lucy or Patience Plant; East Africa] Impatiens gained its name from the impatient way that it expels its seeds – they fly out as if fired from a gun. The genus includes hardy, half-hardy and tender species which are popular houseplants. The hardier types are also much used for summer bedding and containers and are grown as annuals. The tall-growing *I. sultanii* is now out of favour and has been superseded by the many attractive F.1 hybrids which are dwarf (23cm/9in high) and spreading in habit and have large flat flowers. The colour range has also been extended from white, through the soft pastel shades and fluorescent reds and oranges, to wine colours and there are even those with striped petals. Double-flowered cultivars are available but these do not stand up as well to outdoor conditions. Some of the best seed mixtures are 'Elfin' for really dwarf (15cm/6in) or 'Imp' or 'Treasure' for slightly taller-growing sorts. Single colour strains can be obtained, but as cuttings root so easily in water or under close conditions in soil, this seems pointless unless large quantities are needed. Seed should be sown early in the year with bottom heat and the resulting seedlings pricked out into boxes and possibly later moved on into individual pots. They should not be planted out of doors until all danger of frost is past – possibly June in the north. They will flower continuously until the first autumn frost. When only two or three plants are needed they can usually be bought as small plants in May or June. Either sun or shade suits them but they should be kept well watered. Because of their rather sappy nature they do not overwinter well in anything but really quite warm conditions and are really best discarded after flowering in autumn.

Kochia scoparia tricophylla

[Summer Cypress or Burning Bush; Southern Europe/Asia/Australia] This splendid rapidly-growing half-hardy annual can be used much like the permanent conifer to provide a dumpy or pyramid shape of finely-cut feathery foliage. This kochia additionally has a change of colour during the autumn from light green to deep purplish-red. Seeds can be sown directly into the container in May or small plants may be planted out when available. The flowers are quite inconspicuous and appear in the axils of the leaves. Well-tended plants in light soil and full sun will eventually grow to 60-90cm/2-3ft high; the variety 'Childsii' is more globular.

Linum

[Flax; Europe/North Africa] Two hardy annual flax are commonly grown: *L. usitatissimum* of wide distribution and cultivated for centuries as a source of fibre for cloth making. It has beautiful clear blue saucer-shaped flowers and finely divided foliage. The other is the smaller (30cm/1ft) scarlet flax from North Africa, *L. grandiflorum*, at its best in the brilliant red form, 'Rubrum'. Both are easily grown from seed sown in March and April where they are to flower. Seed can be scattered on the surface of the soil, lightly raked in and the spot marked with a sprinkling of sand. Successive sowings from March to June will provide a long display well into the autumn months. Flowers will appear from the first sowing around mid-June. Do not overfeed as they flower best when searching for food. Some sun is appreciated.

Lobelia

[South Africa/Eastern United States/Mexico] A large genus of hardy and half-hardy annuals and perennials, usually grown as annuals, in hanging baskets, window boxes and for edging. *L. erinus* is the lovely blue dwarf lobelia (10-15cm/4-6in) much beloved in bedding schemes, often mixed with white alyssum. It is a low-growing half-hardy perennial which is treated as an annual and planted out around May in hanging baskets and other containers. Some kinds (the Pendula varieties) trail several cm while others are quite squat and dumpy. Varieties include white forms, the 'Cambridge Blue' group and 'Crystal Palace' (dark blue, some with white eyes); there are also varieties with carmine red colours. Small plants should be used in containers wherever possible as they take up very little space and are not greedy. In shade they tend to get a little looser in form than when grown in bright sun. Average soil, kept moist, suits this plant. Seed is very small and should be sown in February in heat. Trays of healthy young plants are always freely available from late April onwards.

L. fulgens (popular name Cardinal Flower) is a red-leaved upright lobelia (30-90cm/1-3ft), very different from *L. erinus*. It has dark crimson foliage, arranged in a low-growing rosette, and a tall flower spike capped by brilliant scarlet flowers. It is hardy if some form of protective covering can be placed over the crowns during the worst winter months, but is not completely reliable. Should a cold frame be available it may be advisable to lift a few crowns and overwinter them there. This lobelia is at its best in rich moist soil and is sometimes grown by the water's edge. There is a particularly fine cultivar 'Queen Victoria' with deep red flowers. Propagate by division of the rosettes in spring.

Lysimachia nummularia

[Creeping Jenny; Europe] The Creeping Jenny is a hardy perennial that is very useful as ground cover in shaded and rather impoverished soil. It has bright yellow flowers set among the green leaves. With rich fare it romps madly away and become an embarrassment. The golden form 'Aurea', however, is much more acceptable and the long trailing stems with yellow leaves will do very well in even the poorest conditions. Bright golden-yellow flowers go very well with the yellowy-green foliage and are produced most of the summer. Plants are sometimes seen growing from the tops of upturned drain-pipes when their growth trails down the pipe in an attractive way; they also trail nicely over the edges of window boxes. Keep the plants on the dry side and never feed them to prevent unwanted spread. Cuttings root easily in spring and summer and the runners take root wherever they touch the soil.

Above: Nemesias in jewel-like colours.
Left: *Lobelia* 'Cambridge Blue'.
Opposite above: *Fuchsia* 'Sunray', variegated ivy, lobelia and impatiens in a trough.
Opposite below: *Nicotiana affinis* 'Sensation'

Matthiola

[Stock or Gilliflower; Europe/Asia] The annual stocks derived from *M. incana* are some of the most valuable of summer-flowering annuals. The Ten-Week Stocks (so called because they can be brought into flower in 10 weeks from sowing the seed under glass) are large-flowering dwarfs reaching between 25-30cm/10-12in high. They flower in June and July from March sowing but have only a limited flowering period. Various colours are available including apricot-pink and dark mauvey-blue. The single and double varieties are distinguishable at an early age; the doubles will have the lighter-coloured foliage. Taller growing stocks (60cm/2ft) which are freely branching can be had and are known as Branching or Giant Perfection strains. They usually give a longer season of bloom, mainly in shades of copper

and yellow. An intermediate kind, the Bouquet Stocks, are midway between the dwarf and tall growers. All of the annual stocks are often raised from seed sown under glass in March for planting outside from the end of May onwards. Do not allow them to become starved prior to planting out as they will not normally recover properly. A rich soil, full sun and approximately 30cm/1ft spacing between plants will ensure good sized blooms. The flower heads, particularly the doubles, are heavy and need some staking with short, thin canes. Brompton stocks are treated as biennials and are planted in their flowering positions in the autumn. Many will produce a few flowers right through the worst winter months in warm climates, but the real show is in the late spring. The deep purple and pale pink kinds are particularly attractive and completely double-flowered strains are also available.

M. bicornis from Greece is the Night-scented Stock and a low-growing hardy annual plant with a heavenly evening fragrance but dull lilac flowers closed up all day. Seed should be sprinkled liberally in small spaces between other plants in early spring for flowers from June onwards. Sun and a well-drained situation suits it.

Nemesia strumosa

[South Africa] This half-hardy annual offers a very wide range of jewel-like colours in the pouched flowers, perhaps unsurpassed by any other single cultivated plant. Red, orange,

yellow and blue bicolours are available. They are easy to grow and often look best when grown on their own in small tubs reaching about 30cm/1ft high. Only one complaint can be levelled against them and that is that they tend to flower themselves to death and have a comparatively short flowering season. They should be given the usual half-hardy annual treatment. At no time should they receive a severe check in growth, otherwise they are inclined to start flowering before they have built themselves up into bushy plants. These would, of course, produce more flowers over a longer period. They enjoy cool moist soil and some sun. There are two groups: the dwarf 'Carnival Mixed' and the taller and larger-flowered 'Sutton's Mixed'. Many strains can be had, some in single colours, such as 'Blue Gem'.

Nepeta

[Catmint; garden origin] This hardy perennial, sometimes listed as *N. mussinii*, is a hybrid correctly known as *N. × faassenii*. It is one of the easiest plants for a hot, dry situation and flowers continuously through the summer from May onwards. A light clipping all over will keep it in good shape and encourage the production of new bushy grey-green foliage. Growth usually reaches between 30-45cm/1-1½ft. The short spikes of lavender-mauve flowers are usually sterile but it is advisable to take them off as they fade. Some stronger-coloured sorts are occasionally available. Propagate by division in spring.

Nicotiana

[Tobacco Plant; Brazil] Decorative tobacco plants are usually grown as half-hardy annuals though they are capable of surviving through mild winters in warm areas. Young plants, however, produce better flowers. The majority of the popular kinds are deeply scented and the pastel colours available have been extended to include scarlets and crimsons. *N. affinis* (now more correctly *N. alata*) is a 1m/3ft tall pure white which opens its flowers at dusk and is very heavily scented. *N. a.* 'Daylight' and *N. a.* 'Dwarf White Bedder' stay open all day. A new hybrid 'Lime Green' is a greenish-yellow and is much sought after by flower arrangers; 'Crimson King' and 'Knapton Scarlet' have red flowers. They seem to do equally well in sun or shade. Young plants can be had in trays when bedding plants first become available and the majority will quickly start to flower and continue doing so until October. Plants can easily be grown from seed in a greenhouse. Tobacco likes plenty of water and some might need a little light staking and particularly so in exposed situations. Rich soil is inclined to make them rather leafy at the expense of flowers.

followed by a long flowerless period. Plants that have bloomed can be cut back and cuttings taken from the tips of non-flowering shrubs in August to provide new plants to be brought into a greenhouse for the winter.

The zonal pelargoniums P. × hortorum have a dark green zonal patch on their leaves and form the biggest group. Flower colour ranges from white to deep red and there are many variations in flower shape and scale. Some of the old varieties are still worth growing but many new ones appear each year and all have a long flowering season. 'Gustave Emich', large semi-double scarlet, 'Rycroft White', double, 'Paul Crampel', single scarlet, and 'King of Denmark', salmon coloured semi-double, have been favourites but are facing serious competition from the new, seed-grown Carefree strain.

The ivy-leaved varieties P. peltatum and hybrids are invaluable for use in hanging baskets and window boxes. They help to break up hard lines in containers. Mauve, pale and rich pink are the predominant colours but 'L'Elegante', bearing white flowers with dark eyes,

Left: Pelargoniums in a window box.
Below left: *Nigella damascena* 'Miss Jekyll'.
Below: Petunias grow in and around an urn.
Opposite top: Sempervivums in a terracotta pot.
Opposite bottom: *Sempervivum arachnoideum*

Nigella damascena

[Love-in-a-Mist; Mediterranean] Love-in-a-Mist is a hardy annual easily grown from seed scattered between other plants in positions where it can be left undisturbed. This can be done in September and in mild areas it will grow through the winter and flower that much earlier the following year or in March or April for flowering in July and August. Overall height is about 30cm/1ft. The foliage of this plant is bright green and feathery and the flowers are sky blue surrounded by feathery spurs. The flower is set in a 'mist' of pale green. The variety 'Miss Jekyll' is a semi-double strong cornflower blue and there is also a white form. Nigella will not survive a second year but it does self-seed and odd seedlings will appear the following year. They really look best when growing in groups of, say, 10 to 20 plants in good soil and full sun.

Pelargoniums

[Geraniums; South Africa] Geraniums, or as they are correctly called, pelargoniums, fall – not too neatly – into several groups. These are the regals, zonals, ivy-leaved, miniatures, variegated and scented-leaved, all of which are tender and half-hardy perennials, much used for summer bedding. Over the years the original species have been interbred, and quite a

number of the most popular varieties could not be said to be thoroughbred, but most do fall roughly into one category or another. The Regal pelargoniums P. × domesticum are shrubby plants with large flowers most of which are blotched with a stronger colour. They range in colour from white with a deep purple eye to deepest burgundy, but the majority of the plants fall in the rich salmon to bright red shades. Regals have a much shorter flowering season than all the others. Flowering is early in the year around April and May indoors or in gentle climates. Their use outdoors is in a way more limited than the rest as they can only be used as temporary plants providing a strong splash of colour for a month or two

additionally has cream-edged leaves which take on a very attractive purple edging in sunny and rather dry conditions, particularly in the autumn. 'La France', double lilac with maroon markings, 'Galilee', rose-pink, 'Abel Carrier', double purplish magenta, and 'Mauve Galilee' are some good choices.

The scented-leaved pelargoniums are more often grown as houseplants but they make particularly attractive plants for sunfacing window boxes especially if the small-growing ones like *P. fragrans*, known as the nutmeg-scented geranium, and its variegated form are chosen. *P. crispum* 'Variegatum' is a beautiful foliage plant even without its lemon scent and quilted leaves and should be in every garden. The flowers of all the scented-leaved sorts are insignificant. The taller growers, up to 90cm/ 3ft, are excellent for balconies, flights of steps and the fronts of mixed plantings. In these positions they are often brushed against and emit a pleasant scent. The miniatures come into their own in window boxes, and varieties such as the single red 'Black Vesuvius' with black-purple foliage (there is also a salmon form), 'Goblin', a deep red double, and 'Friesdorf' with 'butterfly' flowers are winners.

The ornamental and variegated-leaved sorts are fun. 'Bronze Queen', gold with a chestnut zone, 'Happy Thought', soft green with cen-

tral yellow markings. 'Henry Cox', a super red and gold tricolour and 'Filigree', a small busy plant with a spreading habit and lobed silvery-green leaves zoned pink and brown, are but four.

All pelargoniums, despite suggestions to the contrary, do grow in a reasonably rich moist soil containing a high proportion of loam, with occasional feeding. Starved plants will flower more freely but not with the same good-sized blooms: it really is a case of striking a reasonable balance. Set out the plants, in full sun, after frost is over, in May. Tip cuttings of all pelargoniums will root easily in a mixture of peat and sand in August/September but must be overwintered under cover.

Petunia hybrida

[garden origin] These half-hardy annuals are probably the gayest and most enduring of all the plants used in summer bedding. Over the past few years great steps have been taken in their development and double-flowered, frilled-edged, striped and picotee varieties are freely available. Seed can be sown early in the year, or small plants purchased for planting out in late May. They can be used in hanging baskets, tubs and window boxes and the lovely large trumpet-shaped flowers stand up well to bad weather; with dead-heading they flower right through to autumn frost. Baskets filled with large pure white 'White Swan' or other single colour plantings are some of the most effective. The striped varieties are also striking. All colours are very gay and sometimes nothing succeeds more than a generous planting of mixed sorts. The Pendula varieties are trailing and ideal for baskets. A few twiggy sticks may be needed to support some of the taller types (23-30cm/9-12in), but in sheltered positions this is unnecessary. Petunias need copious watering, regular feeding during the whole flowering season and a sunny position. Ordinary soil will do as too rich a soil mix and shade produce more leaf than flower growth.

Sempervivum

[Houseleek; Mountainous regions of Europe] Evergreen succulents, mainly hardy, these grow from tight leaf rosettes. Houseleeks are so called because they are often found growing on the roof tiles of houses. They are a large family and have members ranging from the minute to 8cm/3in high specimens. All have two things in common: a flat rosette shape and after flowering that particular rosette dies. Sempervivums look good in shallow clay pans, in window boxes with a sunny aspect and in troughs and sink gardens. *S. arachnoideum* (the cobweb houseleek) is most attractive with fine white webbing spread all over the low rosette of green leaves sometimes flushed with red. Many original species, gathered from far and wide, are available and dozens of named hybrids have been produced. Some of the wine-coloured varieties are especially attractive. Flowers are small, red, star-shaped and borne on an 8cm/3in stem. They are shallow-rooting and grow in any ordinary soil in lots of sun. Propagation is by offsets, detached and replanted in spring or autumn.

Tagetes

[Marigold; Mexico] This genus is distinct from Calendula, and is usually divided into the African (or American) Marigolds (*T. erecta*), with large-flowered fully double orange and lemon-yellow blooms, and *T. patula*, the French Marigolds with smaller single or double flowers and smaller stature. The divided foliage of all tagetes has a distinctive and, to some, unpleasant scent. Both can be raised from seed sown in heat early in the year or small plants can be bought quite cheaply in boxes in May. Recommended African marigolds include 'Oranges and Lemons', the dwarf 'First Lady' with clear yellow flowers (an All-America seed trials winner in 1968) and 'Toreador' with large carnation-like blooms. Of the French Marigolds, 'Bonita' and 'Butterscotch' (two bronze doubles) and 'Lemon Gem' and 'Paprika' (singles) should be tried. The flowering season of most of the tagetes extends from midsummer to frost. Although they will suffer some shade they produce their best blooms in full sun. Rich soil will encourage large flowers and a continuous display.

Autumn flowering plants

Anemone × hybrida

[Japanese Anemone; China/Japan] The Japanese anemones are fibrous-rooted perennials growing 60-90cm/2-3ft high with three-lobed leaves of a medium-green and delicate 5cm/2in rounded flowers. Listed in catalogues are many named varieties in shades of purple, pink and white such as 'Honorine Jobert', white, 'Kriemhilde', rose-pink. There are some with double flowers and others with crinkled leaves. All grow very well in some shade and most stand up very well to wind and rain. Plants seed freely and can pop up in all sorts of places including cracks in concrete. One of the nicest things about this anemone is that it flowers during September and October at a time when little else is in bloom. Old clumps can be divided in the autumn after flowering. Rich, leafy and moist loam suits them best.

Chrysanthemum

[Asia/Europe] Chrysanthemums used to be plants of the autumn and early winter months, but now they are available throughout the year thanks to dwarfing aids and the use of light control methods. When not in flower they really are very uninspiring and this non-flowering state lasts for about 10 months of the year. The annual species, such as C. carinatum and its numerous named varieties with single flowers in a wide range of colours, and C. coronarium, with single or double flowers from white to yellow, are recommended for pot culture. Because the dwarfed plants look so good and are fairly inexpensive it is suggested that the shallow pans of chrysanthemums sold in bud should be purchased and regarded much like a bunch of cut flowers: looked at, enjoyed, but discarded when past their best. They can be left in their pots, taken out of them and planted in containers, or the shallow pans in which they are bought can be sunk in a mixed container and be replaced by other pots when the first ones are past their prime. Whichever way is employed the soil the plants are in should be kept thoroughly moist. This use of chrysanthemum as temporary container plants might seem an easy way out, but it is very sensible and does give colour

Above: *Tropaeolum majus* 'Whirlybird Gold'
Right: Anemone-flowered chrysanthemum

and interest for a reasonable period because the budded plants last quite a long while if kept out of sunshine and in a cool position. The Charm and Pompon varieties are beautiful and may be grown from rooted cuttings taken early in the spring. Such cuttings will need regular attention throughout the summer, feeding, staking and shaping, but will eventually produce lovely sprays of bloom.

Cosmos bipinnatus

[Mexico] The half-hardy annual cosmos with finely divided leaves and gay dahlia-like flowers of rose, white, yellow and orange shades are perfect flowers for the late summer and very early autumn. Seed can be sown where it is to flower, thinning out seedlings to 23-30cm/9-12in apart. Seed sown in mid- to late-May will flower in September. Sown in the autumn they will bloom earlier. They like a sunny, hot position but will grow in some shade and should be kept well watered. Any type of light soil suits them, but once they have begun flowering some regular liquid feeding will keep them going late into the autumn. Young plants are regularly offered for sale.

Reseda

[Mignonette; North Africa] The hardy annual, R. odorata is a good pot plant for autumn flowering. The loose flower heads, yellow-white and orange, continue well into October, and there are several named forms with red and bronze flowers. Resedas grow best in rich, alkaline soil and in full sun, from seeds sown under glass in early spring or in flowering positions in April.

Sedum

[Ice-plant; Asia/Europe] The hardy perennial, S. spectabile has pale green, succulent, spoon-shaped leaves and flat pink flower heads produced during early autumn. These, on 45cm/18in stems, attract butterflies in large numbers and they will be found 'grazing' on the heads whenever the sun shines. As the flower stems die down towards the end of November they should be snapped off. New shoots emerge to take their place just above ground level early in the year. S. telephium has darker coloured flowers (almost a purple-red); S. maximum 'Atropurpureum' has dark purple flower stems and leaves and pink flowers and 'Autumn Joy' is a robust grower with deep pink flowers deepening to bronze. All sedums enjoy sun and a moist rich loamy soil and will happily produce magnificent foliage and fine flower heads in such a situation. Propagation is by division of the clumps.

Tropaeolum majus

[Nasturtium; South America] The annual nasturtiums are very valuable for autumn when their orange, flame red and yellow flowers seem most appropriate. If seed is sown out of doors in May in full sun and in poor, rather sandy soil (over-rich soil produces too much leaf growth), they will flower from late summer to frost. Both climbing and trailing varieties are available. Some of the dwarf types like the Tom Thumb strain (25cm/10in) are useful in window boxes and hanging baskets and the climbers can be trained up sticks and trellises or be allowed to scramble through evergreen shrubs. Pick off spent flowers to encourage continuous blooming.

Opposite: *Sedum spectabile* 'Autumn Joy' attracts butterflies in large numbers

Winter flowering plants

Bergenia

[Central Asia] The hardy perennial bergenias have handsome glossy, leathery leaves, which often change to shades of red and purple just as winter starts, when colour is most sought after. The blooms of most sorts begin to open from February to April or May according to climate and comprise dense clusters of flowers in many pink shades. *B. cordifolia* has broad glabrous leaves 15-30cm/6-12in in diameter and rose-pink flowers. A variety *B. c. purpurea* has crinkled edges to the leaves and turns almost purple in the winter months. *B. crassifolia* has smaller almost spoon-shaped leaves, and takes on orange to mahogany-red shades in winter. No bergenia likes an open draughty position, all thrive much better when in a sheltered site with a moist rootrun and some shade. When left to develop into large clumps they become very handsome and acquire an architectural quality which fits in very well with most town gardens. Propagation is by division of the clumps.

Euphorbia

[Spurge; Europe/Asia Minor] This large family includes tall-growing plants with rather woody stems, which are best described as sub-shrubs, and smaller-growing hardy herbaceous perennials. The glaucous-green foliage of some of them is much sought after and the flowers are certainly different. Actually the real flowers are practically invisible and it is the unorthodox

Top: Lime green *Helleborus corsicus*.
Above: *Solanum capsicastrum*.
Below: *Bergenia* 'Silberlicht'.

bracts that surround them that are so showy. *E. wulfenii* from Dalmatia is a tall-growing perennial evergreen sub-shrub (1.2m/4ft) with linear leaves and, through the late winter to early spring, sulphur-yellow flowers. *E. myrsinites* is a small trailer with yellow flowers for use in window boxes and similar positions where it can be viewed in close-up. There are many varieties from which to choose, some with brilliant orange colours. *E. robbiae* has rounded evergreen foliage which grows in whorls up the stems and green flowers and bracts. Flower buds are produced in December but the open bracts stay on the plants for months on end. The latter will put up with practically any position and prove interesting all the year round. It is, however, a bit of a marauder and will send its slender rhizomes in any direction that suggests a vacant space Increase by seed, division or by taking cutting immediately after flowering.

Helleborus

[Christmas Rose or Lenten Rose; Europe/Asia Minor] The hardy perennial hellebores are particularly valuable because they are at their best when little else is about. *H. niger* (30cm/1ft) (Christmas Rose) is not by any means the easiest one of the family to grow. The epithet 'black' (niger) refers to the roots for the flowers are white with prominent golden stamens. Care should be taken when purchasing new plants, as any that are dried out seldom recover. A good plant from a good nurseryman is recommended. *H. corsicus* (syn. *H. argutifolius*) is a taller-growing (60cm/2ft), much more shrubby plant. It has a mass of beautifully architectural leaves and pale lime-green flowers from February to May. They stay on the plant and are very decorative even when past their best. *H. orientalis* (45cm/18in) is the Lenten Rose and flowers from February onwards. These can be cream, pink or mauve, all spotted with a contrasting colour. All hellebores enjoy a deep moist soil and shade ranging from light to deep. They also like to be left undisturbed. Beware of slugs and snails and put bait down for them. Propagate by division, but only when absolutely essential.

Solanum capsicastrum

[Winter Cherry; Brazil] Solanums are usually grown as pot plants and offered for sale around Christmas time for use in the home. Although not hardy they are of great value as temporary occupants of winter window boxes where the weather is mild enough. When bought in pots they are usually showing green berries which slowly ripen and remain decorative for about two months. Seed can be sown in early spring in a greenhouse. Young plants in pots can be brought out of doors for the summer when they will flower (quite, insignificant white blooms) and be pollinated. They should be kept well watered for their whole life cycle. Berries will start to plump up in September and to take on colour in late October and November.

Annual climbing plants

Cobaea scandens

[Cathedral Bells or Cup-and-saucer Vine; Mexico] This plant is a half-hardy perennial but is usually treated as an annual and is eminently suitable for a sunny position climbing on some strong trellis support. In good soils it can ramp away and cover a considerable area (up to 6m/20ft in height) in a comparatively short time. It clings by tendrils to either rough surfaces or to any support. The flowers are bell-shaped and open a pale green colour which deepens to violet-blue or mauve as they mature. A white form 'Alba' is occasionally seen. The large seed will germinate easily in a warm and sunny position. Small potted plants are usually offered by nurserymen early in the year and one plant is usually enough for anyone.

Ipomoea tricolor

[Morning Glory; Tropical America] This is the pure blue Morning Glory and possibly the clearest colour in any flower. The flowers, freely produced throughout summer, open in the morning and fade and close during the afternoons.

This half-hardy annual is correctly named *Pharbitis tricolor*. Seed is reasonably easy to germinate after it has been nicked and soaked in water for about 24 hours. Young plants hate being disturbed and seeds should be planted two in a pot, and when a second seed germinates, one should be pulled out and discarded. When the weather outside is sufficiently warm, the young plants should be very carefully planted in the positions they are to flower in, disturbing the roots as little as possible. A sunny position and light soil are best. Support with a light trellis or string.

Lathyrus

[Sweet Pea; Mediterranean] *L. odoratus* first arrived from Sicily in 1699. Today's hybrids would hardly be recognized as belonging to the same family. All types of this hardy annual climber are of value to the container gardener, but perhaps the most suitable are the 'Knee-Hi' (60cm-1.2m/2-4ft) and 'Jet Set' groups. These are small to intermediate growers which need no more staking than a few twigs. They are robust and produce masses of waved and ruffled flowers in a host of different pastel colours. Taller-growing sorts will need canes, stakes or netting (or a shrub to clamber into). The Bijou strain is more bushy, reaching about 45cm/18in and seldom needs support.

Sweet Peas are hardy annuals which can be sown (after chipping each seed) outdoors in autumn or in February or March; small pots of young plants which have been germinated by the nurseryman can be bought instead. They prefer deep soil, well manured or enriched with bonemeal, and will not do well in poor soil nor without adequate attention. Plants should not be closer to each other than 15cm/6in to give each plant a chance to develop fully. All sorts need adequate watering and regular feeding with a general liquid fertilizer. Most of hybrids are scented (an accusation often incorrectly levelled against modern hy-

brids is that they lack scent), but this can certainly be more pronounced in some kinds. Sunny positions suit them best as long as the roots are kept cool. Pick off the dead flowers, otherwise the plants set seed pods and reduce flower production.

Thunbergia alata

[Black-eyed-Susan; South Africa] This half-hardy annual has 5cm/2in flowers in shades of cream yellow and orange with a deep brown eye. They twine around supports and begin to flower in June. Seed should be sown in a little heat in March. These plants are most useful for trailing from hanging baskets and also look effective climbing up canes in a sunny sheltered position.

Tropaeolum peregrinum

[Canary Creeper; Peru] This lovely half-hardy annual has small pure-yellow flowers with frilled throats and blue-green leaves which are finely divided into fingers. It loves to clamber through taller plants when the stalks of its leaves will wind halfway round whatever is to hand. Seeds germinate very easily in some heat in the spring. These are very good plants for difficult positions, tolerating shade although they do best in a sunny and sheltered spot in ordinary soil.

Above: *Tropaeolum peregrinum* will happily clamber up any support.
Left: *Ipomoea learii*

HARDY FERNS

Ferns are among the oldest groups of plants in existence and can be found practically anywhere from just at sea-level to the tops of mountains. Thousands of species are available; many are native plants and these often thrive better than the imported sorts.

There is evidence of a renewed interest in the growing of ferns, both as houseplants and outdoors where the hardy perennials will grow with little attention and in shade. None will endure complete drought and all prefer a cool rootrun and a damp (but not waterlogged) soil which is rich in humus. Ferns do not like to be buffetted by winds nor to suffer drip from overhead trees.

The majority of ferns are evergreen – the new season's fronds unfurling during spring when the old tired fronds can be removed and discarded.

The Hart's-Tongue fern (*Phyllitis scolopendrium*) and its crested form, *P. s.* 'Crispum' (with crinkly edges), are tough plants for town gardens. The Soft-Shield fern, *Polystichum setiferum* 'Acutilobum', is vigorous growing with intricately divided fronds growing to 90cm/ 3ft in length. This last fern develops little bulbils along the midribs of each frond which will grow into little rooted plants: pin the frond down onto a box of finely sieved seed mixture and keep moist and close. Propagation is usually by division in spring.

All ferns should be kept well-watered during the summer months and should receive a top dressing of leafmould or coarse fibrous peat each spring. Many self-sown ferns will spring up in the shady garden provided growing conditions are right.

How to grow Healthy Plants in Containers

The actual planting of container-grown plants has been greatly eased in recent years by their introduction at garden centres. These temporary containers allow plants to be moved to their new sites at most times of the year, and provided that some care is exercised in taking them from their plastic-bags, tin-cans or clay-pots, they need not suffer damage or setback. They should be planted in their new containers at the same depth as before, carefully watered in and attended frequently until established. Open ground plants are a little more difficult to establish due to the unavoidable damage that lifting and subsequent transporting has on the roots. Generally speaking, deciduous shrubs and trees are best lifted from the open ground and planted in the autumn and evergreens are safer if left until April or early May. They need thorough watering in.

Firm planting is essential to all plants and any staking that will be needed should be done at the time of planting. Allow ample space between the level of the soil and the rim of the container for the plants to be given a good drink – there is nothing more annoying than trying to trickle water into a container that is too full of soil and as a result the plants will probably go short. Regular feeding should be the rule with those subjects that are obviously in really active growth – a pot full of petunias clearly should receive attention more often than a very slow-growing conifer. Keep lime away from those plants that demand an acid soil and see that use is made of a proprietary compound to turn a soil that is becoming too alkaline through the use of hard tap water back to being acid.

Try not to grow plants in containers which are too large for them. When given more space than they need, the soil in the pots becomes stagnant and the plant's roots suffer from being in contact with permanently wet soil. Equally there will be problems if things are too tight. Flowers may be induced by underpotting but large shrubs in tiny pots will dry out too quickly, will become starved and most probably die.

The soil used in containers must be of the right consistency – able to hold moisture yet quick draining. When plants are growing freely they will need to be kept moist and this will involve frequent watering. As with

A few containers grouped together will provide a focus in a container garden and could leave space for chairs. But be sure the plants need the same growing conditions. The containers here could be grouped in a sunny corner: (from left to right) *Pelargonium peltatum, Petunia hybrida, Cordyline indivisa, Tropaeolum majus* and sempervivums

other plants there is no single rule for when pots should be watered except that they should be watered when they need it – not before and certainly not when it is too late. Those grown for flowers should have a fertilizer that is low in nitrogen. Nitrogenous fertilizers promote lush green leaves and most of the seaweed-based liquid feeds are pretty much balanced in favour of the flowering plants. Most will benefit from a springtime mulch of well-rotted leafmould, compost or peat but this should be moist at the time of application and should be watered straight away. When dry peat is applied to the surface of soil it often absorbs any water that is applied to it and prevents seepage down to the plant's roots.

Every so often the soil used for all containers will become exhausted and will need complete replacement. The need for renewal will in most cases be obvious by a loss of vigour in the plants and probably by undue yellowing of the leaves. The best time to consider a complete reorganisation is around early March. Enough fresh soil should be to hand, any repairs to or strengthening of wooden containers should be attended to and the division of such plants as need it undertaken.

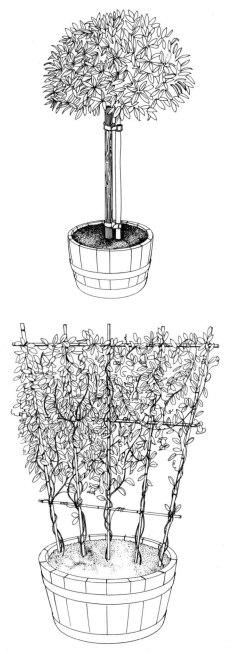

Staking

Some plants might need a little support such as hazel twigs provide. Certainly nigella looks better when propped up and some of the new dwarf sweet peas keep tidier with a few canes and some twine.

Take care to see that half-hardy plants are thoroughly hardened off before they are put outside. This can be done by placing them in a sheltered position for part of a day, then gradually extending the period, but taking them inside at night and finally by leaving them out overnight. Do not finally plant out until all reasonable danger of frost is past.

Shrubs and small trees

It must be remembered that shrubs and trees form the backbone to the container garden. Their needs will have to be considered before those of the more transitory herbaceous plants and climbers. They will in the first instance be more difficult to choose, more expensive to buy, require a longer settling down period and their health must not be threatened by invasive and greedy bedfellows.

Shrubs and trees growing singly in containers are easier to cater for, they can be potted into a mix which suits them, top-dressed as necessary, moved to an aspect they like and be completely repotted periodically. When used in mixed plantings some consideration should be given to all the occupants, but the trees and shrubs should normally win.

Pruning

Some pruning will be needed to keep some shrubs in trim — forsythia and chaenomeles like to be cut back after flowering; camellias and rhododendrons should have faded flowers removed. In the case of some strong growers like shrub roses it may be necessary to have two stabs at pruning — once in autumn to shorten long growths that would be vulnerable to wind damage during the winter months and again in the spring before new growth begins, trimming to shape and removing any dead, weak or damaged shoots. A sharp knife or secateurs should be used for both operations and it is necessary to see for the final pruning that the wood is cut just above a growth bud pointing in the direction in which the new shoot is required to grow.

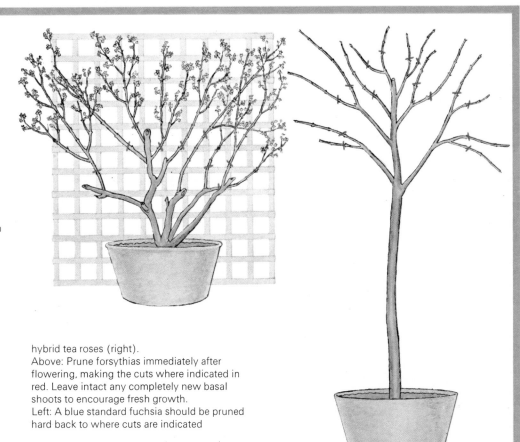

Below: Roses should be pruned after all dead, diseased, weak and inward-growing shoots are removed. The black lines on the centre drawing show how far back to prune in the first spring, and the drawings on either side show where pruning cuts should be made in the second and subsequent springs for floribunda (left) and

hybrid tea roses (right).
Above: Prune forsythias immediately after flowering, making the cuts where indicated in red. Leave intact any completely new basal shoots to encourage fresh growth.
Left: A blue standard fuchsia should be pruned hard back to where cuts are indicated

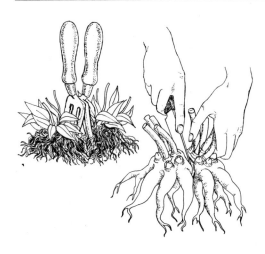

Propagation by division

Plants which are clump-forming will in time become a complete tangle of growth and every two or three years will need splitting up. Do this carefully, discarding the older (inner) part of the clump and replanting the outer pieces in fresh soil.

When a cold frame or heated greenhouse is available it is often a good idea to take a few cuttings of some of the 'not always reliably hardy brigade' such as some of the silver-leaved plants, pinks and chrysanthemums in case of a severe winter and subsequent loss of mature plants. Extra cuttings are always useful both as replacements for older plants and as gifts for friends. Young plants will nearly always do better than tired older ones.

For small entangled plants, pull apart with two hand forks (left). Use a sharp knife to split tough woody crowns

Dead-heading of flowers

Dead-heading of flowering plants is essential in the majority of cases if a continued display is sought. It involves the removal of the spent blooms before they begin to waste the energy of the plants in seed production. Such removal of spent flowers will not only prevent the possibility of seed making and extend the flowering period but considerably tidy up the plants. With some subjects such as pansies this is best done by removing entirely the flower stalks, in others simply nipping off the faded blooms, as in petunias, but it can also, with the woodier type of plant, afford an opportunity of summer pruning.

Plants with sterile flowers such as hydrangeas do not need this attention as they don't set seed and their flower trusses remain attractive for a long time after they have passed their prime. They should, however, be removed before growth restarts in spring.

Herbs, fruit and vegetables in containers

Why not grow fruit and vegetables on your patio or balcony? With a minimum amount of space, a move towards a household being self-sufficient can be made, and, although no great quantity can be grown, the range is wide.

But why grow food crops at all? The reasons are simple – quality, convenience, economy and variety. Quality means that the actual vegetables and fruit are fresh and may be growing until a few minutes before eating. The less usual types and cultivars can be grown, selecting those that have an extra special flavour. Likewise, when that uninvited guest comes to dinner just select a choice specimen from the patio garden for him. On the basis of economy, home-grown food costs next to nothing – the cost of seeds is roughly that of a few days' bread, and from those seeds, or plants, comes such enjoyment and pleasure that the cost is repaid time and time again.

Where to grow them may be a problem, but crops will grow almost anywhere: you can have them growing outside the front door, or amid the dustbins. Some people may think they are unattractive, but asparagus, beet, carrots, celery and sweetcorn all have attractive foliage, and a bedding scheme of vegetables is unique.

The first question is how to grow food crops. If there is a small border of impoverished soil, the solution is to make a raised bed using planks or railway ties and raising the bed by about 15cm/6in. Fill up the space with top soil, acquired at the local garden centre, and incorporate plenty of organic matter such as peat or garden compost.

Many homes, however, have no borders, but only an area of concrete on which to grow plants, while others have a balcony as well as windowsills. Windowsills provide room for window boxes in which tomatoes, pole beans, carrots, cabbages, dwarf beans and chives can be grown, as well as strawberries.

With a little imagination and ingenuity it is amazing how much 'growing area' can be obtained in little space. A series of boxes can be arranged in steps against a wall, and not much knowledge of carpentry is required to erect a frame securing the ends. Length can be adapted to space available, but at least 15cm/6in in depth and in width is advisable.

If boxes of similar size are used they are mounted as in a flight of steps leaving space for air circulation on the wall side, thus preventing damp walls.

The same technique could be used to make a free standing 'bed' of double size, in which case the best position is in a north/south-facing direction, where maximum sun is obtained.

Very large seed trays or 'flats' can be made from good sound lumber and these can be raised on legs, or even mounted on wheels if space allows for movement to catch sunshine at all hours of the day.

Many different types of containers can be used for growing plants – wooden boxes, barrels, wheelbarrows, and old hollowed tree stumps are but a few. Half barrels or tubs may be thought the most attractive to look at, but a herb garden can be made from any suitable sized container and different species such as chervil, coriander, chives, marjoram, mint, parsley, tarragon and thyme can be arranged to produce an artistic bedding scheme.

Salad plants also could be grown in a container with, possibly, a central feature of tomatoes.

Barrels are ideal for strawberries, as are old wooden wheelbarrows, but why not grow the strawberries from the holes in the sides of the container, and utilize the top surface for something trained on a trellis, such as melons?

It is very important that all forms of containers, from the largest to the smallest, should have drainage holes drilled in their base, and the base lined with one inch of drainage 'crocks' (broken pieces of flower pots, clinkers, gravel, etc.). Roughly 2.5sq.cm/1sq.in of drainage holes to every 25sq.cm/10sq.in of container is required.

By combining all features of different containers, a very attractive garden can be made, providing solely food, but with foliage contrasts and interest throughout the year.

FRUIT

Fruit crops can be divided into soft and top fruits, and these groups can be subdivided. Soft fruits include strawberries, raspberries, blackcurrants, red and white currants and gooseberries. Raspberries and other cane fruits can be grown in raised beds, but their cultivation is not ideal for container gardening. Likewise blackcurrants, red and white currants, and gooseberries are not recommended for this type of gardening although by modifying and growing them as cordons or fans against a wall, a crop will materialize with some care and attention – once more raised beds are the solution.

With only a small area of concrete, you can grow a reasonable amount of fruit and vegetables in containers. Above: an arch over a doorway is both decorative and provides a harvest of Golden Hubbard squash. Tomatoes grow in tubs on either.side of the door, and the boxes contain sage and thyme. Right: a mixed planting in tiered boxes and pots will supply salad ingredients – and dessert: carrots and radishes in the higher box, strawberries in the other; tomatoes and chives in the pots. Below: tomatoes again, which provide an attractive focal point, here grouped with peas, red cabbage and lettuce

With a little imagination and ingenuity,
a lot of growing space can be obtained from
a limited area. The small walled garden, right,
is a good example. Against the back wall is
a bay tree with French beans and thyme growing
around its base. The box to the left has marrows
(squash) and the one to the right onions and
parsley. The plum tree next door can be seen
over the wall, and on this side of the wall,
runner beans are flourishing. Golden tomatoes
provide the central interest and are surrounded
by cauliflower, then beetroot, then carrots.
In the foreground is a herb garden containing
coriander, marjoram, balm, thyme, savory,
chives and fennel

Strawberries

The simplest crop to grow is strawberries and they are ideally suited to the whims of a gardener. They can either be grown in beds, or in containers, and the range of suitable containers includes stone troughs, wheelbarrows, hollow tree stumps, and barrels – in fact, anything goes! Before planting, either in spring or in late summer, treat all wooden containers with a wood preservative (not creosote), and replace any broken sections in the process. The most popular container has always been the 40-gallon barrel, which should hold 24 plants in three rows of six, plus six on the top surface. Drill 18 holes of 8cm/3in diameter between the hoops, with the top and bottom rows lined up vertically, staggering the middle row. For drainage six 2.5cm/1in holes should be drilled in the base and the barrel stood on bricks so that it is clear of the ground. Place 15cm/6in of weathered ashes or 'crocks' in the bottom to assist drainage, and a drainpipe filled with sand and rubble vertically in the centre of the barrel. Fill the barrel with a loam-based mixture up to the level of the first series of holes and firm it well.

From the inside push a plant through each hole and firm the roots into the soil; plant up every hole on the bottom row, raise the drainage pipe up a little, and repeat the planting process for successive rings. The drainage pipe is raised after each ring is completed and finally removed altogether leaving a drainage channel in the middle of the barrel.

Runners will be produced and these can either be removed or left to root. Every year the barrel will need a 'once over' when a top dressing of 250g/8oz each of a general purpose fertilizer is worked into the top few cm with a hand-fork. Repair any broken holes or sections during the winter months. Pesticides and fungicides should be applied when necessary, as Grey Mould may be a problem during the fruiting season.

Although the top of the barrel may be planted up with strawberries, alternatives include planting melons, cucumbers, courgettes or zucchini, and marrows or squash to train up a trellis or strings.

The strawberry cultivar choice is wide. Of the standard cultivars, Redgauntlet, Cambridge Favourite, Royal Sovereign, or Templar in Britain; and Fairfax and Harvard 17 (early), Sparkle and Catskill (mid-season), Jersey Belle and Frontenac (late) in the United States can be grown, but the everbearing cultivars seem more suited for container work. Frapendula, Gento, Remont, Ozark Beauty, Streamliner and Ogallala are suitable everbearers fruiting from mid-June to a peak in the autumn.

The range of fruit that can be grown in a container garden is wide. Top: nectarines can be trained up a wall (as here) or grown in a large pot or wooden tub. Strawberries are the simplest fruit to grow. The cultivar Gento, shown left, will produce fruit between June and October that is full of flavour. Suitable containers for growing strawberries include stone troughs, wheelbarrows, hollow tree stumps and barrels, as above. A grape vine, opposite, may not produce enough fruit for wine-making, so choose a cultivar for eating as well

Top Fruit

Top fruit in pots or tubs is a proposition worth considering, but even by choosing a tree on a dwarf rootstock, it is not an economic use of space, although they can be grown successfully. In any case, despite below average yields the enjoyment of home-grown produce will be gained.

The idea of growing a vine or a peach tree may appeal. Buy a one, or at most a two-year-old tree (cultivar Peregrine, Rochester, Bonanza or Hale Haven dwarf) and plant it firmly in a rich mixture with the roots spread out in the hole.

Hand-pollinate the flowers with a fine camel hair brush and thin the fruit when they are 3cm/1¼in diameter, leaving each fruit about 23cm/9in apart.

A peach tree is ideal for growing in a large pot or wooden tub as a 'feature' on the patio or small container garden.

Vines

Grape vines are very hardy, withstanding temperatures as low as —20°C/—6°F, but the young growth and flowers are susceptible to frost and so frost pockets should be avoided. They can be grown as bushes, cordons, espaliers, or fans, but for the highest yield, cordons are used. Grapes are produced on the current year's growth, which is derived from the previous year's shoots. A rampant uncontrolled vine will produce vegetative growth at the expense of fruit. Wood that has finished fruiting is valueless except for propagation.

A rich organic soil is required for vines, so plant them in raised beds specially prepared by incorporating plenty of garden compost or peat. The space required depends on the training method: 1.2m/4ft for cordons, 3m/10ft for espaliers, and 4.6m/15ft for fans. Plant from November to March, placing the roots 10cm/4in below ground level, and firm in thorough-ly. Vines need very little feeding, but phosphates are required to encourage fruiting.

Outdoor grapes are small, but if they are being grown for wine-making, this is of little importance. Thinning will not increase the weight of the bunch, but does mean that the remaining berries are larger, so thin the bunches to maintain the shape, removing berries until none are touching. Use long pointed scissors such as special vinery scissors and do not touch the berries as this damages the 'bloom'.

From a patio vineyard there will probably not be sufficient grapes for wine-making, so dual purpose (table/wine-making/culinary) cultivars are preferred. Suitable cultivars include Precose de Malingre, an early white grape; the standard Concorde, a blue grape; Muscat de Samur, a golden muscat-flavoured grape; Interlaken Seedless; Cataurba, a red grape; Gagarin Blue, a blue-black grape of excellent flavour; and Tereshkova, a purple-red grape.

HERBS

A patio garden composed entirely of herbs may appeal to the home cook, since cooking can be rather dull without herbs and difficulty may be found in purchasing some of them. An interesting idea is to plant the herbs in the shape of an old cart wheel, making the spokes with gravel. If a large tub is used, the herbs can be planted in concentric rings. Suitable herbs include balm, chervil, chives, coriander, fennel, marjoram, parsley, sage, savory, tarragon and thyme. The dwarfer ones can be used as edging to beds or large tubs. When growing mint it is advisable to use a large pot so the roots do not run rampant everywhere.

A moderately rich soil is required for herbs since many are perennials and will not be moved. In raised beds incorporate plenty of organic matter. With herbs there is a minimum amount of essential work. Weak or dead shoots should be pruned out and a bush shape maintained with woody perennials. Camomile is often used to make a fragrant lawn, so try it as an edging plant, taking care that it does not take over the whole bed.

Chives are one of the best herbs to grow. Their mild onion flavour adds interest to salads and soups, and to the gardener it is ideal for edging. Either grow from spring-sown seeds, or by root division, splitting them into small pieces.

Coriander is an annual, the leaves of which are used for flavouring soups, and the seeds used in stews or curries. Seed is sown in place in April, and thinned to 15cm/6in apart.

Lavender is grown for its dried flowers and the dwarf growing species should be planted in April, or propagated from cuttings in July, and used either for edging or in clumps.

Marjoram is used for various culinary purposes from brewing home-made beer to flavouring stews and soups. Dry leaves make a refreshing tea. It is a half hardy perennial, so should be treated as an annual except in warm areas. Sow indoors in February and plant out 23cm/9in apart in May.

Parsley garnishes many dishes including fish and soups, and is reputed to be excellent for indigestion, kidney ailments and rheumatism. Legend has it that it only grows for a woman if she wears the trousers in the family! It can be grown as a biennial or perennial, but to maintain supplies sow fresh seed every July. Suitable strains include Moss Curled, Bravour, Plain and parsnip-rooted Hamburg.

Thyme can be used as a herb and also for ground cover. The upright forms (*T. nitidus*) are used with sage for stuffings and flavouring meats, and bees frequent thyme flowers thus it is invaluable for the apiarist. It can be propagated from heel cuttings in June/July.

Herbs can be planted in a large tub, in the shape of a cartwheel, making the spokes with gravel. The planting here includes balm, chives, marjoram, coriander, sage, thyme, winter savory and parsley

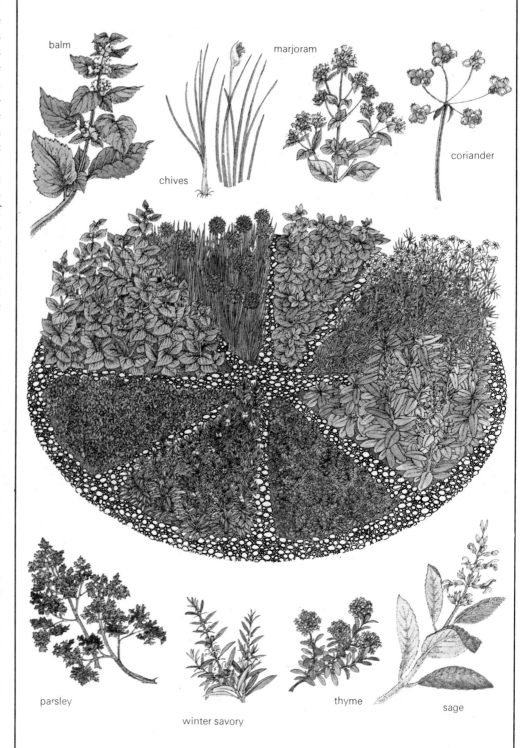

balm

chives

marjoram

coriander

parsley

winter savory

thyme

sage

VEGETABLES

Almost any vegetable can be grown in raised beds or in containers, but even in raised beds some system of rotation should be practised. In some market gardens a four crop rotation is followed, with potatoes being the first crop, followed by roots, peas and finally greens. However, potatoes are not grown in a patio garden, so a three crop rotation is best adopted: greens, roots, and legumes, with other crops such as onions slotted in as a fourth year crop if desired. The reason for rotation is to avoid build-ups of nutrients, pests and diseases, since each crop requires different nutrients – greens need plenty of nitrogen, while root crops need phosphates.

With raised beds and large 'flats' the garden can be divided into sections and a simple rotation adopted. But although rotation is impor-tant, it is often impractical, especially with window boxes, or just a few tubs.

Small Scale Vegetable Growing

Even in a window box, vegetables can be grown by planting two or three rows of plants and having a large plant at each end. Such a window box could have a tomato plant at each end, and rows of carrots, radishes, lettuce or peas, with an edging of chives or parsley. The choice is open, but remember that a window box should have a soil depth of about 25cm/10in, and always choose dwarf or small culti-vars such as 'Tom Thumb' lettuce and 'Little Marvel' pea. For example, there is no point in growing 'Gradus' pea as it is 1.2m/4ft tall.

When using a tub, plant a tomato or pepper in the centre and then grow concentric rings of other crops, or devote the whole tub to salad crops. Alternatively, a tub can be devoted to one vegetable, such as tomatoes or auber-gines or eggplants. The soil mix in the tub must be rich enough to feed crops throughout the growing season, so prior to sowing or planting, incorporate plenty of organic matter, such as peat or garden compost, plus a general purpose fertilizer at 250g/8oz per sq.m./sq.yd.

Crops to Grow

The summarized list on page 205 shows the range of crops that can be grown, but it is im-portant to stress that only certain cultivars of each vegetable are suitable. Careful selection is required when studying seed catalogues, or packets of seed in garden centres, and mam-moth or exhibition strains of most crops should be avoided. In all container gardening the root-run is limited and space is at a premium. Crops such as rhubarb and asparagus should not be attempted unless major sacrifices are made.

Almost any vegetable can be grown in a container garden, and planting in rotation, something will be ready for harvest all year round. Aubergines or eggplants 'Short Tom' (above) and courgettes or zucchini (below) will fruit from July to October

Peas and Beans

Peas and beans are termed 'legumes' and are the most popular group of vegetables grown, since many households consume can upon can of baked beans, as well as numerous frozen packets of green beans and peas.

Peas need a non-acid soil to succeed, so before sowing rake in, or apply, lime – about 125g/4oz per square yard should suffice. Sow indoors in February to March, singly, in 9cm/3½in peat pots if an early crop is wanted, and plant out after the last frost. Peas grow better if sown where they are to develop, and outdoor sowing is done in March or April, spacing 5cm/2in apart. If the plants need support, use a net or a trellis. Although a saturated soil is not wanted, keep the soil moist throughout the growing season. Peas are ready for harvesting when the pods are well filled and firm. Suitable cultivars include Little Marvel, Feltham First, Myzar, Meteor, Kelvedon Wonder, Blue Bantam and Alaska.

Bush beans, dwarf, kidney, French or snap beans are ideal for the small garden, patio, or window box gardening. Sow the seed in place after the last frost, or indoors in small pots for transplanting out, and choose a sunny position and light rich soil. Prior to sowing incorporate organic matter such as peat, plus about 125g/4oz per sq.m./sq.yd. of a general purpose fertilizer. Keep weed-free and well watered. The beans will be ready for harvesting after 2½ months or so when the pods should snap cleanly. Cut the pods off the plant – never pull them or the plant will be torn out of the ground. Cultivars to choose include: Remus, Glamis, Brezo, Masterpiece, Tenderpod, Red Kidney, Long Pod and Dwarf Horticultural.

Pole beans or runner beans make a pleasant feature on a patio growing in a tub. Pole beans like a freshly manured soil, so incorporate farmyard manure or garden compost, plus 125g/4oz per sq.m./sq.yd. of a general purpose fertilizer, firming the soil thoroughly. Sow or 'plant' the seed after the last frost, and once more keep moist. These beans need supports and they can either be grown up a trellis or strings. Top dress the soil around the young plants with a general purpose fertilizer at 125g/4oz per sq.m./sq.yd. To assist pollination and also to keep the beans tender, spray overhead at dusk or dawn with water. (A watering can with a *fine* rose can be used.) Harvest when the pods are over 20cm/8in in length. (Some cultivars have pods of up to 60cm/24in in length, but harvest when they are three quarters of the length stated on the seed packet!) Crusader, Kentucky Wonder, Romano, Blue Lake, Sunset and Streamline are all suitable for tub work.

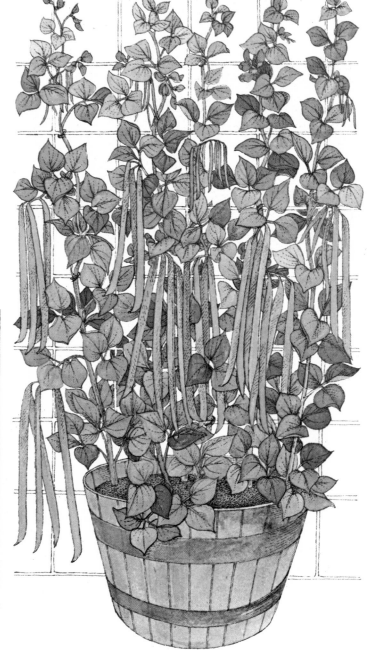

Brussels sprouts (left) should be grown in raised beds. Lettuce, however, is shallow rooting and does not need as much space as sprouts, so it can be grown in any container. Choose a non-hearting lettuce, like the one below, so that a few leaves can be picked as required. Runner or pole beans (right) and peas (opposite) are attractive features in container gardens

Root Crops

When growing root crops a careful selection is important, but remember that the rootrun available is limited to the depth of soil in the container, so select stump rooted or globe cultivars.

Beets are ideal for a container garden, since they have very attractive foliage. Sow the seeds where the plants are to grow, and thin out any overcrowded seedlings. Water in dry weather. Little Ball, Boltardy, Avonearly, Detroit Dark Red, Red-Hart and Red Ball are all reliable cultivars.

Carrots like soil that has not been freshly manured. Sow 'in place', broadcasting the seeds in drifts from March onwards. Thin to 2.5cm/1in apart, and then later to 8cm/3in, using these second thinnings for cooking. Keep moist and weed-free. Suitable cultivars are Early Gem, Amstel, Early Nantes, Early Horn, Goldinhart, Oxhart and Short 'n Sweet.

Radish is a quick-maturing crop, taking about one month from seed, and so successional sowings are required to maintain supply – a little and often. A light sandy soil is best although any non-clayey soil will suffice – always incorporate *well*-rotted organic matter. Cultivars – French Breakfast, Inca, Cherry Belle, Red Forcing, Crimson Giant and White Icicle.

Turnip is another quick maturer, taking about eight weeks from seed to harvesting. Broadcast the seeds, and keep them well watered. Harvest when about 8cm/3in in diameter. An 'open' soil (well drained and yet moisture retentive) is ideal. Early Snowball, Early Red Milan, Goldenball, Foliage turnip and Tokyo Cross are all suitable.

With all root crops, freshly manured soils are better avoided or forked roots will develop.

Leaf and Stalk Vegetables

When using the self-blanching forms, celery is not too difficult to grow. Sow the seeds thinly in pans or boxes, and plant out the seedlings six weeks after the last frost, when the ground has warmed up a little. These seedlings can be kept in the home in boxes or transferred into a frame on the patio. Celery requires plenty of organic matter and even after planting, mulch with garden compost or peat to reduce water loss, and water to keep the soil moist. Harvest the plants from one end of the row. No blanching is required with self-blanching cultivars. American Green, Latham Self Blanching, Golden Self Blanching, Avonpearl and Giant Pascal are all suitable cultivars.

Lettuce is the base of any salad, and very easy to grow. It likes plenty of organic matter and moisture, but as the plants are shallow rooting, only the top few cm need be prepared. This means they are ideally suited for container

Cabbages and Other Greens

Cabbages are one of the easiest vegetable crops to grow, so care in the selection of cultivars must be taken to avoid growing 'footballs' rather than 'cricket balls'. They are greedy feeders and require plenty of nitrogen for leaf growth. Sow the seed in several batches (successional sowings) to avoid a glut. Keep them well watered and four to six weeks after germination, apply a top dressing of 125g/4oz per sq.m./sq.yd. of a general purpose fertilizer. Cultivars worth a try are Babyhead, Copenhagen Market, Earliana, Early Jersey Wakefield, Red Ruby, Suttons Earliest, The Jack and Greyhound. Chinese cabbage – 'Pe-Tsai' – or Michihli can be tried; it is excellent both raw and cooked.

Closely related to cabbages are Brussels sprouts, and these can only be grown in raised beds, as they need at least 50cm/20in square of growing space. Again plenty of water is required in dry weather, and a midsummer top dressing. Sprouts mature from the bottom upwards. Harvest when the sprouts are about 3cm/1¼in in diameter. Peer Gynt, Topscore, Thor, Leda, British Allrounder, Achilles, Jade Cross Hybrid and Long Island Improved are worth trying.

Cauliflower is a third important member of the cabbage family and the flower head is eaten rather than the leaves. Better known as winter broccoli, it is quite hardy. Commercially for an early crop the seed is sown in the autumn with the young plants being overwintered under glass or in frames in the milder climates, but best results in the small garden will be derived from an indoor sowing in March and planting out the young plants in May. An alternative is to purchase transplants. Keep the plants well watered – not saturated. Harvest when the curd or flower head has been visible for a fortnight, and is the size of a tennis ball and larger. Suitable cultivars include Romax, Delta, Cyrano, Dominant, Early Snowball, Purple Head and Snow King Hybrid.

gardening. Sow the seed after the last frost and thin out to 25cm/10in between the plants. Moisture is essential, so water little but often. Lettuce takes as little as six weeks to mature in the summer months, although in the earlier or later cooler periods, 10 weeks is more usual. Successional sowings are recommended to stagger the times of maturity. There are three groups of cultivars – Cos, Cabbage or head and looseleaf. Cos are conical and space-savers. Suitable cultivars are Little Gem, Valmaine and White Paris. Cabbage or head lettuce can be rather large and floppy, but from personal choice the following are suitable: Tom Thumb, Buttercrunch, Minetto, Pennlake, Hilde, Bibb and Great Lakes. Salad Bowl, Grand Rapids, Black-Seeded Simpson and Oak Leaf are looseleaf lettuce producing leaves and no heart, so a few leaves can be picked as required.

An alternative to lettuce is endive. A good rich soil is required so peat or garden compost should be incorporated. Endive likes a cool, moist soil that does not dry out in warm weather. Sow from July onwards for harvesting from late August into early winter. To protect the young heads maturing from late sowings, cover the plants with glass. Endive is blanched so a tie is put around the tops of the plants as soon as they reach maturity – do this carefully so you do not cut through the succulent leaves. After three weeks the head will be crisp and blanched at the centre – perfect for an autumn salad. The major cultivars are Batavian Broad Leaved and Exquisite or White Curled.

Onions

Onions are the mainstay for flavouring stews – no cook can decry their value since they can be eaten raw or cooked; in salads, stews, soups, sauces, pickles, or fried, stewed, boiled or braised.

They need a deep rich soil and so may not be suited for container work, but an adequate yield can be derived from 'sets'. Sets are small onions that have been grown in a warm climate for a few weeks, then dried and stored. Plant the sets in late March to April at a spacing of 8 × 30cm/3 × 12in and firm well. The tips should just be clear of the ground. Keep well watered, and apply a top dressing of general purpose fertilizer at 50g/2oz per sq.m./sq.yd. every two weeks during May, June and early July.

If you choose to grow onions from seed, sow indoors in early March and prick out into boxes or individual pots, planting out in mid May. Once the tops start to yellow, bend over all the top growth to assist ripening. When the tops have shrivelled, lift and dry the onions off thoroughly on the patio. Remove the tops and straggly roots prior to storage in net bags.

For growing from sets choose Stuttgarter Giant, Sturon or Stuttgarter Reisen, although they are often sold only by colour – yellow or white. From seed choose between Ailsa Craig, Superba, Wijbo, Produrijn, Sweet Spanish, Yellow Gable, White Portugal or Red Wethersfield.

Three other forms of onion worth a try are shallots, which are grown in the same way as onions, from sets, but spaced 15 × 30cm/6 × 12in. The second is the tree onion which forms small onions on a stem, and although of little economic value, it is strangely attractive and unusual. The third type is the salad onion, which is grown from seed and produces a quick crop. Sow the seed in April for a summer crop, or in September for a spring crop in warm areas. The cultivars to choose from are White Lisbon, White Bunching, or Evergreen.

Cucumbers, Squashes and Pumpkins

Cucumbers, squashes and pumpkins make an interesting feature in a patio garden. They should be planted in solid garden compost, well rotted farmyard manure, or the richest soil available. Sow the seed in place or indoors in individual pots so the plants do not suffer root disturbance. Because the fruits contain a very high proportion of water, they require frequent watering, soaking the soil thoroughly. Plant either the seed or small plants on mounds,

Above: Moneymaker is a tomato for growing in containers outdoors. When five flower trusses have formed, remove all other growing tips. Below: For the best results from cucumbers, select from among the regular garden sorts

as the mound retains a certain amount of water and also gives space for rootrun. A mound approximately 46cm/18in in height, and 61cm/2ft square is sufficient for one large plant.

For the best results from cucumbers, select from among the regular garden sorts such as Burpless Hybrid, Straight Eight, Marketer, West India Gherkin and Burpee Pickler. To pollinate cucumbers, squashes or pumpkins, pick off a male flower and push the centre of it into the centre of a female flower. Female flowers have incipient 'fruits' behind them, and so can be distinguished from male flowers.

Harvest while still tender unless they are being grown for competition purposes. 'Blowing up' the large squashes and pumpkins is an entertaining ploy for children. Remove all the young fruits except one or two from the plant and then apply water, and more water. A piece of thread can be threaded through the neck of the stem, and placed in a jar of sugar solution, or sugar solution can be used weekly, for watering. This swells the vegetable, but it is virtually inedible!

Summer squash varieties can be chosen from Golden Zucchini, Cocozelle (Italian Marrow), Early Prolific Straightneck and Early Golden Summer Crookneck. For autumn and winter, choose from Acorn, Turk's Turban and Buttercup. Avoid the large field type of pumpkin, selecting Small Sugar or Cinderella.

Fruiting Vegetables

When growing tomatoes outside on a small scale, the choice is once more between buying plants, or raising them from seed. Although there is little choice when buying plants, it must be stated that they should at least be healthy. If one chooses to grow them from seed, sow in February to March indoors and keep warm and moist. When the first seed leaves have expanded, prick out into 9cm/3½in pots and keep them indoors. Repot into 13cm/5in pots if necessary and plant out a week or two after the last frost. Each plant will need a stake as support, but do not tie them too tightly to the stake, allowing for thickening of the stalk in growth. During the growing season apply a top dressing of general purpose fertilizer every month.

Most cultivars need to be side shooted – the exceptions are the bush types. Remove all side growths, and only allow four or five trusses to form; therefore, when five flower trusses are visible, the growing tip should be removed. In Britain the last truss should flower not later than late July. Defoliation of the plants can be practised – this means removing the leaves around the fully formed trusses, to aid ripening. Cultivars are: Pixie, Gardeners Delight, Dobies Champion, Ailsa Craig, Moneymaker, Tiny Tim and Small Fry.

Alphabetical List of vegetable sowing instructions

Since there is such a wide variation in climate from north to south and from sea level to the mountains, it is also well to be guided by the following general rules: the hardiest plants such as cabbage plants, lettuce, onions, peas and turnips may be planted four to five weeks before the last frost date; rather hardy plants such as beets, carrots, lettuce and radishes can be planted two to four weeks before the last frost date; and all tender vegetables such as beans, squash, tomato and pepper must wait until danger of frost is past.

Crop	Sowing time in open	Depth	Distance Apart	Harvest
Beans – Dwarf	May-July	5cm/2in	20×30cm/8×12in	July-Aug.
Beans – Runner	May-June	7.5cm/3in	23×25cm/9×10in	Aug-Oct.
Beets	April-May	2.5cm/1in	15-20×38cm/6-8×15in	July-Oct.
Broccoli	April-May	2.5cm/1in	60×60cm/24×24in	September
Cabbage (Spring)	July	2.5cm/1in	40×45cm/16×18in	April-June
Cabbage (Winter)	April-May	2.5cm/1in	50×60cm/20×24in	Oct.-March
Cabbage (Chinese)	April	2.5cm/1in	23×30cm/9×12in	Aug.-Sept.
Carrots (early)	March	1.2cm/½in	8×30cm/3×12in	May-June
Cauliflower (early)	September	2.5cm/1in	50×60cm/20×24in	July-Sept.
Cauliflower (late)	March-April	2.5cm/1in	60×60cm/24×24in	Oct.-Jan.
Celery	March-April	1.2cm/½in	25-30×30cm/10-12×12in	Sept.-March
Cucumber (Ridge)	March-April	2.5-5cm/1-2in	90cm/36in	Aug.-Oct.
Endive	July-Aug.	2.5cm/1in	25×45cm/10×18in	Aug.-Sept.
Leek	March-April	1.2cm/½in	23×15cm/9×6in	Sept.-March
Lettuce	March-June	Just cover	23×30cm/9×12in	Most of year
Onion	Feb.-March	2.5cm/1in	8×30cm/3×12in	Sept.-Oct.
Pea	March	5cm/2in	8×75cm/3×30in	June-Sept.
Radish	March-July	1-2cm/½in	75×30cm/2×12in	May-Oct.
Shallot	April-May	5cm/2in	15×25cm/6×10in	Sept.-Oct.
Squash	March-April	2.5cm/1in	75×180cm/30×72in	Aug.-Oct.
Turnip	March-June	2.5cm/1in	10×40cm/4×16in	June-Sept.

Crop	Sowing Time INDOORS	Depth	Planting OUTDOORS	Distance Apart	Harvest
Aubergine	March	Just cover	June	38×45cm/15×18in	July-Oct.
Cucumber	March	2.5-5cm/1-2in	April-May	90cm/36in	July-Oct.
Peppers Sweet	March	2.5cm/1in	May-June	45cm/18in	July-Sept.
Sweet Corn	March	5cm/2in	June	38×38cm/15×15in	July-Sept.
Tomato	Feb.-March	Just cover	June	60×60cm/24×24in	—

In milder areas, aubergines or eggplants and peppers can be grown outside. Sow the seeds in March to April in pans indoors, and after germination prick out into individual containers. When there is no risk of frost plant them out, spacing them 1.2m/4ft apart. With aubergines or eggplants, once stunted by cold weather they will rarely grow to fruiting.

Obviously the patio gardener cannot grow all these crops, but modifications can be made, or by choosing certain crops, interest for all the family can be stimulated – pumpkins for the children, dwarf beans for Granny, beetroot, carrot and parsley for the lady of the house, while father can try celery, onions or lettuce.

There are other ideas which can be tried, such as using covers or frames to protect the less hardy crops or to help one to start sowing earlier. One of the principles of protected cropping is to protect the young seedlings which are vulnerable to extremes of weather. Low run plastic tunnels are feasible and can be easily stored when not in use. Sowings can be made up to a month earlier since the small cold frame or the tunnel will keep cold winds off the plants and protect them from frost. The next step is to use a frame, which can be heated by soil warming cables. The final objective will be a greenhouse. As seen earlier on, sun porches are really greenhouses, and many plants can be grown very successfully in sun porches – but nothing is better than your own greenhouse.

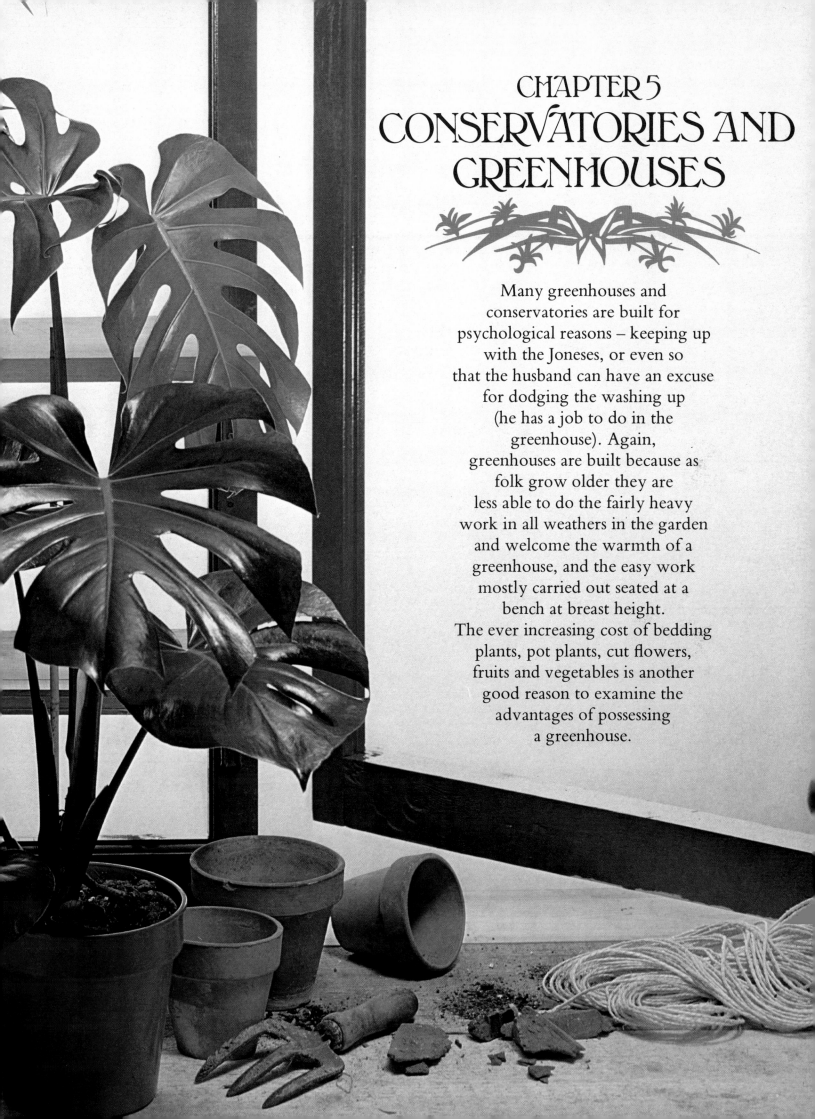

CHAPTER 5
CONSERVATORIES AND GREENHOUSES

Many greenhouses and
conservatories are built for
psychological reasons – keeping up
with the Joneses, or even so
that the husband can have an excuse
for dodging the washing up
(he has a job to do in the
greenhouse). Again,
greenhouses are built because as
folk grow older they are
less able to do the fairly heavy
work in all weathers in the garden
and welcome the warmth of a
greenhouse, and the easy work
mostly carried out seated at a
bench at breast height.
The ever increasing cost of bedding
plants, pot plants, cut flowers,
fruits and vegetables is another
good reason to examine the
advantages of possessing
a greenhouse.

The conservatory

The heyday of the conservatory was towards the end of the last century and in the early years of the present century. It was virtually wiped out by World War One. With it many plants almost disappeared from cultivation – ferns, aspidistras, palms, and such flowering plants as the fuchsia and the pelargonium suffered virtual eclipse. By the mid twentieth century, however, there have been revivals of interest

a hardy plant. It is still, however, a splendid plant for a conservatory.

The number of conservatories built before the wars that are still in existence today is very few. Most of them have fallen into decay and have been demolished, but some still survive.

There is, however, a growing trend for the addition of a conservatory, sun room, lean-to greenhouse, home extension, call it what you

in many such groups of plants, and the conservatory, or garden room, is again a feature of many homes.

Also, and this was particularly true of World War Two, as a result of fuel restrictions many greenhouses were run at much lower temperatures than had been the rule in the past, or were not even heated at all. Thus, to the surprise of gardeners, it was discovered that many plants could survive and even flourish at much lower temperatures than they had normally been given, and indeed many too which did not need any artificial heat at all. One of these plants was *Primula sieboldii* which was to be found in practically every Victorian or Edwardian conservatory in a great range of varieties – 50 or more. Yet this primula is as hardy as a toad, and only now is it staging a comeback as

will, to existing houses. This is splendid; the lean-to greenhouse has in my view always been greatly underestimated, and economic pressures may yet see a considerable upsurge of interest in this type of structure.

The advantages of a lean-to greenhouse, or any glass structure using one wall of the dwelling house, are obvious. It is easy to install electricity and water; the greenhouse gains some warmth from the house wall; it is possible to install some radiators to heat the greenhouse from the domestic central heating system if there is one. Also, it is convenient to have the greenhouse adjacent to the dwelling house – one is more likely to keep a watchful eye on it than if one has to trudge the length of the garden through rain or snow.

Furthermore, if a window of a living room

A conservatory can be simple or elaborate —
from glass shelves across a large window to a
glassed-in window box to a partially or completely
enclosed porch or balcony. When the window
of the living room gives on to the conservatory,
a beautiful display of flowering and foliage
plants can be made: hanging pots of fuchsias,
grape vines, pelargoniums, saintpaulias, cacti
and other succulents, chlorophytum, peperomias,
dracaenas, ficus, ferns, codiaeum, dieffenbachia,
as shown in the conservatories here

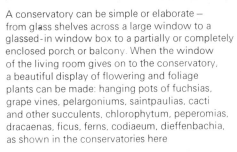

gives on to the conservatory, a beautiful feature may be arranged by grouping flowering and foliage plants so that they can be seen from inside the house, especially if they are illuminated at night.

The decision has to be made whether a glass structure built on to the house is to be used primarily for growing plants, or if it is essentially an extra living room in which some plants may be grown. Obviously if the latter is the case the choice of plants will be limited to those which in the main enjoy the same conditions of heat and humidity as human beings require. This would include the full range of plants that are normally recommended for growing in a normal living room, with the addition of some which require more light than they would normally receive in a living room.

In practice it would be best to concentrate on the plants recommended for the cool greenhouse because the plants for a warm house would probably need more humidity than human beings would find comfortable.

One of the attractions of an extra room or sun lounge is that, provided it can be heated, you can sit and enjoy any sunshine that is going any day in the year. But this means that the heating apparatus is capable of keeping the temperature at around 21°C/70°F for British people, considerably more for most Americans, at least during the periods the sun room is being occupied.

One could have a background heat of about 15°C/60°F with a supplementary heater capable of raising the temperature an extra 6°C/10°F quite quickly. Many plants, most of those indicated as suitable for a cool greenhouse on pp 222–232 will not object to fluctuations of temperature of this order provided the higher temperatures are not maintained for long periods – not more than several hours – and provided that the atmosphere is reasonably humid.

There are various humidifiers on the market – electrically operated types, trays of water to fit over radiators, and of course trays of metal or plastic which are filled with small washed gravel or pebbles and water. The plants are stood on these trays and enough moisture evaporates around them to create a microclimate that is acceptable to them.

Plants in a conservatory, as indeed in a living room, are usually happier when they are grown quite close together so that their foliage forms a canopy, as it were, over the bench or ground upon which they are growing. If the pots are packed around with peat kept always moist, or stood on a sand or gravel tray, which again is always moist, the 'canopy' of foliage tends to keep the moist air from rising too rapidly as it would when plants are dotted about singly.

One very attractive feature of a conservatory could be a series of hanging baskets. There are many plants that really need to be viewed from below if their charm is to be fully appreciated. Among them are the pendulous varieties of begonia, the many brilliantly coloured forms of Christmas cactus – schlumbergera – and, of course, the pendulous types of fuchsia. Other popular plants for hanging baskets, of course, are trailing lobelia, tradescantia and zebrina, ivy leaved pelargoniums, and both the blue and white forms of *Campanula isophylla*.

Watering hanging baskets poses a minor problem, and it is probably best overcome by suspending them on a nylon cord over a small pulley so that they can be raised or lowered as required. Of course, it is not always possible to fix a pulley in the roof of a conservatory or a home extension. But it is usually possible to fix brackets to the rear wall at several heights and suspend the baskets with a nylon cord over a pulley at the horizontal extremity of the bracket. Otherwise you have to stand on a pair of low steps to do the watering.

There are some very ingenious and inconspicuous pot holders available. They consist of a partial circle of green plastic-coated wire, with two hooks at the back. The partial circle can be bent open or closed to accommodate pots of various diameter. Square meshed panels of similar plastic wire are fixed 2.5cm/1in or so away from the wall. The rings are then hooked on to the wire panel, and a delightful arrangement of pot plants can be made against the wall.

Plants in a conservatory are usually happiest when grown close together, as above and above centre, with the lush display of schizanthus, coleus, Begonia rex, salpiglossis, tradescantia and chlorophytum. In a sunroom the plants may be placed for an individual effect, giving more room to sit and relax

One of the great advantages of a conservatory, especially if you can see into it from the house, or enter it without having to go outside as you would have to do with a lean-to greenhouse, is that you can create charming effects with cunning lighting.

There are now available sets of portable lamps operating at 12 volts from a transformer, and which may be moved about safely to illuminate various plants or features that may be in flower at a particular time.

A pool with a small electric fountain and some ornamental fish could be another charming feature of a conservatory. You can even have underwater lighting and floodlighting of the fountain if desired, so the pool can be enjoyed at night.

211

Choosing a greenhouse

To be quite honest, the ordinary dog-kennel-shaped greenhouse, whether it is made of wood or metal struts, is no great thing of beauty. Manufacturers recognizing this fact have produced different designs in wood and metal, notably a 12-sided aluminium house which is elegant and fits into the garden scene as unobtrusively as a well-designed aviary. The trouble with these better-looking houses is that they are more expensive than those of traditional designs.

Choosing a Greenhouse

Choosing a greenhouse is something that should not be undertaken lightly – there are many points that need to be considered.

Let us first look at the claims of glass versus plastic. We now have several types of plastic houses made either with transparent rigid sheeting, or thin PVC sheeting which is stretched over a very light and inexpensive framework. These plastic-covered houses are cheap. The plastic 'envelope' of thin PVC sheeting needs to be renewed every two or three years, but it is not expensive.

These plastic houses, especially the 'tunnel' type, are not very easy to ventilate, and they are probably rather more expensive to heat than traditional glass greenhouses.

Still, a plastic greenhouse has its uses, and where cost is important serious consideration should be given to the various types of plastic clad houses available.

Turning now to the wood versus metal controversy. There are still many old gardeners who are firmly convinced that plants grow better in a wooden house than in a metal one. I do not believe it, having grown plants in metal, wooden, and even a concrete house, for over 20 years. You will be told, no doubt, that metal houses are more expensive to heat than wooden ones because the metal glazing bars conduct the heat out of the house faster than wooden bars do. This is true, but by far the greatest heat loss from a greenhouse is through the glass – that lost through glazing bars, whether of wood or metal, is only a tiny fraction of the total loss, so this criticism can be discounted.

Yet again you will be told by the old die-hards that there is danger of drips of water that have condensed on the metal glazing bars falling on plants. This certainly happened with the early designs of metal houses, but now this problem has been eliminated. So, too, is the danger of glass being broken by the expansion of metal glazing bars; it just does not happen with modern houses. Yet many people still believe this old wives' tale.

There was a time when aluminium or galvanized metal houses were appreciably more expensive than wooden houses. But the cost of timber and the labour of making it into greenhouses have so escalated that aluminium houses are now cheaper than the best types of wooden houses.

My own choice would be an aluminium house without any hesitation, as it will need nothing in the way of maintenance for a lifetime.

Next we have to consider what is an economical sized house to buy. Remembering

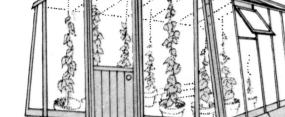
Span-type greenhouse with glass to the ground

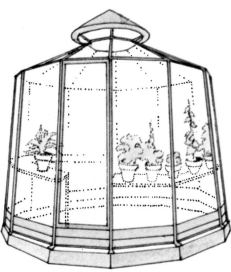

Top left: Lean-to greenhouse with low wooden walls.
Top centre: Span-type greenhouse with low wooden walls.
Top right: Three-quarter span-type greenhouse.
Above: Circular greenhouse with glass to ground.
Left: Greehouse extension to house.

that the object of having a greenhouse is to grow plants in it, we should look for a house that gives us the largest area for growing plants at the lowest cost per square metre/yard of growing area.

One must have a path down the middle of a greenhouse not less than 60cm/2ft wide. So in a greenhouse 1.8m/6ft wide by 2.4m/8ft long you have left on either side of the path 1.4sq.m/16sq.ft of growing space – 3sq.m/32sq.ft in all.

But if you buy a greenhouse 2.4m/8ft by 2.4m/8ft, and you have your 60cm/2ft wide path down the middle, you have 2.2sq.m/24sq.ft each side of your path, 4.4sq.m/48sq.ft in all. This is half as much again as you get in a 1.8m/6ft by 2.4m/8ft house, but a 2.4m/8ft by 2.4m/8ft house does not cost anything like half as much again as the smaller house.

For an amateur I would say that a house 2.4m/8ft wide, which may be extended if desired by adding 1.2m/4ft or 2.4m/8ft sections, is probably the best proposition. But it is always worth looking at the houses in the range that are 3m/10ft wide. One can still have the 60cm/2ft wide path, and the beds or benches on either side at 1.2m/4ft wide are not too wide to be manageable. If you go for a house wider than 3m/10ft then it means having a bench down the middle, and benches on either side, with two paths, which may not be an economic proposition.

The next point to consider is whether the greenhouse should have glass to the ground, or have wooden or brick walls up to say 90cm/3ft above ground. I would say without hesitation that if only one greenhouse is to be built let it have glass to the ground. You can grow plants on the floor of the house; you can grow more plants on a bench at waist height, and still more plants on shelving say 90cm/3ft above the bench. In this way a greenhouse can really begin to show a dividend.

Of course, there is a saving in heating costs if a house has wooden or brick sides up to

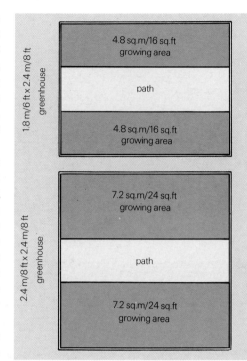

Left: A lean-to greenhouse can provide an attractive extension to the house as well as a place to potter.
Above: The diagrams show how the growing area is substantially increased by choosing a greenhouse that is 60cm/2ft wider

90cm/3ft. But I would think that the value of the plants that can be grown under the benches more than compensates for the extra heating cost.

Siting the Greenhouse

Presumably because a greenhouse is not a very attractive building you see most of them at the end of the garden farthest from the house. This is not the best place because it is not easy to take supplies of electricity, gas or water so far, or if the greenhouse is to be heated by a solid fuel boiler it means a depressing tramp to the end of the garden two or three times a day, probably in the rain or snow and in the dark. Far better to site the greenhouse near the back door, always provided it can receive all the possible sunshine, especially the low-angled sunshine in the early months of the year. This means that the greenhouse should not be overshadowed by the house or by trees.

Whether the house should be sited to run east to west, or north to south depends upon what you want to grow in it. If the house is to be mainly used to grow a collection of foliage or flowering plants, orchids or alpines, it would

probably be best sited to run north-south with the door at the south end.

But if, as is most likely, it is to be a general purpose house intended for raising seedlings of all kinds in the spring, and for growing tomatoes and cucumbers in summer to be followed by chrysanthemums in the autumn, then it is best sited to run east-west with the door at the west end. Sited thus the house will gain the most benefit from the low-angled winter and spring sunlight.

When choosing the site for a greenhouse it is worthwhile spending a little time working out how the supplies of electricity, gas and water may be most easily taken to the house. As we shall see later, electricity is almost essential in a greenhouse if it can be installed reasonably cheaply – even if it is used only to provide lighting. But electricity can be a boon in a greenhouse even if you decide to heat the house by alternative means – by a paraffin or gas heater. It can provide soil warming in a border or on a bench, supplementary lighting for the plants, an extractor fan for ventilation, a heated propagating case, and mist propagation.

So try to site the greenhouse where an elec-

tric cable, a gas pipe and a water pipe may be easily taken to it in the same trench.

While you are thinking about the site for your greenhouse, keep in mind that you may almost certainly wish to extend it one day, or place another house alongside it. Also, you will need some frames to take care of the overflow of seedlings and cuttings produced in the greenhouse until they are ready to be planted out when danger of frost is past. Ideally the frames should be placed on the south-facing side of the greenhouse.

Double-glazing

Now we must look at a very controversial matter – double-glazing. A firm once tried to sell a greenhouse with really complete double-glazing – both walls and roof. It was expensive. The double-glazing effected a saving in cost of heating the greenhouse of the order of about 30-40 per cent.

But plants are not happy in this fully double-glazed house. Even when fitted with an extractor fan for ventilation, the air changes around the plants are neither sufficient nor uniform enough. Hence we get more trouble with

moulds and other diseases. Also, extractor fans and other automatic ventilation systems are activated by some kind of thermostat or device that works by temperature. The thermostat is set to operate the fan when the temperature rises to, say, 10°C/50°F in summer, or 15.5°C/60°F in winter. Now on dull cloudy mornings the temperature in the house may take a long time, several hours, to warm up and start the ventilation. Added to the cool night hours this often gives disease spores time to germinate and enter the foliage while it is still slightly damp from moisture condensed from the air as it cooled during the night.

A traditional type of glass single-glazed house will 'breathe' naturally and, even without the fan or other ventilation working, may have half a dozen air changes an hour through air being drawn in between overlaps of the glass and other places.

If it is really felt essential to effect a cost saving by lining a house with plastic sheeting, it is best only to line it partially. Line say the north and east walls, or line the inside but leave, say, 60cm/2ft at the top unlined to allow moist air to rise to the ridge.

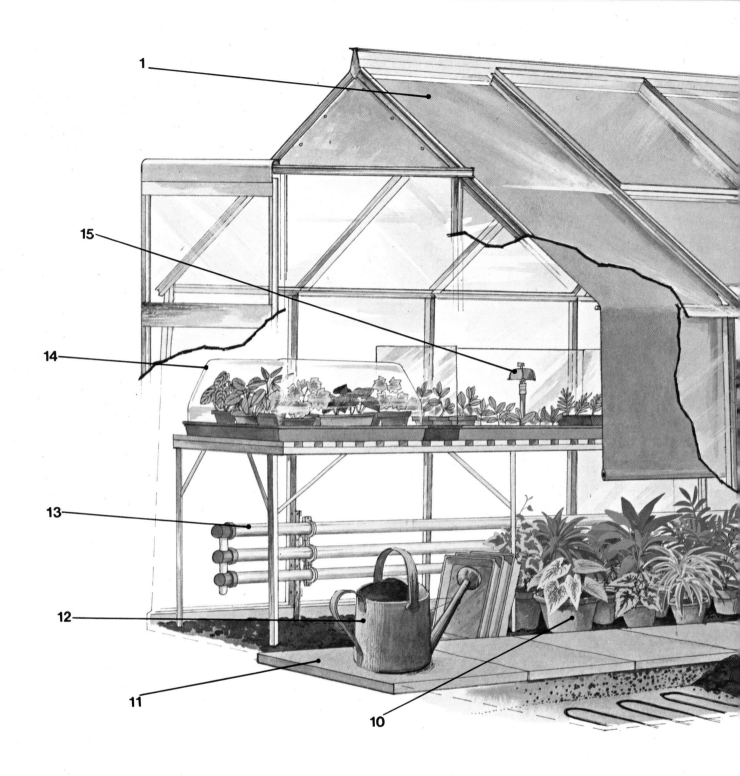

1. Choose a greenhouse that gives the largest area for growing plants at the lowest cost per sq.m./sq.yd. of growing space
2. The greatest heat loss from a greenhouse is through the glass
3. Aluminium houses never need any maintenance
4. A ventilator on either side of the roof is essential, and automatic louvre-type ventilators are a boon
5. Clean the glass every few weeks to be sure light can filter through
6. Young seedlings must be protected from strong sunlight and general shading is required in summer. Expensive green plastic roller blinds can be installed, or a green water borne paint can be used directly on the glass
7. A cold greenhouse (with no artificial heating) can be used to grow alpines, bringing along bulbs and for growing tomatoes in the summer
8. A general purpose greenhouse, for raising seedlings in the spring, tomatoes and cucumbers in the summer, and chrysanthemums in the autumn, is best sited to run east-west. It will then

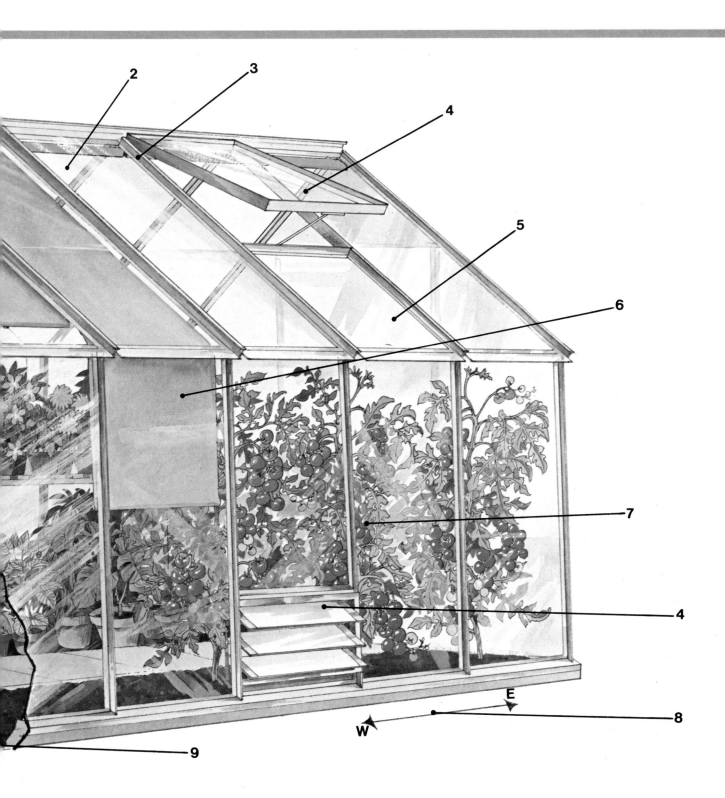

gain most benefit from winter and spring sunshine

9. Electric soil-warming cables enable you to sow seeds earlier and push plants along faster—at an economical cost

10. If you have glass to the ground instead of wooden or brick walls up to 90cm/3ft, you can grow plants on the floor of the greenhouse. These

additional plants should compensate for the extra heating cost

11. A basic requirement is a path down the middle of the greenhouse at least 60cm/2ft wide

12. From early summer to early autumn it is necessary to increase the humidity by 'damping down' two or three times a day

13. Tubular heaters fixed low on both sides of

the greenhouse give a gentle distribution of heat

14. A simple wooden frame covered with glass may be placed on a soil-warmed bench or border to be used for propagation. or a thermostat-controlled propagating case may be installed

15. A mist bench ensures that cuttings or seedlings are always covered with moisture

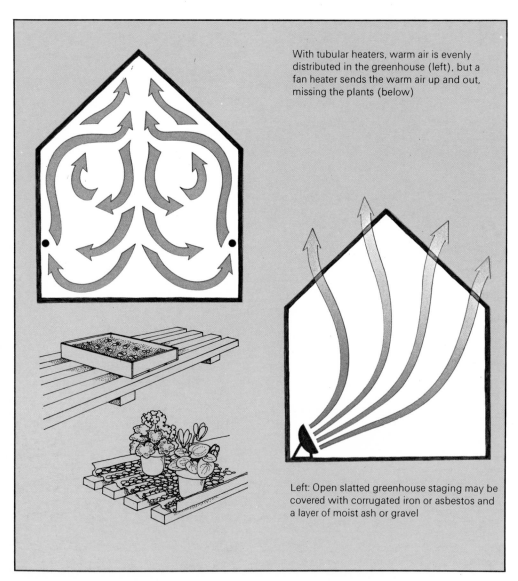

With tubular heaters, warm air is evenly distributed in the greenhouse (left), but a fan heater sends the warm air up and out, missing the plants (below)

Left: Open slatted greenhouse staging may be covered with corrugated iron or asbestos and a layer of moist ash or gravel

Heating the Greenhouse

A cold greenhouse – i.e., with no artificial heating at all – is better than no greenhouse. Indeed, one can make quite good use of it for growing alpine plants, for bringing along bulbs and other spring flowers, also for growing tomatoes in the summer. But heating a house to even a winter temperature as modest as 7°C/45°F night minimum opens up far wider horizons.

The majority of the plants an amateur wishes to grow can be kept happy in such a temperature. If soil warming on benches or in a border can be provided by electric soil warming cables, this makes an enormous difference to the performance of the plants – it enables you to sow seeds earlier, and push plants along faster, but at an economical cost.

The plants we term 'cool house' plants will grow happily with a root temperature of around 13°C/55°F to 15.5°C/60°F. But it is expensive to warm the soil in a border or in pots on benches by keeping the air at these temperatures. By applying soil warming we can still run the house at the economical temperature of 7°C/45°F night minimum. If you

increase this temperature to 10°C/50°F you double the running costs no matter what fuel you use. If you raise it to 12.8°C/55°F you almost double the cost again.

Electricity is the most convenient and versatile fuel for a greenhouse. It is not cheap nowadays, but its use can be controlled very accurately by rod type thermostats, and there is no waste. Also, electricity is excellent for heating propagating cases, for ventilation and for mist propagation where fairly high soil temperatures are required.

It is commonly but erroneously believed that free standing fan-assisted or 'blower' heaters are more effective and cheaper to run than tubular heaters fixed low down to the walls of the house. The fan-assisted heaters are usually stood on the path at the far end of the house, pointing towards the doors, and the fan blows air over the heating elements towards the door. Thus it rises quite quickly and builds up in a layer just below the ridge of the house where the heat quickly dissipates through the glass. It can be that there is a difference of as much as 10°C/14°F between the air at the top of the house and that at ground level. This can be

partially overcome by installing a quite small electric fan near the roof at the end of the house pointing towards the door, downwards at an angle of 10°. This forces the warm air down again and can reduce the difference between the upper and the lower air to about 1°C/2°F.

The tubular heaters give a much more gentle distribution of heat. They are normally fixed to the house walls, and if benches are fitted in the house there should be a gap of about 16cm/6in between the bench and the glass. This allows the warm air to rise and form a protective warm 'blanket', as it were, between the plants on the bench and the cold glass. With a blower heater the air tends to skip over the plants on its way up to the roof, and not to give them the same protection from the cold glass.

Heaters have now been developed using natural gas or propane gas. These systems are cheaper to run than electricity, but not so versatile – you cannot, for example, run soil warming or mist propagation units easily from them. They are, however, efficient, and in the case of the propane type heater excellent where there are no main gas or electricity supplies.

A few hotwater systems are still installed, heated by solid fuel boilers, but these are not very efficient convertors of fuel, and it is not easy to obtain really accurate and steady temperature control as with electric heating.

Advances have been made, too, in recent years with paraffin heaters – automatic supply of paraffin from a large drum, clean burners and thermostatic control.

Not many people are now keeping green-

houses at the temperatures required by many orchids and other tropical plants because of the high cost of fuel. But if it is desired to grow some of these warm houseplants it may be possible to section off a part of the greenhouse at the end furthest from the door, and install some extra heating just in that section.

Ventilation and Shading

Advances have been made, too, in ventilation. Generally small amateurs' greenhouses are not supplied with sufficient ventilators. In a 2.4m/8ft long house there should be one on either side of the roof, and preferably one low down in the wall on each side. There are also various louvre type ventilators which open and close automatically, and equipment which will automatically raise and lower ventilators. This type works by a piston that rises and falls, propelled by the expansion and contraction of a liquid inside the cylinder of the machine.

Shading is a most important part of green-house management. From about the end of March the sun gains rapidly in strength day by day. It is necessary to have handy some news-papers, sheets of brown paper, or a sheet of green plastic to pop over young seedlings to protect them from the heat of the sun in the middle of the day.

From about mid-April it is usually necessary to have some general shading for the green-house. One excellent method, although rather expensive, is to fit green plastic roller blinds inside the greenhouse; these can be raised and lowered as required. But blinds are really only used to best advantage if somebody is there all day to raise and lower them as necessary.

Most people settle for some kind of 'perma-nent' shading – either a kind of whitewash, or a green water borne paint which can be applied to the outside of the glass with a brush or sprayed on. A light application goes on first in spring, and is thickened up with extra coats later as the sun grows in strength.

There is now available a white emulsion which can be rubbed off with a dry duster, but which is not affected by rain, no matter how heavy or how persistent.

Growing Together

We have always to remember that the climate in a greenhouse is an artificial one, and as far as possible we have to see that it adapts to the needs of the majority of the plants we try to grow. It is sometimes said that you cannot grow cucumbers with tomatoes, or carnations with other plants. This is not quite true. You can grow cucumbers in a tomato house, but it would be better to grow them on their own; partition off a small part at the end of the house with polyethelene sheeting so that it can be kept more humid than the rest of the house.

It is probably truer to say that you can grow other plants with carnations, but the carnations will need to be given priority in their likes and dislikes of heat, ventilation and so on.

Left: The hanging basket contains Begonia × tuberhybrida 'Pendula'.
Above: An unusual greenhouse staging in a house extension shows off bromeliads and succulents.
Right: A colourful greenhouse display of Ardisia crispa, Pachystachys lutea, calceolaria, cineraria, pelargoniums and impatiens

Propagation in the Greenhouse

One of the greatest uses of a greenhouse is for propagation, by seed or by cuttings. If soil warming is installed on a bench, or even in a border, a simple wooden frame may be placed on the bench and covered with a couple of large sheets of glass. Or, of course, a more elaborate propagating case with thermostat-controlled air and soil warming may be installed.

Mist propagation is the latest refinement, consisting of a soil warmed bench capable of being maintained at 21°C/70°F. Above this, nozzles are placed capable of delivering automatically a fine misty spray so that cuttings, or even seedlings, are always covered with a film of moisture. Thus, the cuttings never wilt and may be rooted in full sun. Many plants may be propagated by cuttings in a mist bench that would be difficult to root otherwise.

Control of Pests and Diseases

Because the atmosphere in a greenhouse is warm and humid, pests and diseases breed and spread rapidly. Be scrupulous about hygiene. Remove and burn faded flowers, and discoloured or diseased leaves. At the first signs of a disease or pest take action at once, and apply the appropriate control measures – a spray or a fumigation of the house with insecticidal or fungicidal smoke pellets.

Check plants two or three times a week. Turn leaves over here and there as pests and diseases often attack the underside of the leaf. Look too into the heart of young shoots; pests love to cluster down among a tuft of young tender foliage. Sometimes in such cases an aerosol spray is most effective in penetrating among leaves or shoots.

Keep the staging and floor of the house free of green slimy algae by watering the surfaces with an algicide recommended for the purpose. Keep pots clean too, and stir the surface soil in the pots frequently to prevent mossy growth establishing itself.

Staking plants is something that should always be done in good time. If, for example, freesia flower stems bend over and become 'kinked' they will not flower. Staking plants in peat-based mixtures is always more difficult than with loamy mixes, but there are now special wires which may be clipped to the pot and to a cane to keep it upright and rigid in peat.

Dust on plant leaves can be a killer, so spray the foliage on warm days with clear water, or sponge large leaves occasionally.

As mentioned elsewhere, light is more important than heat in winter and the early months of the year. So clean the glass of frames or greenhouses every few weeks with warm water containing a little household detergent.

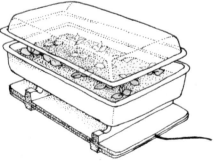

An elaborate propagating case, with soil-warming cables, top, may be installed in the greenhouse, or a simpler propagating frame, as illustrated above, could be used. The newest refinement, a mist propagator, shown left, keeps cuttings and seedlings covered with a film of moisture so they will never wilt

Watering

Of all the arts of greenhouse management the most difficult is watering. It has to be learned by experience and observation. From late spring (April) until early autumn (September) it is usually necessary on sunny days to increase the humidity in the greenhouse by 'damping down' two or three times a day. This means generous watering of the floor, and the shingle or sand covering the benches. Pot plants need checking for water needs mornings and afternoons on hot days. The larger and leafier the plants, the oftener they will need water.

It is easy enough to know when a clay pot needs water. You just tap it smartly with your knuckle, or a cotton reel stuck on a short bamboo cane. If it 'rings hollow' it needs water. If it sounds dull or dead when you tap it, it does not. It is not so easy to distinguish the difference in the sounds with a plastic pot. But with a little experience you can tell how moist the soil is by lifting the pot. A 10cm/4in diameter pot of dry peat-based mixture could weigh around 300g/12oz. When saturated with water it will weigh about 500g/20oz, and you can easily tell the difference.

Peat-based soil mixtures are more tricky as regards watering than loam-based mixes. If a peat mix dries out you either stand the pot in a container of water until it has drawn up all it needs, or you water it from above several times at intervals of, say, 30 minutes until the peat is thoroughly moistened.

In recent years various techniques have been developed to supply the water needs of pot plants by sub-irrigation. Benches are lined with polyethelene and then covered with sand, or a fairly thick fibreglass 'blanket', which is kept permanently moist by various

methods. The pots are stood on this moist base and draw up all the water they require as they need it. Such systems work very well, and of course are ideal for the amateur who may have to leave his greenhouse for a weekend or for longer periods. Houseplants may also be taken out to the greenhouse and stood on a sub-irrigation bench while the family is on holiday.

In the old days we always had a tank in the greenhouse to collect the rainwater. Not so any more. Research has shown that it is better to use clean cold tap water than water from a tank that is almost certain to be contaminated with disease spores. Indeed, some gardeners refer to tank water as 'disease soup'. It is, however, a good idea to have more than one watering can in the house, and fill these in the evening so that the water can warm up a little before being applied to the plants next day.

Sub-irrigation methods ensure that plants receive water as they need it. The automatic watering device illustrated at the top keeps the sand, or fibreglass 'blanket', on the bench moist. The plants draw up the water when they require it. Another automatic device is the trickle watering system, above, which releases water at set intervals from nozzles along the hose. This water may be supplied directly to the plants, or to the sand and taken up by capillary action

Plants for cool greenhouses

Ardisia

[East Indies] Gay little evergreen shrub with bright green leaves about 10cm/4in long and axillary umbels of fragrant white flowers in June. These are followed by scarlet berries. *A. crispa* is the species usually grown. Set plants in 13-15cm/5-6in pots of gritty loamy soil mix and place in good light. Ventilate freely during the growing season and water to keep the soil evenly moist. Spur vigorous growth by feeding every two weeks with dilute liquid manure from April to September. Keep soil barely moist in winter. Overwinter at a temperature of 7°C/45°F. Shade from bright sunlight in summer. Ardisia grows about 91cm/3ft high and 30-46cm/12-18in across. Shorten straggly plants in February: prune side shoots to within 8-10cm/3-4in of the base. Select only the most vigorous shoots to grow on. Raise new plants from seeds in March, in gentle heat, or propagate from side shoots, 8cm/3in long with a heel, in spring and summer.

Beloperone

[Shrimp Plant; Mexico] Curious evergreen shrub valued for its arching shoots tipped with cones of white flowers shielded by overlapping browny pink bracts, resembling shrimps. Growing to about 46cm/18in high and 30cm/1ft across, the 'shrimps' are borne almost continuously from April to December. The one species in cultivation is *B. guttata*.

Set plants in 15cm/6in pots of loam-based soil mix and give ample air in warm weather. Water freely throughout the growing season and stimulate strong growth with weekly feeds of dilute liquid fertilizer from May to September. Shade from strong sun in hot spells. Water sparingly in autumn and winter – just enough to stop plants drying out. Shorten leggy stems by cutting them back to half their length in February. Raise new plants from cuttings of 8cm/3in long half-ripe shoots in spring and remove the first bracts that form, to encourage robust, bushy growth.

Bougainvillea

[Brazil] Lush and shrubby leaf-shedding climber. Bright papery bracts sheath slender stems from July to September. *B. glabra*, 1.5-2.4m/5-8ft high and 1.2m/4ft across, sports rounded green leaves and magenta bracts (which, incidentally, are attractive surrounds to insignificant white flowers). 'Kiltie Campbell', a variety of *B. × buttiana*, is resplendent in coppery red bracts which fade to magenta. 'Poulton's Special' is an outstanding hybrid

Minimum winter night temperature 7°C/45°F.

Bougainvillea 'Mrs Butt'

with bronze leaves. Its fascinating large purple bracts have unusual centres. Another hybrid, 'Mrs Mclean', comes in golden yellow and fades to pink and apricot.

Get the finest plants by growing them in 20cm/8in pots of loamy soil or in the greenhouse border. Train their slender stems over wires or canes. Feed fortnightly with dilute liquid manure throughout the growing season and water freely too. Give less water when the blooms fade, and keep the soil just moist until growth resumes the following March. Syringe the leaves in hot weather. Shorten main growths by one third their length in February and cut back side shoots to two or three buds. Increase from half-ripe cuttings in summer, rooted at gentle heat.

Bouvardia

[Mexico] Evergreen shrub valued for its eye-catching heads of bloom from June to November. *B. × domestica* is usually grown and is about 60cm/2ft high and 46cm/1½ft across. Clusters of fragrant flowers at branch tips are around 15cm/6in across. Varieties 'President Cleveland', bright crimson and 'Mary', pink, thrive in 20cm/8in pots of a loam-based mixture.

Set in good light but shade from sunlight in summer. Nip out growing tips in late spring to encourage nicely branched specimens. Water freely throughout the growing season, but hardly at all when blooms fade and until new growth starts in March. Give a liquid feed once a week from May to September. This little shrub will survive at 7°C/45°F in winter, but does better if a temperature of 13°C/55°F can be maintained. Increase from half-ripe cuttings

with a heel in spring. Shorten previous years' growth to within 2.5cm/1in of the base in February. Repot when roots fill the container. Ideally, raise new plants from cuttings every year.

Browallia

[Columbia] Gorgeous blue-flowered annuals valued for summer and winter colour. *B. speciosa major* has vivid blue, white-throated blooms. *B. viscosa* 'Sapphire' is a neater variety with slightly sticky leaves. At 15-23cm/6-9in high it is about three-quarters the height of *B. speciosa major*.

Set plants in 13cm/5in pots of a loam- or peat-based soil mix. Browallias thrive in good light and benefit from plenty of water in spring and summer and feeds of dilute liquid manure every two weeks when growth is vigorous. Sow in gentle heat in March for a summer display and in August for a winter show. Plant sturdy seedlings singly in 8cm/3in pots of a loamy soil mix and move them into 13cm/5in pots when roots fill the containers. Nip out growing tips to make plants branch freely and flower well. Discard after flowering.

Campanula

[Bellflower; Southern Europe] *Campanula isophylla* is a superb trailing plant for hanging baskets or for setting on a pedestal. The small toothed, heart-shaped leaves are smothered with a profusion of exquisite starry blue or white flowers, 2cm/1in wide, in August and September. *C. isophylla* itself is blue; 'Alba' is a pure white form.

Set this dwarf perennial, which grows around 15cm/6in high with a 46cm/18in spread, in good light. Water freely in the growing season and boost flowering with weekly feeds of dilute liquid manure when the buds are forming. Grow in 13-20cm/5-8in pots of a loam-based potting mix and raise new plants from seed sown from October to November, or in March and April. Alternatively, take cuttings of non-flowering basal shoots in spring.

C. pyramidalis, the Chimney Bell-flower, has imposing 2.5-4cm/1-1½in long blue or white bell flowers borne on short stems to form an impressive spire of bloom 1.2-1.5m/4-5ft high and about 46cm/1½ft wide. This is a perennial best grown as a biennial, as plants tend to look sad and unkempt in their second year. They have attractive heart-shaped leaves. Flowers form in May. Set plants in large pots or tubs of a rich gritty soil mix and feed and water generously while plants are growing strongly. Raise new plants from seed.

Left: The vivid blue blooms of *Browallia speciosa* provide colour in winter.
Bottom: *Beloperone guttata*, the Shrimp Plant, may also be grown as a houseplant.
Below: The exotic *Canna indica* has fiery orchid-like flowers from June to September

Cestrum

[Mexico/South America] Spectacular evergreen or semi-evergreen upright or arching shrubs 1.5-2.4m/5-8ft high. Small glossy-green oval leaves offset attractive terminal and axillary sprays of tubular flowers which appear from February to September. Finest species are *C. aurantiacum*, 1.2-1.5m/4-5ft high; gay

Canna

[Indian Shot Plant; Tropical Asia/Tropical America] Exotic and richly hued spikes of gladiolus or orchid-like flowers thrust up on unbranched stems from broad paddle-like leaves in green, brown or purple. This splendid June-to-September-flowering perennial lights up the greenhouse with its fiery blooms. Plants grow 91cm-1.8m/3-6ft high. There are many hybrids with either green or purple leaves and in a rainbow of flower colours: green-leaved kinds – bright red 'Brilliant', carmine-pink 'Evening Star', red-margined yellow 'Lucifer', canary-yellow 'Richard Wallace'. Brown and purple-leaved kinds – deep red 'America', scarlet 'Feuerzauber', soft pink 'Tyrol', orange-bronze 'Wyoming', orange 'Verdi'.

Water freely once growth starts and feed frequently. Plant tubers in small pots in spring; pot on as growth increases. Finally have plants in 23cm/9in pots or tubs of rich peaty soil. When flowers fade and leaves yellow in autumn, dry off tubers and store in a warm place over winter. Propagate by dividing the rhizomatous rootstock in spring.

orange blooms from February to May. *C. fasciculatum*, salmon-red flowers, 1.8-2.4m/6-8ft, April to June; and *C. parqui*, whose primrose flowers are richly scented at night. This is a summer-flowering low-growing species, 91cm-1·5m/3-5ft high. It is also the hardiest.

Set plants in 20-25cm/8-10in pots of rich loamy soil; alternatively, grow them in tubs or in the border. They demand a good light position but need shelter from bright sunlight from May to September. Overwinter in a temperature of 7-10°C/45-50°F. Water freely throughout the growing season, keep just moist in winter. Feed every two weeks from May to September. Increase plants from half-ripe cuttings taken in July and August. Keep plants tidy and free-flowering by entirely removing two- or three-year old shoots and shortening side shoots to 15cm/6in. Do this in February or March. Repot, if grown in pots or tubs, when roots fill the container.

223

Cineraria cruenta

[Canary Islands] Attractive half-hardy perennial usually grown as a biennial. Imposing heads of richly coloured daisy flowers top stems 38cm/15in to 76cm/30in high. Shoots clothed with large heart-shaped leaves, light to mid green in colour. Bushy, compact growth. Usually a single stem set with one large boss of bloom. Selected forms are 'Hybrida Grandiflora', of which 'Blue Shades', 'Deep Red', 'Light Rose', brick-red 'Matador', 'Old Rose' and 'Pure White' are some of the finest strains that come true from seed. Height: 46-61cm/1½-2ft. More compact and lower growing is 'Multiflora Nana'. A broad-petalled selection equalling the rich colour range of 'Hybrida Grandiflora'. 38cm/15in high. The Stellata strain, with narrow starry-petalled blooms, is represented by 'Feltham Beauty', 61-91cm/2-3ft high. Again, the colours are superb. 'Double Mixed' gives a choice range of colour combinations. Flowers are borne from December to March if a night temperature of 8°C/46°F and a day temperature of 16°C/61°F can be maintained, although lower temperatures have no adverse effects.

Set plants in pots of rich loamy soil, gritty and well-drained. Shade from bright sunshine or leaves will curl and wilt. Do not overwater or plants may collapse. This is a useful plant for a poorly lit windowsill or balcony. It doesn't mind draughts. Feed weekly when flower buds are forming. Raise plants from seed in April to August, in a temperature of 13°C/55°F. Pot on as growth increases until plants are growing singly in 13cm/5in pots of loamy soil. Stand outside in a cold frame in summer and bring into the greenhouse in September or October.

Clianthus

[Parrot's Bill or Lobster Claw; Australia/New Zealand] Startling clusters of brilliant pea-like flowers form in axils between leaves and stems from May to June. Compound evergreen leaves of 12-24 leaflets. Evergreen climbing or ground covering shrubs. Two species are grown: C. formosus (glory pea) is almost prostrate 60-90cm/2-3ft wide, with bright red-beaked flowers each with a pronounced black centre. Leaves are covered with silvery hairs. C. puniceus has clusters of red parrot's bill-like flowers on slender arching stems. Leaves glossy-green fan out from the branches. C. puniceus 'Albus' is a rare white-flowered form. Set C. formosus in a hanging basket of well-drained, gritty loam soil. Ventilate freely in summer, syringe the leaves occasionally in dry warm spells, but water by immersing the basket in a bucket of water. Overwinter in a temperature of 7°C/45°F. Enjoys a growing tempera-

ture of 10-13°C/50-55°F during warm weather.

Unlike C. formosus, C. puniceus is a scrambling climber to 3.6m/12ft high. Grow it in loamy soil in the greenhouse border or in large pots or tubs and train it over a framework of wires or canes to enjoy its flowers to the full. Syringe leaves lightly early in the day on warm days as it grows best in dry air. Overwinter in a temperature of 7°C/45°F.

Raise new plants of C. formosus from seeds in February and C. puniceus from 8cm/3in heeled cuttings of side shoots in June and July. Trim C. puniceus to shape by removing weak stems or cutting back straggly stems to near the base to encourage fresh growth. Do this in June, after flowering is over.

Clivia

[Kaffir Lily; Natal] Impressive clumps of strap-shaped leathery bright green leaves 60cm/2ft or so long form thickly from a fleshy rootstock. Robust stems topped with umbels of trumpet flowers appear from spring to late summer. C. × cyrtanthiflora, a garden hybrid between C. miniata and C. nobilis, produces scarlet flowers in March and April. The popular C. miniata is renowned for its several fleshy flower stems which terminate in imposing heads of trumpet blooms from March to August. The less common C. nobilis is smaller, about 30cm/1ft high and bears orange-red, greenish tipped blooms in May.

Above: *Clivia miniata*
Below: *Clianthus puniceus* 'Roseus'
Opposite: Two beautiful orchids, *Coleogyne cristata* (left) and *Cymbidium* 'Flare × Nam Khan'

Set plants in 15cm/6in pots of loam-based soil in spring. Water to keep the soil evenly moist throughout the spring and summer. Give just enough water in autumn and winter to prevent the soil drying out. Pot on plants annually after flowering so eventually they are in large pots (25cm/10in) or tubs, or in the greenhouse border. Overwinter at a temperature of 7°C/45°F. Divide crowded clumps in spring and pot up offsets in small pots of rich gritty loamy soil. Alternatively, but much slower, raise new plants from seed in early spring.

Coelogyne

[Asia/Pacific Islands] Evergreen epiphytic orchids. Spikes of fragrant blooms borne on upright (20-45cm/8-18in high) or pendulous stems. Flowers, from December to October, range from white and greenish-yellow to brownish and deep salmon pink. Pseudobulbs rounded or flask-shaped; leaves strap-like. *C. asperata* has 20cm/8in flower stems topped with 8cm/3in blooms, buff-green in colour with white or cream lips flecked yellow or red; *C. cristata* thrives in living room conditions as it likes it fairly cool; 15cm/6in flower spikes consist of about seven pure white blooms 5-8cm/2-3in wide with a pale orange lip. December to March. *C. speciosa* has two to three buff-green to salmon pink flowers on a spike; lip with deep brown or yellow crests.

Set plants in 13cm/5in pots or larger pans of orchid soil mix (two parts osmunda fibre, one part sphagnum moss, one part leaf mould) by volume. *C. cristata* flowers better in a crowded pot. Ventilate on warm days in summer but plants thrive in humid atmosphere so do not let air become dry. Water less from November to March. Propagate by dividing plants from March to May. *C. asperata* needs warm house conditions (minimum winter temperature of 14°C/57°F and minimum summer temperature of 22°C/72°F). The others mentioned do well at a temperature of 7°C/45°F minimum winter night temperature, and 14°C/57°F minimum summer night temperature. Shade from bright sunlight in summer.

Cuphea

[Mexico] Curious evergreen perennials and sub-shrubs valued for their massed display of tubular flowers from June to September. The two most decorative for greenhouse decoration are *C. cyanea* and *C. miniata*. The former is a shrub some 46cm/18in high and about 30cm/12in across; the oval hairy leaves clasp stems wreathed at the tips with blooms consisting of yellow and red calyces from which arise violet-blue petals. *C. miniata* is larger, up to 60cm/2ft high; it has more pointed, silvery-haired oval leaves and 2.5cm/1in long scarlet blooms that develop in leaf axils from early summer to late autumn.

Set plants in 13cm/5in pots of loam-based soil, feeding weekly throughout the spring and summer with dilute liquid fertilizer. Keep the soil evenly moist during the growing season. Shade from bright sunlight in summer and overwinter at a temperature of 7°C/45°F. Keep plants trim by shortening leggy growths by one-half to two-thirds their length in autumn or winter. Raise new plants from cuttings of side shoots in March and April. Alternatively propagate from seeds in gentle heat in January.

Cymbidium

[Ceylon to India and Japan/Malaysia to Australia] Evergreen terrestrial orchids, up to 1.2m/4ft high. Sprays of blooms in a wide range of colours in almost any hue apart from black and blue. Handsome flowers last for many weeks when cut. Blooms are borne from February to June. The vast range of colourful hybrids, derived from crossing several species, have to a large extent superseded the original species. Their blooms are 8-13cm/3-5in across and borne on elegant stems. Best known are the white 'Balkis', yellow green 'Miretta', light pink 'Prince Charles' and rose-pink 'Vieux Rose'. There are hundreds more in a splendid range of hues.

Set plants in a mix comprised of one part loam, two parts osmunda fibre and two parts sphagnum moss, together with a little bone meal and crushed crocks for good drainage. (All parts by volume.) Grow in 10-13cm/4-5in pots to start with, but finish off large varieties in tubs or 46cm/18in pots. Water freely during the growing season and shade from bright sunshine in spring and summer. Ventilate freely whenever it is warm and dry. Grow in a temperature of 16°C/61°F in summer and 7-10°C/45-50°F in winter. Increase plants by dividing the fleshy bulbs in March and April. Repot when new shoots are barely 8cm/3in high, after flowering.

Dendrobium

[Tropical Asia to Ceylon/Samoan and Tongan Islands/Northern Japan/ New Zealand] A very large genus of orchids, mostly leaf-shedding epiphytes, but many tropical kinds are evergreen. Mid- to dark green leaves, oval-oblong in shape. They range from tiny plants with just a few flowers to plants many metres high with long stems fringed with blooms in contrasting colours. There are species for both the cool and warm greenhouse. Cool greenhouse: *D. kingianum*; 15cm/6in spikes carrying violet-purple blooms with white flecked lips, 2.5cm/1in across, April and May; *D. nobile*, 46cm/18in high, flowers 5-8cm/2-3in across in January to March. Blooms white with pink or lilac shading. The yellow lip has a velvet maroon blotch and a pink to purple margin. This is a most accommodating species that will even grow on a warm windowsill. *D. speciosum*, 15-38cm/6-15in high with well-clad spikes of scented creamy flowers whose white lips are speckled with purple.

Set plants in 13cm/5in pots or larger pans of soil consisting of three parts osmunda fibre and one part sphagnum moss (by volume). Shade from sunshine from mid-March to October, on bright hot days. Spray with water to keep the air humid throughout the summer. Rest plants by watering less from November to March. *D. kingianum* and *D. speciosum* thrive in cool house conditions (16°C/61°F in summer and 7-10°C/45-50°F in winter). *D. nobile* prefers slightly higher temperatures of 18°C/64°F in summer and 10°C/50°F in winter These are night readings. Increase plants by dividing overgrown clumps after flowering.

Dipladenia

[Brazil] Twining evergreen shrub to 4.5m/15ft high. Mid-green elliptic leaves offset 20cm/8in spikes of rose-pink, trumpet-shaped flowers from June to September. *D. splendens* is the species usually seen. Set plants in large pots (13-20cm/5-8in initially, then shift to 30cm/1ft pots as growth increases and roots fill the pot) of rich loamy soil. It thrives in a minimum winter temperature of 13°C/55°F and needs at least 16°C/61°F throughout the spring and summer. Water just enough to prevent plants wilting in winter, but give more as growth increases in spring and summer. When the flowers drop, keep the soil on the dry side. Syringe leaves daily in hot dry spells in summer. Feed every two weeks with dilute liquid fertilizer if growth is slow. Propagate from 8cm/3in cuttings of young shoots in spring, or lengths of riper shoots, each set with two leaves, in midsummer. Shorten flowered stems hard back, to within 5cm/2in of the previous year's growth, after flowering. But if extension growth is required, let plants grow on and only shorten stems by half their length.

Epidendrum

[Florida to Brazil] Splendid epiphytic orchids, mostly deciduous. They vary considerably from species to species: some have pseudobulbs with leathery leaves, others have cane-like stems. Upright or arching flower spikes are set with one or more flowers. They are fairly easy to grow, happy in cool or warm greenhouse conditions, or even on a kitchen windowsill, provided it is warm enough. Blooms are most intriguingly shaped and the lip is particularly pronounced. Cool greenhouse epidendrums: *E. ciliare*, 25cm/10in. Flower stems carry up to eight blooms with long narrow green petals with contrasting pale blue or white lips, De-cember to January. *E. endresii*, 30cm/1ft. Some 15 or so white-petalled, green or violet-tipped flowers have flecked purple and orange lips and are borne on an erect spike, from January to May. *E. cochleatum* (cockleshell orchid) has a short pseudobulb with blooms with deep purple shell-shaped lips on 30cm/1ft long pendulous stems from January to July.

Set plants in pots or hanging baskets of soil consisting of three parts osmunda fibre and one part sphagnum moss (by volume). Grow in a minimum winter night temperature of 16°C/61°F and ventilate in summer when the day temperature rises above 21-24°C/70-75°F. Propagate from divisions of the rootstock from March to May.

Erythrina

[Coral Tree; Brazil] The common coral tree, *E. crista-galli*, grows 1.2-2.7m/4-9ft high and some 1.2m/4ft across. Herbaceous shoots sprout from a shrubby rootstock. Handsome blue-green leaves consisting of leathery leaflets are widely spaced on the stems. Shiny red pea-shaped flowers, 4-5cm/1½-2in long, form freely on shoot tips from June to July.

Set plants in 20-25cm/8-10in pots of well-drained gritty loam. Water copiously in spring and summer, hardly at all in autumn and winter. Keep the temperature around 4-7°C/40-45°F in winter. Raise to 13°C/55°F when growth starts anew in spring. Ventilate regularly on hot days in spring and summer, syringe the leaves to keep growth fresh and feed every two weeks with dilute liquid manure from March to September. Stand pots outdoors on warm summer days. Plants need good light but protect against leaf scorch by shading in midsummer. Raise new plants from 8-10cm/3-4in heeled cuttings in April. Root in gentle heat. Prune all shoots hard back to 15cm/6in of the rootstock in February, to encourage fresh new growth from the base.

Gerbera

[African Daisy, Barberton Daisy or Transvaal Daisy; Transvaal] Tender perennial daisy, 30cm/1ft high, with long hairy green leaves and many solitary flowers. *G. jamesonii* bears scarlet blooms, but the 'Westwood Giant Hybrids' come in a vivid range of colours including lemon, orange, salmon, flame and purple. The blooms are 8-13cm/3-5in across. There are both single and double flowered varieties. May to August is the flowering period.

Set plants in 15-20cm/6-8in pots of gritty loamy soil and place in good light. Ventilate freely throughout the summer, shade from strong sunlight from May to September and boost sturdy growth with feeds of dilute liquid manure every two weeks throughout the growing season. Maintain a minimum winter temperature of 5-7°C/41-45°F. Increase by splitting up established clumps and repotting in 10cm/4in pots of loamy soil, in March, or raise plants from seed in gentle heat from February to March.

Grevillia

[Australia/New South Wales] Attractive evergreen trees and shrubs, much valued for their striking petal-less flowers, and in *G. robusta*, for its handsome fern-like leaves. *G. banksii* 'Fosteri', also noted for its finely divided leaves, silky-white on the underside, is 3m/10ft. Commonly called dwarf red silky oak, it has vivid red flowers arranged in dense spikes, which appear in spring. Specially useful for greenhouse cultivation is *G. robusta*, another species which has the most eye-catching silky, fern-like leaves. Usually grown as a 91cm-1.5m/3-5ft pot plant, its leaves, 46cm/18in long when mature, start mid-green, then darken as they grow older. With rosemary-like leaves and arresting claw-like clusters of red flowers, *G. rosmarinifolia*, a 91cm-1.2m/3-4ft pot plant, flowers magnificently from May to September.

Set plants in 13-18cm/5-7in pots of lime-free soil such as a mixture of two parts lime-free loam, one part peat and one part coarse sand. Stand pots outdoors from May to October. Overwinter in a temperature of 4-7°C/39-45°F. Water copiously from spring to early autumn, and ventilate freely in winter when weather mild. Keep the soil just moist during the winter and early spring. Feed every two weeks with dilute liquid manure from April to September. Raise new shrubs from 5-8cm/2-3in cuttings of side shoots with a heel, in June, in gentle heat. *G. robusta* is best propagated from seeds, in March.

Opposite left: *Dipladenia splendens*.
Opposite right: Gerberas come in vivid colours.
Above: Ipomoea, the Morning Glory.
Above right: *Grevillia banksii*.
Below: *Hedychium gardnerianum*

Hedychium

[Gingerwort; India] Arresting herbaceous perennial. Stout 91cm-1.8m/3-6ft stems are sheathed with tapered leaves, and topped by cone-like clusters of fragrant orchid-like flowers from June to October. *H. gardnerianum* is most usually grown. Ascending to 1.8m/6ft or more and spreading to 1·5m/5ft, its 25cm/10in long mid-green leaves foil spikes of brilliant yellow, red-stamened flowers from July to September.

Set plants in good light in large pots or tubs of rich gritty loamy soil. Keep just moist in winter but increase watering as growth speeds up in spring and summer. Feed every two weeks from April to September, with dilute liquid manure. Overwinter at a temperature of 7°C/45°F. Pot on plants every other year, or as soon as roots fill their pot. Increase by dividing old rhizomes in March and April. Alternatively, propagate from seed in gentle heat in March.

Hoya

[Wax Flower; India/Queensland] Attractive evergreen climbing or trailing sub-shrubs with handsome leathery green leaves and arresting umbels of starry flowers from May to September. *H. bella* is a low-growing spreader about 30cm/1ft high and 46cm/18in across. Twiggy branches are clothed with pale green leaves often dotted with silver. Umbrellas 5cm/2in across of white, crimson or purple-centred blooms appear from the leaf axils. *H. carnosa* is altogether more vigorous, around 6m/20ft high, with clinging aerial roots and clusters of white flowers. Mid-green, shiny and fleshy leaves. Develops new lengths of stem before the new leaves form on it. Flowers of both are fragrant. Those of *H. bella* are larger, about 8cm/3in across. There are variegated leaf forms of *H. carnosa*: the leaves are edged pink or have green margins with gold centres.

Set plants in pots of a peat-based soil. Shade from bright sunlight in summer. Water freely and syringe the leaves during the growing season. Feed every three weeks from April to September with dilute liquid manure.

H. bella looks best in a hanging basket, but *H. carnosa* should be trained over wires or trellis. Overwinter plants at a minimum temperature of 10°C/50°F. Water sparingly during the colder months. Propagate from 5-8cm/2-3in cuttings in June. *H. carnosa* may also be increased by layering in spring.

Ipomoea

[Morning Glory; Mexico/Tropical America] Large trumpet blooms that open in the morning and fade by evening are characteristic of this family of showy climbing annuals and perennials. *I. horsfalliae*, an evergreen with deeply cut leaves that shine like emerald, has rich scarlet blooms which open freely in winter from December to February. Perennial climber. *I. tricolor*, an annual climber, flowers on 2.4m/8ft stems from July to September. Finest varieties of it include the blue and white striped 'Flying Saucers', blue, white-centred 'Heavenly Blue' and crimson 'Scarlet O'Hara'. Heart-shaped leaves. One other, *I. purpurea*, also with heart-shaped leaves, is a 3m/10ft annual with 8cm/3in blooms of a rich purple colour throughout summer.

Set three plants to a 20cm/8in pot of rich gritty loam and place in good light. Train over canes, wires or trellis. Raise plants from seed in March, in gentle heat. Increase *I. horsfalliae* from layers, as cuttings do not root easily. Water freely and pick off fading blooms to encourage further shoots and flowers. Feed with dilute liquid fertilizer every two weeks throughout the growing season. Discard plants after flowering. It pays to soak the seeds of *I. tricolor* in water for 24 hours to soften them so they germinate more quickly.

Jacobinia

[Brazil] Arresting evergreen sub-shrubs with handsome elliptic leaves and striking cone-shaped blooms of many two-lipped flowers. The flowers are either terminal or axillary. Most popular is *J. carnea*. Reaching 1.5-1.8m/5-6ft high and some 90cm/3ft across, its dark green pointed leaves offset 10cm/4in heads of flesh pink flowers. These look rather like narrow feather dusters and appear in August and September. *J. coccinea* is similar in height and spread, but has scarlet cones of bloom and these form in February. They are also slightly smaller.

Set plants in good light and water freely during the growing season. Feed with dilute liquid manure from March to September. Shade only if the sun is very hot. Plants grow best in pots of loam-based soil. Overwinter at a temperature of 10-13°C/50-55°F and step this up to 21°C/70°F in spring. Admit plenty of air in mild weather. Shorten the previous year's shoots to within 10cm/4in of the base in February. Raise new plants from 5-10cm/2-4in cuttings of young shoots in April. Root in gentle heat. Pinch out growing tips of young rooted cuttings to encourage a well-shaped, well-branched bush.

Lachenalia

[Cape Cowslip; South Africa] Handsome tender bulbous plants forming loose rosettes of mid-green strap-shaped leaves reflexed at their tips. Spikes of downward hanging tubular flowers appear from December to April. *L. aloides*, 23-30cm/9-12in high, has nodding heads of red-speckled green-margined blooms from December to March; 'Aurea', orange-yellow, and 'Nelsonii', yellow and green, are two vigorous varieties of *L. aloides*. *L. bulbifera* (syn. *pendula*), slightly shorter (15-25cm/6-10in) bears stems of 2.5cm/1in blooms from December to February. They may be purple, red or yellow and tipped either red or green.

L. orchioides, also about 23cm/9in high, has scented red or blue-flushed white or pale yellow flowers. Flowering in April, the individual blooms are fairly small but are set closely on a robust spotted stem.

Set five to eight bulbs in a 15cm/6in pot of loam-based soil in August or September. Place in good light in a temperature of 10-13°C/50-55°F. After watering the bulbs in thoroughly, leave to drain, then withhold water until the shoots appear. Continue keeping the soil evenly moist, feeding weekly with dilute liquid fertilizer. When the blooms fade, gradually cease watering. Let the bulbs dry off when the leaves turn yellow. Repot in August – do not dry off the bulbs in winter. Increase from bulbils potted up in August when the parent bulbs are set in pots of fresh soil. This is a fine plant for a hanging basket. Use it, too, for decorating indoors when the blooms appear.

Luculia

[Bhutan / Himalayas / Khasia Mountains] A small family of evergreen shrubs grown for their clusters of fragrant blooms. *L. grandiflora*, 3m/10ft or more high, has elliptic mid-green leaves around 38cm/15in long and 6cm/2½in wide tubular white flowers set in 21cm/8in sprays, from May to July. *L. gratissima*, 1.8m/6ft or so high, bears mauve pink heads of 2.5cm/1in wide blooms tubular in shape but flared into five rounded lobes at the end. Flowers form from November to February. *L. pinceana*, 1.2-2.1m/4-7ft high, is similar to *L. gratissima* but with larger, 5cm/2in wide flowers in white; May to September. Its leaves are narrow and about 15cm/6in long.

Set plants in the border or in large pots (25-30cm/10-12in) of loam-based soil, in good light. Water freely in summer and syringe leaves daily. Feed every two weeks with dilute liquid manure when plants are growing strongly. Overwinter at a temperature of 7°C/45°F. When flowers fade, keep the soil just moist until fresh shoots appear in April. Give plenty of air in spring and summer. Repot every two or three years. Raise new plants from seed in gentle heat in March or April, or take 8-10cm/3-4in cuttings in May. These should have a heel and be rooted in sandy soil in a mist propagator.

Mimosa pudica

[Sensitive Plant or Humble Plant; Brazil] This pretty little sub-shrub which branches thinly to about 60cm/2ft high is grown for its acutely sensitive ferny leaves and pink powder-puff blooms in July and August. When the compound leaves are touched during the day they react by drooping rapidly; the leaf stalks droop as well. They unfold their leaflets and resume their normal positions after a few minutes.

Set plants in a loam-based soil and support them with a short cane or two. Water freely during the growing season and feed weekly with liquid fertilizer. Grow in good light but shade from hot sunshine. Admit plenty of air if the temperature rises above 18-21°C/64-70°F. Syringe the staging and pots to keep the air moist. Usually grown as an annual and discarded after flowering. Raise new plants from seed in gentle heat in February or March.

Nerine

[South Africa] A beautiful race of bulbous plants renowned for their imposing heads of glistening strap-shaped and twister flowers from September to November. The leafless stems are topped with blooms in a range of hues from bright red to white. The narrow green leaves come after the flowers. *N. bowdenii* has striking flowers borne on stems to 60cm/2ft high. The heads of bloom, 10-15cm/4-6in across, are composed of iridescent flowers in rich pink; *N. flexuosa*, 60cm/2ft, has umbels of pink blooms on 60cm/2ft stems: 'Alba' is a magnificent white form. The Guernsey lily (*N. sarniensis*) bears 15cm/6in heads of pale pink to red blooms. 60cm/2ft high. A treasured species is *N. undulata*. Growing some 30cm/1ft high, its distinctive pink heads of bloom are a dainty 8cm/3in across.

Set one bulb to a 9cm/3½in pot or three to a 15cm/6in pot of loam-based soil, with the neck of the bulb just above the surface. Do this in August. Start watering when the flower buds form and overwinter, just moist, at 10-13°C/50-55°F. Give liquid feed when the leaves are fully formed but stop feeding and watering when they turn yellow. A position in full sun will yield best results. Repot every two or three years. Increase plants from offsets that develop round the bulbs – detach them and pot them when they are mature. Alternatively, raise new plants from seed in May, setting them singly in 8cm/3in pots of gritty loam-based soil.

Left: *Jacobinia carnea*
Below: *Lachenalia aloides* 'Nelsonii'
Opposite: the beautifully hued nerines

Nerium

[Oleander; Mediterranean region] Superb upright evergreen shrub to 2.7m/9ft high. From June to October it is aglow with terminal clusters of periwinkle-like flowers in white, cream, pink and red. There are both single and double forms. Broad leathery mid-green leaves form thickly on the shoots. *N. oleander* is the species grown in cultivation. It makes a spreading bush some 3-4.5m/10-15ft across.

Set plants in small tubs or pots in March, in loam-based soil. Water copiously throughout the spring and summer and feed every 10 days with dilute liquid manure. Set in full light and overwinter at a temperature of 7°C/45°F. Give plenty of air at all times of the year, except when it is frosty. Repot once a year in fresh loam-based soil. Raise new plants from cuttings of half-ripe shoots with a heel in June and July, or propagate from seed in gentle heat in April.

Plumbago

[Leadwort; South Africa/East Indies] Valuable long-flowering evergreen shrubs, often grown as climbers. Sprays of primrose-like flowers, 2.5cm/1in across form freely on slender shoots clothed with 8cm/3in long elliptic mid-green leaves. *P. capensis* is a straggly 4.5m/15ft climber if grown in the greenhouse border, or a 1.2-1.5m/4-5ft bush if grown in pots. Support the floppy stems with wires or canes. Charming light blue sprays of bloom form freely from April to November. *P. rosea* is smaller, about 90cm/3ft high and 60cm/2ft across, and bears scarlet flowers on 15-23cm/6-9in spikes from June to late July.

Set plants in 15-20cm/6-8in pots of loam-based soil in good light, but shade from intense sunlight, specially *P. rosea*. Keep the soil moist from April until the flowers fade, then water sparingly throughout the winter. Overwinter *P. capensis* at 7°C/45°F and *P. rosea* at about 13°C/55°F. Repot in early spring each year. Encourage robust growth by feeding with dilute liquid manure from April to October. Propagate *P. capensis* from heeled cuttings in early summer, and *P. rosea* from cuttings of basal shoots in spring. Prune *P. capensis* by reducing shoots by two-thirds their length after flowering, and *P. rosea* by reducing growth to within 15cm/6in of the base, also when the flowers fade.

Polygala

[Milkwort; South Africa] One species enhances the greenhouse – *P. myrtifolia*, of which the only form grown in cultivation is *P. m. grandiflora*. This is an evergreen shrub about 1.2m/4ft high and 60-90cm/2-3ft across. Its upright shoots are clad with roughly oval blunt-tipped, light green leaves. Curious pea-like flowers in bright rose-purple, 2-4cm/1-1½in long, form freely in clusters at shoot tips from May to October.

Set plants in 15-20cm/6-8in pots of loam or peat-based soil. Position in good light but shade from hot bright sunlight. Water copiously throughout the spring and summer months, feeding with dilute liquid manure every two weeks when growth is strong. Ventilate freely in spring and summer. Overwinter plants at a temperature of not less than 4°C/39°F. Prune in late February if plants grow leggy; shorten shoots by half their length and trim to shape. Raise new plants from cuttings of half-ripe shoots, with a heel, in early spring. Root in gentle heat.

Primula

[China] Primulas are among our most charming pot plants for winter and early spring. Large heads of bloom rise on sturdy stems above a rosette of rounded leaves. Most popular are *P.×kewensis*, which bears its scented yellow blooms in whorls on erect stems from December to April; *P. malacoides* (fairy primrose) is a real beauty with whorls of pink, red or white starry flowers, from December to April; *P. obconica* has magnificent clusters of 2.5cm/1in wide pink, red or purplish flowers on shortish stems; and *P. sinensis* is renowned for its huge heads of fringed or cut petalled flowers from December to March; numerous varieties of this species include 'Dazzler', orange-scarlet, 'Royal Blue', purple blue and others in various hues from white to orange. *P. sinensis* has broad leaves, jagged and attractively hairy. All, apart from *P.×kewensis*, are usually grown as annuals.

Start plants in 9cm/3½in pots and shift them to 15cm/6in pots of loam-based soil as growth increases. Stimulate growth as blooms develop, by feeding weekly with dilute liquid manure. Water freely and maintain a moist atmosphere and temperature of around 10-13°C/50-55°F when plants are flowering. Raise plants from fresh ripe seed; sow in July for flowering in small pots. Gentle heat is vital for germination. Plants can also be grown from a February sowing. Plunge pots outdoors in light shade, in a frame, for the summer. Shift to 15cm/6in pots in autumn for flowering in winter.

Rechsteineria

[Brazil] Showy tuberous perennials 23-46cm/9-18in high with attractive, hairy, bright green leaves and clusters of tubular flowers borne at the shoot tips. *R. cardinalis* is a June to August beauty, 25-46cm/10-18in high and 23-30cm/9-12in across. Light purple hairs cover the leaves. Scarlet hooded tubular blooms are borne in terminal out-thrusting heads. *R. leucotricha* is smaller, some 23cm/9in across and high, with broad rounded hairy leaves, often set in whorls round the stem, with a silver sheen to them. Pale pink heads of tubular blooms are borne prettily in the middle of the leaf whorls. They appear from August to October.

Above: The unusual hairy leaves of *Rechsteineria leucotricha* set off the pale pink blooms
Below: Ricinus feature handsome serrated leaves
Opposite above: Streptocarpus have showy foxglove-like flowers in many shades
Opposite below: lovely yellow *Reinwardtia trigyna*

Set tubers in boxes of peat in a temperature of 21°C/70°F in spring to start them into growth. When shoots are, say, 2.5cm/1in high, pot them in 13-15cm/5-6in pots of loam or peat-based soil. Place plants in light shade and encourage sturdy growth in a temperature of 16-18°C/61-64°F. Feed every two weeks with dilute liquid fertilizer if growth is slow. Water copiously while plants are growing strongly, but stop when leaves turn yellow after flowers have faded. Overwinter tubers in a dry place at a temperature of 12°C/54°F. Raise new plants by splitting up tubers when repotting in spring, or root basal cuttings with a small piece of tuber attached, in May. Alternatively, propagate from seed in gentle heat in February or March.

Reinwardtia

[Northern India] Splendid winter-flowering evergreen shrubs, of which two species are in cultivation: *R. tetragyna*, 60cm-1.2m/2-4ft high, spreading, with bright flat yellow flowers foiled by attractive narrowly oval leaves; and *R. trigyna*, also around 60cm/2ft high, loosely branched with tubular yellow flowers 2-4cm/1-1½in long, set in leaf axils or round the tips of shoots. 8cm/3in broadly oval leaves adorn the branches.

Set plants in 15cm/6in pots of loam or peat-based soil and grow as annuals. But if sizeable plants are desired, pot on annually in spring. Water freely while growth is vigorous, feed every two weeks with dilute liquid fertilizer from June to September, and syringe leaves in hot spells. Raise new plants from basal cuttings rooted in gentle heat in April. Prune the previous year's shoots to within 8cm/3in of the base when flowers fade. Encourage sturdy, well-branched young plants by nipping out growing tips occasionally as growth develops.

Ricinus

[Castor Oil Plant; Tropical Africa] A shrubby perennial grown for its magnificent mid-green palmate leaves which are handsomely serrated at the margins. Though perennial, it is normally treated as an annual. Its leaves are greatly admired. One species only, *R. communis*, about 1.5m/5ft high with sturdy upright branches to 1.5m/5ft across, decorates the greenhouse throughout the summer months. It is often grown as an outdoor bedding plant in subtropical schemes. If left to grow on from year to year it can reach 6m/20ft high, but is liable to become very leggy, unless cut back hard each spring. Attractive forms include purplish-stemmed 'Cambodgensis'; the neater-growing, compact, green-stemmed, bronzy-leaved 'Gibsonii'; and the reddish-purple leaved 'Sanguineus'.

Set plants in large pots, tubs or the greenhouse border. Loam-based soil suits them well. Position in good light and water freely throughout the summer. Encourage luxuriant foliage by dosing plants with dilute liquid manure, every two weeks from June to September. Raise new plants from seed in late winter or early spring, in gentle heat. Pot on progressively until plants are finally in 20-25cm/8-10in containers.

Salpiglossis

[Painted Tongue; Chile] Striking, prettily veined, flared funnel-shaped flowers richly coloured in hues of crimson, scarlet, orange, yellow and lavender. They are borne in small clusters at the tips of slender shoots that branch freely to 60cm/2ft high. Blooms are about 5cm/2in across. *S. sinuata* is the species grown. 'Shalimar' is a fine strain with 9cm/3½in wide blooms richly decorated and veined with crimson, pink and orange, with a gold throat. It produces a breathtaking display from July to September.

Set plants in 13cm/5in pots of loam-based soil and place close to the light. Shade from hot bright sunshine and water freely at all times during the summer. Feed only if growth is slow, or too much leaf will form in proportion to the flowers. Discard these annuals after flowering and raise new plants from seed in gentle heat in February or March. Enjoy a winter display by sowing again in September and setting plants singly in 13cm/5in pots. Grow in a temperature of 16-18°C/61-64°F.

Streptocarpus

[Cape Primrose; South Africa] A showy group of evergreen sub-shrubs or tufted plants with hairy strap-like leaves and arching stems of nodding, foxglove-shaped tubular flowers. There are several notable species and hybrids. *S. dunnii* is outstanding because of its one wrinkled hoary green leaf that supports the plant throughout its life and its fairly dense cluster of drooping, 2.5cm/1in long brick-red flowers which appear from May to June. Around 46cm/18in high and across *S. holstii*, a branching plant with erect stems 46cm/18in high, has deep green, opposite leaves which are clearly veined beneath. Flowers purplish in colour, 2cm/¾in across, and shaped like violets, appear from May to June. *S.×hybridus*, a race of hybrids 23-30cm/9-12in high and across, is derived mainly from *S. rexii*. Clumps of strap-shaped hairy green leaves form in rosettes to offset the upright or arching stems of red, purple or white, foxglove-like flowers. Noted varieties are the satiny blue 'Constant Nymph', and the purplish-blue, white-throated 'Merton Blue'. The John Innes Hybrids include cerise, white-throated 'Diana', pink, white-throated 'Fiona', magenta-pink 'Karen' and light pink magenta-marked 'Tina'. Blooms appear from May to October.

Set plants in 13-20cm/5-8in pots of loam-based soil or one based on peat. Shade during hot weather, ventilate freely throughout the summer and keep the compost evenly moist during the growing season. Keep a temperature of 10°C/50°F from November to March, but increase this to 13°C/55°F from April to October. Discard single-leaf plants after flowering as they are monocarpic, that is, they die after blooming. Pot on other kinds annually in early spring. Raise new plants from seed in gentle heat in January, tufted plants from division of the clump in March, or from leaf cuttings, 8cm/3in long, from May and July. Root in gritty soil in a warm place.

Streptosolen

[Marmalade Bush; Colombia] One species represents this genus in cultivation – *S. jamesonii*. Straggling to 1.2-1.8m/4-6ft high and across, this evergreen shrub sports a vivid display of terminal clusters of bright orange flowers, 10-20cm/4-8in long, from May to July. Pale green, softish leaves, 5cm/2in long, clothe the slender shoots. The blooms themselves are tubular with a wide mouth about 2cm/¾in across.

Set plants in 15cm/6in pots of gritty loam-based soil in good light, but shade from intense sunlight in summer. Give them plenty of air and water freely throughout the growing season. Feed weekly with dilute liquid fertilizer if growth is slow. Cool airy conditions are essential from April to September. Overwinter at a temperature of 7°C/45°F. Support the stems with canes or tie them directly to the greenhouse framework. Pot on each year in early spring. Keep growth neat and tidy by shortening stems by one-third when the flowers fade. Raise new plants from 8cm/3in cuttings of flowerless side shoots in March and April. Nip out growing tips to help plants branch freely.

Tecoma

[Yellow Elder or Yellow Bells; West Indies/ Mexico to Peru] An imposing evergreen shrub from the Tropics. Stems are clothed with handsome mid-green leaves composed of many pointed leaflets. Clusters of flared funnel-shaped flowers in bright yellow weigh down the tips of branches, and appear from June to August. *T. stans* is the representative species. The flower sprays are 15-23cm/6-9in long and across.

Set plants in 20-25cm/8-10in pots or tubs of gritty loam-based soil and give plenty of water during spring and summer, but keep the soil just moist in autumn and winter. Overwinter at a minimum temperature of 7°C/45°F. Shoots should be ripened well or few flowers and many leaves may result, so position plants in good light. There is no need to shade from hot sunlight, but admit plenty of air to keep the atmosphere fresh. Pot on annually in March, or as soon as new shoots appear, and boost growth with liquid feeds every two weeks from May to September. Raise new plants from cuttings of non-flowering shoots in gentle heat in early spring, or from seed in April. If plants grow too large for the position they are growing in, shorten growths by half their length in February.

Thunbergia

[South and East Africa/Northern India] A charming group of annual and perennial climbers noted for their gay tube-shaped blooms which open out into attractive discs of flat petals. Most popular is *T. alata* (black-eyed Susan) from South Africa. Twining to 3m/ 10ft, this annual is set with small oval green leaves and chocolate-centred, flat yellow blooms that appear in leaf axils, from June to September. Another, from Northern India, *T. grandiflora*, is evergreen and twines to 6m/20ft or more. Terminal sprays of light purple-blue flowers 5cm/2in across appear from June to September. From East and South Africa we get *T. gregorii*. Also vigorous, to around 3m/10ft, it is usually grown as an annual and its 4cm/ 1½in orange flowers develop singly from axils between leaves and stem. Blooms form from June to September. This is also an evergreen. These are all grown under glass or as houseplants. *T. alata* can also be grown outdoors in containers once frosts are over.

Left: Climbing thunbergia will cover the wall
Below: Bright orange *Streptosolen jamesonii*

Set plants in the border or in large pots and train over netting, trellis or wires. Use a loam-based soil and position plants in good light, shading from hot sunlight in summer. Water freely and feed with dilute liquid fertilizers weekly, while growth is vigorous. Admit ample air if the temperature rises above 16°C/ 61°F. Repot *T. gregorii* each year in early spring. Raise new plants of *T. alata* and *T. gregorii* from seed in March, and *T. grandiflora* from 10cm/4in cuttings of stem pieces (internodal cuttings) in April and May. Shorten leggy plants of *T. gregorii* to within 23cm/9in of the base in spring; thin out crowded stems of *T. grandiflora* and shorten side shoots by half their length. Overwinter evergreen species at a temperature of 7°C/45°F.

Torenia

[Wishbone Flower; Tropical Asia] A superb half-hardy annual for brightening light shade with its massed display of tubular violet-purple, purple and yellow-throated blooms. These form near the tops of shoots from July to September. Growing about 30cm/1ft high, stems are set with small light green, toothed-edged leaves. 'Alba' is a white flowered form. The blooms are remarkable for their delightful velvety texture.

Grow plants in 15cm/6in pots of loam-based soil in good light or shade. Nip out shoot tips in early summer to encourage well-branched plants. Water freely and feed with dilute liquid fertilizer, weekly, if growth is slow. Prop up the slender shoots with twigs. Discard the plants after flowering, but raise new ones from seed in gentle heat in March and April. Pot on progressively as plants develop. Start by pricking out seedlings into 8cm/3in pots. The one species grown is *T. fournieri*. 'Grandiflora' is a larger-flowered form.

Trachelium

[Throatwort; Southern Europe] An attractive herbaceous perennial, this is valued for its airy sprays of tiny gypsophila-like flowers which cloud the tips of 60cm-1.2m/2-4ft shoots. *T. coeruleum* is the species commonly grown. From June to August a haze of violet-blue flowers forms freely at the end of the stems. Arresting double-toothed oval leaves clasp the shoots. 'Album' is white with fragrant blooms.

Set plants in 15-20cm/6-8in pots of loam- or peat-based soil and position in good light. Water so that the soil is fairly moist in spring and summer, but only just moist in autumn and winter. Pinch out leading shoots of young plants to make them branch and flower abundantly. Overwinter at a temperature of 7°C/ 45°F and raise new plants from seed in February and March. Remove weak side shoots to encourage stronger main stems.

Plants for warm greenhouses

Minimum winter night temperature 16 C/60 F.

Angraecum

[Tropical Africa/Madagascar] Upright orchids whose stems replace pseudobulbs. Fans of leathery glossy strap-shaped leaves form in opposite rows on the shoots. Beautiful starry, white, spurred blooms develop on thin wiry stems. August to October-flowering *A. distichum*, from Africa, grows about 30cm/1ft and bears blooms 2cm/¾in across on arching stems; *A. eburneum*, from Madagascar, flowers from December to March, grows some 1m/3ft high and gives rise to pale green flowers on short stalks borne on 60-90cm/2-3ft drooping flower stems; *A. sesquipedale*, from Madagascar, is a very sturdy species with thick, dark green leaves 25-38cm/10-15in long and 5cm/2in wide. From March to May two to four flowers with handsome 30cm/1ft spurs form on 15cm/6in flower stems; the blooms are about 15cm/6in across and quite fleshy. They are ivory-cream tinged with green.

Set plants in pots or baskets of orchid mixture (equal parts osmunda fibre and sphagnum moss) by volume. Give plenty of air from spring to autumn and on mild days in winter. Shade from hot sunshine and water copiously throughout the summer. Overwinter at a temperature of 14°C/57°F. *A. distichum* tolerates lower temperatures down to 10°C/50°F. Raise new plants from 30cm/1ft cuttings of tops of stems in May, or strike basal shoots. Root both in a gritty medium in gentle heat.

Aristolochia

[Dutchman's Pipe; Brazil/Sicily/Algeria] Intriguing evergreen climbers with heart-shaped leaves and solitary flowers which form in leaf axils. The blooms are curiously twisted, tubular in shape and swollen at the base, hooded above.

A. elegans (Calico Flower) is a graceful climber with broadly kidney-shaped light-green leaves. Originating from Brazil, it has 8-10cm/3-4in flowers with pale yellowish-green tubes and rich chocolate-purple lips with white markings.

Set plants in large pots or ideally in the border, in good light. Grow in a loam-based medium and train plants over netting or wires or canes. Overwinter at a minimum temperature of 10°C/50°F. Water freely throughout the spring and summer and shade from bright sunshine. Keep the soil just moist from October to April. Repot each year in early spring and boost growth with doses of dilute liquid ferti-

lizer every two weeks. Increase plants from cuttings of side shoots in May and June. *A. elegans* can be propagated from seed in April. Gentle heat is necessary for both methods. Trim to shape in late winter: spur back shoots of pot-grown plants to 8cm/3in from the base, and cut back shoots of border-grown plants by a half to two-thirds their length. Both plants grow some 2.4-3m/8-10ft high and across.

Asclepias

[Milkweed; Tropical America] One greenhouse species, *A. curassavica* (blood flower) bears orange-red crown-shaped flowers in 5cm/2in heads at the tops of 90cm/3ft shoots. The mid-green, pointed leaves of this woody perennial are set thickly round the stems. Blooms appear from June to October.

Set plants in pots of a loam-based mix or in the greenhouse border, watering freely throughout the growing season and boost growth with dilute liquid fertilizer at weekly intervals from spring to late summer. Raise new plants from seed in gentle heat in February or March.

Brunfelsia

[Brazil/West Indies/Peru] Delightful evergreen shrubs set with attractive mid-green long narrow pointed leaves that handsomely offset the solitary salver-shaped blooms which appear near the top of the plant. Two species are grown. *B. calycina* grows about 60cm/2ft high and 30cm/1ft across, and its magnificent glossy leaves provide a perfect foil to the 5cm/2in wide, scented violet-purple flowers. *B. macrantha* is a superior form with 8cm/3in flowers.

Above: *Brunfelsia calycina* 'Macrantha'
Below: *Asclepias curassavica*

These come from Brazil and Peru *B. undulata*, from the West Indies, towers to 1.2m/4ft and grows around 60cm/2ft across. The white or creamy flowers, 4cm/1½in across, appear from June to October. Each bloom has an 8cm/3in tube which terminates in a flat expanse of petals.

Set plants in 15-20cm/6-8in pots of a loam or peat-based mix in late summer. Damp down among the plants to keep the air moist throughout the spring and summer and shade from bright sunlight. Overwinter at a temperature of 10°C/50°F. Plants will tolerate lower temperatures for short spells. Feed with dilute liquid fertilizer at 10 day intervals from April to October. Raise new plants from cuttings of half-ripe shoots in spring and summer. Keep *B. undulata* trim by cutting back straggly stems in March. Help it to form a well-branched framework of shoots by pinching out shoot tips when these grow extra long.

Cattleya

[Mexico to Southern Brazil] Flamboyant orchids with long pseudobulbs ending in thick strap-shaped leaves. Graceful arching flower stems carry several blooms characterized by a broad, often frilled, tongue-shaped lip. The blooms of some species grow as large as 25cm/10in across. Numerous hybrids derive from crossing the species with one another. Cattleyas in cultivation include *C. bowringiana*, producing two leaves from a pseudobulb, that grows to 60cm/2ft high. The flowering stems around 20cm/8in long bear six to ten flowers each about 9cm/3½in across. The blooms are rosy purple in colour and yellowish white in the throat. They appear from September to December and are native to British Honduras. It is commonly called the cluster cattleya. The queen cattleya, *C. dowiana*, bears but a single leaf, grows some 30cm/1ft high and produces up to five golden blooms with bright purple, golden-veined lips. Each bloom is borne on a 13cm/5in stalk. They appear in autumn. *C. mossiae*, the Easter orchid or spring cattleya, is one of the easiest to grow. Scented lavender pink blooms with a yellow throat and frilled crimson lip, 10-18cm/4-7in across, are produced from March to June. Other species are *C. labiata*, the autumn cattleya, whose 13-18cm/5-7in waxy rose blooms with a frilled crimson lip and yellow throat appear from August to November; and *C. trianaei*, the Christmas orchid or winter cattleya, which develops 18cm/7in pink or white purple-lipped blooms of outstanding beauty.

Set plants in 8-23cm/3-9in pots of orchid medium (two parts osmunda fibre and one part sphagnum moss) or in wooden baskets with open sides, so there is plenty of drainage. Give them a humid atmosphere by spraying down the pots and staging daily in late spring and summer. Water freely, too, while they are making plenty of growth. Ventilate the greenhouse on hot summer days and also provide light shading. In autumn, drop the tempera-

ture slightly to encourage flower buds to form. Overwinter at a temperature of 10°C/50°F apart from *C. dowiana*, which prefers 14°C/57°F. Repot every three years, or when plants become crowded. Raise new plants from divisions of the pseudobulbs when they are repotted in spring.

Clerodendrum

[Africa/Asia] Superb group of evergreen shrubs and climbers grown for their attractive sprays of bell-shaped flowers borne at the ends of branches; upright branching growth. From South East Asia there is *C. paniculatum*, shrubby, around 90cm-1.5m/3-5ft high, with handsome 10-15cm/4-6in lobed, heart-shaped leaves and 23-30cm/9-12in clusters of scarlet bell-shaped flowers with protruding stamens. Blooms appear from July to October. The Java glorybean, *C. speciosissimum*, is a real beauty. Its stems are set with imposing heart-shaped leaves, and immense clusters of fiery scarlet flowers are borne at the tips of shoots from July to September; 90cm/3ft high, 46-60cm/18-24in across. Climbing eagerly in the warmth of a greenhouse, the bleeding heart vine, *C. thomsonae*, produces a massed display of pendulous clusters of starry scarlet flowers offset by attractive white calyces, June to September.

Ideally plant in the greenhouse border, or set plants in 15-20cm/6-8in pots of gritty loam-based mix. Shade on warm days when the sun is intense and water freely while strong growth is being made. Feed every two weeks with dilute liquid fertilizer to encourage flowers. Overwinter at a temperature of 13°C/55°F. Pot on annually in spring. Raise new plants from cuttings of side shoots in spring, rooted at gentle heat. Trim *C. speciosissimum* after flowering; cut back shoots to within 15cm/6in of the base.

Columnea

[Costa Rica/Mexico] Exotic pendulous, thick woolly-leaved stems ablaze with myriads of scarlet or orange-red hooded blooms, these are some of the most colourful evergreen shrubs for the greenhouse. There are sub-shrubs and perennial climbers. *C. × banksii* has 60-90cm/2-3ft long trailing stems with small glossy green leaves and a multiplicity of 6-8cm/2½-3in flowers from November to April. From Costa Rica comes *C. gloriosa*, with similar trailing shoots, but whose flowers, scarlet in colour, have a yellow patch in the throat. 'Purpurea' is a purple-leaved form. Flowers from October to April. Mexico gives us *C. schiedeana*, a climbing or drooping form with 9-1.2m/3-4ft stems, with mid-green leaves and yellow and brown flecked scarlet flowers 5cm/2in long. Flowers from May to July.

These plants look magnificent grown in hanging baskets of a loamy or peat based medium enriched with sphagnum moss. Overwinter winter-flowering kinds at a temperature of not less than 13°C/55°F, making sure the soil remains evenly moist. Summer-flowering kinds need less warmth in winter – 10°C/50°F. Water freely in summer and keep the air moist; feed weekly with diluted liquid fertilizer and shade lightly from bright sunshine from April to October. Ventilate the greenhouse when the temperature exceeds 18°C/64°F. Repot annually, winter-flowering types in summer and summer-flowering species in spring or autumn. Propagate from 8cm/3in cuttings of unflowered shoots from March to June. Root in gentle heat.

Crossandra

[East Africa/East Indies] Handsome evergreen shrubs bearing dense spikes of orange or orange-red flowers from March to November. Spreading shoots have an upright habit. Stems clothed with showy bright green elliptic leaves around 10cm/4in long. From East Africa comes *C. nilotica*, some 60cm/2ft high and 30cm/1ft or so across. It flowers when quite young. Spikes of brick-red blooms unfold over a four to six week period and give a show of colour from March to November. The blooms, clustered, each about 2.5cm/1in across, are composed of a slender tube opening to five rounded petals, the lower three of which form a pronounced lip. *C. undulifolia*, native of the East Indies, grows some 90cm/3ft high and 60cm/

234

2ft across. Its stems are clothed with dark green wavy-edged leaves. The orange-red spikes of bloom are rather larger than those of *C. nilotica* but flower for the same length of time.

Start plants in 10cm/4in pots, moving them successively into larger ones until finally they are in 20cm/8in pots of a peat- or loam-based soil. Water freely throughout the summer and dose with dilute liquid fertilizer once a week. Overwinter at a temperature of 13°C/55°F, keeping the soil just moist. When new growth appears in spring, increase watering. Keep plants shapely by reducing all growths by about two-thirds their length after flowering. Increase stock from seed in March, or from softwood cuttings. 8cm/3in long, in spring rooted in a propagator.

Eranthemum

[Burma/India] Striking winter-flowering sub-shrubs, upright and branching with deep green oval leaves and dense spikes of flared five-petalled blooms in red or blue. The blooms are enclosed by tubular greenish bracts. *E. macrophyllum* is 60-90cm/2-3ft high and 60cm/2ft across, with toothed 13-23cm/5-9in long leaves. The pale blue flowers, about 2.5cm/1in long, are borne on loose spikes. *E. pulchellum* (blue sage) has oval leaves pointed and roundly lobed offset by dark blue flowers enclosed in a whitish calyx. Flower spikes 2-8cm/1-3in long are sometimes borne in clusters. A species with rose-coloured blooms in spikes 13-15cm/5-6in long is *E. roseum*.

Set plants in large pots of loam-based soil. Keep the soil evenly moist throughout the summer and shade from fierce sunshine. Shorten flowered shoots to within 2.5cm/1in of the base when the blooms fade. Then keep plants on the dry side until March, when the soil should be watered freely to encourage strong new growth. Feed fortnightly with dilute liquid manure when growth is strong in spring and summer. Raise new plants from cuttings of young shoots from March to June. Root in gentle heat. Pinch out the growing tips of young plants to help them bush out and produce many flowering stems.

Exacum

[Persian Violet; Island of Socotra] Charming member of the gentian family, *E. affine*, an annual, is grown for its 1-2cm/½-¾in flattish violet-blue, yellow-centred blooms which form freely on branching shoots. Growing 23-30cm/9-12in high and across, flowers appear from July to September. They are sweetly scented. Shining oval leaves form thickly on the stems.

To get the best from this plant, set it in 13cm/5in pots of loam-based or peat-based soil and keep it in a temperature of between 13-16°C/55-61°F. Water copiously from May to October, and keep moist if the plant is over-wintered; shade from hot sunshine and feed every two weeks with dilute liquid manure to encourage sturdy growth. Position in good light. Raise plants from seed in gentle heat in March. Alternatively, produce extra fine, large plants by sowing in August and potting on as growth develops through winter and spring. To keep the plants growing sturdily through winter, maintain a minimum night temperature of 16°C/61°F. Nip out the leading shoots occasionally to encourage a bushy framework.

Opposite above: Attractive sprays of bell-shaped flowers grow on *Clerodendron thomsonae*.
Opposite below: *Cattleya labiata* 'Purpurea'.
Above: The colourful *Columnea gloriosa* 'Purpurea' has hairy leaved stems with myriads of blooms.
Right: Orange-red spikes of bloom are produced by *Crossandra undulifolia* 'Mona Wallhed'.
Below: The popular and charming *Exacum affine*

Gardenia

[Cape Jasmine; China/Formosa/Japan] Beloved for buttonholes, its gloriously scented waxy white, blooms form singly in leaf axils near the tops of shoots. Growing some 90cm-1.2m/3-4ft high and 90cm/3ft across, this is one of the most cherished of evergreen greenhouse shrubs. Handsome glossy green leaves develop in whorls of three round the stems. The double-flowered G. jasminoides 'Florida' is the one met with in cultivation and a particularly fine large-flowered form of it is 'Fortuniana' – its blooms are 8cm/3in across. They appear from June to August. 'Veitchiana' is a winter-flowering variety.

Set plants in 15-20cm/6-8in pots of peat-based soil in good light, but shade from fierce sunshine. Water liberally throughout the spring and summer and encourage sturdy growth by feeding with dilute liquid fertilizer every two weeks during the growing season. Water sparingly in autumn and winter, apart from 'Veitchiana', which needs ample moisture to maintain a flourishing display of bloom. Overwinter summer flowering plants at 12°C/54°F and winter-flowering ones at a minimum of 16°C/61°F. Reduce shoots by half to two-thirds their length after flowering to keep growth trim and shapely. Nip out growing tips of young plants to encourage bushiness. Repot established plants every spring. Raise new plants from 8cm/3in cuttings of un-flowered shoots in gentle heat in February or March. Take care to keep the air moist throughout the growing season by damping down among pots and staging.

Hibiscus

[Rose Mallow; China/Tropical Africa/Hawaiian Islands] Handsome shrubby evergreens with flared trumpet-shaped blooms from which protrude a 'club' of prominent anthers. Developing as large bushes, they add character to the greenhouse when they bloom from June to September. This is the hibiscus of romantic film-makers. Three species are generally grown: H. mutabilis, about 1.8m/6ft high and across, with downy heart-shaped leaves and 10cm/4in lily-like blooms that open white and turn deep red. The flowers last for a week or more and are produced almost continually in August and September. Probably most popular is H. rosa-sinensis. Outstanding varieties are the clear pink 'Hubba' with outward-curving wave-edged petals; pale yellow 'Miss Betty'; and yellow and mauve, purple-eyed 'Veronica'. Bright green toothed leaves offset perfectly the handsome 13cm/5in blooms. A fascinating species, H. schizopetalus, with clusters of luminescent orange-red flowers with long protruding stamens, flowers from August to September. And of South Sea Island fame, H. waimeae has white flowers composed of 11cm/4½in spreading petals which contrast with a long tube of fiery red stamens.

Set plants in 20-30cm/8-12in pots or large tubs of peat-based soil. Place in full light but shade from intense sun. Water freely in spring and summer. Overwinter at a temperature of 7-10°C/45-50°F. Ideally, though, raise the temperature to about 16°C/61°F and water freely. Then plants remain fully evergreen and attractive throughout the winter. Prune by shortening side shoots to within 8cm/3in of the older wood in spring. Raise new plants from 10cm/4in cuttings of side shoots, with a heel, from spring to early summer.

Laelia

[Mexico/Central America to Brazil] Showy epiphytic orchids with jointed pseudobulbs and leathery strap-shaped leaves. Five magnificent blooms appear on each spike that arises from a pseudobulb. Blooms are composed of wide spreading sepals and petals from the centre of which forms a bold-lipped trumpet. L. anceps, represented by varieties such as white 'Alba', with a yellow throat, rose-sepalled, crimson-petalled yellow-throated 'Barkeriana' and white, pink-lipped, yellow-keeled 'Hilliana', carries its flowers on 60cm/2ft stems. The blooms are some 10cm/4in across. This comes from Mexico. Flowering from December to January, it provides glorious colour when it is most appreciated. Another species, L. harpophylla, from Brazil, has 30cm/1ft flower stems set with three to nine blooms some 5cm/2in across; bright orange sepals and petals and an orange, yellow-edged lip add a gay touch to the greenhouse from January to March.

Get the best results by setting plants in open woodwork baskets of orchid mixture, in good light. Shade from hot sun and damp down to keep the air moist. Give plenty of air throughout the summer and water freely during the growing season. Overwinter at a temperature of 10°C/50°F and water just sufficient to stop the tissues from shrivelling. Raise new plants from divisions of the pseudobulbs from March to May. Pot on plants every two or three years or as soon as the pots or baskets become crowded.

Lycaste

[Tropical America] Gorgeous epiphytic orchids with fragrant waxy blooms and hard cone-shaped pseudobulbs topped with leathery deciduous leaves. Flower stems develop freely from the base of the pseudobulbs. Single flowers appear. The outer 'cup' of sepals is larger than the inner petals and the lip is fairly small. There is a wide range of colours in shades of white, pink, brown, green and yellow. An easy house plant, or for the greenhouse, is L. cruenta. Aromatic blooms with greenish-yellow sepals and golden petals,

Above: the flowers of the romantic *Hibiscus rosa-sinensis* last but a single day in bloom
Below: Fragrant orchid *Lycaste cruenta*

5cm/2in across, form on 15cm/6in stems in March and April. Bright green leaves 38-46cm/15-18in long, form a perfect foil. The flowers of *L. macrophylla* are 10-13cm/4-5in across with reddish-brown, green-backed sepals and white petals flecked with pink. They appear from July to November. Enjoying slightly warmer conditions, *L. virginalis* (syn. *L. skinneri*) bears white blooms with a rose-pink lip, 10cm/4in across. Its flower stems are 25cm/10in long. Vivid green leaves contrast effectively with the scented flowers which may appear at any time.

Set plants in pots of orchid mixture in March and April. Use 8-18cm/3-7in pans, or attach plants to soil mixture bound to blocks of wood or cork oak bark and suspend them in the greenhouse. Keep plants cool and moist from April to September. They also appreciate good light, with shade from too hot sun. Water sparingly from October to March, just sufficient to prevent tissues shrivelling. This is their resting period. Overwinter plants at a temperature of 10°C/50°F. Repot when pots are crowded with roots and raise new plants from divisions of the pseudobulbs in early spring.

Miltonia

[Pansy Orchid; Tropical America/Tropical Brazil] Showy orchids with flamboyant pansy-like flowers borne on erect or arching stems. Narrow strap-shaped leaves arise from tapering pseudobulbs. Exotic-flowered hybrids are grown in preference to the species. *M.* × 'Aurora' carries about eight 8-10cm/3-4in white, blotched purple blooms, July to October, each of which have a wide lip and pale yellow throat. *M. regnellii* has 46cm/18in flower spikes bearing around six 5cm/2in white blooms with rose and yellow-crested lips. 'Purpurea' has a richly coloured rose-purple lip. *M. vexillaria*, also with 46cm/18in

Below: Moth-like blooms on the intriguing phalaenopsis orchid, give it its common name
Right: Another orchid, an exotic miltonia hybrid

flower stems, sports around 10 scented, 9cm/3½in blooms to each stem. They appear in May and June and are usually rose-mauve with a buttercup yellow lip.

Get the best results by setting plants in 8-13cm/3-5in pots of orchid mixture and growing them in cool airy conditions. Damp down among the plants on very warm days in summer. Keep the soil evenly moist throughout the year as they have no definite resting period. Shade from hot sunshine. Overwinter at a temperature of 10°C/50°F. Give them a position in good light. Raise new plants from divisions of the pseudobulbs in spring or summer. Repot every two or three years.

× Odontioda

[Bigeneric orchids derived from crossing Cochlioda with Odontoglossum] Erect, then arching spikes of 6-8cm/2½-3in flattened blooms in a wide range of hues appear from October to May. The flower stems vary from 30cm/1ft to

60cm/2ft or so high. The blooms are longer-lasting than those of *Odontoglossum*. Two-leaved pseudobulbs send up long strap-shaped leaves. Finest hybrids include bright red 'Mazurka'; yellow, brown-spotted 'Connosa'; and magenta to pale mauve 'Florence Stirling'. These are epiphytic orchids.

Grow them in large pots or baskets of orchid mixture. Set plants in good light and ventilate whenever possible throughout the year, but not when it is foggy or frosty. Keep the soil evenly moist at all times and spray clear water over the leaves throughout the spring and summer. Shade on extra warm days in summer. These plants do not rest in winter like many other orchids and should be overwintered at a temperature of 10°C/50°F. Raise new plants by splitting up the clumps in spring or in summer.

Phalaenopsis

[Moth Orchid; India/Indonesia/Phillippines/New Guinea/Northern Australia] Highly intriguing epiphytic orchids with rhizomes in place of pseudobulbs, which give rise to short fleshy oblong rounded strap-shaped leaves. Aerial roots form freely and grow quite long. Flower stems may be upright or arching, short or long. Blooms can be small and mothlike or large and typically orchid-shaped; they also last a long time when cut. Noteworthy is *P. amabilis*, bearing about 14 10cm/4in blooms to an arching, branched flower stem. Huge fleshy leaves provide a striking contrast. They are borne on stubby, 2.5cm/1in high stems. The flowers, which appear from October to January, are composed of flattish white waxy petals, whitish sepals, and a red spotted, yellow, lobed lip ending in two backward curving tendrils. *P. rosea* has a 61cm/2ft flower stem set with vivid, 4cm/1½in blooms consisting of

white sepals, rose-coloured petals and a three-lobed lip, with the two outer lobes, rose-purple and the middle lobe, bright rose purple. Blooms form mostly from February to October.

Set plants in hanging baskets of open wooden structure, or on squares of criss-crossed wood packed with orchid mixture. Suspend them in good light, but shade from hot summer sunshine. Keep the air warm and humid. Water freely throughout the spring and summer, feed once a month during the same period, and give plenty of air on mild days from April to October. Overwinter at a temperature of 16°C/61°F. Repot every two or three years, or when clumps are crowded. Divide rootstocks in May and set plants in small pots of orchid mixture. Shade lightly until growth is established.

Ruellia

[Brazil] Striking evergreen perennials or sub-shrubs which merit a place in the greenhouse for their impressive clusters of trumpet-shaped blooms borne at the tips of shoots from November to April. Handsome deep green leaves, narrow and pointed, clothe the stems. Two species are grown: R. macrantha, shrubby, to 90cm/3ft high and 60cm/2ft across. Its leaves are about 15cm/6in long, and rose-purple heads of bloom furnish the upper parts of the shoots from January to April; R. portellae is a spreading perennial making 23-30cm/9-12in of growth. Its 8cm/3in elliptic leaves are set with silvery veins and have a bronzy shine. Impressive rose pink trumpet blooms appear from leaf axils at the top of the plant. It provides a noteworthy display from November to late March.

Position plants in good light and water copiously from spring to autumn, then only slightly less for the rest of the year. Set R. macrantha in loam or peat-based soil in 15-20cm/6-8in pots, and R. portellae in the same mix in 8-13cm/3-5in pots. Feed with dilute liquid fertilizer, weekly, when the flowers are forming. Overwinter at 13-16°C/55-61°F. Repot annually in September, when plants are mature and growth vigorous. Propagate from 8cm/3in cuttings of non-flowering basal shoots in April and May. Prune by shortening R. macrantha to within 8cm/3in of the base after flowering. Nip out growing tips of young plants to encourage bushy growth.

Saintpaulia

[African Violet; Central Africa] Glorious blooms, like wide spreading violets, form freely on short, branched heads 8-10cm/3-4in high from June to October. Rosettes of rounded hairy leaves provide an attractive backcloth. The one species in cultivation is S. ionantha, and this has given us a multiplicity of brightly coloured forms. There is the deep blue 'Blue Fairy Tale', velvety blue-purple 'Diana Blue', 'Pink Fairy Tale', 'White Fairy Tale' and other forms in a wide range of hues. There are single and double-flowered varieties.

Set plants in 13cm/5in pots of peat-based soil and place in good light, but shade from bright sunlight. Keep the soil moist, but not water-logged, at all times; a high degree of humidity is essential and can be achieved by setting the pots in containers of moist peat or on trays of pebbles. Do not water the leaves or they may scorch, as the fine hairs are likely to trap moisture which acts like a lens, concentrating the rays of the sun. Give a dilute liquid feed every two weeks during the growing season. Repot every two years and overwinter plants in a temperature of 13°C/55°F. Raise new plants by rooting the stalks of leaves in water, or inserting leaf cuttings to half their depth in pots of gritty soil. Or sow seed in spring, in gentle heat.

Scutellaria

[Costa Rica] Impressive evergreen sub-shrub. The one greenhouse species, S. costaricana, has dark green, oval, pointed leaves on purple stems and dense terminal clusters of tubular scarlet, yellow-lipped blooms from June to September. Height: 46-60cm/1½-2ft. Set plants in 13-15cm/5-6in pots of loam-based soil. Stand in good light but shade from fierce sunshine in spring and summer. Water freely throughout the growing season, less often in winter, boost growth with feeds of dilute liquid manure every two weeks from April to October. Over-winter at a temperature of 10-13°C/50-55°F. Damp down staging and pots to keep the air moist in spring and summer. Encourage sturdy vigorous growth by pruning the previous year's shoots to within 8cm/3in of the base in February. Pinch out shoot tips of young plants to make for bushy growth. Raise new plants from cuttings of unflowered shoots in early spring. Pot on annually, or discard plants when leggy and raise afresh each year from cuttings.

Stephanotis floribunda

[Madagascar Jasmine; Madagascar] Enriching the air with their sweet fragrance, axillary sprays of tubular white waxy flowers that spread out flat form on twining evergreen shoots from May to October. Broad, oval, 8-10cm/3-4in long leaves clothe the stems. This is a plant whose flowers are grown for buttonholes. Growing some 3m/10ft high and 1.8m/6ft across, it is best trained over wires or trellis.

Set plants in 15-20cm/6-8in pots or small tubs of loam-based potting mix and shade lightly in good light, shaded in summer. Keep the soil moist at all times, slightly less in winter, and maintain a humid atmosphere. Over-winter at a temperature of 10°C/50°F. Repot each year in spring until the plants are in 20-23cm/8-9in pots, thereafter only every three years. Spur growth with feeds of dilute liquid fertilizer every two weeks throughout the spring and summer. Keep plants shapely by removing weak shoots, shortening others by half and spurring side shoots to within 8cm/3in of the base in February or March. Raise new plants from cuttings from non-flowering side shoots in gentle heat in spring and early summer.

Vriesea

[Cuba to Southern Mexico/Northern Argentina/West Indian and Caribbean Islands] Striking foliage plants, terrestrial and epiphytic, bromeliads, valued for their handsome rosettes of thick, glossy green often purple banded leaves, a few cm to 1.5-1.8m/5-6ft high. All collect water in a central funnel or 'vase' of leaves. The sword-like or candelabra blooms of tubular flowers vary from yellow to red and yellow, according to species. Most striking species are V. fenestralis, 76cm/2½ft, whose rosette of darkly veined green leaves spirals upwards; 6cm/2½in long sulphur-yellow blooms are produced in summer on a spike that ascends some 46cm/18in above the foliage. Its common name is 'Netted Vriesea'. King of the bromeliads, V. hieroglyphica, around 60cm/2ft high, has greenish-yellow leaves marked with purple. The greenish-yellow flowering spike reaches 76cm/2½ft high in spring. Probably most commonly grown is V. splendens, the 'flaming sword'. From a rosette of purple-banded green leaves develops a sword-shaped flower spike of red bracts and yellow flowers. These are about 8cm/3in long and appear in July and August.

Set plants in 13cm/5in pots of gritty, peaty soil. Damp down frequently to maintain high humidity and shade from bright sunlight. Ideally, set plants in permanent light shade. Water freely from spring to autumn, making sure to top up the central leaf reservoirs or 'vases'. These plants grow best in a steamy atmosphere at about 18-21°C/64-70°F. Give very little water in winter. Repot every other year, or as soon as roots fill the pots. Raise new plants from seeds, which takes a long time, or ideally from rooted offsets after flowering. These form to the sides of the plant, usually round the base.

Plants for cold greenhouses

Abutilon

[Flowering Maple; Brazil] Handsome evergreen or semi-evergreen shrubs. Arching shoots clad with heart-shaped leaves. Bright, pendulous lantern flowers borne freely singly or in clusters from leaf joints from spring to autumn. Showy kinds are *A. megapotamicum* (1.8-2.4m/6-8ft) with a carmine calyx, yellow petals and protruding red stamens; good varieties include 'Fireball', a gem with large red blooms; its close relation, 'Golden Bell', with golden-yellow flowers. Then there are the variegated-leaved forms – 'Savitzii', whose drooping orange lanterns are foiled by white and green speckled leaves, and *A. striatum* 'Thompsonii', similar but with green and yellow leaves.

Increase plants from half ripe cuttings of side shoots in late spring. Root them in a propagator. Alternatively, raise the species from seed; hybrids do come true. Water freely from May to September, shading lightly from strong sunshine, and ventilate when the temperature exceeds 13°C/55°F. Feed every two weeks to boost flowering growth. Give little water when plants are resting from October to April.

Below: Agapanthus 'Sybil Harton'.
Right: *Camellia × williamsii* 'Donation'.
Opposite: *Ruellia macrantha*

Minimum winter night temperature not falling below freezing.

Keep in good light. Set plants in large pots – 15-20cm/6-8in – or in tubs of a loam-based mix or in the border. They will make from 1.2-1.8m/4-6ft of slender drooping growth and should be supported with canes.

Agapanthus

[African Lily; Cape Province/South Africa/ Natal] Robust clump-forming plants with long strap-shaped leaves. Sturdy flower stems rise above the leaves and are topped by globes of clustered funnel-shaped flowers. *A. praecox* (syn. *A. umbellatus*), deep blue, and 'Albus', white, bloom freely from July to August. There are several hybrids in white, pale and deep blue, but the hardiest is 'Headbourne Hybrid' whose flowers range from violet to pale blue. All grow 76-90cm/2½-3ft high.

Set plants in rich loamy soil in good light. They may be stood outdoors during the summer months and moved into the greenhouse for the winter. Grow in 23cm/9in pots or tubs, potting on from year to year as the clump expands. Propagate from seeds in spring, or divide clumps into well-rooted offsets, also in spring. Water copiously during the growing season. Remove flowered stems from the base and keep fairly dry in winter.

Callistemon

[Bottle Brush; Australia/New South Wales] Intriguing shrubs, bushy with narrow tapering leaves and shoots adorned with bottlebrush blooms of small flowers with brilliant scarlet or yellow stamens. Growing 1.5-1.8m/5-6ft high and across, the two most reliable species are *C. citrinus* 'Splendens', with 5-10cm/2-4in flower spikes in brilliant red, and *C. salignus*, its counterpart in vivid yellow.

These shrubs have a large root system, so grow them in 25cm/10in pots or tubs in good light. Use loamy soil. Water well in spring and summer, feed every two weeks with dilute liquid manure. Ease up on watering in autumn and winter. Propagate from heeled cuttings of half-ripe shoots in July and August. Or raise plants from seeds in March, in gentle heat.

Camellia

[Japan/China] Spectacular winter- and spring-flowering evergreen shrubs. Deep glossy green leaves show off single, semi-double, double and anemone-centred blooms in white, pink, red and variegated colours. Finest varieties: 'Adolphe Audusson', semi-double blood-red,

with brilliant golden anthers; 'Mathotiana Alba', ice-white double with overlapping petals; 'Chandleri Elegans', vivid pink splashed white, anemone-centred; 'J. C. Williams', soft pink single that flowers for months; 'Donation', probably the finest of all with semi-double orchid-pink flowers; 'Contessa Lavinia Maggi' whose double white or pale pink blooms are striped with cerise pink. A highly fragrant form is *Camellia sasanqua* 'Narumi-gata'. Its carmine buds open white.

Making 1.8-2.4m/6-8ft of growth, up and across, set shrubs in large tubs of peaty lime-free soil. Water with clean rainwater, too, or the leaves will be disfigured with limy patches. Shade from strong sunshine, or leaves may scorch. Encourage strong growth by feeding with sequestered iron in spring, watering freely throughout the spring and summer, and mulching with peat to keep the soil cool. Raise new plants from stem, or leaf and bud, cuttings in late summer.

Celosia

[Tropical Asia] Colourful half-hardy annual grown for its red or yellow plumed or crested silky textured flowers July to September. It grows 30-60cm/1-2ft high. The crested kind, *C. argentea* Cristata, called cockscomb, has a flowerhead 8-10cm/3-5in across. 'Jewel Box' is a good variety and comes in many colours. The plumed form, *C. a.* 'Pyramidalis', is available as 'Thompson's Magnifica' in vivid red, and 'Fountains', in a galaxy of hues. The plumes are magnificent – at least 25-30cm/10-12in long.

Raise plants from seed in gentle heat in spring. Prick out seedlings in boxes of loam-based mix and finally set them singly in 9cm/ 3½in pots (for the compact cristate varieties) and 13cm/5in (for the larger plumed varieties). Ventilate freely on warm days and water copiously to keep plants growing strongly and flowering profusely. Feed every two weeks with dilute liquid manure. Discard after flowering.

Cobaea

[Cathedral Bells or Cup-and-Saucer-Plant; Mexico] Vigorous evergreen climber with mid-green pinnate leaves ending in tendrils, and glorious purple or white (depending on species) bell flowers embraced by 'saucers' of green sepals, 3-4.5m/10-15ft high by 2.1m/7ft across. Flowers appear from May to September. *C. scandens* is the only species in general cultivation; the bell-shaped flowers are deep purple. 'Alba' is a white flowered form.

Train over trellis or wires. Excellent for providing light shade for other plants in summer. Grow in 20cm/8in pots of an open loam-based mix and water freely in summer and autumn. Ventilate fully on warm days. The plant is usually grown as an annual and raised afresh each spring, but if a winter night temperature of 5°C/41°F can be maintained, it may be grown on for another year or until it becomes too rampant. Raise plants from seed in gentle heat in March and April.

Crinum

[Cape Coast Lily or Swamp Lily; South Africa] Gorgeous lily-like flowers clustered at the top of sturdy stems 60cm-1.2m/2-4ft high, in July and September. Broad strap-shaped leaves form a thick clump. There are three commonly grown forms of this bulbous plant: *C. × powellii*, pink; *C. × powellii* 'Album', white; and *C.*

moorei, rosy red and white. *C. × powellii* is a garden hybrid.

Water frequently when in full leaf, less so for the rest of the year. Shade from hot sun and repot every three years, or as soon as the crowns are congested. Grow in the greenhouse border or set three bulbs to a 20cm/8in pot of loam-based mix. Increase from offsets taken at repotting time in March or raise new plants from seed in gentle heat.

Diplacus glutinosus

[also known as *Mimulus glutinosus*; Monkey Flower; California] Shrubby perennial related to mimulus. Striking flared orange, salmon or buff trumpet flowers form on shoots 46cm/18in long. Blooms appear freely from April to November. Set plants in a rich gritty loam mix. Keep fairly moist in spring and summer, shade from bright sunlight but keep in good light and reduce growth by half in winter. This encourages bushiness. Water sparingly during the colder months. If growth is weak, feed every two weeks with dilute liquid manure during the growing season. Increase plants from heel cuttings of sturdy young shoots, 5-8cm/2-3in long, in April. Root in gentle heat. Pot on young plants in 9cm/3½in pots and pinch out growing tips to make them branch freely. Pinch out a second time when growth is vigorous.

Eccremocarpus

[Chilean Glory Flower; Chile] Sprays of inch-long, vivid orange tubular flowers mass on vigorous shoots of this short-lived perennial climber, from June to October. One species, *E. scaber*, is grown. Set it in a 23cm/9in pot of rich gritty soil, or in the border and train it over netting or trellis. When the flowers fade they are followed by arresting bunches of black seed pods. Cut back stems to ground level in late autumn. Water copiously throughout the growing season. Raise new plants from a spring sowing in gentle heat. This is one of the easiest greenhouse plants to propagate.

Hydrangea

[China/Japan] Showy deciduous flowering shrubs for summer. There are two types of *H. macrophylla*: the Hortensia group which have domed heads of bloom, consisting almost entirely of flamboyant, sterile flowers, and the Lacecap group with blooms composed of an outer ring of eye-catching sterile florets that surround a centre of insignificant fertile florets. Flowers are either pink or purplish, in limy soils, or purplish blue or deep blue in acid soils. By using blueing powder a pink-flowered variety can be changed to an ultramarine-blue. Of Hortensia varieties there are 'Parsifal', fringed petals, pink; 'Niedersachsen', pink or

purplish blue; 'Altona', deep pink or blue, depending on which soil it is growing in. Charming Lacecaps include 'White Wave' and 'Blue Wave'.

Set plants in tubs or large pots of rich, gritty, loamy, ideally lime-free soil, so the blooms are blue or purplish if they are 'blue' varieties. Shade from hot sun, water well throughout the growing season and cut off spent flower heads when they fade. After flowering, shift plants outdoors and plunge rim-deep in cool soil until January or February, then return to the greenhouse and start growth again. Increase plants from 10-15cm/4-6in shoots in August and September. Prune in March, removing weak shoots and those congesting the bush, also any flower heads.

Impatiens

[Busy Lizzie; East and West Africa/Zanzibar] Few greenhouse plants flower with such abandon as the Impatiens. Pansy-like blooms cluster at shoot tips for most of the year. They are offset by simple heart-shaped leaves and grow 15-38cm/6-15in high and across. Most hybrids such as 'Beauty of Klettgau', fiery salmon; 'Harlequin', scarlet and white, 'Karminrosa', bright rose-pink and 'White Cloud', are derived from crosses between *I. holstii* and *I. sultanii*. Another, *I. petersiana*, is resplendent in narrow bronzed leaves and brick red flowers. There are also many new varieties which are raised from seed and which breed remarkably true. These include the 'Imp', 'Minette' and 'Zig-Zag' strains.

All appreciate ample water in spring and summer, a weekly liquid feed, a position in good light and some shade from hot sun. The plants will survive in a frost-free greenhouse,

if kept on the dry side, although they will probably lose quite a few of their leaves. In a temperature of 13°C/55°F, they will go on flowering all winter. Plants thrive in 13cm/5in pots of peat-based or a gritty loamy mixture. Repot when roots thrust through the pot's drainage holes. Raise new plants from cuttings rooted easily in a jar of water. Pot up singly and move into larger pots as necessary; pinch out growing tips.

Lapageria rosea

[Chilean Bellflower; Chile] Exotic evergreen climber with long leathery deep green leaves and superb square-shouldered bell-shaped blooms. Train over wires, netting or trellis. Flowers brighten late summer and autumn. While *L. rosea*, the species (height up to 4.5m/ 15ft) is commonly grown, an improved form is 'Nash Court', whose blood-red blooms, white spotted within, flower freely for months from July onwards. 'White Cloud' is an albino variety, and the finest white form. It grows best in the greenhouse border, but if space is limited, set plants in 25cm/10in pots. This is a lime-hater, so only use peaty, lime-free soil.

Water liberally throughout the growing season and keep just moist in winter; shade from hot bright sunlight and ventilate on warm days. Propagate from seeds in March and April, or from shoots layered in spring and autumn; remove from the parent plant when rooted, after about 2 years. Incidentally, this is the floral emblem of Chile.

Opposite top: *Lapageria rosea* 'Nash Court'.
Opposite bottom: *Eccremocarpus scaber*.
Below: Impatiens 'Baby Orange'.
Right: *Leptospermum scoparium* 'Red Damask'

Leptospermum

[Manuka or Tea Tree; New Zealand] Erect evergreen shrub or small tree with neat heath-like leaves and shoots which are massed with bright starry five-petalled flowers, somewhat like a myrtle's. *L. scoparium*, around 1.8-3m/ 6-10ft high and 1.2m/4ft across, is most commonly grown. Varieties of it include 'Red Damask', double red flowers; 'Gloriosa', large red; 'Bocconoc', crimson flowers offset by attractive bronzy leaves; and 'Leonard Wilson', the double white Manuka, with green leaves and double white flowers. All flower in May and June.

Grow in large pots or ideally in the greenhouse border, in light well-drained soil and in good light. Ventilate freely in spring and summer, water and feed to keep growth vigorous. Keep in trim by pruning back straggly shoots in April. Increase from half-ripe stem cuttings in June and July, rooted in gentle heat.

Lippia

[Lemon-Scented Verbena; Chile] Arching shrub renowned for its intensely aromatic leaves, which are light green, long and pointed, and its upright spikes of pale mauvish white flowers in July and August. Growing around 1.2m/4ft high and across, it is a very undemanding greenhouse shrub.

There is one species, *L. citriodora*, also called *Aloysia citriodora*.

Set plants in large pots or small tubs of rich gritty soil. Water and feed frequently in spring and summer to encourage robust growth. Ventilate freely in warm weather. Water very sparingly in winter – sufficient to keep the soil just moist. Propagate from half-ripe cuttings of side shoots in June and July. Repot plants when they are root-bound; their roots having filled the pot.

Prune back the previous year's shoots to half their length in April.

Pleione

[Hardy Orchid; Tibet to Formosa] Flamboyant terrestrial or semi-epiphytic orchids with magnificent fringed trumpet flowers that arise from a star of broad petals. The thin pointed leaves are effectively ribbed, and they develop from pseudobulbs, usually after the flowers. Blooms are borne singly or in pairs on 15cm/6in stems and are white, yellow, pink or mauve. The trumpets are flecked with other colours. *P. formosana* (now correctly *P. bulbocodioides*) ranges from white through all shades of pink to mauve. The lip of the bloom, paler in colour, is blotched from brick-red to magenta. Flowers appear from February to June. *P. f.* 'Alba' is a pure white form; *P. f. limprichtii* is a rich purple red, while 'Oriental Splendour' has dark purple flowers and similarly coloured pseudobulbs.

Grow in 10cm/4in pans of a mixture (by volume) of two parts loamy soil and one part sphagnum moss. Plant pseudobulbs one-third deep. Shade from bright sun, ventilate freely and water copiously throughout the growing season. Feed every two weeks from June to September when plants are growing strongly. When leaves turn yellow, dry off plants and store in a frost-free place until the following spring. Then repot in fresh soil if the pot is full of roots. Propagate from offsets (pseudobulbs) in spring when repotting plants.

Punica

[Pomegranate; Iran/Afghanistan] Attractive leaf-shedding shrub or small tree 2.4-3m/8-10ft high and across. Striking 4-5cm/1½-2in long trumpet- or bell-shaped flowers 3cm/1¼in across form freely on slender twiggy shoots from June to September. They are followed by large, orangey, soft, red-fleshed edible fruits. The shining oblong leaves, rather like a myrtle's, turn a golden hue before they fall in autumn. *P. granatum* is the species most commonly grown, but 'Nana', a dwarf form of it, 46-60cm/1½-2ft high and across, makes a superb

pot plant if space is limited. Varieties 'Legrelliae', with large double pink and white variegated blooms, and 'Flore Pleno', double orange, brighten the greenhouse for almost one-third of the year.

Grow plants in large pots or tubs of loamy soil in good light. Water copiously and ventilate freely throughout the growing season; keep just moist in winter and feed with a weak liquid manure every two weeks in spring and summer. Raise plants from seeds of species sown in March, and varieties from heeled cuttings of half-ripe shoots in July.

Sarracenia

[Pitcher Plant; North America] Curious insectivorous plants whose bizarre pitcher-like leaves trap insects lured by their colour and pungent scent. The hollow leaves have digestive juices which quickly 'consume' the victims. Once inside a pitcher, the insect is enticed downwards into the digestive liquid, by secretions of sugary fluid. It cannot retreat because of downward thrusting hairs. Trapped – it is doomed to a watery grave. The plant waxes fat on the decomposing bodies of hapless flies and other winged insects. Kinds most frequently grown to 'entertain' the onlooker are *S. drummondii*, 30-76cm/12-30in high and 23cm/9in across. The 'lids' to the pitchers are white with purple veins; the pitchers themselves are greenish. Yellow to reddish purple blooms some 8cm/3in across appear in April and May. *S. flava*, 60cm/2ft high by 23cm/9in across, has yellowish-green pitchers veined crimson; yellow flowers appear in April and May. *S. purpurea*, 23cm/9in high and spreading

Above: The Bird of Paradise, *Strelitzia reginae*
Below: *Sarracenia purpurea* traps insects

to 30cm/1ft, makes a rosette of purplish-green pitchers. Flowers of the same colour form in April and May.

Grow plants in a mixture of equal parts chopped sphagnum moss and peat. Stand pots, which should be 20-25cm/8-10in across and fairly shallow, in saucers of water at all times to keep the soil permanently moist. Spray leaves in summer to keep the air moist. Repot every two or three years. Propagate from seeds in March or divide and replant healthy portions, at the same time, of well-established clumps.

Strelitzia

[Bird of Paradise Flower; South Africa] Aptly named, for *S. reginae* does indeed closely resemble the head of this exotic bird. Leathery, light green paddle-like leaves around 46cm/18in long, make an impressive, dense clump. In April and May the flowers rise from the centre. They are large, about 15cm/6in long. Shaped like a green, purple-hued boat, from which a crest of orange and blue petals ascend, the bloom is as exotic as you are likely to see.

The greenhouse border is best for growing as there are no restrictions for its roots. It flowers earlier as a consequence. It may also be grown in a large tub or pot of gritty loamy soil. Encourage bright green leaves by feeding every two weeks throughout the growing season. Use dilute liquid manure. Water to keep the soil evenly moist in late spring and summer but fairly dry in autumn and winter. Good light is necessary, but shade from bright sunlight. Propagate from rooted offsets in spring, or raise new plants from seed. It is much quicker to obtain a flowering plant from planting a rooted portion, than by rearing from seed.

Alpines for cold greenhouses

Aethionema

[Asia Minor] Seemingly always in flower, this evergreen carpeter about 10cm/4in high and 30-46cm/12-18in across, bears delightful cross-shaped flowers in abundance in June and July, and sporadically throughout the remaining summer months. It revels in hot dry places in gritty soil. It enjoys lime, so scatter plenty round plants if lime does not occur naturally in the soil. A. × 'Warley Rose' is the finest variety. A profusion of deep pink blooms covers every part of the plant in April and May. A. iberideum is another beauty, making a wide spreading mat of blue-green foliage and showy white flowers.

Set plants in 15-20cm/6-8in pans of gritty soil mix from September to March. Propagate from seeds in early spring or soft wood cuttings in June and July.

Anacyclus depressus

[Mount Atlas Daisy; Atlas Mountains, Morocco] Grown for its attractive 5cm/2in wide daisy flowers, white and yellow with a dull red reverse, from June to August, and 5cm/2in high carpeting fern-like leaves. It forms a neat mat of foliage around 30cm/12in across.

Set plants in pans of well-drained gritty soil mix and do not overwater, as the roots are liable to rot in soggy soil. Place in full sun or light shade. Propagate from seeds in October and from cuttings in March and April or July and August.

Armeria

[Thrift; Spain] Deep green cushions of tight little narrow leaves are a feature of this plant. In May, they are hidden beneath a pink foam of bloom. A. caespitosa makes a tightknit hummock set with stemless pink flowers. A finer form of it, 'Beechwood', has larger heads of bloom on small stems. 'Bevan's Variety' is slightly more hummocky with deeper pink flowers.

Grow in 15-20cm/6-8in pans of rich gritty soil mix. Water freely in dry warm spells, less so in winter. Give as much air as possible. Raise new plants from seed in March and April, or by division when the blooms fade.

Aster alpinus

[Alpine Aster; Europe] Large showy daisy-like blooms brighten the year from mid- to late summer. A. alpinus has deep blue gold-centred blooms on 23cm/9in stems. Grey-green spatula-like leaves provide a neat 'ferny' backcloth. A. 'Albus' is a fine white form, though slightly less vigorous. Both 'Goliath', deep blue and 'Beechwood', mauve-blue, are selected forms; they are vigorous and free-flowering. The plants make an exquisite carpet of intense colour when most rock plants have finished flowering. They spread 30-46cm/12-18in. Set them in good rich, gritty soil in 15-20cm/6-8in pans in full sun. Remove faded flowers and propagate from rooted offsets in October to March.

Crassula sarcocaulis

[South Africa] Curiously ancient-looking shrubby plant with stout gnarled woody stems set with tiny green, often crimson-tinted, leaves. Attractive clusters of crimson buds open to reveal minute pink flowers, from July to September. Enjoying full sun and air, this crassula thrives in a gritty well-drained soil mixture.

Set plants in 8-15cm/3-6in pots. Water well throughout the growing season, from spring to summer, but sparingly in autumn and winter. Raise new plants by cuttings taken from the fleshy leaves. Alternatively, propagate from seeds in spring.

Cyclamen repandum

[France to Greece] Charming species noted for its beautifully marbled heart-shaped leaves, silvered above, reddish below. Height 15cm/6in. In April, pretty miniature cyclamen flowers uncurl from the centre of the corm. They have appealing twisted petals in red, pink or white. They are fragrant, too.

Set a single corm in a 10-15cm/4-6in pot of a loam- or peat-based potting mixture. Alternatively, plant four or five corms in a 20cm/8in pan. Water from the base to avoid wetting the corm, which may otherwise rot. Keep lightly shaded in summer. Raise new plants from seed in September.

Doronicum cordatum

[Leopard's Bane; Balkans/Asia Minor] A spring dazzler with 20-30cm/8-12in stems topped with sunny daisy flowers in golden yellow. Sheaves of kidney-shaped leaves appear in spring. Deadhead this herbaceous perennial when the blooms fade towards the end of May to encourage a second burst of blooms in autumn. Increase plants from rooted offsets in autumn or spring. Water freely, shade lightly and give plenty of air. Plants thrive in deep pots of rich, loamy soil. Split up and replant clumps every two or three years, so they do not become congested.

Erinus alpinus

[Mountains of Western Europe] Tufted evergreen perennial with attractive toothed, spoon-shaped leaves, 8cm/3in high and 15cm/6in across. Starry flowers, 1cm/¼in across, form in airy sprays from March to August. Three forms are usually grown: 'Albus', pure white; 'Dr. Hanelle', carmine-red; and 'Mrs. Charles Boyle', glowing pink.

Set plants in small pans of gritty soil mix. Place in sun or light shade. Water freely throughout the growing season. Increase from seed in April.

Below left: Aethionema pulchellum.
Below: Iberis sempervirens 'Little Gem'.

Gentiana verna

[Spring Gentian; Europe/Great Britain] Striking herbaceous perennial. Rosettes of long oval leaves give rise to deep blue star-shaped flowers on 8cm/3in stems from May to June. Plants have a 15cm/6in spread. Individual blooms 2cm/1in long. *G. verna* 'Angulosa' is the form usually grown.

Set plants in 15-20cm/6-8in pans of limy soil mix and leafmould. Water freely in dry spells while growth is vigorous. Place in full sun or light shade. Propagate from rooted offsets in March, or from cuttings in April and May.

Geranium subcaulescens

[Cranesbill; Balkans] Charming May to October flowering herbaceous perennial. Glowing carmine-red, dark-centred saucer-shaped blooms 2cm/1in across form freely on spreading plants 23cm/9in across and 15cm/6in high. The flowers are offset by attractive grey-green rounded, lobed leaves. 'Russell Prichard' is an invasive variety with magenta-cerise flowers, 4-5cm/1½-2in across. Set plants in full sun or shade in pans of ordinary gritty soil mix. Cut back faded flower stems and increase plants by splitting the crowns and replanting rooted offsets between September and March.

Helichrysum milfordiae

[South Africa] Silver-leaved rosettes 5cm/2in high and 23cm/9in across sport intriguing 2cm/1in diameter wide white flowers in May and June; they are stemless and open from crimson buds. Grow this herbaceous perennial in 15-20cm/6-8in pans of ordinary gritty soil in full sun. Water freely in summer but hardly at all in winter. Raise new plants from cuttings of side shoots 4-5cm/1½-2in long in April to July.

Iberis semperverens

[Candytuft; Southern Europe] Rosettes of dark evergreen leaves spread to 23cm/9in. In May and June they are smothered with close-set cushion heads of white flowers 10cm/4in high. 'Little Gem' and 'Snowflake' are the two neatest varieties. Set plants in pans of ordinary gritty soil in sun or light shade. Water copiously in spring and summer, much less in autumn and winter. Increase from 5cm/2in long softwood cuttings from June to August.

Lewisia

[British Columbia/Cascade Mountains/North West America] Magnificent evergreen. Handsome rosettes of blue-green leaves lie almost flat on the soil. Exquisite sprays of wide trumpet blooms on 8-15cm/3-6in stems arise from their centres. Flowers throughout spring and summer. Finest forms are pink to salmon and crimson Birch Hybrids, large white *L. brachycalyx* 'Angustifolia', brick-red 'George Henley', rose-red 'Rose Splendour', a quite superb variety, and luminous peach-pink *L. tweedyi*.

Plant in March or April, in 15-23cm/6-9in pans of fertile, gritty soil. Place a layer of chippings round their necks to prevent water lying round them and causing them to rot in winter. Water copiously during the growing season, but sparingly when the leaves have faded. Propagate from offsets in June. Root them in a mixture of equal parts moist peat and sand. Or raise from seed in March, although named varieties do not breed true.

Oxalis adenophylla

[Chile] Massed with 2cm/1in wide, satin-pink flowers from May to June, the cup-shaped blooms on long stems have special appeal. Crinkled grey leaves develop from a bulb-like rhizome. Growing 8cm/3in high by 15cm/6in across, the whole plant dies back in autumn. Plant in a good loam-based potting mixture. Thriving in sun or partial shade, propagate this plant by dividing the rootstock in March.

Parochetus communis

[Shamrock Pea; Himalayas] Light-shade-loving herbaceous plant 8cm/3in high and about 50cm/20in across. Handsome gentian-blue, sweet pea flowers form freely from October to March, against a backcloth of small clover-like leaves.

Set plants in shallow pans 15-20cm/6-8in across, using a gritty loamy soil. Alternatively, establish in good soil in the border beneath the greenhouse staging. Water and feed freely from spring to autumn, sparingly from late autumn to late winter. Propagate by dividing and replanting rooted pieces in March and April, or in July.

Phlox douglasii

[Alpine Phlox; Western North America] Superb prostrate carpeter. Its grey-green awl-shaped leaves are almost hidden beneath a froth of starry flowers in May and June. Finest form for pan culture is 'Rosea'. Its compact cushions, 5-10cm/2-4in high and 30cm/12in or so across, thrive in full sun. Set plants in ordinary gritty soil. Water freely in summer, hardly at all in winter. Propagate from 5cm/2in cuttings taken from the base of the plant in July.

Primula auricula

[Auricula; European Alps] Startling heads of brightly hued, flared trumpet blooms arise on stout stems from a rosette of mid-green, broad evergreen leaves. Reaching 15cm/6in high and across, auriculas brighten spring. Sometimes the leaves are dusted with a powdery white farina, adding to their appeal. There are many fine varieties, some with a distinct white eye to the flower. 'Old Yellow Dusty Miller', 'Red Dusty Miller', 'Blue Bonnet' and 'Blue Velvet' – a beauty in velvety blue which contrasts effectively with a pronounced white zone in the throat – are all easy to grow.

Set in pans of gritty soil in sun or light shade. Raise new plants by rooting offsets from June to August, or from seed in spring. Water liberally throughout the spring and summer, but hardly at all in autumn and winter.

Opposite above: *Erinus alpinus*. Below: *Helichrysum milfordiae*. Left: *Saxifraga × apiculata*.
Opposite below: *Phlox douglasii*

Saxifraga

[North Asia/North America/Europe] This large genus includes several species ideally suited to pan culture in the alpine house. *S. oppositifolia* is a colourful carpeter to welcome spring in March and April. Around 2cm/1in high and 30-60cm/1-2ft across, it clothes the soil with wedge-shaped leaves and myriads of short-stemmed cup-shaped flowers. 'Latina' is a variety with close-packed silver-edged leaves; vivid purple-red blooms cover the plant in March. 'Splendens' is the largest flowered variety with red flowers with dark green leaves. Both appreciate a cool position

shaded from midday sun. Set plants in peaty, gritty soil that is quite lime-free. Plant in 15-20cm/6-8in pots. Raise new plants either by splitting up established clumps and planting out rooted divisions, or taking cuttings of non-flowering rosettes, in May and June.

S. × apiculata, of garden origin, is a gem of a cushion plant with tiny hoary green leaves. Soft yellow saucer-shaped blooms smother the plant from March to April. Spreading to 38cm/15in across, it thrives in a 15-20cm/6-8in pan of rich gritty soil containing lime. Set plants in good light. Give as much air as possible. Raise new plants from cuttings of non-flowering rosettes in June. Water freely in summer.

GLOSSARY

alpine: a plant native to the alpine zone, (the top of tree growth to the permanent snow line)

annual: a plant that completes its life-cycle within one growing season

aroid: any plant belonging to the araceae family, e.g. philodendron

axil: the point at which a stalk or branch diverges from the stem or axis to which it is attached; many flower clusters grow in axils

biennial: a plant that requires two growing seasons to complete its life-cycle

blind (non-flowering): failure to produce flowers or fruit; usually from disease, improper nourishment, or too deep or too early planting

bract: a small, leaf-like or membranous organ usually on the stalks of a flower cluster or just beneath the flower itself; in many plants the bracts look like miniature leaves

bulb: a growth bud with fleshy scales, usually underground

bulbils: small miniature bulbs often formed at the base of mature bulbs or on stems above ground

calyx: outer circle or cup of floral parts (usually green)

capillary action: by capillary action moisture is held between and around particles of soil

corm, cormlet: a plant storage organ, composed of a thickened stem base, usually covered with a papery skin; at the top of a corm is a bud from which both shoots and new roots appear

cristate: with a comb-like tuft of hairs or soft bristles, found on petals, in particular some iris species

crown: (1) the basal part of the plant between the root and the stem, usually at or near ground level; (2) the whole upper foliage of a tree

cultivar: plant maintained in cultivation, having arisen, either in the wild or in gardens, as a mutant or hybrid

dead-head: to remove faded flower heads

deciduous: applied to a plant that loses its leaves at the end of the growing season, particularly trees and shrubs

dioecious: plants that have single-sexed flowers on separate plants

division: method of propagation used for all types of plants that increase in size by suckers, rhizomes, or underground growths

epiphyte, epiphytic: a type of plant adapted to live above the soil, usually adhering to tree branches or mossy rocks; orchids and bromeliads provide the best example. Epiphytes are not parasitic and use their hosts only as supports

ericaceous: having the characteristics of the ericaceae (the heath family)

fern: plant without flowers

germination: first stage in development of plant from seed

glabrous: smooth, not hairy or rough

glacous: covered with a white powder that rubs off

half-hardy: applied to frost-tender plants to be grown outdoors only in summer, and to shrubs that may be left outdoors in winter

hardening off: gradually acclimatizing plants grown in a greenhouse to outdoor conditions

hardy: referring to plants which survive frost in the open year by year

heel: the basal end of a cutting, tuber, or of propagative material

herbaceous: non-woody, with no persistent stem above ground

hybrid: obtained by cross-pollination between two dissimilar parents

imbricated: closely overlapping; usually referring to scale, bract or leaf arrangements

inflorescence: the arrangement of flowers in a cluster; inflorescences are classified according to the floral arrangement, as spikes (lavender), racemes (hyacinth), panicles (gypsophila), or umbels (allium)

internodal: the length of the stem between the nodes (joints)

lanceolate leaves: leaves that are more or less lance-shaped

lateral: from the side

lobe: any projection of a leaf, rounded or pointed

midrib: large central vein of a leaf

monocarpic: a term applied to a plant which dies after flowering and seeding

monoecious: stamens and pistils in separate flowers borne on same plant

node: a joint in a stalk where leaves form

pendant: hanging down from its support

perennial: any plant that lives for an indefinite period

petal: flower-leaf

petiole: a leafstalk

pinch out: to remove the growing point of a stem, to promote a branching habit or to induce formation of flower buds

pinna, pinnae: the ultimate divisions or leaflets of a compound leaf which is pinnate, e.g. the leaflets are arranged opposite or alternate from each other on a common axis

pinnate: applied to a leaf that is divided into several pairs of oppositely arranged leaflets

pip: the raised crown or individual rootstock of a plant; pips are sometimes valuable for propagation purposes; also colloquial for small seed

pistil: female organ of a flower

pollen: fertilizing powder at top of stamen

propagation: increase of plants

prostrate: lying flat

pseudobulbs: false bulbs; swollen, bulb-like structures between two stem joints which in some cases resemble bulbs

racemes: unbranched flower arrangements; the individual flowers are stalked and spirally arranged, e.g. hyacinth

rachis: the main stalk of a flower cluster or the main leafstalk of a compound leaf

rhizome: a horizontal, underground stem which acts as a storage organ

rootbound: pot-bound; plants growing in pots or ruts, where the roots are so closely packed that there seems little room for further growth (some plants bloom best in these conditions)

rosette: cluster of leaves radiating in a circle from a centre usually near the ground

sepal: one of the separate parts of the calyx; the sepal is usually green and protects the petals and sex organs

sori: the collection of spore sacks under or in which are the spores; the sori usually occur on the underside of fern fronds, and resemble small, fruiting bodies

spadix: a thick, usually fleshy and crowded spike of flowers, in members of the arum family and a few other plants

spathe: a leaf-like, often coloured bract which surrounds or encloses a flower cluster

sporangia: sacks containing the spores

spore: a minute, dustlike body, composed of a single cell, by which lower plants such as ferns, fungi and mosses reproduce

stamen: pollen-bearing or 'male' organ

succulent: able to store water in stems or leaves

tender: applied to plant which may be frost damaged

terminal: topmost; referring to the upper shoot, branches or flowers

terrestrial: growing in the ground

top-dressing: the application of a layer of soil or compost, usually to plants in pots in a confined space

tuber: a thickened, fleshy root (dahlia) or all underground stem (potato) which serves as a storage organ and a means of surviving periods of cold or drought

tuberous: having a swollen root, usually known as a tuberous root

umbels: flower clusters where all the individual flower stalks arise at one point

variegated: applied to leaves or petals that are patterned in a contrasting colour

247

Acknowledgments

The publishers would like to thank the following individuals and organizations for their kind permission to reproduce the photographs in this book:

A-Z Botanical Collection: 52, 54 right, 77 centre, 201 below right; *Bernard Alfieri:* 169 right, 224 below; *Anglo Aquarium:* 148 above centre and below left; *Aspect Picture Library:* 211 below; *Auto Grow:* 220 below, 220–221 above; *John Bethell:* 107 left, 110 left, 111 left; *Peter Black:* 88, 88–89, 90, 91; *Pat Brindley:* 25 below, 54 left, 87 below centre, 87 right, 97 above, 131 below, 134–135, 136 below, 138, 139 centre left, 156 below left, 156 below centre, 160, 161, 162, 163 above right, 164 right, 165, 167, 169 left, 171, 172 above, 173 above, 174, 175, 176 above, 178–179, 180 below, 182 right, 184 left, 186, 186–187 below, 188, 189, 190 above, 191 above, 201 left, 202 below left, 209 below, 211 above left, 214, 218, 219 right, 222, 227 below left, 228 right, 234 below, 235 below right, 238, 239 right, 240 below, 243 left, 244 below; *W. F. Davidson:* 62, 63 below, 147, 163 below right, 164 left, 173 below right, 178 below, 179 below, 239 left, 240, 244 right, 245 below; *Downward/Crowson:* 198 above; *Brian Furner:* 198 left; *Melvin Grey:* Front and back jackets, 5, 6–7, 10–11, 12–13, 31 above, 65, 96 above, 109 below, 117, 120–121, 121, 125, 126–127, 128–129, 136 above, 137 above, 206–207; *Susan Griggs Agency/Michael Boys:* 81 right, 92, 94, 123 right, 156 below right, 157 above 210; *Angelo Hornak:* endpapers; *George Hyde:* 16 right, 22 below, 24 above, 28 above; *Bill McLaughlin:* 39, 41 above, 45 above right, 72, 104–105, 112, 113, 115 above and below right, 122–123, 148–149 below, 152–153 below, 168, 208; *Marshall Cavendish Publications:* 110 right, 118–119; *Giuseppe Mazza:* 19 below left, 20, 63 above, 68 right, 69 right, 73 above, 78, 79 left, 81 left, 102–103, 190

centre, 228 left; *John Moss:* 16 left, 17 below, 24 below, 27 right, 28 below left and right, 30 below, 32, 33 right, 35 above and below left, 36 below left and above right, 38 centre, 40 right, 41 below, 42 left, 43 right, 72 inset, 74, 135 above; *N.H.P.A.:* 150–151, 181 below; *Frances Perry:* 67, 96 below, 172 below; *Pictor Ltd.:* 61; *John Sims:* 14–15, 17 above, 18 below, 27 left, 29 above, 30 above, 34, 35 right, 36–37, 40 left, 42 right, 43 left, 44–45, 45 left and below right, 48 above, 49 above, 68 centre and below left, 69 left, 73 below, 75 below, 79 right, 80 above, 80–81 below, 100–101, 114 below, 131 above, 133 left, 146–147; *Harry Smith Horticultural Photographic Collection:* 18–19, 19 right, 21, 22 above, 23, 26, 29 below, 31 below, 53, 55, 56 above, 56 below, 57 above, 74–75 above, 84, 85, 86, 87 left, 87 above centre, 95 left, 130, 138–139 above left, 139 below, 139 right, 141, 142, 143, 144 below, 145, 153 above, 156 above, 163 left, 166, 169 below, 170, 173 below left, 177, 179 above, 179 right, 180 above 181 above, 182 left, 183, 184 right, 185, 187 left, 190 below, 191 below, 194, 199, 201 above right, 208–209, 223 above left, 224 above, 225–226, 227 above left, 227 right, 229, 230, 231, 232 right, 233, 234 above, 236, 237, 241, 242, 243 right, 245 above; *Spectrum Colour Library:* 25 above, 57 below, 64, 66, 153 below, 176 below, 203, 204, 212–213, 223 above right and below, 246; *Peter Stiles:* 146, 187 below right; *Sutton and Sons Ltd., Reading:* 95 right, 97 below, 181 centre, 202 above left, 232 left, 234 below left; *Syndication International:* 116, 123 left; *Elizabeth Whiting:* 115 below left, 209 above, *(Steve Colley)* 157 below, *(Graham Henderson)* 38 right, 109 above, 114 above, 118, *(Michael Nicholson)* 133 right, *(Tim Street Porter)* 36 above left, 75 above, 108–109, 152–153 above, 219 left, *(Tubby)* 33 left, 104, 211 above right, 215.

The publishers also gratefully acknowledge the loan of plants for special photography from: Rochford's House of Plants, Hoddesdon, Herts. Selwyn Davidson Ltd., London.
The properties and equipment kindly loaned for special photography were provided by: The Flower House, London; Casa Pupo, London; Rural Crafts Shop, London; General Trading Co., London; Heals Ltd., London, Wrays Lighting Emporium, London.

Illustrations: *David Bryant:* 106–107, 137, 149, 154–155, 192–193, 196–197; *Julia Fryer:* 14; *Ian Garrard:* 216–217; *Hayward Art Group:* 48, 49, 83 above left and centre, 129, 132–133, 193, 214, 218, 221; *Kay Marshall:* 47, 83 above right, below left and right, 120, 158 right, 159; *Tony Michaels:* 71 centre and below; *Marion Mills:* 77, 140, 143, 144; *Virginia Nokes:* 50–51, 59 above and centre, 195 above and below; *Kristin Rosenberg:* 82; *Gwen Simpson:* 92–93, 95, 96, 98–99; *Kathleen Smith:* 46, 58, 60 centre and below, 76; *Prue Theobalds:* 59 below, 60 above, 124, 125, 205; *Elsie Wrigley:* 70, 71 above, 111, 198, 200, 202.